Praise for Ch

'Douglas Hurd has done the impossible. Together with his co-author, Edward Young, he has produced a page-turning book about the history of British foreign policy'   Denis MacShane, *Independent*

'One of the great achievements of this thoughtful and elegant book is to emphasise the thread of continuity running through British foreign policy from the age of Napoleon to the cold war ... a book of great authority and insight'   Dominic Sandbrook, *Sunday Times*

'Highly readable ... I enjoyed *Choose Your Weapons* immensely, particularly the magnificently colourful account of the Bevin and Eden years ... Any future Foreign Secretary would be well advised to read this engrossing book on their first day in office'
Jack Straw, *Observer*

'A highly readable fusion of archival scholarship and personal experience, mixing vivid portrayals of the personalities and private lives of their chosen protagonists with cool analysis of the policy choices they made'   John Campbell, *Mail on Sunday*

'Full of wry, unillusioned wisdom. There are some delicious apercus ... All Douglas Hurd's characters are portrayed sympathetically, even when they fail'   Bruce Anderson, *Independent*

'That Douglas Hurd was once Foreign Secretary lends piquancy to his elegant account of that office ... a very canny, diplomatic book'
Scotland on Sunday

'This elegant examination of the contrasting strands of British foreign policy from the Napoleonic wars to the Suez debacle ... is an entertaining book, enriched by the insights of an experienced practitioner'
Economist

'Elegant, stimulating and shrewdly perceptive'
Sunday Business Post (Ireland)

'This is a fascinating book'   David Owen, *Guardian*

Douglas Hurd is a former diplomat, politician and author. He was an MP between 1974 and 1997, and served as Secretary of State for Northern Ireland, Home Secretary, and Foreign Secretary in Margaret Thatcher's government. He is the author of a highly acclaimed biography of Robert Peel, as well as a number of thrillers and his autobiography, *Memoirs*, published in 2002.

Douglas Hurd was joined in this work by Edward Young, who after gaining a first in history at Cambridge won a Mellon Scholarship to Yale, where he studied history and international relations as part of the Grand Strategy Program. Edward Young has since worked as Assistant Private Secretary and speechwriter to David Cameron and is currently the political adviser to the Conservative Party chairman.

CHOOSE YOUR WEAPONS

✦⇒◉⇐✦

THE BRITISH FOREIGN SECRETARY
200 Years of Argument, Success and Failure

DOUGLAS HURD
and Edward Young

Phoenix

For Judy

A PHOENIX PAPERBACK

First published in Great Britain in 2010
by Weidenfeld & Nicolson
This paperback edition published in 2011
by Phoenix,
an imprint of Orion Books Ltd,
Orion House, 5 Upper St Martin's Lane,
London WC2H 9EA

An Hachette UK company

1 3 5 7 9 10 8 6 4 2

Copyright © Douglas Hurd and Edward Young 2010

The right of Douglas Hurd and Edward Young to be identified as the
authors of this work has been asserted by them in accordance
with the Copyright, Designs and Patents Act 1988.

A CIP catalogue record for this book
is available from the British Library.

ISBN: 978-0-7538-2852-6

Typeset by Input Data Services Ltd,
Bridgwater, Somerset

Printed and bound in the UK by
CPI Mackays, Chatham ME5 8TD

The Orion Publishing Group's policy is to use papers that
are natural, renewable and recyclable products and
made from wood grown in sustainable forests. The logging
and manufacturing processes are expected to conform to
the environmental regulations of the country of origin.

www.orionbooks.co.uk

CONTENTS

LIST OF ILLUSTRATIONS

Section One

'Killing no Murder, or a New Ministerial way of settling the affairs of the Nation!', by George Cruikshank, 1809 (Bridgeman Art Library)

'Delicious dreams! Castles in the air! Glorious prospects!', by James Gillray, hand-coloured etching, 1808 (National Portrait Gallery, London)

George Canning, by Sir Thomas Lawrence, oil on canvas, 1829 (The Royal Collection © 2009 Her Majesty Queen Elizabeth)

Lord Castlereagh, by Sir Thomas Lawrence, oil on canvas, 1809–10 (National Portrait Gallery, London)

'Amusement at Vienna, alias Harmony at Congress', by Charles Williams, 1815 (The Trustees of the British Museum)

'The Congress of Vienna', by Jean-Baptiste Isabey, pencil and watercolour, 1815, Louvre, Paris (Lauros / Giraudon / Bridgeman Art Library)

Emily Castlereagh (Mary Evans Picture Library)

George Hamilton-Gordon, 4th Earl of Aberdeen, by Sir Thomas Lawrence, oil on canvas, 1808, Haddo House (National Trust for Scotland)

Catherine, Countess of Aberdeen, by Sir Thomas Lawrence, Haddo House (National Trust for Scotland)

Lord Aberdeen's Daughters, Jane, Caroline and Alice, by George Hayter, 1815, Haddo House (National Trust for Scotland)

Harriet, Countess of Aberdeen, by Sir Thomas Lawrence, Haddo House (courtesy of Lord Aberdeen)

Henry John Temple, 3rd Viscount Palmerston, by Thomas Heaphy, watercolour and pencil, 1802 (National Portrait Gallery, London)

Emily Mary, Countess Cowper (later Viscountess Palmerston), print, after painting by Sir Thomas Lawrence (Bridgeman Art Library)

Princess Lieven, by Sir Thomas Lawrence, oil on canvas, 1812–20 (Tate Gallery, London)

Sarah Sophia, Countess of Jersey, lithograph (Bridgeman Art Library)

Palmerston, by John Partridge (Broadlands Trust, Hampshire / Bridgeman Art Library)

Aberdeen, from a photograph c.1860 (Getty Images)

'Aberdeen on Duty', *Punch*, vol. XXV, July–December 1853, p. 259 (Punch Ltd)

Henry Stanley, 15th Earl of Derby, 1875 (Getty Images)

'Augurs at Fault', *Punch*, vol. LXXI, July–December 1876, p. 63 (Punch Ltd)

Congress of Berlin, 1878, by van Werner (Rischgitz / Getty Images)

Robert Arthur Talbot Gascoyne-Cecil, 3rd Marquess of Salisbury, by Sir John Everett Millais, oil on canvas, 1883 (National Portrait Gallery, London)

Section Two

ACKNOWLEDGEMENTS

A literary partnership (this is my third) needs strong foundations. Edward Young and I had worked strenuously together on my biography of Robert Peel. We formed the habit of pooling historical ideas and impressions, a haphazard collection at first, which gained gradually in coherence and bred much fierce, enjoyable argument. We divided the writing, but each was conscious that the other stood at his elbow.

This process advanced a stage when my wife, Judy, and I went to a conference at Knowsley organised by Professor Charmley of the University of East Anglia. The theme of the conference was appeasement as a continuing strand in Conservative foreign policy rather than as a term of abuse. The hero of that occasion was John Vincent because of his brilliant editing of the diaries of Disraeli's Foreign Secretary, the 15th Lord Derby. I was fascinated by Derby's intelligent but resolutely inactive approach to foreign policy, and wanted to know more.

Shortly after this, Ed Young enjoyed two years at Yale on a Mellon Scholarship from Clare College, Cambridge. He was wafted up into the heady heights of the Grand Strategy program at Yale under the benevolent gaze of veteran prophets and grand viziers such as Paul Kennedy, John Gaddis, Charles Hill and Ted Bromund. As part of that exercise, the participants enacted as triumphs of theatre their analyses and solutions to the world's main problems. In quieter moments Ed wrote an essay about Castlereagh, Canning and the tension between their different concepts of British foreign policy.

Other influences came to bear. I had always been fascinated by Anthony Eden, who was Foreign Secretary when I joined the Foreign Service. The contrast between his successes as Foreign Secretary in 1954 and the disaster of Suez two years later still grips and cautions me today. Ed and I both read Ferdy Mount's stimulating novel, *Umbrella*, about the sad, mild, Lord Aberdeen, whose passion for conciliation we already knew from our work on Peel. Other fragments of knowledge and argument began to form a pattern in our minds. Some of the issues were well to the fore in public discussion as Britain and America digested the awkward lessons of the Iraq War.

It was, I think, during a visit to Saudi Arabia with a quite different agenda that we decided to pull our thoughts together into a book about eleven British Foreign Secretaries. Having divided the work, we had to immerse ourselves in a mass of already published material. Copious lists of reading suggestions came from Yale. I must in particular thank again the Library of the House of Lords for the speed and efficiency with which they gathered what I wanted, and their patience in letting me keep it until the pressure from the next customer became overpowering.

But we also needed to tackle primary material in archives, particularly to glean telling facts which previous historians had passed over, and partly to equip ourselves to make shrewder judgement of the published material. I twice visited the great archive at Hatfield and am grateful to Lord Salisbury and his archivist Robin Harcourt-Williams for their welcome and hospitality. Judy, Ed and I spent two nights at Harewood House in Yorkshire, Lord Harewood having arranged that the Canning papers could be brought there for consultation from their usual home in the West Yorkshire Archives. We are grateful to Lord and Lady Harewood for their hospitality and to Lynn Tungate, Terry Southern and the staff of the Archives for all the trouble they took in carrying out this manoeuvre. Likewise, we thank Lord and Lady Derby for putting us up at Knowsley, as well as the staff of the Liverpool Record Office, for their co-operation in guiding us through the Derby papers. The archivists at the Special Collections in Birmingham University were particularly helpful in making available what we needed from the Chamberlain and Eden papers. The Public Record Office at Kew and the British Library gave indispensable help on Edward Grey, Ramsay MacDonald and Ernest Bevin.

We need to thank many individuals for their generous co-operation: the Countess of Avon discussed with me Anthony Eden's method of working, along with his distaste for jacket covers on books. Philip Bobbitt nobly agreed to have lunch with us on his birthday where he educated us about Castlereagh and the rule of World Law. Niall Ferguson also offered energy and insight over a Travellers' Club lunch, while Max Hastings, Denis MacShane, Andrew Adonis, David Marquand and the Foreign Office Chief Historian, Patrick Salmon all gave wise advice at various intervals. Ted Bromund led us to fascinating material by John Kent on Bevin's African ideas; Nick Humfrey was an intelligent source of help; Rebecca Jackson displayed patience, perceptiveness and fast typing skills; Martha Varney, Naomi Wiseman, Fiona Petherham and Tom Corby all clubbed in with assistance at crucial points. Meanwhile, across an ocean, Evan McCormick had subtle thoughts on Clausewitz and Thucydides. The Master of Davenport College at Yale provided Ed with a congenial apartment for his learned visit there after leaving Yale, while the Arthur Vining Davis summer research grant provided funds which helped Ed to prepare the original submission.

It was exceptionally good of Sir Michael Howard, John Jefferies of Warwick School and my son Nick to read the text for us and provide valuable, searching comment. As before, we have depended on the wise encouragement and advice of Michael Sissons, our agent, and Ion Trewin, our editor at Orion. We are in debt to the whole team at Orion, in particular Bea Hemming who took charge of much of the spadework of production and Linden Lawson who examined our text with her usual scrupulous care. We were fortunate to find in David Smith an illustrator of rare talent who turned an underlying notion of ours to good effect. We warmly thank Chatham House for their generosity, and in particular Camilla Seymour, for all her hard work in organising our launch party.

The book was written partly by me in longhand, partly by Ed on his laptop. The task of pulling the results together into an intelligible whole fell largely on Pauline Glock; we are deeply in her debt for many long and hard hours. She and I work together for Hawkpoint, the independent financial advisory firm at 41 Lothbury, behind the Bank of England. Hawkpoint kindly tolerated my decision to turn my office there into a writers' studio, permanently littered with papers and the occasional bottle. Through 2007 and 2008, Ed and I met there in the evenings to compare ideas and drafts. We also wrote at weekends on the long medieval table in my library at Westwell. Ed, who has a full-time job, often laboured through the small hours in the flat which he shares in St John's Wood, unloading on me the next day what he was pleased to call the wisdom of the night.

We spent two weekends, separated by fifteen months, at St Deiniol's, the library founded by Gladstone close to his home at Hawarden in Flintshire. St Deiniol's provides a magnificent library and simple welcoming atmosphere for all kinds of study or relaxation, being frequented alike by exhausted rectors in need of a rest, eager theologians and Liverpool football fans. We are most grateful to the staff there for their encouragement.

On our last visit to St Deiniol's, I was allotted Room 15, the Lindisfarne Room. An attractive book by my bedside about the Lindisfarne Gospels told me that there are two mistakes of calligraphy by the Anglo-Saxon monk who copied and illustrated the texts – deliberate mistakes designed to underline the truth that only God can achieve perfection. We hope that any mistakes in this book will be forgiven on the Lindisfarne principle.

This book is dedicated to my wife Judy, who was a staunch and perceptive companion through twenty-six years and the making of many books; who knew exactly when to criticise and when to encourage; whom I greatly miss; who took the last chapter into hospital with her in October 2008 but sadly was not given time to read it.

DOUGLAS HURD
London, June 2009

PRELUDE

'In history a great volume is unrolled for our instruction,
drawing the materials of future wisdom from the past errors
and infirmities of mankind'
                    Burke, *Reflections on the Revolution in France*

This is a book written not in despair, but certainly in disquiet.
Despair would be foolish when in its time the human race has
overcome so many difficulties which at one moment seemed
overwhelming. But disquiet is in order, as we see a world apparently adrift among many simultaneous threats. Climate change,
shortages of food, water and energy, pressures of population,
financial collapse, in many places political chaos, bitterness and
war all crowd the agenda. Because the last of these groups has
been our particular study and experience we concentrate upon it.
Within the wide range of bloody disorder between and inside
states, we focus upon one country, our own. Within the British
story, we select one period of a century and a half between 1807
and 1956 during which Britain climbed to its peak of Empire and
became for a few decades chance guardian of the globe. Within
that period, we focus upon a selection of those who held just one
office, the British Foreign Secretary.

We have chosen eleven British Foreign Secretaries who varied
greatly in fame and effectiveness. Some, like the 15th Earl of Derby
and Austen Chamberlain, we have rescued from virtual oblivion
because we think them in their own way remarkable. Some Foreign
Secretaries found themselves relegated to the side of the stage by
their own Prime Minister. During our period, this happened mainly
in wartime. Since then, in an age of summits, this relegation has
become almost normal, though the story of Prime Ministerial essays
in foreign policy from Lloyd George through Chamberlain, Churchill
to Blair has been one of effort rather than success.

Our chosen Foreign Secretaries have varied in character. Some have been by nature noisy, others quiet. Some have enjoyed and believed in working with foreigners, others have particularly relished defiance. Some have accepted the importance of public opinion; others despised it. Lord Salisbury did both. Some saw their job as essentially that of a mountaineer, seeking peaks on which to hoist the flag of their country and indeed of themselves. Others have seen themselves more modestly as a pilot employed to steer a craft through rapids, seeking a reputation simply from the avoidance of shipwreck. All worked hard. We suspect that all enjoyed their position though some pretended, including to themselves, a passion for a quiet life without official boxes. Only with one, Edward Grey, was there a genuine yearning for birds and fish as opposed to office. We believe that each of them, famous, infamous or neglected, was in his own way a vivid character whose story is worth retelling. It is not, we think, our fault that our chosen period includes no female Foreign Secretary.

We have another purpose besides the sketching of characters. We begin the book with Canning and Castlereagh, two great men whose personal ambitions escalated and clashed to the point of fighting a duel on Putney Heath. They hated each other, but the clash was not simply one of personalities. The two men illustrated, the first with eloquence, the second with persistent diplomatic skill, different answers to the questions which run through the policy-making of the whole period. These questions are not peculiar to the period or to Britain. Any study of another country or another modern period would reveal them in different guise.

What should be the balance between the interests of a nation and the ideals which its leaders or its people profess? Is an ethical foreign policy a contradiction, or a hypocrisy, or a realistic ambition? Should it be the aim of Britain or any other major power to exert itself on behalf of a particular form of government in other countries, whether based on democracy or some alternative legitimacy? Can this aim extend to intervention by force? What is the role of alliances between nations? Of international institutions with rules binding all? How important is national prestige and how is it best expressed and sustained?

The circumstances in which these questions were posed varied greatly as the nineteenth century evolved through two world wars towards the twenty-first. In one form, they faced Canning and Castlereagh as they brought Britain to a decisive victory over Napoleon and then had to decide what to build on the ruins of Europe. In another form, they faced Eden and Bevin who after another victory, against Nazism in 1945, undertook a similar task among a new pile of ruins.

We cannot disregard the differences made by time. We must resist the temptation simply to recruit our characters into one of two opposed regiments of thought. But in different shapes, those questions persist.

They face us again today. Under brilliant American leadership, Eden and Bevin helped to build a set of international institutions which, though by no means perfect, provided answers for the post-war world to the questions we have defined. Those institutions, in particular the UN family and NATO, have to some extent evolved in the last sixty years, but not fast enough. Indeed, the whole concept of Darwinian evolution does not apply to institutions. They are not species, but rather buildings built to provide shelter. The institutions in which we still shelter, in particular from war between states and disorder within them, are no longer fit for the purpose. Storms break through the roofs and make the world wretched. We patch and repair as best we can and make a great many speeches. But it often seems that the deterioration advances faster than the repair work as Iraq, Afghanistan, Darfur, Congo follow Bosnia and Rwanda. The questions belong to the same family as those which confronted Castlereagh and Canning after the Napoleonic Wars, Austen Chamberlain and Ramsay MacDonald between the two World Wars, and Eden and Bevin at the end of the Second World War.

History provides no automatic system of navigation for our leaders. Knowledge of history does not change politicians into statesmen. But ignorance of history is foolishness. The most dangerous form of ignorance is that smidgeon of shallow knowledge which lacks any understanding of the characters or context of past decisions. The false analogy can be more disastrous than the blank mind. But some greater understanding of how our predecessors wrestled with principles and problems painfully familiar to us may edge us, however slowly, to answers more adequate to our own generation. We feel, therefore, that it would be cowardly to leave the lessons embedded in history. In our last chapter we are bold enough to draw some conclusions for today.

CHAPTER I

CASTLEREAGH AND CANNING

'So that in the nature of man we find three principal causes of quarrel. First, competition; secondly, diffidence; thirdly, glory. The first maketh man invade for gain; the second, for safety; and the third, for reputation.'

Thomas Hobbes, *Leviathan*

We are told that Lord Castlereagh discussed the opera as he made his way to the duel. He entertained Lord Yarmouth, his cousin and second, by humming tunes made famous by the soprano, Catalani, as their curricle trundled over the bridge. They arrived on Putney Heath just as dawn was breaking on Thursday 21 September 1809 and disembarked from the carriage with duelling pistols in hand.

They were met on the Heath by two more men. There were discussions, a final attempt to call the whole thing off, before the seconds agreed on a distance of twelve paces – the longest for which there was any precedent. Castlereagh then took up his position. Standing across from him in the autumn morning was the proud, slightly balding figure of George Canning.

The seconds handed the duellers their weapons. 'I must cock it for him for I cannot trust him to do it himself,' Canning's second explained to Lord Yarmouth. 'He has never fired a pistol in his life.' The men took aim. Lord Castlereagh was asked if he was ready: His Majesty's Secretary of State for War and the Colonies

I

replied that he was. Mr Canning was asked if he too was ready: His Majesty's Secretary of State for Foreign Affairs said yes.

Canning fired first, off target. Castlereagh responded and also missed. There was a pause, and some discussion. Perhaps past grievances could now be laid to rest. But Castlereagh insisted on a second attempt. Canning's second shot skimmed by Castlereagh's chest, taking a button from his coat; Castlereagh's bullet passed through Canning's nankeen breeches and punctured his leg somewhere along the 'fleshy part' of his thigh.

Canning's second ran up to him and began to help him away. Hobbling from the field, Canning stopped suddenly. 'But perhaps I ought to remain.' There was no response. He repeated himself, turning to his opponent. 'Are you sure we have done?' Before Castlereagh could speak, Yarmouth intervened, assuring Canning and also Castlereagh that indeed they had done. Castlereagh then approached Canning, took his arm and helped him to Yarmouth's house where a surgeon was waiting.

Standing close by as they limped away from the Heath was the house in which William Pitt the Younger had died three years before. The two men had been his close disciples. He had taught them many of the arts of politics but not that of working together. At the time of the duel Castlereagh was forty years old, Canning thirty-nine.[1]

For four decades up to this moment the lives of Robert Stewart, Viscount Castlereagh, and George Canning had run together in counterpoint.*

Born into Anglo-Irish families – Castlereagh in 1769, Canning in 1770 – they were each brought up on radicalism and religious dissent. Castlereagh ended one letter in October 1777 with a well-known call to revolution: 'I am still a true American,' he told his uncle, dismissing any doubts on the subject that an eight-year-old might have.[2] He abandoned his undergraduate studies before taking his degree and spent most of his second year at Cambridge attending the trial of Warren Hastings in London. The calling to

---

* For the sake of simplicity, Robert Stewart, Viscount Castlereagh will be referred to as Castlereagh throughout, although in April 1821 he became the 2nd Marquess of Londonderry when his father died.

account of the great proconsul for his deeds of peculation and misgovernment in India became the focus of political and social attention, and Castlereagh was gripped. By July 1790, Castlereagh had been elected to the Irish Parliament as an independent Whig representing County Down.

As a teenager, George Canning wrote Byronic poems before Byron, lamenting the slavery of Greece. He formed close links with the leading Whigs in England, and rumours, probably exaggerated, of his republican sympathies as a student are supposed to have reached and alarmed George III. He shared many of Castlereagh's early views on politics and society, and both men would later be joined by their belief in the need for Catholic Emancipation.[3]

But if the early political views of the two duellists were fairly similar, their childhood lives were worlds apart. Castlereagh's family had been prosperous and successful for as long as they had been in Ireland. His education may not have been sensational – the list of alumni at the Royal School in Armagh is not adorned with the names of great statesmen – but his upbringing amongst the Presbyterian gentry of Ireland was stable, landed and happy.

None of this applied to the early life of George Canning. His father had led a motley existence as a lawyer-cum-literary figure who then failed badly in business. Canning's father lost his inheritance when he married a penniless eighteen-year-old in 1768, and then he died just a year after Canning's birth. Canning's grandfather compounded one catastrophe with another, refusing to restore the inheritance his grandson was entitled to, and severed the existing pension of £150 per year. Mrs Canning's solution to her impending penury was to take to the stage. After a period of moderate success, she hitched herself to a dramatic rascal called Reddish who ended up drinking himself into dementia and died in York Asylum in 1785. She then found another failed businessman, Mr Hunn, married him, and persuaded him to become an actor as well.

Canning was rescued from this ramshackle childhood by the intervention of an actor called Moody, who wrote to all of Canning's relations warning them that the boy was 'on the road to the gallows'. In 1778, Canning's uncle, the merchant Stratford Canning, took charge of the eight-year-old and bundled him off to study at Eton. Here, George Canning began to shine, for he had a gift, inherited from his mother, which he liked to deploy as a way of impressing his teachers and friends. At Eton, and later at Oxford, he dazzled his colleagues with fiery displays of oratory and journalism.[4]

The event which altered both men's lives and opinions more than any other took place across the Channel. Castlereagh, like Canning, was initially in favour of the French Revolution. He visited the Continent in the summer of 1791, and met French émigrés in the Austrian Netherlands. 'It was', he complained, 'impossible to convince them that matters never could be reinstated as they formerly were ... that to escape disappointment they must moderate their views.' From the Netherlands he went on to Paris and attended debates at the Legislative Assembly. He was amazed at the deputies' 'inconceivable fluency of language' but he worried that there was a 'tumultuous pedantry' to France's new leaders and that the changes would lead to chaos.[5]

As the Revolution became more destructive and violent, Canning's views moved in the same critical direction. At a debating society one evening in the early 1790s, Canning turned to the President of the Club and explained to him and the audience that Mirabeau, the famous leader of the Revolution, was 'like the beverage, Sir, which stands so invitingly before you – foam and froth at the top, heavy and muddy within'. From November 1797 to July 1798, Canning dedicated the force of his wit and erudition to mocking the Revolution in a satirical magazine, the *Anti-Jacobin*.[6]

The two men, now convinced of the dangers of the French Revolution, disagreed about how to defeat it. For Canning, the French Revolution was the climax of a pan-European clash of opinions; it was a contest to be won by skilful arguments and dramatic exploits. By contrast, Castlereagh came to see that the Revolution had turned into a clash of European populations – that ideas had taken second place to thoughtless passions and pride. In 1793, the French Republic proclaimed its famous 'levée en masse', mobilising a whole nation to resist the counter-revolutionary forces. A month later, Castlereagh wrote that the 'tranquillity of Europe is at stake, and we contend with an opponent whose strength we have no means of measuring. It is the first time that all the population and all the wealth of a great kingdom have been concentrated in the field: what may be the result is beyond my perception.' Years later, Clausewitz analysed over several hundred pages what Castlereagh had discovered: the French were attempting total war.[7]

While Canning cracked jokes about the French Directory and its curious new calendar of ten classical months in each year, Castlereagh spent the 1790s exploding insurrectionary plots in Ireland, personally involving himself in many of the arrests. In March 1798, he was appointed Chief Secretary in Ireland, in effect deputy to the Viceroy. Within months, a French expeditionary force arrived in Ireland, expecting the country-wide insurrection which had been promised by Irish exiles in Paris. Although the invasion and the uprisings failed, they called into question the whole basis of the British Constitution. An all-Protestant Irish Parliament sat in Dublin representing the dominant Anglo-Saxon minority, and there was no Irish representation at all at Westminster. This structure began to look rickety. It now seemed that the only way to secure the British Isles was to formalise the Union between Ireland and Great Britain and centralise power in London. It fell to Castlereagh to pursue that logic to its conclusion: he was required by Pitt to persuade the Irish Parliament to vote for its own dissolution. He set about this with great determination, using methods which just about stayed within the rules of the day, but were later denounced as unscrupulous.

Events in Ireland took their toll on the way Castlereagh thought about human beings. One letter, written a decade later, when his focus had shifted across the Irish Sea as a loyal Tory and Member of Parliament, shows the pessimistic flow of Castlereagh's opinions as he travelled through Britain. 'To observe the wealth, the industry, the comfort of the country, which I have passed through since I left London, and to know that there are people ready to hazard all these blessings [through sedition] does astonish, if we did not know what human nature always has been and will be.'[8] What was needed, as Castlereagh saw it, was a benign but cool-headed aristocracy, led by men who were strong enough to be uninterested in public opinion, and sensible enough to govern without pride.

These views were firm but not unfeeling. 'There is no bloodshed for which he does not grieve,' Castlereagh's Private Secretary reflected after the Irish Rebellion was over, 'and yet he has no tendency to injudicious mercy.' Castlereagh kept any unhappiness carefully hidden; he only released his emotions when playing Handel on his 'cello or in letters to his wife, Emily, who remained dotty but devoted to the end. The public drew their own caricatures – a wise young man, able and dedicated, but cold in his manner and with 'a limited intercourse'. Meanwhile, the pessimism which ran through Castlereagh's character extended to his views about himself. 'I feel no confidence in myself', he told his uncle in 1796, 'beyond a general disposition for business, which perseverance and experience might ripen so as to qualify me to discharge the duties of an active situation.'[9] The famous clumsiness of his prose style was already apparent.

In England, Canning's confidence was blossoming. To confidence was added optimism about his fellow men. He was elected to the House of Commons in 1793, and by 1798 he was lecturing Parliament about the 'talents which God has given us for the benefit of our fellow creatures'.[10] Mankind, he thought, was perfectible, and the world might yet be improved. This would happen more quickly if he were in charge. He became obsessed with politics. In 1800, he fell in love with and married an heiress called Joan Scott. Her money gave him the independence he required. As repayment, he treated her as his closest confidante, sending her long and complicated letters analysing every coming in, going out, and piece of intrigue that he laid his hands on each day.

As talented young sceptics of the French Revolution, Canning and Castlereagh abandoned their Whig colleagues during the 1790s and became supporters of William Pitt. They were two of about a dozen disciples and followers, all around the same age, who had gathered together under the Prime Minister, and followed the master loyally in and out of office. Each was impressed by the sheer determination of a man vastly more talented than most others in Parliament, who seemed at times to be holding together the entire country as it was assailed by the revolutionary tide. But where Canning was drawn to Pitt out of loyalty and admiration for the man he christened the 'pilot who weathered the storm', Castlereagh never shook off his intellectual debt to a Prime Minister who was pragmatic, skilful and strong in adversity.

Pitt's death in 1806 left the two men in an alliance which was destined to fall apart. The Pittites excluded themselves from the new Government – the Ministry of all the Talents – under Lord Grenville and agreed to stay together as a Pittite faction in floating Opposition. But when the Talents fell in March 1807, after abolishing the Slave Trade but achieving little else, each of the Pittites began to scurry around anxiously to secure his own return to high office.

By five o'clock on Wednesday 25 March 1807 the matter was settled. Canning sent a letter to his wife from the Foreign Office. 'Is my own dearest Love satisfied with this date? Will she be still more satisfied, when she hears that her letter quite decided me? I was nearly decided before – But I had a battle to fight & an intrigue to defeat, & to assert myself boldly – which I did – & here I am.'[11] Just as Canning was settling in as Foreign Secretary, Lord Castlereagh was a few yards away in Whitehall, acquainting himself with his own new responsibilities as Secretary of State for War and the Colonies. Both men were to be led by the Duke of Portland, whose qualifications as Prime Minister were his advanced age, his modesty and the fact that his appointment would offend the smallest number of people.

This was not an auspicious moment to become Foreign Secretary. Certainly, the prospects for survival against Napoleon were brighter than in the darkness of the early 1800s. Britain's naval supremacy had been confirmed by Nelson's victory at Trafalgar; the threat of a French invasion now seemed unreal. But on the Continent, Napoleon looked unbeatable. After victories at Austerlitz and Jena, Napoleon had reached a new summit of supremacy. This was illustrated in November 1806 by the inauguration of a 'Continental System', which banned all British goods from Europe. The French thought this blow would be crippling; the Continental System would cut off the sources of Britain's strength by distorting her trade, while adding to the discontent which was growing among merchants and industrialists in the north of England.

It fell to Canning to turn this situation around. For a long time he had argued that the key to Napoleon's downfall lay in the resistance of his conquered subjects. He had spoken in the House of Commons in December 1798 of risings against the French in Holland and Spain as proof that loyalty cannot be sustained by the sword. In this same spirit Canning outlined his foreign policy to the Commons on 15 June

1807: 'We shall proceed upon the principle that any nation of Europe that starts up to oppose a power . . . the common enemy of all nations, whatever be the existing political relations of that nation, it becomes instantly our essential ally.'[12] In practice, this meant supporting states that declared war against Napoleon of their own free choosing, but refusing to bribe countries into alliances before they had themselves declared war.

Canning never doubted that Britain was strong enough to defeat Napoleon. He argued that the key to England's international power lay in the self-reliance of its imperial economy. No Continental System could seriously affect this. Canning explained:

> If ever the period should arrive when Great Britain being excluded from all Continental intercourse . . . the nations who now flatter themselves that they are the most necessary to her existence, who fancy that their commerce is one of the main springs of her power, would perhaps be the first to feel that that power is not created by foreign commerce . . . that this country has in itself in its own consumption and its own colonies ample means of self-existence; and that in her intercourse with other nations she bestows more benefit than she receives.[13]

Unfortunately, a depression set in after the Continental System had been erected and after the British Government had established retaliatory measures. Canning had spent too long studying the Classics and not enough time reading Adam Smith. But it was this breezy confidence and sweeping vision which gave him the strength to face the first serious test of his ministerial career.

On 14 June 1807, Napoleon won a devastating victory over the Russians at Friedland. In so doing, he obliterated his last serious opposition on the Continent. Worse was to follow for Britain. Napoleon carried forward his victory by meeting the Russian Czar, Alexander, on a raft on the River Niemen, near the town of Tilsit in Russia, to discuss the terms of his defeat. There Bonaparte deployed to the full his ability to charm and frighten; Alexander was bewitched. In secret articles and agreements at Tilsit, Napoleon arranged with Alexander that if Britain did not restore to France all maritime conquests made since 1805 and make a series of major economic concessions, Russia would wage war on Britain. If this happened, France and Russia would then compel the Danes, the Swedes and the Portuguese to join the Continental System and declare war upon Britain.[14] In this way, the remaining neutral states in Europe would be subsumed within a huge Napoleonic front against England. One way or another, the Danish and Portuguese navies would fall into Napoleon's hands, threatening that control of the seas on which Britain's security depended.

For several weeks, the new British Government had no idea about any of this. On 29 June there were rumours in London of a great battle in which the Russians had been involved. On the 30th it was clear to Canning that there had been some kind of disaster. By 7 July, the full nature of the defeat was apparent and news of an armistice filtered through.[15] But Canning, Castlereagh and the rest of the British Cabinet could only guess at what had gone on on that raft on the River Niemen, and had only a vague notion of the threats they now faced. Reports soon began to filter over to Britain about the cordiality of the Tilsit exchange. Spies, agents and ambassadors wrote from across Europe warning about some kind of Franco-Russian alliance. There was nothing uniform about their advice. They hypothesised about mysterious plans and cryptic commitments, basing their information on whispers and hearsay. Their reports were collated into dramatic dossiers of 'Secret Intelligence' and launched on to the Foreign Secretary's desk.[16]

We cannot tell how these reports affected Canning's idea of what had happened at Tilsit or his views on how Britain should react. Everything hung on the instincts and character of the new Foreign Secretary. By 10 July, Canning had 'no doubt that Bonaparte reckons on the Danish fleet at a fit time as an instrument of hostility against Great Britain'.[17] On 14 July, the Cabinet agreed to send a strong force to the Baltic.[18] Five days later, Lord Castlereagh wrote to Lieutenant-General Lord Cathcart, repeating Canning's warning in his own clunking prose: the 'most serious apprehensions' had arisen that the naval power and resources of Denmark 'may at no distant period be turned against this Country'. These apprehensions were to be explained to the Danes in full, but 'which explanations and representations however to have their due Weight, it is considered should not be entered upon until they can be supported by an adequate naval and military force assembled on the Spot'.[19]

The pace quickened when Canning received a letter on 21 July from the Count d'Antraigues, a peripatetic French émigré who bustled about lobbying for tougher action against the revolutionary French regime. His travels had taken him from France through Austria to Saxony, and into Russian pay. By 1807 he had settled in London, loosely attached to the Russian Embassy as a propagandist and spy.[20] Perhaps he was not the most reliable and objective source of intelligence to rely on when planning a dangerous operation – but in the shifting and confused world of the Napoleonic Wars, Foreign Secretaries had to make do with what they got. The letter d'Antraigues sent to Canning on 21 July reads like many of his other letters at the time. It was long and complicated, with a great deal of blather about his own affairs. But it began with a message which D'Antraigues claimed to have received from a Russian general close to the Czar. This general, while aboard the raft on the River Niemen, had heard plans for 'a maritime league of this country [Russia] against England and the unification of the Russian squadrons with those of Sweden and Denmark [as well as] the forces of Spain and Portugal in order to attack England at close quarters'.[21]

The information blew away any lingering caution in Canning's mind. He added a footnote to a letter he had been writing to Lord Gower, the British Ambassador in Russia: 'Since I finished my letter to you at two o'clock in the morning I have received intelligence which appears to rest on good authority, coming directly from Tilsit, that, at a conference between the Emperor of Russia and Bonaparte, the latter proposed a maritime league against Great Britain to which Denmark and Sweden and Portugal should be invited or forced to accede ... If this be true our fleet in the Baltic may have more business than we expected.'[22]

The new information demanded tougher action. Just over a week later, a large expedition of ships and soldiers set sail. Canning made his instructions simple: 'the possession of the Danish fleet is the one main and indispensable object to which the whole of your negotiation is to be directed'. The Danes would be asked to give up their navy in exchange for subsidies and security. If the Danes rejected these offerings, more decisive measures would be required.[23] 'I am sure if we succeed we do a most effective service to the Country,' Canning scribbled in a letter to his wife on Friday 31 July. 'But the measure is a bold one & if it fails – we must be impeached I suppose & dearest dear will have a Box at the Trial.'[24] The following day, Canning wrote to his wife about the one aspect of his Danish policy which was still bothering him:

> ... a mail which I received in the House last night, just at the moment when I sat down, brought me the account of the French being actually about to do that act of hostility, the possibility of which formed the groundwork of my Baltic plan. My fear was that the French might not be the aggressors – & then we would have approved a strong measure fully justifiable I think & absolutely necessary, but without apparent necessity as justification. Now the aggression will justify us fully: & yet be so timed as to give us all the merit (which we have a right to) of having foreseen & made preparation in time. I am therefore quite easy now as to the morality & political wisdom of our plan. – Now for the execution.[25]

Canning slept badly during the next few weeks, alert with excitement and anxiety while waiting for news of the Danish mission. The diplomacy failed, the fighting started, and a naval bombardment of Copenhagen began. After three relentless days and considerable damage to life and property, the Danes asked for a truce. They agreed to give up the fleet if Britain evacuated its forces from Denmark.[26] The British sailed away accordingly, with the Danish fleet in tow.

When news of the attack reached London the reaction was mixed. George III had always been uneasy about the mission, complaining to Canning that it was 'a very immoral act. So immoral that I won't ask who originated it.' The Opposition were equally unimpressed and launched their own attacks on Canning in the House of Commons. Thomas Moore, the poet, tried to explain Canning's policy with an esoteric rhyme – 'If Grotius be thy guide, shut, shut the book. In force alone for law of nations look' – while the caricaturist Gillray drew a cartoon to celebrate the Copenhagen campaign. On balance, praise for the bold move outweighed the criticisms; even William Wilberforce concluded that the expedition was a justified measure of self-defence. But the arguments rumbled on into the following year, and in early February Canning had to defend the expedition in full. In a speech lasting almost three hours, Canning pledged his honour to the accuracy of the intelligence and defended every action he had taken. Paying close attention was a young MP, Viscount Palmerston, who described Canning's speech as 'very witty, very eloquent and very able'.[27]

Canning argued that the Danish expedition was a pre-emptive measure to defuse an imminent threat. The imminence may have been exaggerated. Much of the intelligence Canning received was false, and some of it may have been planted by Napoleon to force Britain into a rash decision.[28] But Napoleon is said to have been furious when he heard about the British attack on Copenhagen, strongly suggesting that he did have some kind of Danish plan. This is confirmed by the secret articles of Tilsit which show that Napoleon intended to incorporate Denmark within his system of European alliances and client-states, and turn that mighty coalition against Britain.

Even before the Copenhagen expedition was over, the Tilsit tryst had begun to bear fruit in another part of Europe. The secret articles had referred to Portugal as well as Denmark, and by implication the Portuguese fleet. By six o'clock on 26 August 1807, Canning had reached his own conclusion about Napoleon's plans. 'We have more work upon our hands. Lisbon <u>ought</u> to be another Copenhagen.' Canning worked hard to persuade the Portuguese Royal Family to flee to Brazil before Napoleon exerted a stranglehold, but the Portuguese Regent wavered. On 26 November, the Royal Navy were instructed to blockade the Tagus unless the Royal Family agreed to escape with their navy to Brazil. At last, and with French troops closing in on Lisbon, the Regent joined the British on 28 November; the Portuguese fleet sailed the following day for Brazil under British escort. 'Huzza, Huzza, Huzza,' Canning wrote joyfully, 'Denmark was saucy and we were obliged to <u>take her</u> fleet. Portugal had confidence and we rescued hers.'[29]

With his typical swagger, Canning skirted over any regrets. Yet the larger question lingers on: were the bombardment of Copenhagen and the blockade of the Tagus just acts of war? The Catholic Church, embellishing Aquinas, tells us that a war must fulfil several criteria if it is just: it must be waged by a lawful authority; it must be fought for a just cause and underpinned by good intentions; the use of force should be proportional; and it should also be a last resort. The Copenhagen mission was launched on what were plausible grounds of future self-defence. The threats in the Treaty of Tilsit were real enough; Nelson had destroyed nearly twenty men-of-war at Trafalgar, while Canning rescued more than thirty from Denmark and Portugal.[30] Force was employed only after diplomacy had failed and lasted no longer than was necessary. Many innocent people died in Copenhagen in September 1807, but if Canning had left the Danish fleet to Napoleon, he would have run the risk of far greater casualties when Napoleon challenged the Royal Navy and attempted a new invasion of Britain.

One hundred and thirty-three years later, Britain again stood in desperate danger. Again, an ally had collapsed in defeat. Once again, a powerful fleet seemed about to fall into the hands of the enemy; again, the British Government decided on a pre-emptive strike. On 3 July 1940 Admiral Somerville was ordered by Churchill, after negotiation had failed, to attack the French fleet at its base at Oran in Algeria. There were differences. Denmark was neutral, France had been an ally. The operation in Copenhagen was successful, the entire Danish fleet being captured, whereas in 1940 the battleship *Strasbourg* and other French ships escaped to Toulon. Copenhagen was bloodier; thousands of citizens were killed in the bombardment of the city. In each case there were some misgivings at home; but in each case the attack was justified by a certain danger and gave necessary proof of ruthless determination at a moment of weakness and doubt.

In the autumn of 1807, the British Government responded to Napoleon's Continental System. Orders in Council obliged all foreign ships to call at a British port to pay duty before visiting European ports from which British ships were excluded.[31] The effects were chaotic. During the course of 1808, international trade wound down to a standstill. In Britain, there were economic slumps and peace protests. In America, where trade was faltering, there were war-cries and some talked about an invasion of Canada. None of this seems to have had much effect on Castlereagh and Canning. They were both staunch advocates of the Orders in Council, and more worried about the dangers from Europe than from Yankee rebels who hated Britain already. Besides, by the spring of 1808, the problem was overshadowed by new developments in Spain.

Just when it seemed as though Napoleon might be unbeatable, he made the first of his big mistakes. In the spring of 1808, he decided to make his brother, Joseph, the new King of Spain. Revolts, already brewing, now erupted across the Peninsula and Napoleon was forced to pour thousands of French troops into Spain. The crisis, an irritation to Napoleon, was for Canning a source of new hope and drama. He decided to support the struggling Spaniards with arms and equipment, while ignoring Joseph Bonaparte and recognising the Bourbon Ferdinand as the Spanish King. Some weapons captured from the Armada in 1588 were dusted down in the Tower of London and shipped back to Spain.[32]

In July 1808, a British army was dispatched to the Peninsula. Over the next months, erratic progress culminated in General Sir John Moore's Corunna campaign. Moore, a stern critic of the Government who was particularly baffled by Castlereagh's military dispatches, questioned the strategy but managed to carry out a series of delicate manoeuvres before Napoleon turned on him and chased him halfway across Spain. At Corunna, Moore fought a valiant rear-guard action, allowing his troops to evacuate peacefully, but he was mortally wounded. Both Castlereagh and Canning had to defend the expedition in Parliament. Castlereagh gave a pedestrian defence of the plans; Canning followed with a dazzling speech, but it is said that his words were eclipsed by the spectacle shining through the Commons' windows of Drury Lane Theatre burning down.[33]

In the spring of 1809, the Government was caught up and embarrassed by a scandal involving the sale of Army commissions by the Duke of York's mistress. The Duke resigned as Commander-in-Chief of the Army, but Canning's patience was wearing thin. He wrote a long letter to the Prime Minister complaining about the entire conduct of the war. In particular, he worried about the Government's 'spirit of compromise', the lack of a daring strategy, and the way that the Government had lost public confidence by its handling of the war in Spain. It was, he felt, his duty 'fairly to avow to your Grace, that the Government as at present constituted does not appear to me equal to the great task which it has to perform'. The Duke of Portland, worried by what this statement might imply, invited Canning to discuss his concerns with him in person. Over the course of several days Canning's ultimatum became clear: there would be 'a change in Castlereagh's department, or mine'.[34]

Panic set in. Portland, anxious to avoid confrontations of any kind, scrabbled around for a compromise. Others were consulted – first Lord Bathurst, then Castlereagh's uncle, Lord Camden, even the King who devised complicated schemes by which Castlereagh might remain in Government but in a new position. But no one quite had the confidence to suggest any of these ideas to Castlereagh, and the problem stewed through the summer of 1809.

Perhaps the Duke of Portland should be forgiven for the loose and colluding part he played in those months. For several years, Canning and Castlereagh had sat calmly beside one another in Parliament. It is true that there had been tension between them and Canning had held a low opinion of Castlereagh's abilities for a long time.* But this had always seemed compatible with the normal current of rivalry which runs through all political careers. Now Canning had infected that rivalry with an ultimatum much more ruthless than before. We cannot know whether expunging Castlereagh from the Government was Canning's main goal, or merely a tool to accelerate his own career. Either way, Canning was playing outside the normal rules of politics and the Duke of Portland was not a strong umpire.

Meanwhile, in Europe, the Austrians had turned on Napoleon and won a major victory at Aspern. Somehow, the British Government had to find a way of pressing home the advantage. The plan which they came up with – an amphibious expedition up the River Scheldt to seize the island of Walcheren, destroy French lines of communication, and attack Antwerp – was not new, but it was greeted with a flurry of fresh objections from the senior military advisers to the Government, who worried that the operation was unfeasible and based on faulty intelligence. These were minor details for someone like Canning; he and Castlereagh brushed off the military concerns. Something had to be done quickly before the French regained the

---

* One particularly alert biographer of Canning found a table drawn up by Canning in 1807, charting the motley abilities of his colleagues. This fierce piece of analysis placed Castlereagh at the bottom of the pile. See Dixon, *Canning*, pp. 98–9.

initiative. On 21 June, the Cabinet gave the go-ahead to the Walcheren plan.

The Castlereagh-Canning dilemma now reached new levels of complexity. One Cabinet Minister was insisting on the dismissal of another; yet both were at a crucial stage of essential work. No one in the Cabinet wanted to upset the War Secretary while the Walcheren expedition was getting under way; everyone was equally desperate to stop Canning leaving the Government. Lord Eldon, Lord Chatham, Lord Harrowby, Lord Liverpool and Spencer Perceval were all drawn into the confusion. Castlereagh, consumed by hard work, knew nothing of what was afoot.

On 21 July, news reached England that the Austrian army had been defeated by Napoleon at Wagram, bringing to an end the resistance to French domination in Central Europe. The whole basis for the Walcheren expedition now evaporated – but the Cabinet ploughed on. On 28 July, Castlereagh, Canning and Spencer Perceval travelled down to Deal to see the British force of 40,000 troops set sail for Walcheren. The Duke of Portland now decided that something could be done to solve the Castlereagh problem. A plan was agreed: Castlereagh would be moved out of his post and into the House of Lords; Lord Camden would break the news to his nephew. But Camden could not bring himself to do it. Canning became more and more irritated by the concealment – but refused to remove his demand. At last Portland agreed to say something to Castlereagh; soon afterwards, he suffered an epileptic fit.[35]

What should be done with Castlereagh? Who should be the next Prime Minister? These two questions tangled with each other. The Chancellor of the Exchequer, Spencer Perceval, and Canning were the obvious candidates; they tested each other's ambitions carefully, like prize fighters poking for weaknesses. Meanwhile, the news that Flushing had been successfully taken by the British expeditionary force reached London, driving Castlereagh into new convolutions: 'so hazardous and critical an operation (danger of navigation included) as our expedition to Antwerp is, I believe never was before attempted – so God send us a good deliverance'.[36]

But God sent no deliverance. With heavy rainfall slowing the expedition, the French opened the dykes on the waterways; the

British troops were already up to their knees in water. The water spread a fever peculiar to the region, and soon huge numbers of British soldiers were sick. The Commander-in-Chief of the Walcheren expedition, Lord Chatham, now admitted that it would be impossible to move on and attack Antwerp. This was the final straw for Canning. He demanded that Castlereagh be removed immediately. But Spencer Perceval and Lord Liverpool were reluctant to offend Castlereagh and set out a more cautious approach. They suggested a general reshuffle and persuaded the incapacitated Duke of Portland to resign. The Duke accepted this solution, but warned Canning that Castlereagh could not be dismissed out of hand. Canning responded by hinting at his own resignation, and refused to attend Cabinet the next day.

At this point, during the Cabinet meeting on 7 September, Castlereagh began to suspect that something was going on. It must have been sheer pressure of wartime work which had blunted Castlereagh's usual shrewdness up to then. Sir Thomas Lawrence thought Castlereagh was particularly downcast during his portrait session later that same afternoon. In the evening, Castlereagh asked his uncle, Lord Camden, to explain the situation. The story began to come out. Castlereagh resigned the following day, agreeing to carry on administrative business at the War Department for the time being but refusing to take part in policy. In Walcheren, the situation continued to deteriorate. By 11 September, almost 11,000 troops were ill.[37]

On 13 September, the King sent for Canning to consult on the formation of a new Ministry. Canning initially suggested Spencer Perceval as Prime Minister, but was willing to undertake the job if His Majesty so wished. The King refused the offer and later described the conversation as the 'most extraordinary he had ever heard'. Canning continued to wait hopefully, although now worried by the 'constant meetings and co-jobberations' at Spencer Perceval's house. It was also curious – or so Canning thought – that Castlereagh had somehow disappeared 'as thro' a trap door'.[38] But Castlereagh had not disappeared. On 16 September he wrote a long-winded letter to his old colleague, Edward Cooke: 'If my colleagues (whose support and confidence I had no reason to doubt accompanied me throughout my late anxious and laborious duties) are either <u>unable</u> or <u>unwilling</u>

to sustain me in that situation [the War Department] I desire in that case only the privilege of being allowed to defend out of office my own public character and conduct.'[39]

Three days later, Castlereagh wrote to Canning directly: 'You continued to sit in the same Cabinet with me, and to leave me not only in the persuasion that I possessed your confidence as a colleague, but you allowed me, tho' thus virtually superseded, in breach of every principle both public and private to originate and proceed in the Execution of a new Enterprise of the most arduous and important nature, with your apparent concurrence and ostensible approbation.'[40] Apparently, this was an unavoidable challenge to personal honour. At half past ten the following morning, Canning sent the following reply: 'The tone and purport of your Lordship's letter (which I have this moment received) of course precludes any other answer, on my part, to the misapprehensions and misrepresentations, with which it abounds, than that I will cheerfully give to your Lordship the satisfaction that you require.'[41]

News of the duel travelled quickly. Within days, Londoners could choose from a full selection of rhymes and satires about the contest. There were also serious conclusions to be drawn. The Whig *Morning Chronicle* voiced one of them: 'To suppose it possible after the disgusting exhibition they have made, to form out of their dispersed and disordered ranks a Government that could stand, is the height of absurdity.' It was indeed absurd. Both Canning and Castlereagh slunk off to the back benches; on 4 October Spencer Perceval was appointed Prime Minister; twenty-two days later the long-suffering Duke of Portland died; finally, on 4 November, the order was submitted to evacuate the island of Walcheren.[42]

Castlereagh wrote to the King to apologise for his part in the duel, but denied that Canning had had any grounds to complain about his work as Secretary of State for War. Canning tried to defend his own actions by publishing the correspondence which had led to the duel, but the attempt backfired. Yet Canning did have a case. Castlereagh's administration of the military effort had been clumsy as well as unlucky. But Canning had pushed the argument too far and at the wrong time; the wide support he once had now deserted him.

Historians and observers would later take this duel as the high point of the argument between the two men. Their two most famous biographers, Sir Charles Webster and Harold Temperley, filled the pages of a renowned journal in 1929 with a learned dispute about its causes and consequences. But this had been a duel of ambitions not ideas; fierce personal competition rather than ideological rancour had been the animating force. The strange and interesting part of the Castlereagh and Canning story followed the physical contest. The intellectual dispute became sharp and real. As the personal relationship was slowly restored between Castlereagh and Canning, a series of political arguments broke out between them about Britain's position in the post-war world. These arguments reached back to their earliest ideas and drew on each man's instinctive beliefs. They unfolded in an altogether more stimulating manner than any violent quarrel about jobs.

During the next two and a half years George III faded into a final, incurable bout of madness. The Prince of Wales at last achieved those powers of Regency which his Whig friends, led by Lord Grey, had long hoped for. He at once let them down. Instead of appointing a new Whig government as expected, the Regent kept in place the existing Tory Administration under Spencer Perceval. Perceval abandoned his attempt at bringing Whigs in to his Government and now looked back to older friends. On 18 February 1812, at the second time of asking, some twenty-nine months after he handed in his resignation as Secretary of State for War, Lord Castlereagh agreed to return to the front benches as the new Foreign Secretary. Canning, still condemned to the back benches, had paid the heavier price for the duel.

Not much had changed in the world. Napoleon continued to dominate most of Europe. Britain had found a new military hero in Arthur Wellesley, who later became the Duke of Wellington, but even he had made only a stilted progress in Spain. Meanwhile the pressure of unrelenting warfare continued to fuel disgruntlement across England. As the economic effects of the Orders in Council became steadily more erratic and controversial in Britain and also in America, an Inquiry into the Orders was proposed in April 1812. But before any headway could be made in reforming the system, fate changed the game. As Spencer Perceval was walking through the lobby of the House of Commons on his way to the Inquiry on 11 May, he was shot through the heart and killed. The assassin was an insane businessman called John Bellingham who had been financially ruined by the Orders in Council.*

The tragedy suspended the normal functioning of Government. The Regent flailed around in search of a new Prime Minister. After several false starts and widespread confusion he chose Lord Liverpool on 8 June 1812. Castlereagh was to continue as Foreign Secretary and now also as the Leader of the House of Commons. From the Peninsula, Wellington wrote to Lord Liverpool with typical terseness to welcome him to his new Office. 'You have undertaken a most gigantic task, and I don't know how you will get through it . . . However, there is nothing like trying.'[43]

Within a fortnight the gigantic task had become titanic. On 16 June a motion was put forward to repeal the Orders in Council. Under pressure, the Government conceded. But unaware of this retreat, and furious after years of being bullied by the Royal Navy, the Americans declared war on Britain two days later.

The American war was always going to be a sideshow to the European conflict, and it did not resolve any of the issues which had caused it. The Americans invaded Canada, where they sacked the city of York, now Toronto; the British burned Washington in revenge. The conflict then sank into a fierce stalemate. The tenacity of the Americans surprised even cautious observers, but the war did not have the devastating effect on Great Britain's struggle against Napoleon which most wars on two fronts are supposed to have.

No one could have predicted this when the fighting broke out in 1812. With Britain now at war on two continents and the Government in a state of general disarray, the Regent decided to intervene. The Government needed politicians who could hold their own against the Opposition, with skills of oratory and 'especially of retort'. The Prince took it upon himself to broker an agreement between Castlereagh and Canning in order to get Canning back into Government. Surely, as he explained to Castlereagh's half-brother,

* Today, John Bellingham's descendant Henry Bellingham is a bastion of respectability as the Conservative Member of Parliament for North West Norfolk.

Sir Charles Stewart, there was nothing between Castlereagh and Canning 'which the weighty, enormous and difficult crisis of the country ought not to soften down and bury in oblivion'.[44]

But even the weighty, enormous and difficult crisis of the country was not enough to soften Canning's pride. Canning met Castlereagh; they shook hands; they agreed to let bygones be bygones; but they could not agree about how they could work together in Government. The offer which Castlereagh made to Canning was generous. He would relinquish the Foreign Office to Canning, but keep the Leadership of the House of Commons and also assume the Chancellorship of the Exchequer. Yet Canning could not bring himself to agree on the grounds that by keeping the Leadership of the House of Commons Castlereagh would technically be his superior.

Canning had made a huge mistake. On 24 June Napoleon had launched a massive army of around 600,000 French troops across the River Niemen to invade Russia; six months later only 40,000 would drag themselves back. After so many ripples and eddies this way and that, the tide in Europe had finally turned but Canning was not there to profit from it in his own career. Some years later, Canning would look back ruefully on Castlereagh's offer – 'the handsomest ever yet made to an individual'.[45]

After defying the French invaders, the Russian Czar, Alexander, decided to rescue the rest of Europe from Napoleon's claws. Castlereagh dispatched Lord Cathcart as the new Ambassador to Russia. His instructions were vague: 'Whatever scheme of policy can most immediately combine the greatest number of powers and the greatest force against France ... before she can recruit her armies and recover her ascendancy is that which we must naturally desire most to promote.' With the help of Nathan Rothschild, who worked hard to raise cash on Castlereagh's behalf, the British began to persuade the other powers in Europe to join yet another alliance against Bonaparte.* On 27 February 1813 a treaty was

---

* Nathan Rothschild played a remarkable role in Britain's war effort, providing finance as well as an impressive intelligence network for the allies. A year later, Castlereagh received a note from Lord Liverpool which ended with a quiet statement of Rothschild's importance: 'P.S. – Mr Rothschild has been a very useful friend. I do not know what we should have done without him last year.' See Charles Webster, *The Foreign Policy of Castlereagh* (London: G. Bell, 1931–4), Vol. 1, pp. 38; 543.

signed with Prussia; in June Castlereagh managed to pass a treaty of alliance with Sweden which granted subsidies as well as the use of the Royal Navy in annexing Norway if the Swedes sent 30,000 troops to Germany. In the same month Wellington won a decisive victory in the Peninsula at Vittoria and Joseph Bonaparte was bundled out of Spain. Weeks later the Austrians declared war against France.[46]

Canning's career unravelled at almost the same speed as Napoleon's. There was small profit in opposing a victorious government. Half-hearted attacks on the Government's 'half-afraid' war with the USA came to little. The Norwegian conquest 'filled him with shame, regret and indignation', but he could do little about it beyond quarrelling with Castlereagh in Parliament.[47] He began to think about leaving politics altogether. In 1814 he decided to travel to Portugal to improve the health of his eldest son. The Ministry learned of his plans and asked him to become the British Ambassador in Lisbon. Canning accepted the posting under pressure. He did not return until 1816.

Years of chaotic and exhausting warfare with Napoleon were reaching their final climax. The man who had controlled most of Europe for a decade was at last on the run. His opponents sensed blood and drove forward. Castlereagh grasped the opportunity which opened up before him and focused his energy and expertise on bringing the long conflict to a close. He was ably supported by the new Prime Minister, Lord Liverpool, who began to show himself as a man of cautiousness, plain sense and determination.

Castlereagh was confronted by two major problems as he pursued his task. The first was how to draw the various strands of counter-offensive against Napoleon into a coherent campaign. It was clear that what was needed was a new system of co-operation. The individual interests of the allies had to take second place to their shared interest in beating Napoleon. But achieving this would require levels of discipline and self-restraint which had been absent in the earlier coalitions, and a new, intense and regular pattern of consultation. As Castlereagh put it in August 1813, 'before Lord W[ellington] forms his future plans, he must know what is to happen in Germany; his whole policy must be governed upon that of the Allies'. This did not mean abandoning the work in Spain, but co-ordinating the effort there with a powerful thrust against Napoleon in Central Europe. We have done wonders in the Peninsula,' Castlereagh told Lord Cathcart, 'but don't let the experiment be tried of a single combat again in that quarter. We may sink before the undivided power of France: and if we do, Germany, and even Russia, will soon resume their fetters.'[48] From this desperate need for European co-operation against Napoleon flowed the whole philosophy of a Concert of Europe, which in different forms strongly influenced the diplomacy of the next hundred years.

The first problem led naturally to the second. Europe had been in tumult for two decades; years of conquest and upheaval had wiped out the structures which had defined the old order. Victory against Napoleon would have to be followed by diplomacy and reconstruction on a scale unknown since the Peace of Westphalia in 1648. But the allies each had their own ideas for what Europe should look like after the wars. There was a particular argument about whether Napoleon had to be removed from the French throne or whether Europe could be liberated without regime change in France. The Austrians favoured the second option because of the check Napoleon would have on the other powers in Europe, and because he was married to their Emperor's daughter. But, slowly, Castlereagh came to realise that there could be no peace in Europe with Napoleon in power. 'Fatal would it be for them, and for the world, if they could for a moment think of seeking their safety in what is called a Continental peace.'[49] A lasting peace would depend on whether the European powers could agree on some kind of system, some new alignment of nations and empires in Europe which could withstand the competing forces and rivalries which had contributed to Napoleon's rise.

As wise men do when faced with great difficulties, Castlereagh looked to the past; as a good Pittite, he wondered what his master would have done. His research came to rest on a thoughtful but winding memorandum on the 'Deliverance and Security of Europe' which Pitt had drawn up in 1805.[50] The plan had come to nothing at the time but it fitted Castlereagh's worldview. He sent a copy to Cathcart in April 1813. 'As an outline to reason I send you . . . a dispatch on which the confederacy in 1805 was founded,' he explained. 'I well remember having more than one conversation with

Mr Pitt on its details before he wrote it.' The 'main features we are agreed upon', Castlereagh told Cathcart, were 'that to keep France we need great masses'.

Occasionally in history we come across documents which achieve little in their own right but which articulate something so powerfully that the central ideas take on a life of their own. There was no penetrating rhetoric or imaginative prose in Pitt's memorandum, nor was the basic tenor of his proposal particularly new. France had to be kept in check, and this meant surrounding it with 'great masses', creating territorial balances and power blocs around it to deter fresh expansion or daring attacks. But the rigour and completeness of Pitt's memorandum lifted it above others of its time. First Castlereagh, and then, much later, a Harvard academic called Henry Kissinger saw it as a template for ending the Napoleonic Wars. Indeed, as Dr Kissinger illustrated, 'the Pitt plan became the blueprint of Castlereagh's policy'.[51]

There was also a hidden subtlety to Pitt's memorandum, and it was this which Castlereagh seized and deployed to maximum effect. Pitt had realised that in the clashing world of revolutions and mass warfare it was not enough just to shift around territories and armies, as if playing a game of Risk. The 'great mass' foreign policy, with its border changes, power blocs, empires balancing empires, could only be part of the solution. It had been the bread and butter of eighteenth-century diplomacy, but it was not quite palatable now. New devices were needed to keep revolutionary France from spreading its ideas abroad using force; Pitt had sketched these out in his usual meandering way:

> ... in order to render this Security as complete as possible, it seems necessary, at the period of a general Pacification, to form a Treaty to which all the principal powers of Europe should be Parties ... and they should all bind themselves mutually to protect and support each other, against any attempt to infringe them – It should re-establish a general and comprehensive system of Public Law in Europe, and provide, as far as possible, for repressing future attempts to disturb the general Tranquillity, and above all, for restraining any projects of Aggrandizement and Ambition similar to those which have produced all the Calamities inflicted on Europe since the disastrous era of the French Revolution ...[52]

By adapting the ancient instruments of guarantees and defensive treaties to create a European alliance which would exist in peacetime, Pitt had sowed a new seed in diplomacy, and it now began to take root in Castlereagh's mind. By the end of 1813 Castlereagh and the Cabinet were drawing up proposals for a treaty 'not to terminate with the War, but to Contain defensive Engagements with eventual obligations to support the Powers attack'd by France, with a certain extent of Stipulated Succours'.[53] With this talk about defensive Engagements and Stipulated Succours, we see the start of modern collective security.

Such was the plan; putting it into practice would be a quite separate matter, made more difficult by the standard of British diplomacy on the Continent. The young and austere Earl of Aberdeen had been sent by Castlereagh to represent Britain to Austria. He was equipped with few qualifications but a profound sense of personal tragedy – orphaned as a child, widowed as a young man and haunted, quite literally, by his loss. He quarrelled with his British counterparts about protocol and they failed to establish a clear voice with the European powers. By December 1813, the European allies had grown tired of incoherence and sent a request to London for a single negotiator. This caught Castlereagh off-guard. No one except the Foreign Secretary was equipped to negotiate on such a basis. He would be gone for months, and much of the time would be spent on the road. Yet Lord Liverpool saw the problem and urged him on. Over the Christmas period of 1813, the Cabinet drew up a memorandum setting out the basis for Castlereagh's negotiations. The *sine qua non* of his negotiating position were to be '1st the Absolute Exclusion of France from any Naval Establishment on the Scheldt, and Especially at Antwerp and 2ndly The Security of Holland being adequately provided for under the house of Orange by a Barrier, which shall at least include Juliers and Antwerp as well as Maestricht with a Suitable Arrondisement of Territory in Addition to Holland as it stood in 1792'. To this was added that 'the Monarchies of the Peninsula must also be Independent under their Legitimate Sovereigns. Their Dominions at least in Europe being guaranteed against attack by France.'[54]

At first sight, these instructions seem slightly surprising. It is hard for us to appreciate today the overriding importance of geography on Britain's security in the nineteenth century. Airpower has diminished the significance of distance, and nuclear weapons and terrorism mean that immovable forces such as oceans and deserts are redundant as a defence against attack. None of this was true in 1813. In particular, the deepwater ports on the coast of north Europe were a long-standing anxiety to British statesmen. An enemy naval base at Flushing or Antwerp was a red alert for invasion. As Castlereagh told Aberdeen, leaving Antwerp in the hands of France would be 'little short of imposing upon Great Britain the charge of a perpetual war establishment'.[55]

Castlereagh set off, accompanied by a motley entourage which consisted of his wife, Emily, her niece and nephew, his Private Secretary and two other clerks. After a cold and choppy crossing, they arrived at Hellevoetsluis on 5 January 1814 where they were greeted by cheers and a burst of jubilant gunshots from the recently liberated Dutch.[56] It was the first time a serving British Foreign Secretary had set foot abroad.

Without a pause Castlereagh rattled off across Europe in pursuit of the allies. His aim at this stage was not to negotiate peace but to keep the coalition together. He detached himself from his wife so that he could travel faster. He reached Frankfurt six days after leaving The Hague, spending only one night in an inn. He got to Freiburg on 17 January 1814 but the Allied Headquarters had moved on to Basle. He was there within twenty-four hours, only to be told that the Czar had already left to join his troops in France.

Metternich, the Austrian Minister, was still at the camp in Basle when Castlereagh arrived. There, the two statesmen met for the first time. Metternich had hitherto manoeuvred on behalf of his empire with agility and total lack of scruple between submitting to Napoleon and trying to outwit him. From now on, his own views became clear. Metternich shared Castlereagh's instinctive distaste for war and belief in rational diplomacy based on courtesy and shared interests. In Castlereagh, however, there still existed vestiges of the English Whig respect for constitutional institutions acceptable to the people and for the rule of law. By contrast, Metternich believed that only Legitimacy – by which he meant the exercise of power by hereditary monarchs – provided a principle which could keep Europe in peace. But both men at this moment saw the need for a new balance of power; and both men thought that the way to achieve this was through calm diplomacy. It was no surprise when Metternich said after the meeting, 'I get on with him as if we had spent all our lives together.'[57]

Within days, Castlereagh was off again, heading through the snow for the allied lines just north of Dijon. There, he found the allied leaders at serious odds. The Czar had decided that after the war Poland should no longer be partitioned between Russia, Austria and Prussia but reunited under his own sovereignty. The land which Prussia would lose in Poland could be substituted by Saxony; Austrian losses could be made up in Italy. It was not a great start to collective diplomacy and the Austrians were particularly alarmed. Slowly, Castlereagh imposed some order on the proceedings. The joint pursuit of war was continued; the allies agreed to discuss all contentious issues later, at a congress which would be held in Vienna after the war. Castlereagh drafted a memorandum to his plenipotentiaries in Europe, charting a course for British diplomacy in the final stages of war: 'The interests of Great Britain neither require to be asserted with chicane nor with dexterity – a steady and temperate application of honest principles is her best source of authority.'[58]

Castlereagh now planned the next move to Châtillon where negotiations with the French could begin. Before leaving, he wrote one of many letters to appease his wife as he travelled across Europe. Emily was still cooped up in the Low Countries, and increasingly irritated by the separation.

> I have now made acquaintance with all the great wigs here. The Emperor Alexander would be your favourite. He has 30,000 Guards here that are the finest soldiers I ever beheld. When I can calculate at all movements or events, you shall have my plans. Till then, don't stir, lest I should give you the slip and return by Paris.
> I am quite well. Work is hard – and I never see a single princess.
> So God preserve you,
> C.[59]

These conjugal complications were but potholes on the winding road towards peace. Greater difficulties lay ahead. The Czar was becoming distracted by the prospect of victory. As Castlereagh put it, the Czar 'has a <u>personal</u> feeling about Paris'. This feeling focused on a vision of triumph and magnanimity. 'He seems to seek for the occasion of entering with his magnificent guards the enemy's capital, probably to display, in his clemency and forbearance, a contrast to that desolation to which his own was devoted.' At Châtillon, there was no holding him. The Czar ordered that all negotiations be suspended as he charged forward into France, throwing allied diplomacy into disarray.[60]

Castlereagh set off again. At Troyes he met the Czar and on 13 and 14 February tried unsuccessfully to bring him back to sanity. He returned to Châtillon and was met by the news that Napoleon had launched a series of massive counter-attacks and was advancing on Troyes. This news had a predictable effect on diplomacy. The French negotiators, sensing a comeback, dispensed with the compromises that had been carefully drawn up in the preceding days and prepared to fight to the finish. The arrogance of the allies dissolved into an excessive humility. For several weeks, their spirits were only held together by Castlereagh. He urged strength on his failing friends, and reminded the other powers how close they still were to beating Napoleon. In early March the battles again began to flow in the allies' favour and Castlereagh found himself able to negotiate the four-power treaty he had hoped for all along. On 9 March 1814 the Prussians, Austrians and the Russians signed a treaty with Britain at Chaumont, agreeing to keep 150,000 men each in the field against Napoleon until peace was settled collectively. Britain would finance the alliance to the tune of £5 million, paid in monthly instalments until a month after a peace treaty had been signed.[61]

The Treaty of Chaumont transformed an uneasy alliance into an unstoppable force. Yet the deep significance of this treaty lay behind the military requirements, in its prescriptions for peace. The treaty, 'having for its object the maintenance of a balance in Europe ... and to prevent the invasions which for so many years have devastated the world', bound all four of the signatories to act together and protect Europe from aggression for the next twenty years. Thus the thought planted by Pitt at last bloomed into reality: here was a firm basis for European collective security after the war. Castlereagh was delighted. 'What an extraordinary display of power. This, I trust, will put an end to any doubts as to the claim we have an opinion on continental matters.'[62]

28

Napoleon, still defiant, saw France in ruins around him. Castlereagh had noticed more people dead than alive as he travelled between Troyes and Chaumont. In the face of defeat, Napoleon launched another set of counter-attacks against the allies. But it was too late. The final battle was fought at Montmartre on 30 March 1814. Paris surrendered before Napoleon could get back to save it and on the 31st the Czar rode into Paris, a fantasist at last basking in reality. Soon afterwards, the French Senate formally deposed Napoleon, and a provisional Government was established under Talleyrand. On 4 April Castlereagh wrote a letter from his resting place in Dijon to his long-suffering wife:

> My Dearest Em,
>   The victories of the Allies . . . all lead me to hope that we may meet without further delay at Paris . . . I flatter myself that the Declaration of Paris will tranquilize the peasants and make the roads safe . . .
>   I have laid in a stock of silks and old Sèvres china for you here, but you must come for it, or else I will give it *en débit* to some belle in Paris.
>   God bless you dearest friend, I am a bad boy but you will forgive me when we meet which I trust will be in the fewest days possible.
>   Ever yours,
>   C.[63]

By the time Castlereagh reached Paris on 10 April 1814, Czar Alexander had already been wreaking his own peculiar brand of havoc. He decided that Napoleon could both keep his imperial title and spend the rest of his days as the sovereign of Elba – an island with a good harbour and within easy sail of France. Castlereagh was appalled at these hazy acts of generosity; Metternich, who had also been absent during the negotiations, was likewise outraged. Napoleon himself was nonplussed by the offer. He wanted to move to England. For Castlereagh, this was a bizarre and faintly alarming prospect; yet with few alternatives by early May he had begun to take Napoleon's request seriously. He wrote to Liverpool asking 'If his taste for an asylum in England should continue, would you allow him to reside in some distant province? It would obviate much alarm on the continent.'[64] But the Czar's decision proved to be unshakeable;

Napoleon settled down to his new kingdom of Elba in the same month. His departure was followed by the arrival in France of the Bourbon King, Louis XVIII, who assumed the throne of his dead brother, Louis XVI. At long last, France would be led by the sort of ruler whom everyone could trust – moderate, mundane and mediocre.

The central task of reorganising Europe now moved to the top of the agenda. A peace settlement with France was drawn up, settling the most urgent questions of territory and defence. Castlereagh managed to satisfy Britain's vital interests early on in the negotiations. He ensured that the Low Countries would be strengthened against France by joining Holland and Belgium, and that the key city of Antwerp would be kept as a commercial port without fortifications. 'I have secured the assent of France to the incorporation of the Low Countries with Holland,' Castlereagh explained, because 'I felt it of the last importance not to go to a Congress without having this most essential point acquiesced in by that Power.'[65] These agreements, crucial in prohibiting any future invasion of the British Isles, added an element of independence to Castlereagh's negotiating hand. Now that the key national interest had been fulfilled, he could use the power of Britain as a mediating force in the negotiations and try to broker a more sustainable peace.

It is hard for us now to appreciate the complete control which Castlereagh had over British foreign policy at this moment. We are used to Prime Ministers scurrying across the world to announce new decisions and initiatives. Nowadays, Foreign Secretaries hold the preliminary meetings which may or may not be relevant to the result; they hover in the background of the main event, bursting with advice which may or may not be used. By contrast, Castlereagh's remit during the negotiations at Paris was very wide indeed. Week after week he toiled away, writing to Liverpool every so often, and then as a partner in policy-making rather than an inferior. The relationship which developed between Prime Minister and Foreign Secretary is by our standards extraordinary. It is summed up by the Prime Minister's letter to Castlereagh on 16 May 1814: 'We have heard nothing from you since the 5th but I conclude you are too hard at work to have much time to write . . . As your treaty is to be definitive, there would be some advantage if it were possible that we could see it (to guard against <u>minor errors</u>) before it was actually agreed.'[66] The Prime Minister and Cabinet had been reduced temporarily to proof-reading.

The treaty which became the First Peace of Paris on 30 May 1814 was remarkably even-handed. Anxious to do nothing which would make the new Bourbon regime unpopular at home, the allies granted France the generous borders of 1792 as well as most of its old colonies. There were no major reparations, no embittering disarmament clauses, and no long-term plans for an occupying force. Castlereagh returned to Britain on the day the treaty was signed. He arrived at Dover on 3 June to crowds cheering on the beach.[67]

The feeling in Britain was one of relief rather than pride in victory, but it was no less powerful for that. For a few weeks, Castlereagh was a hero. In June, the Regent awarded him the Order of the Garter. In the Commons the peace treaty was received with wide applause – until William Wilberforce rose to speak. Something crucial had been forgotten. Wilberforce turned the mood of the House and the country on its head. 'I cannot but conceive I behold in his hand the death-warrant of a multitude of innocent victims, men, women, and children, whom I had fondly indulged the hope of having myself rescued from destruction.'[68] With these words, the campaign for universal abolition of slavery was rekindled. Up and down the country, petitions were assembled and posted off to Parliament, demanding an end to slavery by all the European powers. It was not clear how this could be accomplished. Castlereagh had exacted some abolitionist concessions from France during the peace negotiations in Paris, but Talleyrand had been reluctant. Whatever the difficulties, the political message was clear. Castlereagh, who had neither spoken nor voted on that night in 1807 when the abolition of the slave trade passed the House of Commons, had been charged with carrying the abolitionist mission forward at the Congress in Vienna.*

In June the allies visited London for further negotiations. The

---

* Castlereagh's argument in 1807, widely shared at the time, had been that the Abolition bills would achieve little apart from allowing other countries to increase their own slave trade. It is typical of the man that he believed that Britain by itself could not abolish the slave trade, and instead ought to work with other powers to secure an international agreement on stopping the trade. See Wendy Hinde's *Castlereagh* (London: Collins, 1981) for more on this theme, pp. 126–30.

visit was marked by few advances in the big questions of reorganising Europe, but in small things the tone had been set for the coming Congress of Vienna. The days and nights were awash with receptions and parties; the Czar's eccentricities caused general confusion; and progress was made on details of the union between the Belgians and the Dutch. At no point, then or later, does it seem to have struck Castlereagh as important that the Belgians were unhappy at being lumped together with the Dutch. For Castlereagh the case was unanswerable: 'to make Holland and Belgium capable of sustaining a real independence, upon the confines of France, they must form one state'.[69] Throughout the next twelve months of diplomacy, Castlereagh sustained and acted on the doctrine that national feelings were less important than the need to maintain a territorial balance of power.

On 16 August 1814 Castlereagh set off for the Congress at Vienna. He stopped off along the way in Ghent, where peace talks between the American and British commissioners had bogged down. He stayed long enough to tell the chief British negotiators that moderation and compromise were the key, and then set off again via Paris for Vienna. The Congress began on 1 October. Hundreds of princely families swooped on the city, eager to see a piece of the action. Like Castlereagh, they realised that 'never at any former period was so much spoil thrown loose for the world to scramble for'. Unlike Castlereagh, only a few of them were interested in building 'a just equilibrium in Europe'.[70]

Castlereagh showed himself a master of various waltzes and reels at the balls which formed the backdrop to the negotiations. Emily, who had accompanied him to Vienna, continued the practice she had established in Paris of holding nightly dinner parties for friends and acquaintances. But neither of them was at ease in Vienna. They disapproved of the frivolities which took place on the Sabbath and were reluctant to associate themselves with the low moral standards of European high society. The Continental Establishment was itself rather unimpressed with Emily. Snooty ladies complained by turn that she was fat, talkative, badly dressed and gigantic. The Austrian police drafted reports about the Castlereaghs' novel and amusing habit of browsing rather than buying items in shops. By and large, these social tensions simmered beneath the surface. The only real disaster came when Emily decided to go to a ball wearing her husband's Order of the Garter as a decoration in her hair.[71]

The Polish and Saxon questions dominated the Congress. The Czar was determined to swallow Poland whole. This disturbed the complex geographical equations which Castlereagh and Metternich were playing with, and it had particularly gloomy implications in Germany. But half a million Russian troops stood between the diplomats in Vienna and a free Poland, and it was difficult to see how the Czar could be denied.[72] These bleak prospects for Poland were the culmination of a long period of decline and dislocation. By contrast, the proposed annihilation of Saxony — which was a codicil to the Czar's Polish plan — would mark a dramatic turnabout in German history, following years of Saxon power and prestige during the Enlightenment. The King of Saxony was vulnerable: he had continued to support Napoleon long after most others had deserted him. But wiping his kingdom off the map and subsuming his territories within Prussia, as the Czar was suggesting, would alter the balance of power in Europe and create a large tilt in the centre of Europe away from Austria and towards Prussia. This would have to be balanced by more changes elsewhere — and so the possible sources of discontent multiplied. From far away, George Canning worried about the effect on national feelings: 'we do not wish to see Saxony annihilated as an independent State. It would create serious discontent, and ill blood throughout Germany.'[73]

Castlereagh did his best to deter the Czar, drawing up a memorandum to remind him that the European powers 'avowedly fought for their own liberties and for those of the rest of Europe, and not for the extension of their dominion'. But by early December 1814, Castlereagh was issuing warning notes to London that in the confused and unhappy climate a new war was possible — and Britain would not be able to stay out.[74] Meanwhile, news of the impending dismantlement of Saxony had begun to filter through to Britain, stirring up widespread concern. Liverpool wrote back to Castlereagh, his sentences now heavy with worry and reluctance:

> ... if war should be renewed at present I fear that we should lose all that we have gained, that the revolutionary spirit would break forth again in full force, and that the Continent would be plunged in all

the evils under which it has groaned for twenty years. A war now, therefore, may be a revolutionary war. A war some time hence, though an evil, need not be different in its character and its effects from any of those wars which occurred in the seventeenth and eighteenth centuries before the commencement of the French Revolution. In short, this appears to me to be the precise period in which the sentiment of Cicero, so often quoted by Mr Fox, is really in point: *Iniquissimam pacem justissimo bello antefero* [the most unfair peace is better than even the most justified war].[75]

It was as difficult for Liverpool in 1814 as for Churchill in 1945 to contemplate leading an exhausted Britain into war against her greedy Russian ally.

For the moment, Liverpool and Castlereagh had no leverage. There was no longer a British army on the Continent and many troops were still occupied in the American war. Castlereagh was stuck, but he had no one to turn to except possibly France. Signs of sympathy were hardly forthcoming from that quarter. 'Lord Castlereagh is like a traveller who has lost his way and cannot find it again,' Talleyrand wrote.[76]

An unexpected event brought the crisis to an end. From the negotiators at Ghent, messages arrived on New Year's Day 1815 that a peace treaty had at last been signed between the British and the Americans. Months of exhausting negotiations had at last given way to unspectacular compromise. This altered Britain's negotiating position and lifted Castlereagh out of his dead end. 'We have become more European, and by the Spring we can have a very nice army on the Continent.' Two days later, Metternich's Austria and Talleyrand's France signed a new tripartite defence treaty with Britain, providing for mutual aid in case of attack. This meant that if war did break out, Russia and Prussia would be outnumbered – even the Czar was realistic enough to see that. On 4 January Castlereagh wrote to Liverpool in triumph: 'I have every reason to hope that the alarm of war is over.'[77]

Unfortunately, Liverpool now had new grumbles. Castlereagh had been away too long. Chastened by the war scare, and in need of Castlereagh's leadership in the Commons, Liverpool sent a request for Castlereagh to return to London at the end of January. But Castlereagh stayed on, desperate to complete the Saxon negotiations.

Not until the second week of February was a compromise reached. Poland was split after all between Austria, Prussia and Russia, with the Russian part, the largest, to be turned into a semi-autonomous kingdom under the Czar. The King of Saxony managed to hold on to most of his old territory. The rest – including parts of the Rhineland – went to Prussia.

Throughout this period, Castlereagh continued to lobby the Great Powers of Europe for stronger commitments to the abolition of slavery. He was both irritated and inspired in this task by the heat of British public opinion. 'It is impossible to persuade foreign nations that this sentiment is unmixed with the views of colonial policy,' Castlereagh complained, 'and their Cabinets, who can better estimate the real and virtuous motives which guide us on this question, see in the very impatience of the nation a powerful instrument through which they expect to force, at a convenient moment, the British Government upon some favourite object of policy.' British professions of disinterested virtue have through the years quite often been genuine but rarely believed. Yet Castlereagh did make some progress. A declaration which condemned the slave trade as inhuman was signed by all the powers and inserted into the Final Act of the Congress. Even Wilberforce seemed satisfied with Castlereagh's efforts.[78]

On 15 February 1815, Castlereagh left Vienna for Britain. Shortly after arriving back in London, he heard that Napoleon had escaped from Elba. Castlereagh geared himself for another brutal campaign. 'If we are to undertake the job,' he told Wellington, 'we must leave nothing to chance. It must be done upon the grandest scale ... you must inundate France with force in all directions.' The Government set aside another £5 million for financing a new coalition; at Waterloo, Wellington played the part for which he had been destined all along. The victory was narrow but final, and it was not followed by the feared French civil war.[79]

The Castlereaghs were back in Paris by 6 July for new peace negotiations. There, Castlereagh was met by Wellington. The Duke was becoming a legend and Lord Liverpool had appointed him as co-plenipotentiary. It was a marriage of minds. In each man, a natural pragmatism had been reinforced by magnanimity; they worked hard to establish a reasonable and lasting settlement with France. 'Nothing could go on better than Wellington and I did to the last,' Castlereagh recorded. 'I do not recall a single divergence of opinion between us throughout the whole.'

This spirit of co-operation was not shared by the other European powers. The peace negotiations had to last longer than in 1814 because of strong disagreements among the allies. The Prussians in particular wanted harsher reparations from France; Castlereagh and Wellington maintained their calls for restraint. On 12 August Castlereagh wrote to Canning in an attempt to explain to him the 'very arduous task, yet to be effected, in which our Efforts are to be made on principles somewhat contradictory, namely to require for Europe Securities against France, without injuring essentially the Position of the King, whose authority if it is to be preserved, is in itself the greatest of all the Securities to which we can look for the Cessation of the Revolutionary Calamities of Europe'.[80] The final peace treaty which was signed in November 1815 was a product of these difficulties. The French were pushed back within their 1790 borders and ordered to pay a 700 million franc indemnity. Wellington would now maintain an occupying army, and all the works of art looted by Napoleon during the wars had to be returned. This last requirement infuriated proud Frenchmen; they hissed Wellington when he went to the opera to hear Catalani perform.[81]

The hissing was one problem, the Czar another. A year on from his entry into Paris, he set off on another crusade. He spent a great deal of his time visiting a mystic called Madame de Krudener and, inspired by her sessions, he entered a new spiritual phase in his life. The effects were mixed. He foresaw a new type of partnership in Europe, a Holy Alliance led by the monarchs of the Christian powers, and summoned the British plenipotentiaries to tell them of his plans. Castlereagh and Wellington found it difficult to listen with 'becoming gravity' to the Czar, and eventually managed to fob him off on the grounds that the British constitution forbade the Regent from making such a commitment. The plan was, as Castlereagh thought, 'a sublime piece of mysticism and nonsense'. 'The fact is that the Emperor's mind is not completely sound.'[82]

At Paris, the allies renewed their Quadruple Alliance and the defensive guarantee set up at Chaumont. They also agreed that Bonaparte and his family should be perpetually excluded from the

French throne. Under the provisions of the Sixth Article of the Quadruple Alliance, the signatories agreed to meet regularly to confirm that the terms of the peace treaty were being carried out. Castlereagh added that these meetings should include wider discussions of common interest. It is not true that this article marked the birth of what we now call global governance. The provision was too vague for that. But for the first time in history, the major powers of Europe had accepted the principle that there were issues which needed to be discussed collectively and on a regular basis in peacetime.

Castlereagh returned to London shortly after the agreements were signed. 'I do not find any cavil or critique, except the general nonsense of the Morning Chronicle, afraid that our Treaty of Alliance will enslave mankind.'[83]

A few months after Waterloo, Castlereagh wrote a classic dispatch to all British diplomats which established the principles of post-war diplomacy. 'There is no longer any object which the Prince Regent can desire to acquire for the British Empire, either of possession or fame . . . his only desire is, and must be, to employ all his influence to preserve the peace, which in concert with his Allies he has won.'[84] This was a turning point. From now on Britain was a satisfied power, anxious above all to preserve her possessions in peace. Colonial ventures later in the nineteenth century were always subordinate to that central fact in the minds of Britain's Foreign Secretaries.

Britain had climbed to the top of the mountain, but there were still tremors below. Castlereagh had defeated the French but the spirit of revolution lived on. At a mass meeting in London on 15 November 1816 rabble-rousers waved the tricolour and carried a cap of liberty on top of a pike. Two months later, the window of the Prince Regent's carriage was broken by a missile of some kind – possibly a bullet. In the summer of 1817 there was an uprising in Derbyshire. Throughout the period, secret Government committees were presented with evidence suggesting that Britain was under siege from a co-ordinated conspiracy.[85] But in Britain, the roots of discontent were economic not revolutionary. Peace did not bring the prosperity many had hoped for; the combined effects of the Corn Laws, a depreciated currency, the national debt and a run of bad harvests added to the natural problems of transition from war to peace.

The leaders of all the major powers in Europe felt similar quaking in their own countries, and they were anxious above all to keep control. Metternich found in the paranoia of the Czar a new audience for his theory of Legitimacy. Both men began to see in the Concert process of diplomacy a tool to protect the status quo. For the Czar, this became a pious as well as a practical necessity. The Holy Alliance which he had sketched in Paris came into being as a band of reactionary autocrats who met under the auspices of the Congress system and were committed to rolling back revolution wherever it might occur. Thomas Macaulay, Whig writer and historian, felt these blows to freedom keenly. The doctrine of Legitimacy was 'but Divine Right brought back under an assumed name, like a thief from transportation'.[86] For his part, Castlereagh disliked the fierce and ideological turn taken by the European Concert but continued to believe that Britain had to work closely with the leaders of the main European powers if the Vienna Settlement was to be maintained.

Against this strained background, an old voice now began to make itself heard again. Canning's long exile from Government had come to an end two years earlier when Liverpool asked him in 1816 to join the Cabinet as President of the Board of Control and share the responsibility for running India. Canning had marked his return by closing the last wounds of personal conflict with Castlereagh. He spoke thoughtfully in Parliament when challenged about the rivalry, referring to the 'real substantive equality' in which all true statesmen exist. 'In a free country like ours', he explained, 'it is for the man to dignify the office, not for the office to dignify the man.'[87] Yet, as the personal relationship healed, a new fracture was exposed. Quietly at first, and always politely, Castlereagh and Canning argued about Britain's new role in the world.

Canning had disagreed with a great deal of what had gone on at Paris and Vienna. He outlined his own view on the new European order in a speech in Liverpool in 1822:

Gentlemen, in the times in which we live there is . . . a struggle going on – in some countries an open in some a tacit struggle – between the principles of monarchy and democracy. God be praised that in that struggle we have not any part to take. God be praised that we have long ago arrived at all the blessings that are to be derived from that which alone can end that struggle beneficially – a compromise and intermeddling of those conflicting principles.[88]

But Canning's views went further than praise for the Glorious Constitution of 1688. Like Castlereagh, Canning thought that history was being shaped by a new force of freedom. Unlike Castlereagh, Canning approved. 'I see the principles of liberty are in operation', Canning explained a few years later, 'and shall be one of the last to attempt to restrain them.' Castlereagh, on the other hand, had set out his thoughts on liberty in 1814: 'I am sure it is better to retard than accelerate the action of this most hazardous principle which is abroad.'[89]

Canning believed that Europe needed new institutions to reflect the principles of liberal nationalism. The annexation of Poland and the union of Norway and Sweden had appalled him because they rejected the powerful forces of nationhood. No other structures could provide for peace or stability in the long term. At this time, Canning rejected the idea that the use of arms could have any long-term effect on these developments. History was moving in a liberal direction, but 'sixteen thousand bayoneted philosophers' could not 'suddenly produce the effect, which in England had been the result of the Revolutions and the accumulated wisdom of ages'.[90]

Somewhere between Canning and Metternich, Castlereagh set out his own plan. He did not agree with Canning that what was needed in Europe were liberal changes or national structures. 'It is not insurrections we now want in Italy, or elsewhere,' Castlereagh had written in 1814, 'we want disciplined force under sovereigns we can trust.'[91] Nor did he agree with Metternich and the Czar that all change had to be resisted at any cost. Instead, he remained pragmatic in his policies and faintly pessimistic about human progress. He pondered without any trace of enthusiasm the idea of a new union which could bring about positive change in the world: 'The Problem of an Universal Alliance for the Peace and Happiness of the world has always been one of speculation and of Hope, but it has never yet been reduced to practice, and if an opinion may be hazarded from its difficulty, it never can.' Two years later, he varied the same theme: 'Dissertations on abstract principles will do nothing in the present day.' Yet careful co-operation between the powers, carried out in a spirit of decency and moderation, could relieve immediate difficulties and might preserve a long-term peace. If the leaders of the European empires could agree to meet in quiet but regular diplomacy, then stability could be maintained. 'I am quite convinced that past habits, common glory, and these occasional meetings, displays, and repledges, are among the best securities Europe now has for a durable peace.'[92]

At the Congress of Aix-la-Chapelle in 1818, these three visions of world order headed into their first collision, with Castlereagh trying to reconcile the complicated schemes of Metternich and the Czar with the scepticism of Canning back home.

The Congress began on 29 September and proceeded with an earnestness which had been absent from Vienna and Paris in 1815. An army of altruists campaigned on the fringes of the main event. Men such as the social reformer Robert Owen flocked to advance their various causes. Sir Thomas Lawrence skirted around the scene, trying to snatch vacant afternoons for his own project, commissioned by the Regent, to paint all the leading men of Europe. The subject matter reinforced the seriousness. The rehabilitation of France topped the agenda. Discussions also ranged over a number of new themes, including the Barbary pirates, the revolting Spanish colonies in South America and enforcing the bans on the slave trade. A group of senior Prussian generals chanced their hand with an idea for a European army led by Wellington. For Castlereagh, though, it was the process not the policies which was interesting. Here, assembled together for the first time in peace, were the leaders of the major European powers to discuss matters of general interest. If they co-operated usefully at Aix, then perhaps a new era of diplomacy could begin. Instead of wars and mass revolutions, the dispassionate processes of diplomacy would decide the chief issues of the day.

On 20 October, after three weeks of negotiations, Castlereagh spelled out the future to the Prime Minister in London in a letter of rare clarity and elegance:

At all events, it is satisfactory to observe how little embarrassment and how much solid good grow out of these reunions, which sound so terrible at a distance. It really appears to me to be a new discovery in the European Government, at once extinguishing the cobwebs with which diplomacy obscures the horizon, bringing the whole bearing of the system into its true light, and giving to the counsels of the great Powers the efficiency and almost the simplicity of a single State.

The prophet did have his followers on the Continent and in London; but in courts and Cabinets on both sides of the Channel, his message was dismissed. On the same day in October that Castlereagh was eulogising about new discoveries in diplomacy and a single European State, Lord Bathurst, the Secretary of State for War and the Colonies, was writing to the Foreign Secretary to warn of a very different picture which had been painted in Cabinet earlier that day:

We were all more or less impressed with the apprehension of great inconvenience arising from a decision being now publicly announced of continued meetings at fixed points. It is very natural in you to feel a strong wish that they should continue, from having experienced the advantages which have been derived by this which has taken place; but even if we could be sure that the subsequent meetings would be equally cordial, is there any advantage in fixing beyond the next period[?] ... The objections which Canning feels on this subject are not confined to the inexpediency of announcing a decision of meeting at fixed periods, but to the system itself ... He thinks that system of periodical meetings of the four great Powers, with a view to the general concerns of Europe, new, and of very questionable policy; that it will necessarily involve us deeply in all the politics of the Continent, whereas our true policy has always been not to interfere except in great emergencies, and then with a commanding force. He thinks that all other States must protest against such an attempt to place them under subjection; that the meetings may become a scene of cabal and intrigue and that the people of this country may be taught to look with great jealousy for their liberties, if our Court is engaged in meetings with great despotic monarchs, deliberating upon what degree of revolutionary spirit may endanger the public security, and therefore require the inter-ference of the Alliance ... I have only to add that, if you write a circular letter to the other Powers, it will be very desirable for you to have a draft of it sent over here, if possible, as these are compositions which often lead to much unnecessary discussion in Parliament, unless they are carefully worded.

Yours very sincerely,
BATHURST[93]

The polite tone and friendly phrases could not hide the disagreement. Castlereagh had lost his supremacy in making policy. The Cabinet as a whole and Canning in particular were set on changing his stance. Their critique was not just of what Castlereagh was doing, but also of what Metternich and the Czar were planning for the Congress system. Already, the Czar and his Foreign Minister, Capodistria, were drafting proposals that all European powers should guarantee each other against any political changes. Bathurst had talked opaquely in his letter about the danger of joining this conservative club; three days later, the Prime Minister followed this up with a warning which was more acute: 'Bathurst's despatch and letter of Tuesday, and my letter of today, will put you entirely in possession of our sentiments upon the present state of the negociations. The Russians must be made to feel that we have a Parliament and a public, to which we are responsible, and that we cannot permit ourselves to be drawn into views of policy which are wholly incompatible with the spirit of our Government.'[94]

Castlereagh was now caught in the crossfire of ideas. On one side were the complaints of the Cabinet in London; on the other, the plans of his allies in Europe. He had loyalties on both sides. He was in Aix as an ambassador and representative of His Majesty's Government. Yet he had no desire to dismantle the architecture of European co-operation which he had erected and which still seemed to be working fairly well. On 9 November he responded to further missives from Downing Street by trying to minimise the use of the European vocabulary which caused such trouble in London:

> I received your letter from Walmer of the 3rd, with Canning's notes enclosed, and shall do what I can to profit by your joint suggestions. Some of them have already been, as you will see, attended to. There is no difficulty about the word *solidarité*. They will, I dare say, leave it out . . . Some of them, such as *legitime* and *constitutionelle*, you will find, have been admitted by us in some of our joint notes in 1815,

in Paris, and are *sacramental* words in the Russian Chancellerie used *as often as possible*. I have, however, endeavoured to reconcile them to reduce, if not expunge, this species of matter ... The expressions in allusion to the Holy Alliance, I think Canning, if he reads the Prince Regent's letter to the Sovereigns at Paris, will feel we could not object to; and, if we are to go on with Russia for any time, I fear it is in vain to hope for a pure vocabulary.[95]

Such exchanges will be familiar to any recent Foreign Secretary who has had to negotiate texts in the Council of Ministers in Brussels.

The letter did not bring the argument to a close, but practical agreements were reached on how best to restore France to its necessary position in Continental affairs. Castlereagh left the Congress feeling cheerful, still confident about what congresses could achieve. 'We have done more business than in double the time at any of our former reunions, and all are gone home in good humour and vowing eternal peace and friendship.'[96]

In the eighteen months which followed the Congress at Aix, the Vienna Settlement began to creak and groan. Peace prevailed between the leaders of the European powers, but each faced strife at home. The situation in Britain was almost as bad as in the rest of Europe. On 16 August 1819 a mass meeting in St Peter's Square in Manchester ended with the local yeomanry killing eleven and wounding hundreds more in a moment of nervous confusion. Six months later, police agents discovered a conspiracy drawn up by plotters in Cato Street led by a man called Thistlewood to assassinate the entire Cabinet while at dinner one evening. Castlereagh thought that the Cabinet ought to meet at dinner as usual and take on the assassins in a hand-to-hand battle. He was dissuaded from the plan by Wellington's expert advice – 'we thought it better to stay away from the festive board and not suffer it to go to single combat between Thistlewood and Marshal Liverpool,' he later admitted when in a more realistic mood.[97]

Firmer steps were also being taken during these years. We cannot be sure how much Castlereagh co-operated with the monarchs of Europe in setting up a network of spies. But by April 1820 he was writing to the French Prime Minister about plots to free Napoleon and sending him the details and addresses of the Irish individuals involved. He urged '*precaution* and *surveillance*, and not ... punishment', while asking Lord Sidmouth, the British Home Secretary, to investigate and track suspicious individuals living in London. At the same time, Castlereagh was sharing stories of Britain's struggle against Jacobinism with his old friend Metternich: 'Your Highness will observe that, although we have made an immense progress against Radicalism, the monster still lives and shows himself in new shapes, but we do not despair of crushing him by time and perseverance.'[98]

Perhaps it was Castlereagh's own fault that he came to be associated in public opinion with the worst instincts of a reactionary autocrat. His cold manner and close relationship with the harsh regimes in Europe did him no favours. But a disproportionate amount of blame fell on Castlereagh's shoulders for the problems in Britain. As Leader of the House of Commons, Castlereagh had to defend the Government's policies in Parliament. This made him dangerously unpopular. The conspirators at Cato Street had fought between themselves for the right to kill him. After the tragedy at Peterloo and years of incomprehensible entanglements with the despots in Europe, the poets turned on him as well. *The Masque of Anarchy* is not Shelley's finest poem; its phrases are crude as well as unfair. But the images it conjures up are unforgettable:

> I met Murder on the way –
> He had a mask like Castlereagh –
> Very smooth he looked, yet grim;
> Seven blood-hounds followed him.
>
> All were fat; and well they might
> Be in admirable plight,
> For one by one, and two by two,
> He tossed the human hearts to chew
> Which from his wide cloak he drew.

Meanwhile, inside the Cabinet, the argument about Britain's role in the world was hardening. By 1820 it was clear that some statement of policy had to be agreed on before the next congress took place. The State Paper that Castlereagh produced on 5 May 1820 was the first step away from co-operation in Europe. Under pressure in Cabinet, especially from Canning, Castlereagh pronounced His Majesty's verdict on the Quadruple Alliance which Castlereagh had erected with the other European powers. It was a 'union for the Reconquest and liberation of a great proportion of the Continent of Europe from the Military Dominion of France ... It never was intended as an Union for the Government of the World, or for the Superintendence of the Internal Affairs of other States.'[99]

In later years, Canning would claim these statements and Castlereagh's Paper as the foundation of all that he worked for. Recent academics see in that Paper a final healing of his rift with Castlereagh, a joint expression of patriotic agreement about Britain's role in the world. The facts suggest otherwise. Twenty-three days after the Paper was published, Canning's cousin, Stratford Canning, scribbled in his diary: 'I congratulated him on the line which I knew had been taken ... and as I had reason to believe from a former conversation with him, in obedience to his suggestions. "Yes," he said, "we shall have no more congresses, thank God!"'[100] The State Paper was Canning's first victory over Castlereagh since he had been shot in the thigh during the duel; unhappily for Canning, it was short-lived.

A month and a day after the State Paper, the various domestic and foreign difficulties afflicting the Cabinet came together in a new and peculiar form. Earlier in 1820, the long decline of George III had come to a quiet end and the Prince Regent became King. The news had raced across Europe until it reached the ears of Caroline, the new King's estranged wife and exiled Queen. On 6 June 1820 she drove back into London cheered on by the mob and a phalanx of liberal supporters to press her regal claims on George IV and his unfortunate Government. London was gripped by the sensation. Princess Lieven, well-known wife of the Russian Ambassador, wrote in her diary: 'The Ministers are in a most dangerous position ... they have triumphed over the greatest difficulties, foreign and domestic, that have ever confronted a government; and now they are going to be defeated by a woman.'[101]

Caroline's return was relevant for both Castlereagh and Canning. Shortly after he had separated from his wife, the Regent had organised a special commission to follow her about and collect proof of her transgressions. Castlereagh became involved. The Austrian Government was called on to co-operate, using its own expertise in surveillance to monitor the Queen in northern Italy. The key, as Castlereagh explained to his brother, was to get 'ocular demonstration of the Princess's frailties'. When the Queen returned to London in June 1820, this evidence was assembled and deployed. A Bill of Pains and Penalties was hastily assembled to deprive the Queen of her duties; the evidence of her infidelity was brought before Parliament. For months on end, the material was analysed in the House of Lords. Out of the salacity came new examples of the dark arts of Castlereagh's intelligence system, feeding the radical illusion that Castlereagh was involved in a despotic league.[102]*

Meanwhile Canning was suffering his own embarrassment. Ever since his earliest days in politics, Canning had been close to and supported by Caroline. Now he found himself sandwiched between repaying that loyalty and his responsibilities to a Government that was committed to condemning her. At first he tried to resolve the conflict by avoiding it. He fled to Italy but it was not far enough. Suspicion and rumour fused in the new King's mind into a furious rage. There was no strong evidence to confirm that Canning had slept with Caroline in his youth. But the King was convinced and Canning's authority disintegrated. In December he sloped back to London, and handed in his resignation once again.

The Queen lingered uncertainly until the following June, when she attempted to enter George's official coronation at Westminster Abbey but was barred from taking her place at his side. Three weeks later, she died suddenly. There were riots as her coffin passed through the streets of London, but these were overshadowed, at least for Castlereagh, by new dangers in Europe.

Eleven months earlier, in July 1820, Naples had erupted in revolution. The monarchs who had joined the Czar's Holy Alliance came together to stamp out the sedition. In November Austria, Russia and Prussia met at Troppau and signed a protocol promising to intervene whenever they saw a dangerous and illegal change of government inside one of their neighbours. The doctrine of Legitimacy was acquiring teeth. Castlereagh objected to the protocol and detached

* Upon her return to London, Caroline took up residence in a house near Castlereagh's on St James's Square. The mob soon invaded most of the street. Castlereagh moved a bed into his rooms at the Foreign Office in order to escape the mayhem.

himself from the Congress at Troppau, as well as a second meeting at Laibach. He set out his feelings in a letter to his brother. 'If they will be theorists we must act in separation. I shall personally grieve for any schism in an alliance to which I am so cordially attached . . . [but] better [to] look our difficulties in the face, than get entangled in the labyrinth to which the protocols will conduct us.' Castlereagh's absence from the congresses was an empty protest. The Holy Alliance summoned King Ferdinand of Naples to Laibach in order to 'free the will of His Majesty' so that he would renounce the new constitution he was sworn to uphold. In March, the Austrians intervened. A further revolt in Piedmont fizzled out when Russian troops arrived. Two months later the Laibach Congress concluded with another declaration: 'Useful or necessary changes in legislation and in the administration of States ought only to emanate from the free-will and the intelligent and well-weighed conviction of those whom God has rendered responsible for power.'[103] No such language had been heard in Britain since Stuart times; no British Foreign Secretary could put his name to it.

The wartime alliance which had defeated Napoleon had finally come apart, but Castlereagh could not let go. He defended the intervention in Naples to the House of Commons in order to maintain the 'cordiality and harmony of the Alliance'. But the Congress system was not the only thing that was breaking. In the autumn of 1821, Castlereagh travelled to Hanover with the King for a royal visit to George's dynastic possession. The visit was successful but Castlereagh was unwell. 'I don't know why, or when I have been so low.'[104]

The pace of events in Europe gave him no opportunity to stand back. In March 1821 Greek rebels had struck out against Turkish domination in the Ottoman Empire. It was the first stirring of a problem which would confound British Foreign Secretaries for the next century – the dreaded Eastern Question. In theory, the Ottoman Empire ruled by the Sultan from Constantinople was a divine construction of Islamic civilisation on earth; in practice it was chaotic and bizarre. British sensibilities were offended by the distasteful oppressiveness of a disorganised regime. But realistic observers were aware that the Ottoman Empire played its part as a barrier to Russia; the integrity of that empire was thought to be essential to the balance of power. The result was an unsolvable dilemma. For a hundred years, British statesmen would struggle to cope with it — in the clumsy slide into war in 1853, during the Bulgarian atrocities of 1876 and the war which followed, in the Balkan commotions leading up to 1914. Castlereagh was the first to try his hand at solving it, as the Greeks fought for their freedom in 1821.

The Greek uprising swiftly distinguished itself from other revolts in Europe. Rather than attempting to resolve the specific complaints of the Greeks and check the spread of revolution, the Sultan had hardened the confrontation by killing the Greek Patriarch in Constantinople. The Christian sympathies of Europe and the sentiments of Czar Alexander had been aroused in support of the Greeks. An act of revolution which, had it occurred anywhere else in Europe, would have been condemned and crushed by the Holy Alliance, now reawakened those Christian principles which had captivated the Czar six years earlier in Paris. It turned out that Legitimacy could only be invoked by Christian monarchs; the Sultan need not apply.

Castlereagh responded to these developments with a subtle initiative. The Czar, in one of his sporadic bursts of generosity, had promised Castlereagh at Aix-la-Chapelle that if ever the interests of Europe were seriously threatened, Castlereagh could bypass proto-col and write directly to him. In July 1821, Castlereagh decided to play this card. 'In obedience to the King my Sovereign's command, and under a deep sense of the importance of the present crisis,' Castlereagh began, 'I now presume to address your Imperial Majesty upon the affairs of Turkey.' Castlereagh's advice to the Czar was pragmatic. He urged him to 'observe rather than to intermeddle in the endless and inextricable mazes of Turkish confusion'. Of course, the Ottoman Empire left a great deal to be desired. But it was vital for European safety that no steps were taken which might inflame the confrontation. He reminded the Czar of his fears of revolution:

> I am confident that the dreadful events which now afflict that portion of Europe are not regarded by your Imperial Majesty as constituting in the history of these times either a new or an insulated question. They do not originate in the conflicting and inflammable elements of which the Turkish Empire is composed; but they form a branch of that organized spirit of insurrection which is systematically propa-

48

gating itself throughout Europe, and which explodes wherever the hand of the governing power, from whatever cause, is enfeebled.[105]

There were no signs of a resolution in Greece as 1821 drew to a close, and the Czar hovered on the cusp of intervention – whether or not restrained by Castlereagh's letter, it is impossible to know. But in Britain, something was changing. Today we are used to the erratic ebb and flow of public opinion in its sympathies with afflictions far away. Indeed, faraway countries of which we know little may now command greater sympathy than those nearer at hand. At the start of the 1820s these feelings were largely unknown. But now, with Britain's own survival assured after the defeat of Napoleon, British public opinion began to focus on Turkish atrocities in the Ottoman Empire. Across the country, people raised the cry of freedom for Greece.

Castlereagh could not grasp the development. To his cautious mind, the campaign in Britain appeared emotional and impetuous – if anything, a dangerous new turn. He continued to press for nonintervention. In December he sketched the outlines of a new letter to the Czar. Illness and exaggeration came together in sweeping statements about the revolutionary tide. It 'is impossible that the Emperor should not see that the head of this revolutionary torrent is in Greece, that the tide is flowing in upon his southern provinces in an almost uninterrupted and continuous stream from the other side of the Atlantic'. The energy of his analysis drove him to new conclusions. For years he had resisted the illiberal doctrine of Legitimacy which Metternich had championed. But now his resistance collapsed. He continued his letter by advocating Russian intervention against the Greeks: 'If I am right in regarding the revolutionary movement in Greece as the true danger ... the question is, What course ought the Emperor in wisdom to pursue? I have said above, that, in any other case, his Imperial Majesty would decide at once, and if necessary, act against the Greeks and in favour of the legitimate authority of the country.'[106]

The problem rumbled on into 1822, growing in uncertainty and wider interest. In January, Castlereagh delivered a state of the nation address in his capacity as Leader of the House of Commons. The speech was vast, covering all the major aspects of Government.

Naturally, he took great care over foreign affairs, and he spoke defensively about the Congress system. The 'maintenance of the general peace of Europe', he explained, could only be ensured by 'the personal amity of sovereigns, and by a system of mediation'. But the most thoughtful part of his speech came when he turned to America. He spoke sensibly about the interests which were shared between the two countries, and in particular of trade. He ended with a peroration which attracted no attention at the time, but as a statement of co-operation was far-reaching and insightful about the future course of Anglo-American affairs.

> It will be time enough, a century hence, to think of contending interests. It is the absence of a friendly spirit to anticipate, amidst peace and good-will, the possible condition of rivalry and hostility. The sea is open to both nations, and assuredly there is no disposition in England to appropriate this highway of the world. America has a territory, and a new and virgin territory, almost as spacious as the face of the seas themselves. She is of the same stock, and has the same materials of greatness and future glory with Great Britain. Let her use the example we have set her, and run the same race.[107]

Even as Castlereagh's system of co-operation was collapsing around him, he seemed to have cemented his authority as Foreign Secretary. Canning's hopes of returning to high office in England had all but disappeared. In March 1822, Canning resigned himself to his fate and accepted an offer to travel to India as Governor General. It would be a glittering but empty end to a career which had promised much and delivered little. Over the spring and into the summer, he prepared for his last adventure. The clarity of his argument with Castlereagh began to slip away.

A new congress was planned for the summer of 1822 to discuss the Ottoman question. On 7 August the Cabinet came together to approve Castlereagh's instructions. Strangely, the Foreign Secretary made no contribution to the discussions. Wellington thought he 'appeared very low, out of spirits, and unwell'. The following day, Castlereagh put his hand over his temple and told his domestic servant, 'I am quite worn out here.' For some weeks, people had been noticing that something was wrong with Castlereagh. In June, Princess Lieven had written that Castlereagh 'looks ghastly. He has aged five years in a week; one can see that he is a broken man.' Yet Castlereagh went on, wrestling with his own demons and the demented state of affairs in the East.

Two days after the August Cabinet meeting, Castlereagh was seen wandering along Pall Mall, dishevelled and apparently in a daze. He broke down in front of the King later that day. He said that the police were after him because he was 'accused of the same crime' as the Bishop of Clogher, who had recently been arrested for homosexual behaviour with a young soldier in a Westminster pub. Castlereagh showed two letters to the King detailing the allegations and told him that he would flee to France. The King, baffled by the display, lamely mentioned the Congress. Castlereagh replied: 'Sire, the time has come to say goodbye to Europe. You and I alone have known Europe, and together we have saved her. There is no one left after me with any knowledge of Continental affairs.' Castlereagh left the King and met Wellington, who told him flat out that he was mad. 'Since you say so, it must be so,' Castlereagh replied. Wellington offered to postpone his own trip abroad in order to stay with Castlereagh. The offer was refused. Meanwhile the King had instructed Castlereagh's surgeon, Bankhead, to inspect his patient. Bankhead bled the Foreign Secretary, producing a substance which Emily thought looked like jelly but no diagnosis of what was wrong.

The Castlereaghs left London the same day for their home at North Cray in Kent. Over the years, their estate had developed an eccentric appeal. Emily had assembled a small zoo consisting of several kangaroos, emus, ostriches, an antelope and a tiger given by Wellington. But Cray's charms produced no change in Castlereagh's mood. Shortly after rising on the morning of 12 August, he took a knife to his neck and severed his carotid artery. Within a minute, he was dead.*

The catastrophe has only been partially clarified by history. Castlereagh certainly had gone mad, but murkier waters ran beneath that verdict. Thanks to the work of a recent scholar, we now know that Castlereagh had in his youth suffered from a form of syphilis contracted at Cambridge. There is a possibility that

* Castlereagh's home at Loring Hall in North Cray is today used as a care facility for adults with learning difficulties.

this permanently affected his brain, making him depressed and paranoid.[108]

There is also another story, which emerged many years after Castlereagh's suicide. One night in 1819 Castlereagh seems to have been solicited by a whore on his way from Parliament to his house in St James's Square. We do not know whether Castlereagh made a habit of taking up these offers, but it seems that this time he may have followed the whore back to a nearby house. There, the whore began to undress, revealing that she was in fact a man. At this moment, so the story goes, a group of men rushed into the room and seized Castlereagh, threatening to expose him as a sodomite. Castlereagh escaped by giving them money. But the blackmail seems to have continued; in 1822 Castlereagh still believed he was being pursued. Eventually, he relayed his nightmare to Wellington and his colleague, Lord Clanwilliam. He did not take their advice of admitting the story and arresting the blackmailers. In the end, it looks as though he went mad and killed himself rather than reveal what happened in 1819.

None of this was apparent in the weeks after his death. Within hours, the rumours reached London. Anonymous notices went up across the capital, suggesting that the body of a suicide would desecrate Westminster Abbey. Byron celebrated the moment in verse.

> So *He* has cut his throat at last! – He? Who?
> The man who cut his country's long ago.

An inquest was set up to establish the cause of death. Its conclusion – death under the influence of delusion – rescued Castlereagh from an inglorious end. Castlereagh, the man who had done what Pitt had failed to do and built up a successful coalition against Napoleon, was laid to rest in Westminster Abbey while the mob cheered in satisfaction outside.

The reaction in Vienna was different. 'The man is irreplaceable', was Metternich's response. He 'was devoted to me in heart and spirit, not only from personal inclination but also from conviction. He was my second self.'[109]

*

For seven years, Castlereagh had defined the direction of British politics – caution at home; co-operation abroad. His death not only halted that direction but choked the motor too. The Government stood at a standstill for three weeks as it wrestled with the inevitable but unappetising choice of successor.

George Canning had still not sailed for India. He had accepted the post of Governor General but his departure had been delayed. When the news broke that Castlereagh had killed himself, people started to wonder whether Canning might return to the Foreign Office again. There was no serious competitor for the post and the Government badly needed an injection of energy and intelligence. But the King and the Cabinet were loath to reappoint a man whose talent was matched by the trouble he tended to cause. There was something deep in Canning's character which attracted distrust alongside admiration. There were questions too about seniority. Should Canning receive both of Castlereagh's positions – Leader of the House of Commons and Foreign Secretary – or could he be satisfied by the Foreign Office alone? There were negotiations, rumours, at last the only possible conclusion. On 8 September, Canning was offered both posts.

He did not need long to make up his mind. For a brief moment he flirted with an imagined self-pity – 'I would that this offer had not come. The sacrifice of personal interest which I make to public duties is enormous' – and then accepted the offer. He vented his true emotions in an impassioned letter to his wife. 'Do not let us fall into the traces of 1812 dearest love! The fatal decision which blasted all my prospects – threw away the goodwill of the Sovereign, the Ministry, and the House of Commons, and forfeited for me the most splendid situation in this country – in Europe – and in history.' Although in the future he would occasionally daydream about what life on the subcontinent would have been like, 'governing some eighty or a hundred millions in the shades of Barrackpore', the choice was easy. Staying in England gave Canning the chance to complete unfinished business. He may have missed out on redrawing the map of Europe in 1815, but he could at least chart a new course for Britain. 'Ten years have made a world of difference and prepared a very different sort of world to bustle in than that which I should have found in 1812,' Canning admitted to his friend, Sir Charles Bagot, in

November. 'For fame, it is a squeezed orange; but for public good there is something to do ... You know my politics well enough to know what I mean, when I say for Europe I shall be desirous now and then to read England.'[110]

Canning returned to the Foreign Office just as the unease which had been spreading through Europe was hardening into a new global divide. Britain stumbled awkwardly between alternatives. On the one hand, the forces which had inspired the American and French Revolutions continued to gnaw at ancient traditions, asserting themselves with particular energy in the South American rebellions. On the other hand, a new wave of reaction was sweeping through the Continent, propelled by Metternich, the Czar and Bourbon France. Castlereagh had tried and failed to reconcile these irreconcilables by close co-operation with the leaders of Europe. Now liberals and nationalists in Britain and Europe saw in Canning a chance for real change. 'Canning is a genius, almost a universal one ... and no man of talent can pursue the path of his late predecessor,' Lord Byron explained.[111]

The drama resumed with a crisis in Spain. A liberal revolution had forced a new constitution on the Bourbon monarch, King Ferdinand; the European powers sharpened their talons and stirred themselves to intervene. A congress had been arranged to try to resolve the situation but in April 1823 the French invaded in support of Ferdinand and against the liberals in Madrid. The formula the French came up with to justify the intervention has since become familiar: the policy was simultaneously 'toute Européenne et toute française'.[112]

Canning had achieved no more than Castlereagh in allaying the fears and calming the tempers of the conservative powers; he found himself able to do little more than flail about as an annoyed spectator while the Spanish liberals were crushed. But at moments of great difficulty, new ideas are formed; frustration and anger came together to refocus Canning's vision. If Britain was not strong enough to get its way inside Europe, then it would have to influence Europe from outside. What Britain lacked on the Continent, it could make up on the sea through the power of the Royal Navy. If the Holy Alliance dominated the politics of Europe, Britain could at least stop its reach from spreading across the Atlantic.

The French intervention in Spain convinced Canning that the Congress system had to go as soon as possible. He announced that he would 'get rid of the Areopagus and all that'. Even if there still remained such a thing as a common European interest, no European power could be trusted to pursue it. They were each driven by their own political neuroses, and France was especially suspect. By the end of 1825, Canning had reduced French foreign policy to two rules of action: 'to thwart us wherever they know our object, and when they know it not, to imagine one for us, and set about thwarting that'.[113] In abandoning the Congress system, Canning homed in on another idea. The reactionary trend in Europe was not an isolated phenomenon, but part of a wider struggle stretching across the Atlantic. The ambitions and anxieties exhibited by the monarchs in Europe were not limited by borders, nor were the new forces they were challenging defined by any map. The same conflict between tradition and change was present in South America where colonial uprisings were breaking up the empires of Portugal and Spain. But whereas in Europe Britain's capacity to influence the struggle was limited, across the Atlantic Britain's naval power and trading links gave her the edge.

In 1823 the South American question was bubbling towards boiling point, but it was not yet a general European concern. In October 1818, the Americans had told the British Minister in Washington that Europe owed it 'to the welfare and prosperity of Old Spain – to acknowledge the complete independence of such of the American provinces as had proved themselves competent of self-government'. Castlereagh's response had been cool. He told Lord Liverpool that 'we have never been so efficiently advanced upon details to render it prudent to bring forward, at least on our part, any proposition relative to Buenos Aires'. Moreover, he added, 'our taking the lead would only have exposed us to additional jealousy'.[114] By 1823, Peru and Cuba alone of Spain's American possessions could still be described as a part of the Spanish Empire. Colombia, the modern Argentina, Chile and Mexico were all irretrievable. But the arrival of French troops in Spain seemed to suggest that the Bourbon dynasty still had plans to reassert some influence over the fledgling nations in South America.

On 25 September 1823 Canning told Wellington that he was

'morally convinced' that if France were allowed to 'get a sway in Spanish America, not only will our ministry be overturned, and I think deservedly, but the reputation of this country will be irretrievably lowered'.[115] In this spirit, he began work on his new strategy to restore the reputation of Britain and restrict the ambitions of France. From Thursday 9 October to Sunday 12 October 1823, Canning met the French Ambassador, the Prince de Polignac, in close conference to settle the Spanish American question. That conference resulted in five conclusions, each a small earthquake in its own right, set out in an artful and articulate memorandum which was then circulated across the globe.

First, Canning persuaded the Prince de Polignac that 'any attempt to bring Spanish America again under its ancient submission to Spain, must be utterly hopeless'. It is unlikely that the French had any serious intention of reconquering South America, but Canning played a menacing hand against this possibility – 'the junction of any foreign Power in an enterprise of Spain against the Colonies, would be viewed by them as constituting an entirely new question; and one upon which they must take such a decision as the interest of Great Britain might require'. With this vague phrase, Canning showed himself prepared to use the Royal Navy against any Bourbon attempt to reassert control in the Western Hemisphere. Second – and significant for all those students who read in Britain's history the story of a ruthlessly expanding empire – the British Government 'absolutely disclaimed, not only any desire of appropriating to itself any portion of the Spanish Colonies; but any intention of forming a political connection with them, beyond that of Amity and Commercial Intercourse'.

The third point set out the ultimatum. His Majesty's Government 'would consider any foreign interference by force or by menace in the dispute between Spain and the Colonies as a motive for recognising the latter without delay'. This was followed by a rebuke to Metternich and the Holy Alliance: 'Mr Canning without entering into any discussion upon abstract principles contented himself with saying that however desirable the Establishment of a Monarchical Form of Government in any of the Provinces might be, he saw great difficulties in the way of it, nor could his Government take upon itself to recommend it.'[116] The final point was a message of pointed irony: 'Mr Canning further remarked that he could not understand how a <u>European</u> Congress could discuss Spanish American affairs without calling to their Counsels a Power so eminently interested in the result, as the United States of <u>America</u>.' No one could imagine Metternich sitting in a congress with the United States.

The Polignac Memorandum coincided with the launch of another of Canning's devices in Washington. For several months, Canning had been working on a way of linking his policy for undermining the Holy Alliance with an understanding with the USA. In August, he had presented an idea for an Anglo-American partnership against European intervention in South America to the American Minister in London. Surprise at the offer and suspicion of the old enemy had combined to cripple the move in Washington. President Monroe consulted Thomas Jefferson and James Madison about Canning's initiative. Both men agreed that the offer put forward by Canning was 'the most momentous which has ever been offered ... since independence'; both men urged the President to accept it. The President called his Cabinet to discuss the offer on 7 November; there, the idea was shot down by the clever, alert, sceptical Secretary of State, John Quincy Adams. In its place, Adams and Monroe planned an independent move. A month later, the President delivered a speech to Congress stating that the United States opposed any involvement by the European powers in the Americas: 'we should consider any attempt on their part to extend their system to any portion of this hemisphere as dangerous to our peace and safety'.[117]

This speech set out what we now know as the Monroe Doctrine – a statement by the United States of America that Europe could no longer interfere with its New World. But both the President's speech and the safety of the Americas would have been impossible if Canning had not already decided that Britain would resist attempts by foreign nations to reassert control over South America. There was nothing charitable or generous about Canning's policy. He disliked the growing power of the Holy Alliance and wanted to protect Britain by limiting its spread; the United States was too weak to police its own waters, so it was in Britain's interest to do this on America's behalf. The choice the Americans had to make was whether to formalise these shared interests into a concrete alliance. By turning down Canning's offer, President Monroe missed an opportunity to open up new areas of co-operation both in Europe and America, but he did not alter the fundamental behaviour of either side. The independence of the Americas was preserved not by the words of the President, but by the force of the British fleet. Indeed, when news of Monroe's speech reached Britain, the London newspapers reacted favourably. *The Times* congratulated the Americans on a policy 'so directly British'. For Canning, it was all grist to his mill. The 'effect of the ultra-liberalism of our Yankee co-operators on the ultra despotism at Aix-la-Chapelle of our allies, gives me just the balance I wanted'.[118]

The effects of these decisions gradually began to filter down to South America. Canning, developing a tactic which became a trademark of publishing his diplomatic papers for popular effect, arranged for copies of the Polignac Memorandum to be dispatched to South America. There, the document caused a sensation; the authorities in Chile gave Canning the title 'Redeemer of Chile'.[119] In Britain, there were some doubts about Canning's answers to the South American question. Some liberals accused him of acting only out of commercial interest; the Whig Earl Grey grumbled that 'the whole policy . . . is that of stock-jobbers and commercial speculators'. Traditionalists and High Tories complained that the policy was dangerous and revolutionary; George IV was especially uncertain and took steps to slow it down. His problem, as Canning explained, was that 'it sanctions what he conceives to be a very revolutionary principle. It cuts him off from his dearly beloved Metternich . . . and it exposes him to the risk of having a cocoa-nut coloured Minister to receive at his Levee.'[120]

The King found some sympathy for these concerns, and even more for his dislike of Canning, in the capitals of those Continental powers who made up the Holy Alliance. Encouraged by the King's indiscreet criticism of the Foreign Secretary, Metternich concocted an intrigue to have Canning removed from office. George seems to have been a willing plotter in the conspiracy and a constitutional crisis threatened, prevented only when Wellington told the King that no ministry could stand without Canning. Indeed, Canning had prepared a resignation speech which would have announced that he had been driven out by the Holy Alliance, and by implication, the collusion of the King.[121]

Slowly, Canning carried his South American diplomacy through to its natural conclusion. In July 1824 Britain opened formal commercial relations with Buenos Aires. In December, the Cabinet agreed the same for Mexico and Colombia. More sluggishly, Chile and Peru moved in the same direction. Every so often in these months, Canning took time out from his diplomacy to marvel at his own omnipotence: 'I did, while I lay in my bed at the Foreign Office with the Gout knawing my great toe, draw up the Instructions for our Agents in Mexico and Colombia which are to raise those States to the rank of Nations . . . The thing is done . . . an act which will make a change in the face of the World almost as great as that of the discovery of the Continent now set free.'[122]

It all sounded very exciting, but Canning's policy was not all that he claimed. Trade did increase with South America, greatly to Britain's advantage. For the people of South America, British support was crucial in their campaign for recognition. But the material impact on Britain's strategic position was small, and much less important than Canning claimed.

Instead, Canning's South American policy had a powerful impact on Canning himself. In its original form, the South American strategy had been designed as a way of rebalancing power in Europe. Years later, Canning looked back on this diplomacy with deep thoughtfulness. He spoke intelligently about the fluid and shifting components which make up a balance of power. A balance of power was not a fixed and unalterable structure, but a 'standard perpetually varying, as civilization advances, and as new nations spring up, and take their place among established political communities'. With new states, different types of governments, the ebb and flow of opinions and ideas, the methods required to adjust a balance of power 'became more varied and enlarged'. That was why, when the French invaded Spain in 1823, Canning decided to find other ways of redressing the balance than war or traditional European diplomacy. He said that he had 'looked another way – sought materials of compensation in another hemisphere. Contemplating Spain, such as our ancestors had known her, I resolved that France had Spain, it should not be Spain "with the Indies". I called the New World into existence, to redress the balance of the Old.'[123]

The blend of logic and nuance behind Canning's policy is captivating. But Canning had become a victim of his own cleverness and success. By focusing so closely on the Americas, he began to exaggerate their significance on the world stage. There was no truth in the argument that 'American questions are out of all proportion more important to us than European', but as early as November 1822, that was Canning's view. Exaggerating the importance of the Americas is not in itself a crime; Canning's mistake was that he reached this conclusion because of his over-emphasis on ideas. He had been correct to recognise that the world of the 1820s had been split into ideological camps, but he was pushing things when he claimed that the next war would be 'a war of the most tremendous character – a war not merely of conflicting armies, but of conflicting opinions'. He inflated the argument further when he suggested that that war would be based on 'a division of the world into Europe and America, republic and monarchy, a league of worn out governments on the one hand, and youthful stirring nations with the US at their head on the other'.[124] Canning's ideas had distorted his sense of geography.

This affected his whole assessment of Britain's place in the world. 'England should hold the balance,' he declared, 'not only between contending nations, but between conflicting principles.' What did this mean? Canning seemed to be suggesting that Britain should and could decide the direction of history – that it could shape the ideological direction of the world. He gave no clue about how this could happen. As his South American policy drew to a close, this gap became exposed, first in Greece and then in Portugal. In arguments about ideology, there was a limit to what Britain could do.

The Greek War of Independence proved the limits of Canning's rules. There was no balancing the Old World with the New in the Ottoman Empire; the opportunities for Britain to decide between conflicting principles were few and far between. Here was a war waged by a nationalist minority against imperial oppression in which neither Canning nor the Holy Alliance took a clear side. Privately, Canning sympathised with the Greeks, although there 'is no denying that they are a most rascally set'; in public, he held back from supporting them and worked hard to ensure that Russia did the same. In 1824 the Ottoman Sultan called on his vassal, Mehemet Ali, the Pasha of Egypt, to suppress the Greek infidels. Through 1825 the Pasha's son, Ibrahim, rampaged through the Peloponnese in a ruthless counter-attack. Meanwhile, support for the Greeks had grown to new levels in England. Lord Byron made his way, sighing, to fight for the Greeks. The Greeks lobbied Canning for greater assistance but achieved nothing beyond embarrassing him when they asked how Britain could still be neutral to a struggle in which British nationals were taking part.

Two events changed the nature of the conflict. In the autumn of 1825, the Russian Ambassador, Count Lieven, showed Canning a report which alleged that Ibrahim was planning to convert the Greek population to Islam or deport them into slavery in Africa. Once Morea had been cleansed of the infidel, Ibrahim would repopulate it as a Muslim colony. This story was confirmed by Canning's cousin, Stratford, the new envoy in Constantinople. Canning was stirred. He sent a message to the Turks that Britain would 'not permit the extension of a system of depopulation which exceeds the permitted violences of war'. He told the commander of the British Navy in the Mediterranean to warn Ibrahim that Britain would resist attempts at removing Christians from Greece.[125] This move was unexpected; it was one of the first attempts by a foreign nation to enforce limits on a faraway war for humanitarian reasons. But it did not follow that Britain would use its force to help the Greeks secure their independence or to protect them from defeat. Instead, the path to peace was opened up by another event which took place in December 1825 – the death of Czar Alexander I.

Canning had already been planning a new alliance with Russia over Greece before Alexander died. On 7 December, some eleven days before he heard of Alexander's death, he had written to Bathurst about Cabinet discussions for a 'straitforward & single handed' concert with Russia on the issue, and discussing why France was not suitable for the joint effort.[126] When the news of Alexander's death reached Canning soon after this, the chances of success were raised. For decades Alexander's erratic behaviour had reduced the chances of co-operation with Russia. Now, and after some uncertainty, a new

Czar, Nicholas, appeared on the throne. He was well known in London; he seemed straightforward and predictable. Canning sent Wellington to St Petersburg where he reached an agreement with the new Czar about the East. Both Britain and Russia disclaimed any territorial or commercial designs on Greece, but agreed that Turkey should be offered mediation with the aim of establishing an autonomous province in Greece.

Byron had died, Missolonghi had capitulated, but with this agreement, the possibility of Greek freedom had been restored. Britain and Russia had accepted that the status quo was untenable. In so doing, they had sided with the Greeks. The following July, the Protocol became the basis of a much firmer tripartite treaty with France. The three powers called for an armistice and Greek autonomy, while writing secret clauses into the treaty which allowed a joint allied naval force to break the Ottoman supply lines from Egypt if the Turks did not co-operate.

The Anglo-Russian Protocol and the Treaty of London were ambivalent victories for Canning. Liberalism in the East seemed to have been reconciled with the balance of power. But this had only been possible through co-operation with the other European powers. By accepting the need for diplomacy, Canning had reluctantly returned to Castlereagh's approach. 'Europe' rather than 'England' had done the trick. After the Protocol had been signed in 1826, Canning made his feelings plain in a letter to his cousin: 'I am not quite satisfied with the prospect of our co-operation,' he admitted, 'but it was worth the trial; and it affords the only chance of bringing things to a conclusion without a war.'[127]

By the time Canning wrote this letter he was already preoccupied with another part of the world. The Portuguese had been tumbling in and out of crises for a number of years. The instability was mostly of their own making, as their leaders wrestled indecisively with the idea of constitutional reform. But, as with other disputes of its time and character, the Portuguese problem became the focus of foreign mischief as European powers, and France in particular, tried to capitalise on the uncertainty for their own purposes. Amidst the confusion, the Portuguese had called on Britain to restore order but Canning's early responses had been calm and cool. When the Portuguese Foreign Minister asked for help in July 1823 Canning had argued that sending troops would mean intervention in an internal matter, whereas Britain always operated on a principle of non-intervention in contrast to the interfering doctrines of the Holy Alliance. Over time, though, Canning whittled down his objections until Britain was diplomatically involved. By 1825 he was interfering in Portuguese politics while the Royal Navy kept watch close by. 'The truth is', Canning explained, 'that the successive military occupations of Piedmont, Naples, and Sicily have gradually wrought a change in the view of international rights and duties; and have led to the Greater Powers ... and the smaller ... to look upon the introduction of a foreign force in a country as one of the ordinary resources of a weak government and one of the natural good offices of a powerful neighbour in cases of international danger and alarm.'[128]

In 1826 the situation deteriorated seriously. King John VI of Portugal died in March. His heir, Dom Pedro, decided to renounce the throne in Portugal to carry on as King of Brazil. He left the Portuguese his eight-year-old daughter, Maria, as Queen, his sister Isabella as Regent, and a new constitution to protect the liberties of them all. This act of abdication shattered the calm which had existed since 1825 and threw Portugal back into civil war. The struggle was bitter and complicated; the leaders of the rival parties were all related to one another. Isabella and Maria were locked in a struggle with Maria's uncle, Miguel, who in theory was also Maria's fiancé. Liberals and constitutionalists rallied behind the two ladies, Churchmen and conservatives turned to Miguel.

Since 1373, Britain had been joined in an alliance with Portugal which bound both parties to mutual support.* Towards the end of 1826, this alliance suddenly blazed with new relevance as Isabella, Maria and the constitutional Government found themselves fending off armed bands of rebels who invaded Portugal from Spain. The Portuguese Government sent a request for assistance to London in December. Within days, Canning had made up his mind. Five thousand troops had already been mobilised and a message of support had been sent to Portugal by the time the issue was debated in Parliament.

Canning's speech on granting aid to Portugal on 12 December 1826

---

* The alliance is still active at the time of writing, making it the oldest in the world.

need not have been a remarkable occasion. The Cabinet had made its decision to intervene in the conflict, and it was difficult to see how the Whig Opposition could vote against a policy which was designed to support liberalism abroad. On top of this, Canning was unwell. Hansard had recorded the previous day how Canning 'spoke in tones so feeble, that his words were very indistinctly heard'. Expectations would not have been high, and nor could they have been exceeded by the plodding first half of Canning's speech. Yet as he went on, Canning rediscovered some of his old rhetorical flair.

> Some years ago . . . I said that I feared that the next war which should be kindled in Europe would be a war not so much of armies as of opinions. Not four years have elapsed, and behold my apprehension realized! It is, to be sure, within narrow limits that this war of opinion is at present confined; but it is a war of opinion that Spain (whether as government or as nation) is now waging against Portugal; it is a war which has commenced in hatred of the new institutions of Portugal.

From here, he drove on towards his conclusion, offering his listeners a new and chivalrous path –

> Let us fly to the aid of Portugal, by whomsoever attacked, because it is our duty to do so; and let us cease our interference where that duty ends. We go to Portugal not to rule, not to dictate, not to prescribe constitutions, but to defend and to preserve the independence of an ally. We go to plant the standard of England on the well-known heights of Lisbon. Where that standard is planted, foreign dominion shall not come.[129]

The speech was a sensation and the intervention was greeted with wide support. Listening carefully that evening was a long-standing fan. 'I heard that speech with peculiar interest,' Lord Palmerston declared. '[I]t is most gratifying to hear avowed by the Ministers of the country as the guide to their conduct those principles which one feels and knows to be true.' In Vienna, Metternich responded with his usual indignation. Canning had sided with 'the revolutionary party and goes to moral war against us'.[130] Quietly forgotten in the furore were Canning's earlier concerns about intervening with force in foreign disputes. True, he was sending troops to Portugal not to change a system of government but to preserve one. True, the Portuguese had asked for help. But the 5,000 troops he dispatched into a civil war were 'bayoneted philosophers' all the same.

British troops arrived to great cheering in Lisbon later that month. They engaged with the conservative revolutionaries before the year was out. By January 1827, the Miguelists had been defeated. Britain's first attempt at liberal intervention looked to have been a success.

It was at this moment in early 1827 that Lord Liverpool suffered a paralytic stroke. Within weeks it became clear that he could neither recover nor continue as Prime Minister. During fifteen years of high drama and near catastrophe, Liverpool had somehow held the Government and country together. Cynics would mock him later, but at that point in 1827 he seemed irreplaceable.

Canning had never given up on becoming Prime Minister. His chances had plummeted after the duel and then slowly recovered. Now, in the spring of 1827 and some twenty years after his name had first been touted, there were few alternatives. His only serious challenger was the Duke of Wellington. As before, there were movements and machinations. As usual, there were misunderstandings and wounded pride. At last, on 10 April 1827 George Canning became Prime Minister, the culmination of a chaotic career.

It was a fleeting victory. The old distrust which he inspired crippled his attempt to form a strong Government. More than forty members of the Government – including the Home Secretary, Robert Peel, and the Duke of Wellington – resigned rather than serve under him. Canning was forced to invite several Whigs to join his Government, thus deepening the rift in the Tory Party between Left and Right. As Foreign Secretary, Canning appointed an intelligent nonentity, Lord Dudley, and continued to exert his usual control. From afar, the Greek Archbishop looked at the new Administration and predicted that 'the new English government is for nations in general and not for Aristocracy alone'.[131]

The most serious damage to Canning was physical. For many months, Canning had complained of ill-health. In January he had been one of several senior members of the Establishment struck down by sickness after the Duke of York's funeral. In April he was still struggling to shake it off. Now the experience of putting together a Government was too much for him. He struggled to carry out responsibilities in three fields as Prime Minister, Chancellor of the Exchequer and Leader of the House of Commons but became seriously ill. Meanwhile, matters were far from settled in Portugal. In April, Canning came to an agreement with France that British troop withdrawals would depend on the French withdrawing from Spain. But inside Portugal the uncertainty continued and the regency relied for its survival on British support.

By early August, Canning's life was in danger. The Duke of Devonshire lent him Chiswick House to recover, but there things only got worse. On 8 August Canning died. He had been Prime Minister for only 119 days – the shortest premiership in British history. A few days later, his funeral took place in Westminster Abbey. There was none of the disruption or cheering which had greeted Castlereagh's funeral. Instead, there was sadness and mourning for the hero who had struck a more liberal path. Palmerston wrote one epitaph when the news reached him that Canning was dying: 'What a loss! Not merely to parties, but to nations; not to friends only, but to mankind.' Metternich wrote another epitaph in Vienna. Canning had been a 'malevolent meteor'. His death 'was an immense event, for the man was a whole revolution in himself alone'.[132]

Canning's immediate record was sealed by the contrasting conclusions to his policies in Greece and Portugal, both of which occurred after his death. On 20 October 1827 the Turkish fleet was wiped out by the allied forces following a skirmish in Navarino Bay. This cut the lines of supply and communication between the Ottoman Empire and Egypt. In effect, it guaranteed Greek independence. By contrast, the British withdrawal from Portugal was followed by a return to civil war. By July 1828, the conservative Miguel had returned with Metternich's support and became King. In the case where Britain had acted independently and with force to intervene in an internal dispute, there had been no resolution. In the case where Canning had co-operated with allies and based his intervention on a strong degree of consensus among the local population, a lasting solution had been found.

*

We are left with two imperfect models of diplomacy, the one falling down where the other succeeded.

Castlereagh operated a traditional policy based on the balance of power, but he ignored the forces of change which were active underneath. He remained the man of facts and acts, whose view of power was traditional, territorial and top-down. The peace settlement which he erected after the defeat of Napoleon established forty years of peace between the Great Powers. But it could not prevent half a century of uncertainty within those powers. In Austria, Metternich was aware of the changes which were present inside Europe, and turned his energies to crushing them. Castlereagh, by contrast, spent years of his career denying the changes without destroying them. In the end his Congress system was unable to cope.

Canning recognised the forces of change which were running through Europe and America. His achievement was to develop a system of foreign policy which accepted these changes and sought to shape them to good effect. In South America, in Portugal, in Greece, as in the wars against Napoleon, Canning saw the advantage that could be gained by encouraging liberal and popular national movements. He also realised that in the new world of European politics, often what mattered was not what a Foreign Secretary did, but how he did it. He contrived to make people – the press, the enfranchised, the soon-to-be enfranchised, the mob – believe that what he was doing was right. Canning realised that the choice of means had a big impact on the ends, and that popular support could define his success. But too often Canning's rhetoric was greater than the reality. He laid too much emphasis on the power of ideas. His argument that Britain should preserve a balance of opinions between Europe and America sounded good on the floor of the House of Commons, but never really moved on from there. In the end, Canning was forced to return to Castlereagh's processes of co-operation in order to get results.

The competing visions of Castlereagh and Canning are the prototype for all subsequent dilemmas of British policy during the time of greatest British power. On the one hand, a Canningite school of foreign policy emerged: unilateral, noisy, vaguely idealistic, believing in progress and liberal intervention. On the other, a separate school developed from Castlereagh, emphasising diplomacy, skilful workmanship, and the building of alliances and institutions to maintain peace and stability. These arguments eventually culminated in the consensus which emerged after the Second World War and a balance between international rules and national power. For over a century, the arguments would move back and forth in and among the two factions, beginning with the long and oscillating argument between Lord Palmerston and the Earl of Aberdeen.

CHAPTER II

ABERDEEN AND PALMERSTON

'... you know as well as we do that right, as the world goes, is
only in question between equals in power, while the strong do
what they can and the weak suffer what they must'
Thucydides, *History of the Peloponnesian War*

'How shall I describe the entrance into this town? For three or
four miles the ground is covered with the bodies of men and
horses – many not dead – wretches, wounded, unable to crawl,
crying for water amidst heaps of putrefying bodies – their screams
we heard at an immense distance and still ring in my ears – the
living as well as the dead are stripped by the barbarous peasantry
who have not sufficient charity to put the miserable wretches out
of their pain.'[1]

George Gordon, 4th Earl of Aberdeen, wrote this letter from Leipzig
on 22 October 1813. A few days earlier, he had witnessed at first
hand the slaughter which came to be known as the Battle of the
Nations. More than half a million men had for three days manoeuvred, marched, charged, bombarded and slaughtered each other
in the largest battle of the Napoleonic Wars. The French forces,
outnumbered by the allies, had eventually collapsed into a chaotic
retreat, a defining moment in decades of conflict, the clearest omen
yet of Napoleon's final defeat. In the first flush of victory, Aberdeen

had written excitedly that the deliverance of Europe was at hand. The awful human cost dawned on him a few days later. 'Our victory is most complete . . . it must be owned that a victory is a fine thing but one should be at a distance.'[2]

Lord Aberdeen was twenty-nine years old at the time of the battle. Other men might have been hardened by the death and suffering of those bloody days. Not so Aberdeen, whose sense of pathos had been reinforced by two decades of harrowing personal misfortune.

Born on 28 January 1784, Aberdeen's early years were chequered by the loss of his father when he was seven, then of his mother when he was eleven. His grandfather, the 3rd Earl, was a distant figure and he was left to the care of two men who later became his guardians, Henry Dundas, Lord Melville and William Pitt. The connection to these two pillars of English political life was a source of huge pride and advantage to the young Scot. With their support, Aberdeen breezed through Harrow and St John's College, Cambridge, forming a close circle of friends and a love of scholarship and antiquity. He seized the opportunity presented by the Peace of Amiens in 1802 to carry out a grand tour of Europe and while in Paris spent several evenings dining at Malmaison with Napoleon and Josephine. His travels extended into the Ottoman Empire; in an academic way, he roughed it round Greece and the Levant, trying his hand at the fashion of locating the site of Troy. He returned to Britain in 1804. Within two more years his life was upended again. Melville was impeached for financial irregularities; Pitt's health collapsed for the last time, the loss almost breaking Aberdeen, who wrote, 'I have lost the only Friend to whom I looked up with unbounded Love and Admiration.'[3]

By this time, Aberdeen had found a new source of comfort in the arms of Catherine Hamilton, a daughter of the 1st Marquess of Abercorn. Pitt had introduced Aberdeen to Abercorn and his family at Bentley Priory after the young man had returned from his European travels. There, Aberdeen had fallen completely in love with Catherine and the two had been married on 28 July 1805, each aged twenty-one. Catherine, or Cat as Aberdeen called her, was beautiful, open-hearted and kind; Aberdeen thought that she was the 'most perfect being whom God in his power ever created'.[4] The couple lit up even the cynics of Regency London with their devotion to each other and their happiness together.

For several years this happiness prospered, pushing aside the earlier tragedies. Bentley Priory became a scene of laughter and entertainment as Aberdeen took part in a run of amateur dramatics in the small theatre there. In 1806 Aberdeen took Catherine up to his estates at Haddo House in Aberdeenshire, where he began to plant some fourteen million trees. Catherine gave birth to a baby girl, Jane, in 1807, followed by two more girls, Caroline and Alice, in the succeeding years. There was a moment of sadness in 1810 when Catherine gave birth to a baby boy who lived less than an hour, but this did not disrupt the warm atmosphere of family life for too long. In a quiet way, Aberdeen pursued his own interests, collecting classical pieces with a particular focus on coins. He translated his love of classical buildings into friendship and commission for the architect William Wilkins, who carried out large alterations to Aberdeen's London residence, Argyll House.

It was probably in the spring of 1811 that Catherine showed the first signs of tuberculosis. For several weeks her health hovered, not recovering but not obviously getting worse. As the weeks turned into months, Aberdeen began to panic, trying a range of doctors and cures without success. By the autumn, it was clear even to Aberdeen that Catherine was fading. In his anguish he wrote to an old family friend, the academic William Howley, desperately searching for some peace of mind. 'The true cause of the frightful and overwhelming nature of the impressions which this makes on my mind is . . . a want of an active and lively belief in the truths of revelation . . . Could I, from a rooted trust in the truth of revelation, feel sure of her being translated to Heaven, as I ought to do, my situation would be comparatively happy; but at present it is only some general feeling which tells me that virtue and innocence like hers must lead to bliss.'[5]

Catherine died on 29 February 1812, entertaining Aberdeen even in her last hours with a playful discussion of the new novel, *Sense and Sensibility*.* For at least a year afterwards, Aberdeen saw Catherine in

---

* Published the previous year, the first of Jane Austen's novels, but under the *nom de plume* 'A Lady'.

ghostly apparitions, recording each occasion in his journal with Latin notes – 'Vidi'; 'Vidi, sed obscuriorem'; 'Tota nocte vidi, ut in vita'; 'Verissima dulcissima imago'.[6]

Politics and diplomacy became for Aberdeen a way out of this confused and morbid world. He had inherited from Pitt a vague belief that public office was a decent and indeed vital profession, but not the abilities which in most men make politics enjoyable from day to day. He was a bad speaker who had fluffed his maiden speech in the House of Lords by failing to deliver it when the moment came. He never developed a taste for the sound of his own voice and his speeches, when actually delivered, were often inaudible. Throughout his life he disliked the crude abrasions of parliamentary politics; at the height of his career as Foreign Secretary many years later he wrote that he found his office irksome and had 'no wish ever to enter the House of Lords again'.[7] But at this moment in 1812, a political appointment held certain advantages, among them a means of escape.

Aberdeen was too young to be counted in the first rank of Pittites, but he had strong relations with many of them, in particular the new Foreign Secretary. He kept up a close relationship with Castlereagh, founded on strong mutual respect. After the duel with Canning in 1809, Castlereagh had written carefully to Aberdeen to solicit his sympathy and support. The idea of Aberdeen taking up a foreign diplomatic posting had been floated from time to time; in 1813 Castlereagh offered and Aberdeen accepted the task of reopening relations with the Austrian Empire.

In this new incarnation as Ambassador to Austria, Aberdeen was not an outright success – although some of the harsh criticism levelled then and later was unfair. He was too easily flattered by the attention he received from the Austrian Emperor, Francis, who 'insisted on my dining and supping with him every day', and he persuaded himself that he had a unique hold over Francis's Minister – 'Do not suppose me arrogant when I think that I have considerable personal influence with Metternich.'[8] More serious were the annoying quarrels with the other British Ambassadors in Europe, Lord Cathcart (Russia) and Sir Charles Stewart (Prussia) about matters of precedence. But in itself, the act of hurtling across war-wrecked Europe to rebuild an Anglo-Austrian link was no mean achievement and one for which Aberdeen had been well prepared by his earlier travels around Greece. Indeed, his thoughts must have returned to that expedition when at one point he and Metternich were separated from the main allied party and had to spend the night together in a hay loft.

The time Aberdeen spent in Europe had a profound and lasting impact on him. Like Castlereagh later, as he travelled he drew the conclusion that ideological changes led to senseless bloodshed and strife. 'Instead of imitating Bonaparte, we ought to pursue a conduct directly opposite, and avoid everything of a revolutionary tendency,' he told Castlereagh. 'Let us restore everything to the right owners ... it is clear that we ought to put down as much as possible the mischievous effects produced by these speculating philosophers and politicians.'[9] Throughout his life, Aberdeen had no interest in nationalist movements or the feelings which accompanied them, except for a lurking admiration for the struggle in Greece.

After Castlereagh arrived in Europe in 1814 to grip the diplomacy, Aberdeen fell in more closely with the man and his methods. There was 'a soundness and right headedness about him which has had great effect'.[10] As an observer and participant in those months of fevered diplomacy, Aberdeen drank with Castlereagh the heady potion of intense personal diplomacy mixed with an understanding that Britain was a Continental power. Aberdeen, like Castlereagh, became a firm Europeanist, believing that Britain's interests coincided with those of a peaceful Continent.

In Aberdeen's case, this drink was laced with one conclusion which was peculiarly his own. As he moved through Europe, Aberdeen saw roads and rivers choked with dead bodies. In Teplitz, Aberdeen took a walk one evening in a private garden and fell over a heap of amputated arms and legs. But in spite of, or perhaps because of, his earlier acquaintances with high tragedy, Aberdeen distilled from these experiences a deep and lasting horror of war, underpinned by a raw feeling that nothing, no idea or value, was more important than life. Along with the Duke of Wellington, he would many years later become one of only two men in the nineteenth century to become Prime Minister with first-hand experiences of war.[11] Unlike the Duke, he did not find that the sacrifices made in battle were outweighed by the honour or prestige gained. A week on from his letter after the battle at Leipzig, he wrote again – 'Much as I have seen of these horrors, I have not yet grown callous to them.'[12]

Aberdeen returned to Britain in June 1814. Maria, his sister-in-law and the recipient of the Leipzig letters, had by this time followed her sister Catherine into tuberculosis and death. On arriving back in London, Aberdeen was told that Catherine's brother, Lord Abercorn's heir, had also just died. He left behind him a beautiful widow, Harriet, and three children of her own. Abercorn applied the necessary mixture of hints and pressure and the following year Aberdeen and Harriet were married.

The marriage, which had been overshadowed by a new catastrophe when Aberdeen's own brother was killed at Waterloo, proved to be fraught and unsteady. Aberdeen may have remembered the verdict he had expressed several years previously that Harriet was 'certainly one of the most stupid persons I ever met'. There was some comfort in the bedroom which resulted in four sons and a daughter, as well as a series of rather honest letters about sex. But Harriet was irritating and neurotic; Aberdeen had to confirm repeatedly that he loved her – 'You ask if I think of you when I go to bed in our room. I have told you dearest that I always do.'[13]

For Aberdeen, the domestic tragedy still had several acts left to run. One by one, his three daughters by Catherine fell ill with tubercular complaints. Aberdeen withdrew from public life to care for them, feeding them medicines, monitoring their symptoms, looking after them as best he could. Caroline died in 1818; Jane in 1824; finally Alice fell ill as well. Aberdeen took her abroad to try and cure her, personally supervising much of her care. For a time there were signs of improvement, but on 29 April 1829 Alice passed away. Aberdeen locked himself away for several days afterwards, unable to come to terms with his grief. It is hard for us to imagine the accumulated burden of bereavement in his life.

In these years, Aberdeen had been watching rather than taking part in the major decisions of State. Joining him in these observations, although not sharing his analysis, was one of Aberdeen's contemporaries from Harrow, Henry Temple, now the 3rd Viscount Palmerston.

Palmerston had been born some nine months after Aberdeen, on 20 October 1784. His family was prosperous but not especially prominent, and his childhood was distinguished chiefly by the visit his entire family made to Paris in 1792. Palmerston's father, a respected but not spectacular Member of Parliament, was received at the Tuileries and became one of the last Englishmen to be presented to Louis XVI and Marie Antoinette before they were deposed. This visit was followed by several slightly fraught years travelling around revolutionary Europe, before the Palmerston family returned to England and established their eldest son at Harrow, where he came across the young Aberdeen. Two stories, improvised if not apocryphal, survive of Palmerston and Aberdeen during their school years. The first records the young Henry Temple devastating George Gordon in a pillow fight. According to the other, George once locked his rival in an unlighted room until Henry began to bleat – 'Lighten our darkness, we beseech thee, O Lord.'[14] Palmerston was a sicklier child than is often imagined; his mother was always worrying about his health. Like Aberdeen, he followed Harrow with studies at St John's College, Cambridge, although in his case delaying his arrival there by three years of study in Edinburgh with the political economist Dugald Stewart. There, he consumed and digested the ideas of Adam Smith, becoming an unstinting believer in free trade.

As an Irish Peer, Palmerston was eligible to stand for the House of Commons; after several attempts he was elected in 1807 as Member of Parliament for Newport on the Isle of Wight. In 1809 Spencer Perceval offered him the post of Chancellor of the Exchequer, a relatively minor position at that time, but, showing a caution which gradually deserted him, Palmerston turned it down and took a junior position as Secretary at War. The post was in a bureaucratic way important; Palmerston mastered the brief rigorously and well. But it did not occasion great speeches or, until 1827, entitle Palmerston to a Cabinet seat. So Palmerston devoted himself to extra-curricular pursuits, namely horse-racing and beautiful women.

As a boy, Palmerston had written to a friend telling him that, while he did believe in marriage, he would be 'by no means precipitate about my choice'.[15] In the event, Palmerston did not get married until 1839 when, aged fifty-five, he married Lady Cowper

75

who had been his mistress for the previous thirty years. During these decades, Palmerston's life was a sustained collection of ladies and extramarital affairs. He was well dressed, good-looking and confident; one biographer wrote later that his 'air was more that of a man of the drawing room than of the senate'.[16] He probably fathered three of Lady Cowper's children while she was married to Earl Cowper, but he was by no means faithful to her, then or later. In June 1863, when he was seventy-eight and Prime Minister, Palmerston seduced the young wife of an Irish journalist when she came to visit him at home. Later that year her husband filed for divorce, citing Palmerston as the co-respondent.

The love affairs of 'Lord Cupid' helped to cement Palmerston's reputation as a jaunty, easy-going cad. He was frequently in debt and rarely paid his creditors. Even after he was married, he would be embarrassingly late for social engagements – wits and socialites noticed that the Palmerstons always missed the soup.[17] There was a folksy iconoclasm in his manner, an almost deliberately non-intellectual charm. Victor Hugo met Palmerston and thought that he was a man of fiction rather than history. Marx became strangely obsessed with Palmerston; in 1853 he wrote a rather exhausting exposé of this exploiter of the masses who was always popular. 'In his eyes, the movement of history itself is nothing but a pastime, expressly invented for the private satisfaction of the noble Viscount Palmerston of Palmerston,' Marx complained. Queen Victoria and Prince Albert, who had their own reasons for hating him, called Palmerston 'the immoral one'.[18]

None of these observers noticed the huge industry and discipline which Palmerston imposed on himself in office and on those working for him. They did not know that Palmerston rarely stayed in bed after seven and worked long past midnight on his papers and dispatches, standing at a special writing desk to prevent him falling asleep.

Like Aberdeen, Palmerston started off as a Tory, but he was a follower of Canning rather than Castlereagh. His maiden speech had been about Canning's Copenhagen expedition, where he had defended the use of secret intelligence. He shared Canning's joyous patriotism; he later wrote that he did 'not blame the French for disliking us. Their vanity prompts them to be the first nation in the world; and yet at every turn they find that we outstrip them in everything.' By default, he also inherited Canning's faith in nationalism – 'Providence meant mankind to be divided into separate nations.' He was not, however, personally close to Canning, nor did he share his master's chief attribute. He was never a very strong speaker and in this respect was rather like Aberdeen. But while Aberdeen thought too much about speaking, Palmerston too often spoke without thought. He would stutter and stammer his way through half-finished sentences, waving his handkerchief around while searching for a word.[19]

In terms of Party allegiance, Palmerston was more liberal than Canning and would later leave the Tories for the Whigs. But he did not share Canning's optimistic faith in human nature and he could be quite cynical about ideas. Aberdeen claimed many years later that Palmerston was no more radical than he was, 'but being entirely without principle, he does not hesitate to follow whatever may seem most conducive to the popularity of the moment'.[20] This was slightly wide of the mark. Palmerston was always a moderate liberal; he wanted other countries to have their revolution, but it needed to be 1688 not 1789. Besides, the tide of public opinion was to him much more interesting and important than any ideas.

Like Canning, Palmerston believed that public opinion in any country could materially affect the balance of power. As he explained in 1829, 'those statesmen who know how to avail themselves of the passions, and the interest, and the opinions of mankind, are able to gain an ascendancy, and to exercise a sway over human affairs, far out of all proportion greater than belong to the power and resources of the state over which they preside'.[21] This notion stayed with him all his life. 'Opinions', he told the House of Commons in 1849, 'are stronger than armies. Opinions, if they are founded in truth and justice, will in the end prevail against the bayonets of infantry, the fire of artillery, and the charges of cavalry.'[22]

While Palmerston took great care to shape and follow public opinion, Aberdeen tended to see it as a weathercock pointing towards what not to do. Palmerston fed newspapers with news leaks and articles; Aberdeen turned the other way. He thought the media an erratic and unhelpful guide to diplomacy, on the whole increasing the chances of war. 'The English people know little, and care little' about foreign relations, Aberdeen wrote at the end of his life, 'but when mischievously directed, they can be quite as unjust and as aggressive as France or Russia.'[23]

But as with Castlereagh and Canning, the argument between Palmerston and Aberdeen ran deeper than their views about public opinion. Their quarrel focused on the utility and justice of war; it was born out of their different interpretations of human nature. Aberdeen thought that deep down men wanted peace and safety, although this could occasionally be forgotten in the heat of a fevered press campaign. 'After all, the great mass of mankind care much more for their personal safety than for Constitutional privileges,' he once said.[24] Palmerston thought that 'unfortunately man is a fighting and quarrelling animal; and that this is human nature is proved by the fact that republics, where the masses govern are far more quarrelsome, and more addicted to fighting, than monarchies, which are governed by comparatively few persons'.[25] This was a fundamental disagreement between two able statesmen which no discussions or debates could ever resolve. Through the 1820s and 1830s, this argument unfolded in a series of proxy battles about intervention and the use of force. We should note, though, that Palmerston denied the use of the word 'intervention', on the grounds that it was supposed to be French. He would interrupt speeches in the Commons by explaining that British politicians should use the word 'interference' instead.[26]

For a brief period in 1828, both men served in the Duke of Wellington's Cabinet, Aberdeen as Chancellor of the Duchy of Lancaster, Palmerston still as Secretary at War. These were not easy months as the Cabinet squabbled over the two foreign crises which Canning had bequeathed. With Greece, the skeleton of a settlement had emerged from the Treaty of London and the crushing Turkish defeat at Navarino. The critical issue at stake now was the size and precise status of Greece. Palmerston recorded in his journal Cabinet meetings which divided down the old Castlereagh-Canning lines – 'the Duke, Ellenborough, and Aberdeen being for cutting down the Greeks as much as possible; Huskisson, Dudley, and myself for executing the treaty in the fair spirit of those who made it'.[27] Quietly, though, Aberdeen maintained his old belief in Greek independence and his differences with Palmerston on this issue grew out of a different theme. When Palmerston raised in Cabinet the plight of thousands of Greeks who had been kidnapped into slavery, the Duke treated the matter coldly and Aberdeen 'as a thing which we had no right to interfere with'. Others took an even firmer line, Bathurst viewing the ethnic cleansing as 'the exercise of a legitimate right on the part of the Turks; and Ellenborough, as rather a laudable action'.[28] But the dispute between Palmerston and Aberdeen was a dispute over principle – whether Britain could or should interfere in the internal policies of a foreign state. This argument was particularly prominent over Portugal. Aberdeen's stern belief in non-interference and Wellington's own suspicions led to the withdrawal in 1828 of those troops dispatched with such verve by Canning the previous year, driving Palmerston to distraction and despair. Miguel soon regained his ascendancy and threw out Queen Maria and the constitutionalists.

A controversy over domestic reform in 1828 led to a final split between the Tories and the Canningites. Palmerston resigned from his post at the War Office, to the delight of his staff who were overjoyed to see their strict master go. Over the next year, he assembled his critique of Wellington and the new Foreign Secretary, Aberdeen. On 1 June 1829 Palmerston deployed his arguments in the House of Commons. 'If by interference is meant interference by force of arms, such interference, the Government are right in saying, general principles and our own practice forbade us to exert. But', he went on, marking a distinction he would himself later erode, 'if by interference is meant intermeddling, and intermeddling in every way, and to every extent, short of actual military force; then I must affirm that there is nothing in such interference which the laws of nations may not in certain cases permit.' He mocked the absurd proposals for 'a Greece which should contain neither Athens, nor Thebes, nor Marathon, nor Salamis, nor Plataea, nor Thermopylae, nor Missolonghi', before rounding things off with a Canningite statement of Britain's proselytising role in the world. Canning had fashioned England as a friend of liberty 'because it was thought that her rulers had the wisdom to discover that the selfish interests and political influence of England were best promoted by the extension of liberty and civilization'. Yet Wellington and Aberdeen wrongly

79

assumed that Britain's advantage lay 'in withholding from other countries that constitutional liberty which she herself enjoys'.[29]

These arguments were soon overtaken by new events. In July 1830, revolution broke out again in Paris; Charles X abdicated and was replaced by a constitutional government under King Louis Philippe. Palmerston was overjoyed and wrote letters marvelling that a nation of maniacs and assassins had transformed themselves into heroes and philosophers. 'This event is decisive of the ascendancy of Liberal Principles throughout Europe; the evil spirit has been put down and will be trodden under foot. The reign of Metternich is over and the days of the Duke's policy might be measured by algebra, if not by arithmetic.'[30]

Wellington's Government was indeed on the way out. George IV had died in June 1830 and the Tories did badly in the election which followed. Wellington made some effort to bring Palmerston into his weakening ranks but, in the autumn, his Government collapsed and was replaced by a new Whig Government under Lord Grey. After some uncertainty, Grey asked Palmerston to succeed Aberdeen at the Foreign Office; on 22 November, Palmerston left the Tories and assumed the post which made him famous throughout the world.

For Aberdeen the extraordinary run of personal tragedy continued out of office. His wife, Harriet, succumbed to tuberculosis in 1833; the following year Frances, her daughter by Aberdeen, died. Finally, in 1835 Aberdeen's brother Charles died of a brain haemorrhage. Years of relentless sadness had acquainted Aberdeen with grief, but given him no skill in handling it. He was so distraught that he could not bring himself to attend Frances's funeral. After Harriet's death he had turned once again to his old friend Howley, now Archbishop of Canterbury, for advice. 'Although I have been severely schooled by misfortune, I have still much to learn.'[31]

Palmerston quickly gripped the complex fallout from the upheaval in France. Revolution had spread to the Low Countries; the Belgians demanded a break from Dutch rule. Aberdeen in his last days at the Foreign Office had set up a conference to discuss the crisis in London. Palmerston made himself master of all the relevant facts and worked on a settlement which would free Belgium without increasing the power of France. There was extreme tension in the summer of 1831 when French troops entered the Low Countries to throw back the avenging Dutch. But in a crafty fashion, Palmerston disabused Louis Philippe of any grandiose plans by hinting to him that unless the French drew back they would find themselves at war with Britain. By the end of the year, an independent Belgium was agreed under an acceptable monarch, King Leopold. The Dutch continued to be stubborn, refusing to sign the agreement until 1839, when Belgian neutrality was guaranteed by all the European powers – a guarantee which would be invoked fatefully in 1914.

Meanwhile, Palmerston was struggling to keep up with the other troubles on Europe's plate. Shortly after he became Foreign Secretary, the Poles had broken out in revolt against the Czar. In Portugal, Miguel had begun to consolidate his rule, banishing Maria and her father to an island in the Azores. Yet in neither case had Palmerston moved to intervene. Nicholas I crushed the Polish rebellion and wiped out those freedoms that had been granted by the Treaty of Vienna. From separate parts of the House of Commons, criticism of Palmerston mounted. The Tories, who disliked Palmerston for changing parties, taunted him for re-empowering a revolutionary France; the Radicals mocked him for his weakness against Russia and his lack of support for the Poles. A writer calling himself Runnymede, whose real name was Benjamin Disraeli, incorporated both critiques in his articles for *The Times*. Palmerston was 'the Lord Fanny of diplomacy'; he spent his days 'cajoling France with an airy compliment and menacing Russia with a perfumed cane'.[32]

Perhaps Palmerston was merely discovering that in diplomacy there was a limit to what he could actually do, particularly when it came to Poland; perhaps he was waiting for things to calm down before establishing a new stance. We know that Palmerston spent a great deal of time reorganising the Foreign Office to meet his own standards of diligence. He exerted himself to stop the clerks from flashing mirrors at the girls who worked in the dressmakers shop across the road. He also demanded new handwriting skills, refusing to accept anything less than large and clear letters crafted in thick black ink. Clerks were expected to work long into the evening, finishing at ten o'clock. There was no smoking and staff had to be prepared to work on Sundays.[33]

In 1832, Palmerston cautiously began to change the style of his foreign policy. As before, a speech set out the new approach. There was a debate about German politics; liberal Members were unhappy with the repressive politics practised by Metternich and his friends. Palmerston spoke out for freedom and a new foreign policy – 'Constitutional states I consider to be the natural allies of this country,' he declaimed.[34] The following year, the old Holy Alliance was put back together when Austria, Russia and Prussia announced at Münchengrätz that they would stand firm together to suppress revolution. From afar, Aberdeen commended the conservative approach. 'It is on the cordial and intimate union of the Northern Powers that the chance is afforded of preserving the tranquillity and happiness of Europe against the disorganizing and revolutionary policy of the present Governments of England and France.'[35] Palmerston seized the challenge laid down by Aberdeen and the Conservative powers and turned his attention to a crisis which was again breaking out in Spain. As before, so again the conflict arose out of a violent, unsteady competition between the forces of reaction and reform. For a moment, the dividing line of the argument, often obscured by the complexity of events, became sharp and clear.

In the spring of 1834 Palmerston pieced together his own alliance between the constitutional monarchies of France and Britain together with the two young Queens in Portugal and Spain, both struggling against autocratic uncles. This Quadruple Alliance aimed to restore peace under the two Queens in the Peninsula, and to put into place Palmerston's doctrine that constitutional states were Britain's natural allies. Interventions of a kind followed in the Peninsula. Palmerston did not send troops into Spain. Instead, he encouraged British volunteers to go and fight for the Spanish Government, offering what Aberdeen described as British mercenaries rather than a fully fledged invasion.[36]

This was pure Canning all over again, with the one difference that Britain now found itself working with allies. Palmerston was thoroughly pleased with his new alliance – 'a capital hit, and all my own doing' – and defined the intervention in Canning's own terms. It was Spain, he argued three years later, which would decide 'that great contest between opposing and conflicting principles of government – arbitrary government on the one hand and constitutional government on the other – which is going on all over Europe'.[37] The policy shared the same defects as Canning's earlier activity. The intervention led to the surrender of the two uncles in Portugal and Spain, but that was not the end of the story. The Spanish absolutist, Don Carlos, soon escaped and found fresh recruits for a new and terrifying campaign. In Portugal, the liberal Queen made a hash of things ten years later, becoming rather dictatorial herself and precipitating a fresh civil war in which Palmerston again had to intervene. In both countries, the lesson had to be learned again – liberal intervention depended for its success on strong, if not overwhelming, support among the population.

None of this was necessarily clear when Palmerston and the Whigs went out of office at the end of 1834. Indeed, Palmerston had built up a considerable reputation as the protector of foreign liberties and the architect of a free Belgium. The new Prime Minister, Robert Peel, appointed Wellington as Palmerston's successor in his minority Government, but Palmerston did not have to wait long before he and the Whigs were back in power.

Palmerston's second stint as Foreign Secretary was dominated by the series of crises he confronted at the end. But through this period and later he worked hard to suppress the transatlantic slave trade. We have seen how Castlereagh managed to secure an agreement from the powers at Vienna that the slave trade was immoral; but new rules and institutions were only as useful as the will and power to back them up. A British naval squadron was deployed off the African west coast to intercept slave shipping. New treaties were secured, occasionally granting Britain unilateral powers to search certain vessels suspected of carrying slaves. Two pieces of evidence, one academic, one anecdotal, suggest that Britain's actions had a strong effect. In a 'quantitative analysis of the impact of British suppression policies on the volume of the nineteenth century Atlantic slave trade', Phillip LeVeen has shown how British naval activity restricted the slave trade by increasing its operating costs and restricting supply. The number of slaves exported from Africa to America had increased after the Congress of Vienna. But when the Royal Navy started to police West African waters the slave trade began to abate. Many thousands of slaves were rescued in the half-century of intense naval activity in which Palmerston led the charge and dominated the scene.[38] More casually, Palmerston also observed the effect the Royal Navy was having. He noted that slave trade shipping clearly increased when British ships were briefly removed from Africa at the end of the decade to take part in the first Opium War.[39]

But for Palmerston this was never at the heart of foreign policy. It lacked those elements of drama and competition which made European diplomacy worthwhile. By the late 1830s, the focus of that drama was again swinging to the East. Here, the cause of political liberty was almost entirely submerged beneath more pressing and dramatic concerns – the balance of power, trade and prestige.

For most of the nineteenth century Britain's rivalry with Russia was rather distant and indirect. There was no real possibility that either nation would seek to conquer one another; Anglo-Russian relations therefore lacked the fierce uncertainty which affected Britain's dealings with France. Instead, the rivalry focused on secondary objects – the safety of Constantinople and the passage to India. Palmerston in the late 1830s found himself drawn into new entanglements on both of these fronts.

The long uncertainty in the Ottoman Empire over Greece had come to an end in 1832. The Sultan soon managed to engineer fresh catastrophes for himself and his empire. He annoyed his violent vassal, Mehemet Ali, Pasha of Egypt, by refusing to give him Syria as well as Crete in reward for his attempts at suppressing the Greeks. Mehemet Ali replied by sending his son Ibrahim to seize Syria and inflict further mayhem on the battered empire. In desperation, the Sultan appealed for assistance; Palmerston urged the Cabinet to go to his aid. The French regarded Mehemet Ali as a rather talented protégé, and so his advance in the Middle East had gloomy implications for the British position in Asia. The 'mistress of India cannot permit France to be mistress directly or indirectly of the route to the India dominions', Palmerston explained.[40] But Palmerston still had not the necessary strength or popularity to carry the Francophile Whigs with him in an operation of this kind, and Britain left the Sultan to find help elsewhere. In a Faustian pact, the Sultan turned to the Czar who agreed to help him restore calm. The new alliance was cemented in the Treaty of Unkiar Skelessi of 1833, when the Turks paid for Russian protection by granting the Czar key naval rights and a say in Turkish foreign policy. This was a blow to Britain and a blow to Palmerston personally. But there was no collapse of Constantinople, and the Ottoman Empire limped on.

In 1839, the situation blew up again. The Syrians revolted against Ibrahim; the ageing Sultan decided to try and regain his lost lands. The Turks were a fascinating and unpredictable fighting force in the nineteenth century, often rather ferocious in adversity, but useless when on the attack. This time was no exception and the onslaught was easily repelled. The Turkish navy decided that their chances of survival were better if they switched sides; they deserted and joined Mehemet Ali's force. Before the news had come through of these setbacks, the Sultan died. His successor was an eighteen-year-old boy.

Palmerston had already loaded himself up with new arguments. He stirred himself to save the collapsing Ottoman Empire. 'Half the wrong conclusions at which mankind arrive are reached by the abuse of metaphors . . . all that we hear every day of the week about the decay of the Turkish empire and its being a dead body or a sapless trunk, and so forth, is pure and unadulterated nonsense.'[41] Through the winter of 1839 he worked on a new agreement with the European powers to intercede on the Sultan's behalf and emasculate Mehemet Ali's mini empire based in Egypt. For Palmerston, the canvas was empty and awaiting a new display of British influence and prestige. But the French refused to act against Mehemet Ali and objected to Palmerston's ideas. In London, the Cabinet hesitated at the prospect of acting without France and refused to approve Palmerston's plan. Palmerston, now backed by boisterous personal support in the press and almost a decade of experience at the Foreign Office, threatened to resign rather than do nothing. Reluctantly, the Whigs gave way.

In France, public opinion flew into a rage when it became clear that Palmerston was ready to move without her and in concert with Austria, Prussia and Russia – the autocratic powers whom France and Britain had formed the Quadruple Alliance to frustrate. Rash words were spoken and even sensible people predicted war between Britain and France. But the French were not prepared to stop Britain from applying pressure in the Middle East or from bombarding the Syrian coast. Ibrahim was removed from Syria and Mehemet Ali confined to Egypt. The following July, Palmerston brought the affair to a close by involving France in a new convention covering the navigation of the Dardanelles in which Russia waived those advantages gained by the Treaty of Unkiar Skelessi. In this way, the Ottoman Empire patched itself together, storing up its rotten apples for another day. Several of Palmerston's old critics now turned to applaud. Disraeli found it difficult 'to fix upon a page in history a superior instance of moral intrepidity'.[42]

If Palmerston had through stubborn determination thrown back Russian influence in the East, he felt obliged to take more drastic measures in Central Asia in order to protect the northern approach to India through the Caucasus. He focused his efforts on Persia, Afghanistan and the Punjab. Britain's and Russia's dealings in those regions tended to be high in intrigue and low in reward. In the complicated manoeuvres which unfolded, Palmerston decided to replace the reigning Dost Mohammad in Afghanistan with a more pliable ally from the Punjab. This regime change stirred up serious controversy with the Radicals in the Commons and MPs demanded that the relevant diplomatic documents be laid before the House. Palmerston ruthlessly mutilated the key dispatches to defend his own policy. Criticism and contrary advice given by the Foreign Office were simply removed, leaving the impression of a rather tame agreement among Britain's men on the ground about the need for an aggressive policy. The results of the invasion of Afghanistan became clear after Palmerston had left the Foreign Office in 1841. The Afghans launched a successful resistance movement against the British and their client king; the British author of the doctored dispatches was murdered by a mob in Afghanistan; and in retreat, a British army of 15,000 men was massacred – only one soldier survived.

The chaos in Afghanistan ought to have permanently discredited Palmerston. Instead, it was overshadowed by another, much more popular war.

Britain did not have official diplomatic relations with China. This was because the Emperor of China knew that he was the ruler of the world. There was no question for him of dealing with barbarian nations on terms of equality. This did not inhibit the entrepreneurial spirit of British commerce and around a sixth of Britain's overseas trade was with China. It did, however, make regulating that commerce rather tricky, particularly when a large proportion of it involved the distribution of illegal opium.[43] When the Chinese authorities decided to enforce the ban on opium in 1836, the thin veneer of stability began to peel away. The Chinese seized a large haul of opium from British merchants in 1839; this coincided with a drunken outrage and the death of a Chinese man at the hands of some English sailors. The various pieces of the confusion came together and by the end of the year, Britain and China were at war.

This time, it was the Tories not the Radicals who led the torrent of complaints against Palmerston. Many Tories drew from the traditions of the old Country Party which had opposed Marlborough and Chatham, as well as from their own instincts – High Church morality, cautiousness, respect for subtle diplomacy between sensible men – a deep reluctance to accept noisy foreign policy and unnecessary wars. Chief among these critics in the late 1830s was an earnest young Tory called William Gladstone, still a long way from those Liberals he would later join. He condemned Palmerston for protecting drug dealers in an 'unjust and iniquitous war', but slipped up on a detail about whether the Chinese had or had not attempted to kill British merchants by poisoning the water wells.[44]

Palmerston's chief concern during the conflict was the ease and security of British trade. He pressed a series of demands on the Chinese, including compensation for the confiscated opium and trading concessions, by which British merchants would have official access to Chinese markets. But Palmerston was no mercantilist; he did not believe in the pursuit of fixed and exclusive markets abroad. What Palmerston wanted was freedom of trade in China – markets which were open to all foreign goods. The European market was saturated and discriminated against British manufacturing goods; it was therefore necessary to find new outlets for British products. Britain did not demand any unfair advantages; she was competitive and there was no need for discriminatory access. Unfortunately, this decent case was damaged by the fact that the quarrel had developed from the sale of an illegal drug.

The Chinese war ended after Palmerston had left office; it only secured some of the objectives he had laid out. Five ports were opened to international commerce by the Treaty of Nanking, but there was no wider opening of trade and opium was still classed as illegal by the Chinese. Palmerston was not interested in the one piece of territory which Britain gained from the war: Hong Kong was 'a barren Island with hardly a House upon it'.[45]

Palmerston and the Whigs left office in August 1841 after Peel and the Conservative Party won the general election a few weeks earlier. The Whig Government had run out of steam and almost bankrupted the country with a huge budget deficit. Palmerston left Britain in the middle of two faraway wars and with two broken relationships elsewhere. With France, there had been no quick return to the co-operation which had led to the partnership in Portugal and Spain. More dramatically, Britain's relations with America were on the verge of another breakdown. Throughout his life, Palmerston disliked Americans because he thought that they were rather like himself – confident, persistent and often irritating, with a tendency to think a lot about themselves. Palmerston had threatened war in his last months in office over the arrest in New York of a Canadian man called McLeod. McLeod had been involved in the burning of an American ship, the *Caroline*, which had been used to promote rebellion in Canada; the New York authorities accused him of murder. Although the man was eventually acquitted, the affair had ignited violent passions on both sides of the Atlantic. The anger now settled on two territorial disputes between the United States and Canada, one in the north-east of America, the other in the north-west. These disputes and the ongoing entanglements in China and Afghanistan meant that Palmerston's successor would have a great deal of work to do. The foreign ambassadors in London, exhausted by years of dealing with Palmerston, breathed a collective sigh of relief when Robert Peel asked Aberdeen to take up the post. 'What he says is solid, true, and carries the seal of integrity,' the Russian Ambassador remarked.[46]

Peel's administration from 1841 to 1846 is not remembered for its record in foreign affairs. The repeal of the Corn Laws and a string of financial reforms overshadow Aberdeen's efforts abroad. Yet the courteous and considered diplomacy which Aberdeen attempted was a key counterpart to Peel's pragmatism at home, the two policies part of one vision for a decent and more orderly world. What Aberdeen offered in those years was rather bold: an attempt to break away from the noise and bombast which foreign nations were coming to associate with British foreign policy. The method owed something to Castlereagh and his personal diplomacy, much more to Aberdeen's dislike of conflict and his conservative respect for peace. The policy was focused in particular on three countries whose relations with Britain Palmerston had done his best to wreck. America, France and to a surprising extent Russia were all treated as objects in Aberdeen's experiment to restore peace and quiet to the world.

First, Aberdeen sent the banker Lord Ashburton to America to negotiate with the Secretary of State, Daniel Webster, on all topics in dispute between the two countries. In August 1842 he reached a major agreement with the Americans about the contested territory around Maine, dividing the land between America and Britain in a seven-five ratio. The second slab of land covering Oregon in the north-west later proved to be more difficult. President Polk ran his election campaign in 1844 on the slogan 'Fifty-four Forty or Fight'; in the end a boundary was fixed across the 49th parallel just before Peel's Government fell in 1846. This amounted to a considerable concession by Aberdeen and Britain, but the Government's priorities were clear when Peel commented that a month of Anglo-American war would have been 'more costly than the value of the whole territory'.[47]

Aberdeen's most famous achievement in these years was to invent an *entente cordiale* between Britain and France, the phrase as well as the policy. Together with the cautious and respectable French Minister, the historian Guizot, Aberdeen rebuilt a pattern of diplomacy with France and crowned the relationship with a series of royal visits between Queen Victoria and Louis Philippe. Victoria, on her first visit to France in 1843, was the first British monarch to set foot there since Henry VIII. These rounds of personal diplomacy did not alter the basic rivalry between the two powers and there was a cantankerous set-to in 1844 about missionaries in Tahiti. But they did drain away some of the venom which had been building up in France since Waterloo, and at the highest levels of State there was now a sympathy which reduced the chances of an impulsive war.[48]

The third buttress in Aberdeen's new bridge of diplomacy ought to have attracted more sceptical attention. Much more than his contemporaries realised, Aberdeen travelled far down the treacherous road to a Russian *détente*. In December 1844, he wrote to Gladstone at the Board of Trade about the policy. 'Notwithstanding our <u>entente cordiale</u> I very much wish to improve our Russian connection.' He identified a change of mood inside Russia – 'liberal opinions, at least in affairs of commerce, are rapidly gaining ground'; once again, personal connections confirmed his own views: 'There is no doubt that a desire has existed for some time in the most influential quarters in Russia to bring about a great change in our Relations. This is the wish of the Emperor himself, as he repeatedly assured me.'[49]

The main offshoot of the new diplomacy was a long and frank discussion in 1844 between Aberdeen and Czar Nicholas during the Czar's visit to London in June 1844. Aberdeen was probably too cavalier in the meeting; he kept no formal record of what was said. But for the Czar, the discussion was of high significance. After his return to Russia, he sent Count Nesselrode back to London to put down on paper what Aberdeen had told him about the dissolution of the Ottoman Empire. In the memorandum which Nesselrode drafted after his own meeting with Aberdeen, Britain and Russia set out how they would act together once the Ottoman Empire collapsed to create a new settlement around the Mediterranean. The emphasis on cooperation is typical of Aberdeen; the easy talk about dismantling the Ottoman Empire is not. Perhaps something in Aberdeen's personal diplomacy got lost in translation.

Palmerston found his five years in Opposition difficult to navigate. The loss of office was a harsh personal blow, not least financially, as Palmerston and his wife had come to rely on his ministerial salary to pay off his debts and host their popular dinner parties. But the fundamental difficulty was political. Some interpreted Palmerston's savage attacks on the new diplomacy as the crude outbursts of a self-serving man. Aberdeen was especially rattled. He later grumbled that 'no one could have acted with more hostility, or more unfairly, than he did towards me during the whole time I was in office'.[50] There was no hint of constructive support in Palmerston's attitude to his successor. His attack on the Ashburton agreement with America was particularly unhelpful, not least since Ashburton had actually secured more for Britain than Palmerston had been ready to accept when Foreign Secretary himself. Yet on the whole, Palmerston's critique of the new policy was thoughtful and consistent; it flowed naturally from the basic difference of opinion between the two men. He identified correctly the moral foundation of Aberdeen's policy – an overriding desire to avoid war – and had some success in knocking it down. If 'a nation once establishes & proclaims as its Rule of Conduct, that any Sacrifice of Interest is preferable to war', he thundered, 'it had better at once abdicate its Independence and place itself under the Protection of some less Quakerlike state'. In private, he invoked comedy in support of his critique. 'We yield to every foreign state and power all they ask, and then make it our boast that they are all in good humour with us,' he told his brother in 1843. 'This is an easy way of making friends, but, in the end, a somewhat costly one.'[51]

Aberdeen did not deny that his main aim was to avoid a major war. On the contrary, he revelled in the fact. 'I believe I may conscientiously say that no man ever filled the high situation which I have the honour unworthily to hold, who felt more ardently desirous than I do to preserve to the country the blessings of peace, or who would be disposed to make greater sacrifices, consistent with propriety, to maintain it,' he told the House of Lords. Nor did he mind that the media crassly lampooned him. 'I am accustomed almost daily to see myself characterized as pusillanimous, cowardly, mean, dastardly, truckling, and base . . . I feel perfectly satisfied that these vituperative terms are to be translated as applicable to conduct consistent with justice, reason, moderation, and with common sense; and therefore I feel . . . really not indifferent, but positively satisfied, when I see such observations.' None of these critics, including Palmerston, understood why war was such a catastrophe. 'My Lords, I consider war to be the greatest folly, if not the greatest crime, of which a country could be guilty, if lightly entered into; and I agree entirely with a moral writer who has said, that if a proof were wanted of the deep and thorough corruption of human nature, we should find it in the fact that war itself was sometimes justifiable.'[52] In the sober sanctuary of the House of Lords, these words were received with several murmurs of support; events later would suggest that Aberdeen was partly, but only partly, correct.

Palmerston and the Whigs returned to Government in the summer of 1846, with Lord John Russell replacing Robert Peel as Prime Minister after the Tories had split apart while repealing the Corn Laws. Palmerston quickly became embroiled in a pointless and rather medieval furore about royal marriages in Spain with which we do not need to concern ourselves. More interesting are the insane ramblings of a man called David Urquhart who had convinced himself that Palmerston was a treacherous agent in Russia's pay. Urquhart had reached this conclusion while serving as a diplomat in the 1830s; he then managed to get himself elected to Parliament in 1847. There, he called for impeachment proceedings against Palmerston for treachery. His harangues produced nothing of substance, but did occasion a memorable response from Palmerston. On 1 March 1848, Palmerston met Urquhart's arguments with a new statement of Britain's role in the world. 'I hold that the real policy of England – apart from questions which involve her own particular interests, political or commercial – is to be the champion of justice and right; pursuing that course with moderation and prudence, not becoming the Quixote of the world, but giving the weight of her moral sanction and support wherever she thinks that justice is, and wherever she thinks that wrong has been done.'[53]

This became the theme of Palmerston's third period at the Foreign Office. As a talented and good-looking politician in the early 1830s he had set himself up as the champion of liberty; now, greying and in his sixties, he merged that liberalism with a Providential view of Britain's role in the world. He argued that Britain's crusading mission was the natural corollary to a stern pursuit of British interests. The year before his retort to Urquhart, he had informed the House of Commons that Britain's duty and vocation was 'not to enslave, but to set free ... we stand at the head of moral, social, and political civilization. Our task is to lead the way and direct the march of other nations.'[54] He found no incompatibility between this and the firm protection of Britain's material interests. He closed his speech in March 1848 by referring again to his old mentor – 'if I might be allowed to express in one sentence the principle which I think ought to guide an English Minister, I would adopt the expression of Canning, and say that with every British Minister the interests of England ought to be the shibboleth of his policy'.[55]

The results of this vision were slightly thin on the ground. When revolutions broke out in 1847 and 1848, Palmerston wriggled his way through the mayhem, talking much but doing little. Only twice, initially in Switzerland and later in the protection of Hungarian refugees in Turkey, did he play a serious part in the liberal movements of those months. He liked to point out to the various deposed autocrats that Britain had warned them to make timely reforms before revolution broke out. 'Those Governments, those Powers of Europe, have at last learned the truth of the opinions expressed by Mr Canning, "That those who have checked improvement, because it is an innovation, will one day or other be compelled to accept innovation, when it has ceased to be improvement".'[56] But Palmerston's own contribution to the events of 1848 was minimal; his grandiloquence came after the fact.

Aberdeen's heavy cautiousness weighed down his own analysis of these violent months. The revolutions reinforced his conservatism and he thought that Palmerston had inflamed the danger through his posturing. His old allies in Europe fed him stories of Palmerston's attempts at sedition; he mobilised the material to excoriate his rival. Palmerston's policy had been 'shuffling, inconsistent, and shabby. With a constant leaning to Radicalism; but with the pretence of supporting monarchical government,' he complained.[57]

By the end of 1849 the revolutionary chapter in Europe had come to an unsatisfactory close. Metternich in Austria, and Guizot and Louis Philippe in France had become its most prominent victims. All three sought refuge in Britain; Louis Philippe moved to Claremont Park in Surrey, Guizot took up residence in Brompton, and Metternich bought a house in Richmond. But apart from in France, where a new republic was established under a President, the revolutions had not set down permanent roots. These failures were most prominent in Italy, where Austrian shackles were briefly lifted only to return forcefully later, and in Germany, where liberals tried a new national parliament in Frankfurt but saw their efforts wither and fade away.

Palmerston, largely untested by these dramas, looked for new opportunities for vigorous action. He fastened on a collection of British complaints against Greece, of which the most prominent was the case of a Jewish man called Don Pacifico who had been born in

Gibraltar and held a British passport. In 1847, Pacifico's house in Athens had been pillaged by an anti-Semitic mob; he had appealed for redress from the Greek Government but received none. Now Palmerston decided that the time had come to secure justice for Don Pacifico. He ordered a British fleet under Admiral Parker to sail to Athens and extract compensation from the Greeks. The fleet arrived off the Piraeus on 15 January 1850. Demands were made for payment within twenty-four hours. No response came from the Greeks, and Admiral Parker imposed a blockade.

The first outcries of major protest came from Russia and France. Nesselrode, perhaps knowing his Thucydides and the Melian Dialogue, accused Palmerston of introducing a violent precedent into European affairs. From now on, he argued, powerful states would 'recognise towards the weak no other rule but their own will, no other right but their physical strength'.[58]

A sense of outrage entered and infected the House of Lords. Aberdeen, who had since 1846 been the leader of the Peelite faction of the Conservatives in the Lords, joined with the Protectionist leader, Lord Stanley, in a motion of censure. They combined their arguments in an attractive critique, Stanley making jokes about Don Pacifico, Aberdeen tracing the disturbing progress of Parker's fleet through Europe during the revolutionary months. 'When I look back but four short years', Aberdeen moaned in closing, 'and recollect that this country was then honoured, loved, and respected by every State in Europe . . . I confess I do not look with any very great satisfaction even at this new species of friendship which the noble Lord has discovered to exist between us and other countries.' The motion was carried by 169 votes to 132, although Palmerston may have been comforted by the support of many bishops.[59]

With this vote, the crisis became political, threatening the stability of Lord John Russell's Government. By careful arrangement, the Radical MP John Roebuck tabled a motion in the Commons praising Palmerston and his foreign policy. The hope was that this would give Palmerston wide scope for saving himself and the Government. For four feverish and intoxicating nights in June 1850, the Commons dissected Roebuck's motion. One of the impressive curiosities of mid-Victorian politics is the way in which small events in faraway countries could provoke impassioned arguments about the entire nature and purpose of foreign policy. The trait is surprising and satisfying when placed alongside some of the political debates we hear today. Today, events of huge complexity and importance are often summed up in a few opposing soundbites. These are then flung against one another; the result is a numbing deadlock. Any hint of an interesting disagreement is hidden behind a crashing platitude. The debate about Don Pacifico in the House of Commons is a *locus classicus*. A small crisis inspired deeply felt and closely argued debate about the direction and ethics of policy. The focus fell on the question of whether and how political freedom should be spread abroad. The chain of argument extended from Don Pacifico, who had nothing to do with the advance of liberty, to Palmerston's didactic brand of diplomacy, which allegedly did. Various methods were analysed, bits of history were deployed on all sides.

Palmerston spoke on the second night of the debate. Two oranges and a glass of water stood beside him when he rose at 9.45 on 25 June; they were still in place when he sat down again at 2.20 in the morning of 26 June. He dealt efficiently with the Don Pacifico question, saying that he was entitled to justice and that Britain was entitled to help him. He dismissed out of hand the insinuation that 'because a man is of the Jewish persuasion, he is fair game for any outrage'. From here, he moved on to the essence of the case against his foreign policy. 'We have been accused – I especially, have been accused – of "running amuck" through Europe, interfering here and there in the internal affairs of every other county.' He defended the old Quadruple Alliance – an 'act of forcible interference, for the purpose of giving to Portugal the blessings of representative government' – and rejected the argument which had been levelled earlier in the debate that his liberalising efforts there had failed. But he denied that he had incited violence and upheaval in 1848; he wanted only cautious and constitutional reforms.

These were nitpicking details, not the sort of thing which would win a major debate. What was needed was a sweeping statement of principle, and this duly arrived at the close. Palmerston had defended his own policy; what the Commons now had to decide was whether 'as the Roman, in days of old, held himself free from indignity when he could say Civis Romanus sum; so also a British subject, in whatever land he may be, shall feel confident that the watchful eye and the strong arm of England will protect him against injustice and wrong'.[60]

That emotional evening was followed by two more nights of exacting debate. On 27 June, Gladstone brought together high intellect and even higher conscience in his own peculiar type of attack. It was one thing to oppose absolutism, he argued, but quite another to propagate one's opinions abroad. The problem with doing so, interfering with the way other governments ran their countries, was that every other state would then claim the right to do the same thing. This was a dangerous, indeed a crippling principle to introduce into international affairs and ought to be avoided at all costs. The role of a British Foreign Secretary was not to be a 'gallant knight at a tournament' but 'to conciliate peace with dignity'.[61]

Two more hammer blows landed on Palmerston the following night. Palmerston always shared something in common with the Manchester School of politicians, led by middle-class Radicals like Richard Cobden and John Bright. Like these men, Palmerston believed that free trade was an instrument of progress, building new relationships with states and merchants abroad. But he powerfully denied the notion, put forward by Cobden in particular, that free trade would lead naturally to world peace. This dispute became the theme of Cobden's own speech on 28 June. Once again, he put forward an alternative to Palmerston's bombastic policy. Free trade could bring people together from all over the globe; mighty empires and armies would then fade away. 'I believe the progress of freedom depends more upon the maintenance of peace, the spread of commerce, and the diffusion of education, than upon the labours of cabinets and foreign offices,' Cobden explained. Wrongly, Cobden assumed that economics trumped politics in governing the affairs of the world; rightly, Cobden realised that in spreading liberty, there was a limit to what any government could do.

That same evening, Robert Peel rose just after one o'clock from the back benches to deliver his verdict. In the discerning and practical manner in which he had conducted his politics throughout his life, he exposed the gaps in Palmerston's plan. It was easy to talk about spreading liberty, difficult to pin down what that should mean. There were millions of oppressed people in China; perhaps Lord

Palmerston would free them next. And what about Britain's subjects in India? Where they in line for liberation as well? But the real problem with Palmerston's philosophy was the basic concept itself. 'It is my firm belief that you will not advance the cause of constitutional government by attempting to dictate to other nations ... If you succeed I doubt whether or not the institutions that take root under your patronage will be lasting. Constitutional liberty will be best worked out by those who aspire to freedom by their own efforts. You will only overload it by your help, by your principle of interference.'[62]

The following day, Peel was thrown from his horse while riding up Constitution Hill. For several days he lingered in agony before dying on 2 July. The loss of this close political friend and ally was an unbearable blow for Aberdeen. During the day, he displayed a rigid calm; at night his whole body was attacked by crippling spasms of grief.[63]

The Government breezed through the vote on Roebuck's motion with considerable ease. The cheers which had accompanied Palmerston's speech drowned out the calmer reasoning which Peel, Gladstone and Cobden had displayed. Almost all the Radicals, except those of the Manchester School, voted for Palmerston. He was invited to a celebratory dinner at the Reform Club where he told the audience that Britain would always spread freedom around the world.

But Palmerston had picked up one enemy in these months who showed no signs of going away. The Queen, supported by her husband and guide, Albert, had been disgusted by Palmerston's antics over Don Pacifico and wanted him sacked. Albert raised the issue with Russell in July, drawing at the same time on a very different story from many years before. One night in 1838, while staying at Windsor Castle, Palmerston had set out on one of his nightly escapades. He crept into the bedroom of one of Victoria's ladies-in-waiting. He locked one door and barricaded the other before closing in on his target, a woman called Mrs Brand. But Mrs Brand was not so keen on Palmerston. She screamed for help and frightened Palmerston out of the room. The gossip travelled through the Castle, eventually reaching the Queen. It is possible, indeed quite likely, that Palmerston had simply entered the wrong room. But this could hardly be explained to the Queen, and she had never forgotten the incident. Now, Albert explained to Russell, the Queen could no longer consent 'to take a man as her chief adviser ... who as her Secretary of State, and while under her roof at Windsor Castle, had committed a brutal attack upon one of her ladies'.[64] The difficulty was that Don Pacifico had made Palmerston so popular that he could not be immediately removed, and so Russell delayed the execution to a more auspicious time.

This came a year later. In France, the President of the Second Republic, Louis Napoleon, dissolved the National Assembly and carried out a successful coup by which he made himself Emperor Napoleon III. Palmerston made a mess of the politics by privately congratulating the new Napoleon but then backtracking when the Cabinet took a neutral view. There was a dispute over dispatches with the British Ambassador in France; it emerged that Palmerston had sent off one particular note without waiting for approval from the Queen. The sending of unapproved dispatches was always a source of huge irritation to the Queen. She seized on the error and called on Russell to dismiss Palmerston. This he did promptly, bringing to an end Palmerston's long career as Foreign Secretary.

The interruption of our story by a storm over protocol and personalities is a reminder that even in the midst of a highly subtle argument about progress and human nature, relationships and processes always remained central in a Foreign Secretary's career. Queen Victoria's haphazard interest in diplomacy was a particular obstacle which each of her Foreign Secretaries had to clear. But the theme which links all the men in our story, and which is worth a moment's reflection during this hiatus in Palmerston's career, is the relationships they had with their superiors in Downing Street.

The relationship between Foreign Secretary and Prime Minister over the two centuries has depended overwhelmingly on personalities rather than constitutional principle. At one end of the spectrum there were a tiny number of Prime Ministers, such as Bonar Law and Baldwin, who took little interest in foreign affairs and left their Foreign Secretary to get on with it. We have already seen how Lord Liverpool allowed Castlereagh an extremely generous hand in drafting treaties, occasionally asking to see copies '(to guard against minor errors)' before they were signed. A different flavour entered the relationship when Prime Ministers, without previous experience, developed a passionate interest in foreign policy. These included Disraeli, Gladstone, Lloyd George, Neville Chamberlain, Churchill, Thatcher and Blair. These were highly complex characters with wildly contrasting views on the direction which foreign policy should take. What they had in common was impatience and a distaste for the detailed niceties of the Foreign Office. They also liked to convince themselves about their personal charm and ability to get important things done.

The ease of modern communications has altered the structure of the world's diplomacy and propelled Prime Ministers into prominence, whether they wish it or not. Summit meetings are no longer extraordinary events. For many years now, summits have been routine occasions, whether at the UN, NATO or the European Union, attended by Prime Ministers either eagerly or with resignation according to their temperament. Margaret Thatcher and Tony Blair, through long years as Prime Minister, thus acquired as much knowledge of the details of the main foreign affairs issues as successive Foreign Secretaries. While complaining copiously of the burdens laid upon them, both these Prime Ministers in fact enjoyed escaping from the roughness of domestic politics into a world where they were treated with proper respect. But the ideal relationship consists of a partnership where the Prime Minister takes an intelligent interest in foreign affairs but uses it to support his or her Foreign Secretary at crucial moments while for the rest of the time keeping a distance. This was essentially the relationship between Peel and Aberdeen, and between Attlee and Bevin.

After Aberdeen and Palmerston had left the Foreign Office, their own attitudes changed. Until 1851 both men believed that the Foreign Secretary should be held on a fairly loose leash. After 1852, as their careers moved into their final stages with late bursts at the top job, they decided that their own views on diplomacy were too valuable to be sullied by new Foreign Secretaries who might or might not have peculiar new ideas of their own.

With Aberdeen at least there was no hint of ambition behind this zealous search for control. He was an unlikely Prime Minister; if anyone had suggested that as his aim during the late 1840s he would have greeted the idea with sour surprise. Yet when Derby's Government fell at the end of 1852, a year after Palmerston had been removed from the Foreign Office and some ten months after the Whig Government had itself collapsed, it was to Aberdeen that the Queen entrusted the task of forming a new Government. Patiently, he pieced together a coalition out of the shattered remnants of Peel's Conservative Party and the Whigs. To survive, his Ministry would need to tap into a broad cross-section of public opinion; one solution was to recruit Palmerston. But Aberdeen could not contemplate having him at the Foreign Office. Now that he was Prime Minister, Aberdeen saw a new opening for a refined and cautious approach. So instead Aberdeen arrived at, and Palmerston agreed to, the idea of becoming Home Secretary while Aberdeen employed first Lord John Russell and then Lord Clarendon as Foreign Secretary.

It is not true, as is sometimes suggested, that Aberdeen's Government was a failure from start to end. Walter Bagehot wrote later that Aberdeen's Cabinet was the ablest since the Reform Act and at least in the first part of 1853 there was evidence of this. Aberdeen made Gladstone his Chancellor of the Exchequer and Gladstone rewarded him by producing a budget of huge competence and importance, reducing tariffs on a wide range of consumable goods. Even the relationship with Palmerston started off fairly well. There was a cordial exchange of letters about defence planning. Palmerston and Aberdeen agreed that with Napoleon III in charge across the Channel, there was once again a threat of a French attack. Palmerston suggested new fortifications and regular meetings with the Commander-in-Chief; Aberdeen endorsed this politely. Right up until the crisis which engulfed them, everything seemed to be in hand.

Aberdeen could have blamed the French for the confusion which resulted in the Crimean War. The new Napoleon had sparked off fresh uncertainty in the Ottoman Empire when he claimed various rights for Roman Catholics in the Holy Land. Early in 1853, Czar Nicholas countered by making religious claims of his own for Orthodox Christians. Once again but in a new form, the Eastern Question clunked into view. This time the Russians had larger objectives in mind. Remembering the memorandum drawn up by Nesselrode following the Czar's conversation with Aberdeen in 1844, Nicholas seems to have decided that the dissolution of the Ottoman Empire was now likely, and that Aberdeen would co-operate with him in bringing this about. Aberdeen had never been entirely happy with the cruel and unchristian policies which governed the East. In February 1853 he explained to Russell that the Turkish 'barbarians hate us all, and ... we ought to regard as the greatest misfortune any engagement which compelled us to take up arms for the Turks'.[65] But even he still grudgingly accepted the belief shared by all Foreign Secretaries that the Ottoman Empire was vital for the balance of power. The crisis hardened when the Russians invaded the Principalities of Moldavia and Wallachia – now modern Romania. Pressure grew for a firm protest from Britain and France. The French were keen to press the issue; but Aberdeen faltered, reluctant to get involved in the crisis, keen above all things to avoid a European war.

The exchange of letters between Aberdeen and Palmerston from July 1853 shines a light on the confusion which consumed the Cabinet in the second half of that year.[66] It is odd that this dispute between the Prime Minister and his Home Secretary bypassed almost entirely the Foreign Secretary, Clarendon. But reading these letters side by side, vivid portraits of the two protagonists emerge. Palmerston was driven by his passion and erratic eyesight into using too many capital letters. Like a German, he set out his nouns – particularly those relating to key principles – in the upper case. Aberdeen, meanwhile, worried himself by cautiousness and self-doubt into using too many commas. There is at no point any hint of adrenalin or sense of event in Aberdeen's prose. Palmerston's letters, on the other hand, are always probing, eager to act, perhaps too quickly inflamed. These letters identify one of the fundamental questions running through our book. There are no final answers to the question of whether a just war is a necessary war, or whether a necessary war will itself prove useful in the long run. But Aberdeen and Palmerston in these months tackled the question with particular unease.

On 4 July 1853 Palmerston opened his barrage, laying out the tactics he thought that Aberdeen should pursue. British and French naval squadrons should be sent up to the Bosphorus, and if necessary into the Black Sea. This would deter the Czar and his advisers from attempting anything more. Besides, he informed the Prime Minister, this was what public opinion demanded and the fleet movement would have a powerful political effect.[67]

The same day, Aberdeen responded, criticising the tactics and underlying logic of this approach. 'I fear that on the whole, it would not be favourable to the cause of peace, which is that about which I am most interested.' He closed his letter by dismissing Palmerston's political point, mobilising his love of the ancients against popular opinion. 'In a case of this kind I dread popular support. On some occasion, when the Athenian Assembly vehemently applauded Alcibiades, he asked if he had said anything particularly foolish! Ever sincerely yours, Aberdeen.'[68]

The argument revived a week later. The Cabinet had agreed to send a fleet into the Dardanelles but no further. The Russians had issued a bombastic circular, justifying their own actions and harshly criticising those of Britain. Palmerston composed an angry memorandum. It is 'in the nature of men whose influence over events & whose Power over others are founded on intimidation & kept up by arrogant assumptions & pretentions to mistake forebearance for irresolution, & to look upon inaction & hesitation as symptoms of fear, & forerunners of submission', he complained. 'Thus it has been in regard to Russia on the one hand, & England & France on the other.' He was driven by his anger into composing a vivid simile. The 'Cabinet of St Petersburg not content with bullying Turkey, threatens & insults England & France, & arrogantly pretends to forbid the Ships of War of those Powers from frequenting the waters of another Power over whose waters Russia has no authority whatever ... It is the Robber who declares that he will not leave the House until the Policeman shall have first retired from the Court Yard.' Once again, he urged Aberdeen to send the two squadrons up to the Bosphorus; once again the request was denied.[69]

When Aberdeen replied a day later, he reminded his colleague of one element which he had forgotten in his hasty arguments. Diplomacy was on the move at Vienna; a conference between the powers seemed to be making some headway. 'There is at last every probability that our endeavours to preserve peace are now on the point of being attended with success. We have prepared a form of Convention between Russia and the Porte* which is cordially supported by the French Government. It preserves the dignity of the Sultan, and gives to the Emperor everything he can reasonably demand.' Besides, Aberdeen quibbled with Palmerston's geography. The key British concern was not Moldavia and Wallachia, but Constantinople, and Constantinople 'is not now in danger, nor is it threatened'. Sending a fleet into the Bosphorus would achieve nothing beyond 'empty Bravado'.[70]

Rather surprisingly, two days later Palmerston backed down. 'I admit that as we have launched Proposals for peaceful arrangement it would be better not to endanger the negotiation by throwing into it any fresh element of difficulty.' Aberdeen grasped the hint of consensus as swiftly as possible and replied to Palmerston that same day – 'it gives me the greatest pleasure that all polemique should cease between us on this matter', he wrote. Both men agreed with one another that the Russian invasion of the Principalities was a *casus belli* by which the Turks were entitled to declare war on Russia; both men also agreed that it would nevertheless be dangerous and inexpedient for the Turks to launch such a conflict at such a delicate time.[71] The conference at Vienna had ended in a conciliatory Note which the powers at Vienna, including Russia, accepted. At some point in that month, Aberdeen sat with his daughter-in-law and told her calmly that everything was settled. But the Turks rejected the compromise Note on 20 August, gambling that Britain and France would feel obliged to support them in a showdown with the Russians.

The epistolary dispute between Aberdeen and Palmerston died down for several months as the crisis simmered. Meanwhile public opinion in Britain was evolving into a thoughtless clamour for war. Leading the charge and sculpting the rhetoric was that master of invective, Disraeli. As early as June 1853, he was putting Aberdeen under heavy literary fire. 'His mind, his education, his prejudices are all of the Kremlin school . . . His hesitating speech, his contracted sympathies, his sneer, icy as Siberia, his sarcasms, drear and barren

* The Porte was the name given collectively to the Sultan and his Government.

as the Steppes, are all characteristic of the bureau and the chancery, and not of popular and aristocratic assemblies animated by the spirit of honour and the pride of gentlemen.' The caricature became more absurd and pointed in the following days. Aberdeen, Disraeli drawled, 'plagues the most eminent of his colleagues with the crabbed malice of a maundering witch'. Aberdeen did, however, have one firm friend in his support. Gladstone wrote to remind Aberdeen that he personally saw 'no other man in the Cabinet, who combined calmness, solidity of judgment, knowledge of the question, & moderation of views, in a manner or degree . . . sufficient to have held our course so nearly straight, and to insure an air so steadily declining to flatter or inflame the warlike sentiment in the country'.[72]

By October it was becoming clear that the Turks were confident enough of the French and British interest in their own survival to declare war on Russia. Aberdeen despondently surveyed the bleak turn of events; his mood must have plummeted further when he received a new letter from Palmerston on 7 October. Briskly, Palmerston informed the Prime Minister that he intended to propose to Cabinet that day that two squadrons should be sent into the Black Sea with orders to seize Russian vessels and hand them over to the Turks.[73]

At two o'clock, Aberdeen responded with a hurried note of high alarm. 'I have only this moment received your letter . . . I have therefore not time to enter into any discussion of the subject before we meet. I cannot say however that I think the present state of the Russo Turkish question would authorize such a proceeding . . . as that which you intend to propose.'[74] That afternoon, the Cabinet rejected Palmerston's policy. Four days later, Turkey declared war on Russia, yet Britain still had no clear policy which might prevent the crisis turning into a wider European war.

While Aberdeen and his Cabinet pulled in different directions through the storm, a new sailor now decided to stick in his oar. Prince Albert's memorandum on the Eastern Question was fascinating and entirely impractical. The idea of breaking up the Ottoman Empire and erecting a new Greek empire nonetheless appealed to Aberdeen, speaking to his classical instincts and his suspicion of the fanatical Turks. He sent the memorandum on to

Palmerston for his perusal.[75] He should have known that this would be a mistake. He was duly punished on 1 November by another letter from Palmerston.

One by one, Palmerston dismantled the arguments of Albert and Aberdeen. All the Great Powers had agreed to uphold the Ottoman Empire. It was in Britain's own interest that the independence and integrity of the empire be preserved. For this reason, and others, Britain's duty according to Palmerston now lay in helping Turkey out of her difficulties 'by negotiations if possible' and, if the negotiation failed, 'by Force of Arms'. Once again, the arguments between Palmerston and Aberdeen crystallised into an argument about the ethics of war. 'Peace is an Excellent Thing, & War a great Misfortune. But there are many things more valuable than Peace, and many things much worse than War. The maintenance of the Ottoman Empire belongs to the First Class, the occupation of Turkey by Russia belongs to the Second.'[76]

In his reply, carefully drafted and redrafted, Aberdeen did not meet Palmerston at this level. He did not make the argument, which clearly lurked somewhere in his general philosophy, that few if any wars could be justified. But he refused to accept that Britain should violently involve itself in this particular crisis. The Ottoman Empire was 'radically vicious and abominable'; its inhabitants were mainly 'barbarians'. Of course, preserving the Ottoman Empire 'at this moment is a European necessity', but the empire would not be preserved by fighting – indeed, war would make its dissolution all the more likely. In a thin hand, clearly as an afterthought, Aberdeen added – 'Quiet is the only salvation of the East.'[77] To the man who had witnessed the slaughter of Leipzig and suffered innumerable private griefs, quiet was a quality to be prized beyond anything Palmerston could conceive.

Both men were losing patience with one another. Meanwhile, Lord John Russell, now lacking a clear purpose in the Government, had turned his nitpicking energy to the issue of political reform. Palmerston steamed himself up against Lord John's proposals. They became linked in his mind with the Ottoman crisis as an excuse to resign. He wrote to Aberdeen on 10 December floating this possibility and reiterating his idea of British and French ships capturing Russian vessels in the Black Sea. Aberdeen wrote back three days later, hinting, in his opaque way, that the time had come for Palmerston to keep his thoughts to himself. 'As I have very recently written to you on the subject of Eastern affairs, I should not have thought it necessary to trouble you again.'[78] Soon after this, Palmerston resigned.

Meanwhile, the news was travelling fast from Turkey of a massive naval disaster at Sinope. A Russian force had sunk a large Turkish flotilla, with the loss of thousands of lives. Public opinion in Britain flew at the outrage and demanded action. This time Aberdeen and the Cabinet obliged, ordering the British fleet into the Black Sea alongside the French. This belated Palmerstonian move reassured Palmerston; on 23 December he wrote to Aberdeen not to request, but to inform the Prime Minister that his resignation was rescinded and that he would return to his post as Home Secretary. He gave a complex explanation about misunderstanding the reform proposals and then added casually that 'the decision which I am informed the Cabinet came to yesterday to accede to the Proposal of the French Government, whereby the British & French Squadrons will have the Command of the Black Sea, greatly enters into the Considerations which have led me to address this letter to you'.[79]

Aberdeen responded on Christmas Eve, clearly put out by the whole affair. He quibbled about the protocol of withdrawing Palmerston's resignation after it had been formally submitted, and then wondered how Palmerston could have misunderstood the Cabinet's position on reform. He closed the letter by welcoming Palmerston back into office with a barbed paragraph. 'Although not connected with the cause of your resignation, I am glad to find that you approve of a recent decision of the Cabinet, with respect to the British and French fleets, adopted in your absence. I feel assured you will have learnt with pleasure that whether absent, or present, the Government are duly careful to preserve from all injury the interests and dignity of the country. Ever truly yours, Aberdeen.'[80]

With this letter, one painful chapter came to a close and another chapter of much greater suffering opened. Through January and February came the slow but inevitable slide into war. Aberdeen thought about resigning but Gladstone persuaded him to stay on. On 27 February 1854, Britain and France sent an ultimatum to Russia for withdrawal from the Principalities which she had invaded. There was no reply from the Czar; on 28 March Britain and France declared war.

Once started, a war tends to bring out new qualities of fierceness and tenacity in even the most feeble and reluctant of men. This did not happen with Aberdeen. He could not work himself into an angry frenzy, let alone inspire his colleagues or countrymen. Victoria, who was devoted to Aberdeen but a keen supporter of the Crimean War, was exasperated by the even-handedness and calm tone of his speeches. The public 'is impatient and annoyed to hear at this moment the first Minister of the Crown enter into an impartial examination of the Emperor of Russia's character and conduct', she complained.

Aberdeen's plight as a wartime Prime Minister can be compared to that of Neville Chamberlain between September 1939 and May 1940. Both men found themselves leading Britain in a war which they hated. Both men had seen their efforts to save the peace frustrated. Neither man was by temperament a warrior king. Both men found at their side in Government a powerful colleague, full of ideas and enthusiasm, who was eager and well equipped to take their place. But there is a fundamental difference which frustrates the comparison. Chamberlain was rightly blamed for trusting a dictator who had forfeited all trust. Aberdeen had made no such mistake. His offence, a lesser one, was that he had not thought the ambiguous Ottoman crisis worthy of an armed intervention. As a result, he failed to put in place the robust policies which might have stopped it escalating into a European war. Aberdeen's case was not helped by the tortured progress of the military campaign. The final irony of twelve months of failed diplomacy came when the Russians withdrew from the Principalities in May, not because of any particular misfortune in battle, but as a boon to keep the Austrians out of the war. Yet still the conflict continued, becoming irretrievably bogged down and bloody.

The decision to send a British army to the Crimea to try and seize the Russian naval base at Sebastopol was based largely on Palmerston's plan. It was an unhappy move and the objective was not secured until September 1855. *The Times* sent out William Howard Russell to report on the conflict, the first journalist who was in the modern sense a full war correspondent. His dispatches and articles from the horrible scene of the conflict awakened public opinion in Britain, not so much to the futility of the military enterprise, but to the general mishandling of the war. Yet Palmerston, like Churchill during the Second World War, managed to lift himself above the criticism of a war policy which he had himself designed and approved. The hunt for culprits instead homed in on the Secretary of State for War, the Duke of Newcastle, and on Aberdeen. Early in 1855 Lord John Russell, still idle and irritating, resigned in protest at the management of the war. In the Commons, a motion for an inquiry into the war was carried by a large majority. This was the end of the road for Aberdeen; on 30 January 1855 he and his Government resigned.

The Queen did everything she could to avoid turning to Palmerston. But on 4 February he was summoned to Buckingham Palace and asked to form a Government; he was now seventy years old. 'I am', he told his brother, 'for the moment, l'inévitable.' Disraeli, a close observer, thought that Palmerston by this point was 'at the best only ginger-beer and not champagne'.[81]

Without changing very much, Palmerston supervised the Crimean War as it slowly came to a close. Peace negotiations had already opened in Vienna; in March 1855 Czar Nicholas died and was succeeded by his son, Alexander II. In December 1855, the Austrians forced the pace of the negotiations by threatening to join the war against Russia unless the terms were accepted. On 25 February 1856 a congress opened in Paris to end the conflict; on 30 March the Treaty of Paris was signed. The Treaty was more notable for what was not settled than for any of its sparse achievements. The Black Sea was demilitarised by agreement, but there was no solution to the Eastern Question. Perhaps this was to be expected; but it was short-sighted of the negotiators at Paris not to attempt some new diplomatic institution or concert which might help to manage the Ottoman Empire's slow decline.

For Aberdeen, the last year of the Crimean War was particularly hard. Gladstone wrote a long and perhaps too gushing letter to Aberdeen after he had left office. 'Your whole demeanour has been a living lesson to me,' he explained. 'I feel as if a dear friend was dead.'[82] But the sources of personal comfort were few and far between. Aberdeen's wives, all his daughters and almost all of his brothers and sisters were dead. He found no solace in solitude and tormented himself about the decisions made in 1853 and early 1854. 'I fully admit that the cause of war was just,' he wrote to Gladstone, 'and if we could have controlled events, it might not have been altogether impolitick; but with such vague objects in view, and with the certainty of such serious complications being produced, as well as what Bright calls the immoral & filthy despotism on whose behalf we are contending, it was a most unwise proceeding.' He ransacked his mind and vocabulary for new ways of understanding what had gone wrong. 'I assure you that often in the silence of the night, this fatal decision weighs heavily on my conscience. I know that much may be said in palliation; but when a man acts contrary to his own clear convictions he cannot escape severe self reproach.'[83] It was a hard cross to bear.

The anguish accompanied Aberdeen into the last years of his life. He wrote bitterly about Palmerston and the 'system of meddling and arrogance by which we draw upon ourselves the hatred of the whole world'. The public 'call Palmerston the modern Chatham, which is no great praise in my eyes, as I believe the Great Commoner to have been one of the most unprincipled and profligate of the publick men of his day'. Only one political hope stayed with him in these last years. He cared little for the Whigs and less for Palmerston; he admired Lord Derby but had grave doubts about some of his Tory friends. Gladstone seemed to offer a new approach to politics. 'You are the person to whose future I look forward with hope & confidence; & with so much to command ultimate success it cannot be long delayed.'[84]

Sadness had descended into senility by the time the curtain fell on Aberdeen's tragic life. He died on 14 December 1860 and was buried between Catherine and Harriet in the Abercorn family vault. There was no display of popular mourning, only a coda which seemed to come from the grave. In the last months of his life, Aberdeen had come under pressure from his son and daughter-in-law to rebuild the parish church on his Scottish estates. He resisted this although no one could understand precisely why. It was some time after Aberdeen's death that his family started to find scraps of paper scattered among his possessions in his house. Each bore the same Old

Testament text from the Chronicles, copied out in Aberdeen's hand: 'And David said to Solomon, My son, as for me, it was in my mind to build an house unto the name of the Lord, my God: but the word of the Lord came to me, saying, Thou hast shed blood abundantly, and hast made great wars: thou shalt not build an house unto my name, because thou hast shed much blood upon the earth in my sight.'[85]

After becoming Prime Minister during the Crimean War, Palmerston and his policies exaggerated themselves into a caricature. At times, the high point of Palmerstonian politics had arrived; at other times, so had its nadir.

The year 1857 disproves the argument later adapted by Woodrow Wilson and the internationalists that public opinion is rational and clings to peace. There were fresh conflicts in Persia and China. The crisis in China had begun in October the previous year when Chinese authorities boarded a British-registered ship called the *Arrow* and arrested a dozen of its crew. As it happened, the ship's registration had lapsed, but this did not prevent the crisis escalating into war. In the Commons, the controversy provoked a motion of censure on Palmerston's policy. Once again, Palmerston's chief critics were Cobden and Bright. Three years earlier Palmerston had mocked Bright for his tendency to reduce 'everything to the question of pounds, shillings and pence'. Now he turned on Cobden; by his standard, 'everything that was English was wrong, and everything that was hostile to England was right'. But the Tories backed up Cobden's criticism of Palmerston with a powerful demolition job of their own. Disraeli ended his speech by calling for a general election – 'I should like to see the programme of the proud leader of the Liberal party – "No Reform! New Taxes! Canton Blazing! Persia Invaded!"'.[86] An election duly followed: Palmerston romped to victory; both Bright and Cobden lost their seats.

Ten months later, public opinion became more Palmerstonian than Palmerston himself. Napoleon III was almost killed by a bomb hurled by an Italian Count called Orsini; Napoleon escaped but it emerged that there was a link in the conspiracy to a factory in Birmingham. Palmerston tried to tighten the law against foreign conspiracies in

Britain; public opinion erupted at this submission to foreign despots. Palmerston and his Government were defeated in the storm and he was forced to resign.

Palmerston returned to office as Prime Minister in 1859. From this point until 1865, the various strands of his foreign policy slowly unravelled around three crises which severely altered the balance of power. In each case, Palmerston found himself unable to do much except observe. Lacking any supporting system of alliances or institutions, Britain was isolated as well as ignored. Palmerston learnt late in the day that as all power in all nations has limits, something more lasting than seapower and rhetoric was required to carry an influence over unexpected events.

After French intervention against Austria and the Battle of Solferino, the long quest for Italian unification entered its final phase. Here Palmerston paraded his sympathies without offering much in support. His contribution to the cause in which millions of British men and women believed was minimal, but he paraded himself as the architect of Italy anyway.

This was followed by the bitter dilemmas presented by the American Civil War. Britain's material interest seemed to lie with the South, whose states were important to England for cotton. There is some evidence that Palmerston, despite his distaste for slavery, personally wanted to see the South succeed. Yet he held the British Government off from any intervention, diplomatic or military, while maintaining a strict respect for the limits of what Britain could do to stop the slaughter and paying close attention to the unfolding events. When Russell, now his Foreign Secretary, and Gladstone, once again Chancellor of the Exchequer and now also a committed Liberal, pressed for mediation early in the autumn of 1862, he resisted on the grounds that the 'whole matter is full of difficulty, and can only be cleared up by some more decided events between the contending armies'.[87] On the Tory front bench, the mood was much the same. Lord Derby's son, Edward Stanley, who displayed a careful interest in foreign affairs, systematically picked holes in the arguments for doing anything at all. 'It is premature to recognize the southern confederacy. We can't even get at them ... Mediation is impossible. The offer of it is useless unless you want to provoke insult from the North ... if we want to protract the war – to stimulate the combatants to the utmost, let us talk of interfering to stop it. If we want it to die out, let us carefully stand aloof.'[88] Britain did indeed stay aloof but achieved little by its handling of the crisis beyond adding to that bitterness which soured Anglo-American affairs.

The final crisis of Palmerston's career arose from a matter of huge technical complexity. Palmerston said afterwards that only three people understood what the Schleswig-Holstein Question was about: Prince Albert was dead, the German professor was in a lunatic asylum, and he himself had forgotten. Between 1863 and 1864 the reappearance of this old question indeed baffled most observers, but not the key participant.

Otto von Bismarck had become Prussian Chancellor in 1862. Here was an antagonist with more patience and strategic vision than Palmerston; he moved carefully towards the objectives of a considered long-term plan. Part of this plan involved seizing the Germanic territories in Schleswig-Holstein which were at the time ruled by the Danish King. In the spring of 1863, Frederick VII of Denmark played into his hands by attempting to absorb both Duchies of Schleswig and Holstein into Denmark. There was a strong reaction in the German Diet; the possibility of Prussian military intervention arose.

On 27 July, Palmerston tried to ward off the crisis in the House of Commons. 'We are convinced, I am convinced at least, that if any violent attempt were made to overthrow those rights and interfere with that independence, those who made the attempt would find in the result that it would not be with Denmark alone with which they would have to contend.'[89] It was a dangerous attempt at bluff through bluster. This was not the way to deal with Bismarck.

The crisis was complicated by a new uprising in Poland during the same year. For Napoleon III, it seemed as though the entire Vienna Settlement established in 1815, which he thoroughly disliked and which proscribed his family from the throne he occupied, was now under siege. Napoleon suggested a congress to address the central issues in turn. But Palmerston rejected the proposal. He had forgotten the rule he had set himself in 1836: 'England alone cannot carry her points on the Continent. She must have allies as instruments to work with.'[90]

Frederick VII's death without male offspring in December 1863 brought the crisis into an open conflict. Bismarck folded Austria into his strategy and together they invaded Schleswig-Holstein. Popular opinion in Britain rallied behind the poor Danes, spurred on by sympathies from the recent marriage between the Danish Princess Alexandra and the Prince of Wales. The Danes had heard Palmerston's speech in July and felt confident that he would come to their aid. But he did nothing, more suspicious of France and Russia than Prussia, and without a large enough army to act alone. Russell made some futile gestures, but the Cabinet was divided and Palmerston did not even send the fleet to show support for Copenhagen. Schleswig-Holstein quickly fell into Austria's and Prussia's hands.

Palmerston's bluff had been called in an embarrassing way. Disraeli put down a motion of censure on the Government's policy. 'Within twelve months we have been twice repulsed at St Petersburg. Twice have we supplicated in vain at Paris. We have menaced Austria, and Austria has allowed our menaces to pass her like the idle wind. We have threatened Prussia, and Prussia has defied us. Our objurgations have rattled over the head of the German Diet, and the German Diet has treated them with contempt.'

Palmerston struck up a nimble defence on the final night of the debate. Once again, a crisis had sparked searching argument about his foreign policy. This time, though, some of the logic was topsy-turvy. People were blaming Palmerston's interventionist habits for his failure to intervene in Schleswig-Holstein. So Palmerston found himself defending a policy which, in this instance, he had not actually used. It was complicated stuff but Palmerston brushed it off airily. 'What, then, is the use of our influence if we are not to interfere?'

Cobden condemned Palmerston's constant interferences in other countries by making a link between them and the need to sustain the balance of power. To Cobden, the whole concept of a balance of power was an illusion invented at the Congress of Vienna. Palmerston met this argument head-on. 'Then we are told that the balance of power is an exploded doctrine belonging to ancient times. Why, it is a doctrine founded on the nature of man. It means that it is to the interest of the community of nations that no nation should acquire such a preponderance as to endanger the security of the rest.'[91]

Palmerston was on solid ground here, but the rhetoric could not disguise the ineffectiveness of his policy on the Danish Question. In the end, the Government was saved by the lucky timing of a helpful amendment; they squeezed past the motion of censure without actually voting on it.[92]

Palmerston's policy may have been jaded, but his popularity was not. He won another general election in the summer of 1865, aged eighty. Physical strength, though, was at last deserting him. He caught a severe chill in October which soon carried him off. His doctor had asked him as he lay dying whether he believed in man's redemption through Jesus Christ. 'Oh, surely', was Palmerston's reply. For Victoria, the news of Palmerston's death evoked feelings of immense relief. 'I never liked him or could ever the least respect him, nor could I forget his conduct on certain occasions to my Angel.'[93]

People drew two conclusions from the late failures of Palmerston's career. The first concerned the balance of power; in its purest distillation it was accepted by only a narrow range of men. John Bright illustrated the thesis in a vivid form. He said that the balance of power was 'a ghastly phantom which . . . has loaded us with debt and with taxes, has sacrificed the lives of tens of thousands of Englishmen, has desolated the homes of millions of families, and has left us, as a result of the profligate expenditure which it has caused, a doubled peerage at one end of the social scale, and far more than a doubled pauperism at the other . . . that foul idol has at last been thrown down'.

This was wrong and careful men knew it. The balance of power had not disappeared, either as a description of or an instrument for managing international affairs. But the pillars on which the balance of power existed – finance, communications, technology, the size and energy of the relevant states – these were now in flux. Palmerston's mistake had been to assume that, in the new atmosphere, all he needed to do was keep up his enjoyable policy of crafty diplomacy combined with the occasional bombastic tirade. As a new generation of politicians came of age, they brought with them new thoughts on how to manage a balance of power. Gladstone combined Aberdeen's deep belief in European diplomacy with his own moralising brand of ideas; Disraeli conjured up from Palmerston's wreckage a picture of Britain as an illustrious imperial power whose real strength lay in Asia and on the seas.

Both of these men inherited political parties which had largely come to agree on one specific point. The Queen, who had an instinctive feel for these things, identified this second conclusion which flowed from Palmerston's haphazard last years – 'we have done too much, been too active, done ourselves no good'. Cobden reached the same destination in a more elaborate way. There is 'one great change amounting to a revolution which has been accomplished in our foreign policy', he wrote in November 1864. 'After the fiasco last Session on the Danish question, our Foreign Office will never again attempt to involve us in any European entanglements for the Balance of Power, or for any dynastic purpose. Henceforth we shall observe an absolute abstention from continental politics. Non-intervention is the policy of all future governments in this country.'[94]

By this inverted logic, Palmerston's failure to intervene in Schleswig-Holstein convinced many politicians from all sides that intervention was wrong. Perhaps it was natural to draw this conclusion; non-intervention was the traditional doctrine, stretching back over many centuries. But this missed the real heart of Palmerston's problem. Palmerston's crime was not his doctrine of interference, but the thoughtless way in which it was deployed. He made no attempt to combine his sporadic interventions with a longer-term plan.

In these years, Britain had reached the highest vantage point of its power; within a few more years, that relative power would slowly begin to fade away. Of course, there were achievements to show for this supremacy, not least in suppressing the slave trade. But inside Europe, Palmerston's policy had been almost entirely reactive, responding to rather than shaping events. He built no new institutions which might have allowed Europe to evolve safely or given Britain a chance to adapt to the new challenges.

These, though, were not the conclusions drawn by those who followed Palmerston. Through the 1860s and into the 1870s, Britain stayed glumly aloof from Continental politics. There was no meaningful attempt to interfere with Bismarck's wizardry of 1866–70 which resulted in German Unification, no direct influence over these decisive events. Instead, and without any bow to its chief architect, Aberdeen's old policy of non-intervention became ascendant in the decade after his death.

CHAPTER III

DERBY (AND DISRAELI)

'To subdue the enemy without fighting is the acme of skill'
Sun Tzu, *The Art of War*

Disraeli was never a man given to outward rejoicing. He was seventy and subject to gout when he won the general election of 1874 with, for the first time, a clear majority. Now at last at the top of the greasy pole, he had the power to do what he wanted.

But what was that? If you had pressed Disraeli on this point he would have looked at you in amused puzzlement. To *be* Prime Minister had always been his goal. The theatre of Parliament and Cabinet, the almost daily dealings, half-comical half-chivalrous, with the Queen, the delights of political manoeuvre, the pleasures of patronage lay at the heart of Disraeli's ambition. Compared to these amusements, the business of passing laws or guiding the Budget were prosaic duties which he appointed dull, competent men to handle, middle-class worthies like his Home Secretary, Sir Richard Cross, or his Chancellor of the Exchequer, Sir Stafford Northcote. But if you had pressed him further on his own role as Prime Minister he might have quoted from his novel *Endymion*. 'Look at Lord Roehampton – he is the man. He does not care a rush whether the revenue increases or declines. He is thinking of real politics: foreign affairs: maintaining our power in Europe.' For Disraeli, foreign policy was real politics; it was played out on the big stage, with a huge audience for the talented performer. The reputation and the fate of nations were at stake. Nor did he despise the trimmings. Disraeli thoroughly enjoyed the flutter of a Court, the robes of a Cardinal or Archbishop, the subtlety of a diplomatic conversation, the splendour of a banquet and the flow of general ideas among intelligent people. It followed that as Prime Minister he would wish to dominate the foreign policy of his government, to ensure that it was vigorous, even dramatic, and to play a vivid personal part in carrying it out.

Canning, with similar boldness and sense of theatre, was the natural model for Disraeli. But Canning had been Palmerston's model too, and in Palmerston's old age the policy which followed that tradition was beginning to look frayed. It was a long downhill path from the triumphant Don Pacifico speech of 1850 to Palmerston's inability in old age to save Schleswig-Holstein for the Danes or Poland for the Poles. Disraeli believed that this slide could be corrected. Disraeli in Opposition had tried to exploit Palmerston's twilight difficulties, but he intended to imitate the boldness which the great man had shown in his prime.

But there was a difficulty. Disraeli did not agree with Canning and Palmerston about the way the world was going. Both these men had believed in and admired the growth of nationalism as a driving force, at least among European peoples and others of European origin in the United States or Latin America. Just as Canning had encouraged the Latin American rebels against Spain, so Palmerston sympathised cautiously with the cause of Italian unity. By contrast Disraeli almost alone refused to meet the Italian hero Garibaldi when he was lionised in London in 1864. For Disraeli, Garibaldi was a noisy upstart; the Austro-Hungarian Empire was a more interesting and worthwhile entity than any contrived Italian state. Disraeli, the novelist turned politician, believed in a world of empires, sustained by the skill of princes, priests, beautiful women and secret societies.

Britain had no ally in Europe and no army strong enough to be deployed against any of the main European states. Disraeli did not believe that these weaknesses should prevent Britain from following a vigorous foreign policy. Increasingly he justified his confidence by speaking of Britain as an imperial country. When he used the phrase, for example in the famous Crystal Palace speech of 1872, he was thinking only partly of the colonies scattered across the globe, though he played with imprecise suggestions of an imperial tariff and a representative council based in London.¹ 'The Queen of England has become the sovereign of the most powerful Oriental States,' he said at the Free Trade Hall in Manchester in 1872. 'These are vast and novel elements in the distribution of power ... there never was a moment in our history when the power of England was so great and her resources so vast and inexhaustible. And yet, gentlemen, it is not merely our fleets and armies, our powerful artillery, our accumulated capital and our unlimited credit on which I so much depend, as upon that unspoken spirit of her people, which I believe was never prouder of the Imperial country to which they belong.'²

His main preoccupation was with Britain as an Asiatic power. When referring to Oriental states he meant, of course, British rule over India, but as the years passed he became equally preoccupied with Britain's unique relationship with the decaying Ottoman Empire. Canning had talked of a New World redressing the balance of the Old World in Europe. Disraeli thought of redressing that balance yet again, through British influence in an Eastern world more ancient than Europe and much more interesting than Latin America. Memories of his own visit to Palestine as a young man mingled with his fascination as a Jew and novelist with the kaleidoscope of Eastern faiths and mysteries.

These preoccupations with Asia did not mean that Disraeli wanted Britain to stand aloof from European affairs. Rather, our standing in the wider world was our card of entry into the heart of Europe. He was determined, like Canning, not to allow a group of Continental monarchies to dominate the European scene. He did his best to disrupt the uneasy alliance of Germany, Austria and Russia known as the Dreikaiserbund, League of the Three Emperors.

The main issue in European diplomacy for Disraeli and his successors was the Eastern Question. This vague phrase covered a multitude of hatreds and ambitions, both of the big powers and of the fractious peoples inhabiting the Balkans. It centred around the continuing slow decay of the Ottoman Empire based on Constantinople, and the contest for the different morsels of territory which from time to time fell away from its rule. We have seen how Canning handled the Greek struggle for independence. He had to reconcile on the one hand his own liberal instincts combined with the popular cult of Byron and classical Greece, and on the other the inadequacies of modern Greek leadership and the need to keep the Russians from using the Greek cause to further their own ambitions. Palmerston found himself protecting the Ottoman Empire, first against an Egyptian rebel, then against the Christian distaste felt by Prince Albert and Lord Aberdeen, and finally from Russian aggression during the Crimean War. By 1874 the image of Johnny Turk as a gallant ally had faded against the reality of brutal Turkish rule in the Balkans. Bosnia, Bulgaria and Macedonia lacked the inherited glamour which had helped the Greeks. The European powers had pressed on their behalf for decent treatment rather than independence. Decent treatment was consistently denied, but Britain was reluctant to press or let others press the Turks too hard in case their empire collapsed and the route to India was put at risk. This concern for Constantinople as the way to India would have made no sense to Canning in the 1820s and was discredited before Grey came to handle the Eastern Question after 1905. But it was crucial to British thinking about foreign policy in Victorian times.

The Eastern Question was a painful dilemma for many, but for Disraeli an excitement. On this stage Britain was a main actor, with a much more impressive part than anything she could claim in the (to her) mini dramas of Poland or Schleswig-Holstein. Disraeli was determined to play the part with the utmost boldness. In 1875 he wrote to Lady Bradford, 'I really believe "the Eastern Question" that has haunted Europe for a century . . . Will fall to my lot to encounter . . . dare I say settle.'[3]

There was nothing collective about Disraeli's idea of foreign policy. It required not a daring Cabinet but a single daring leader, himself. A Foreign Secretary was needed for the humdrum purposes of diplomatic and parliamentary routine with which the daring leader could not be bothered. Disraeli made no effort to find a soulmate as Foreign Secretary. He chose a man who had been a political ally, but through force of circumstance rather than similarity of temperament or philosophy. Edward Stanley, who became the 15th Earl of Derby, had already been Disraeli's Foreign Secretary in the brief Government of 1868. But their alliance went back much further. Stanley had worked closely with Disraeli since first entering Parliament in 1848. He had served as the first Secretary of State for India under the new arrangements which Disraeli helped him to introduce after the Mutiny. Both men had to manage a difficult personal relationship with Edward Stanley's father, the 14th Earl, who led the Conservative Party and was Prime Minister in the minority Conservative Governments of 1852 and 1858–9 and 1866–7. Together Disraeli and Stanley had edited a weekly Conservative journal called *The Press*. Together they had moved the Party away from protectionism; together they persuaded their reluctant colleagues to plump for the radical parliamentary Reform Bill of 1867. The two men often talked and dined together, in company and alone. Disraeli knew that Derby was loyal, hard-working, conscientious, unimaginative, low in personal ambition. These were the qualities needed in a field of policy where the dash and imaginative courage would be provided by himself. It was a miscalculation which created a crisis and destroyed their friendship.

Stanley, at the age of forty-nine, had inherited in 1869 one of the great titles of England, together with a load of debt. The 14th Earl of Derby had been an aristocrat in the high style, devoted to translating classical literature and training racehorses. He accepted the premiership three times but lacked the driving personal ambition or the administrative talent which might have prolonged these opportunities and made him a great Prime Minister.

Father and son both called themselves Conservatives but otherwise had little in common. The new Earl at once set out on a different course. He sold his father's racehorses to reduce expenditure, and the family's Irish estates in Munster to pay off debt. By nature he was a worrier; he worried about money, of which he had plenty, and about his health, which was generally good. He worried about the Conservative Party and about the future of Britain. On these wider matters, after worrying, he usually concluded that there was not much to be done, at least by sensible people such as himself. We can trace the course of the 15th Earl's worries in his diaries, brilliantly edited by Professor John Vincent.

From these painstaking entries emerges a portrait quite different from that provided by his critics at the moment of crisis in his political life. He does not come across as stupid or lazy but intelligent and hard-working, held back from memorable achievement by his natural pessimism. He was psychologically divided between, on the one hand, the position and some of the instincts which he inherited and, on the other, the modernising spirit of the Victorian age to which he belonged.

Derby believed in the British middle class. Though very different by birth, he possessed most of the solid progressive virtues which that class embodied. He once remarked after meeting a group of northern businessmen that he knew no class in English life to equal them.[4] He admired John Stuart Mill and was a friend of Charles Darwin and an enthusiast for science. He was a sceptic in religion, sometimes going to church as a social duty, but impatient of doctrinal argument and strongly critical of clerical privilege. He chaired the Peabody Trust which produced decent housing at low rates in the big cities, particularly London. He took pride in the 11,000 rooms for 20,000 occupants which the Trust had provided by 1888. Derby wanted the Conservative Party to base itself firmly on centre ground. He worried that Disraeli privately despised the middle class, having never quite shed the early novelist's dreams of an alliance between good-looking young aristocrats and the workers. He urged middle-class Ministers on Disraeli, in particular his protégé Richard Cross, who became a successful Home Secretary and author of several of the social reforms for which, when he remembered, Disraeli took credit.

Derby was a good landlord who planted two million trees. Physically he was dumpy and unimpressive. His favourite exercise was walking, and he never lunched. He preferred his smaller houses in Kent and Surrey to the traditional family seat at Knowsley, increasingly beset by the fog and fumes of Merseyside. As Foreign Secretary he enjoyed commuting to London from Kent by train. His study was kept as neat as a lady's boudoir.[5] Old Jolyon and indeed Soames Forsyte would have recognised and welcomed him.

Yet ancestral attitudes lurked in the background. Derby still owned 57,000 acres in Lancashire as well as 11,000 elsewhere. He valued his position there, and in particular his popularity in

Liverpool.[6] For thirty years he conscientiously carried out his duties as a local magistrate. As head of one of the most ancient families of England he was connected by marriage with another, having married Mary, widow of the 2nd Marquess of Salisbury. He was devoted to her, and she to politics; they had no children. This background shaped the way he thought and expressed himself. For example, he liked living in the south because 'the peasantry of Western Surrey are better looking and better mannered than those I meet with elsewhere'.[7] His criticism of a Russian envoy was easily summarised. 'In one word, he is not a gentleman.'[8] Another of his strongest prejudices had an aristocratic base. As a Stanley he felt no particular reverence for a Hanoverian Queen, who spent her time in bizarre places like Balmoral and was served by men like John Brown. He pitied rather than envied Disraeli for his attendance on Victoria, whom he found self-centred and dangerously unbalanced.

Derby lacked that thrust of personal ambition which can propel a politician out of a morass. He once explained why he continued as a politician in terms which deserve a record for lack of enthusiasm. Resignation would mean 'loss of a kind of employment which habit has made not uncongenial and which, if sometimes disagreeable, keeps off mere vacancy and weariness'.[9] Derby was a Minister because he worried that otherwise he would be bored.

This is not the stuff of magnetic leadership. Derby felt no need to prove himself. He was no arriviste; from the moment of his birth he had arrived. These characteristics played across to his handling of foreign affairs. Most British politicians and almost all Foreign Secretaries believe in an active policy under their guidance. They are swayed by different motives. Cobden was clear that free trade was God's diplomacy;[10] diplomats need only break down protective trade barriers and universal peace would follow. Gladstone, at least when in Opposition, believed that his own passion for freedom and against injustice was the only defensible basis for policy. Disraeli and Derby agreed that Cobden was wrong and Gladstone a pernicious humbug; but from that point on they differed. As we have seen, Disraeli believed in diplomacy as a theatrical entertainment, part comedy and part tragedy, in which Britain should take the leading role. The interests of Empire should be protected and indeed advanced by a national policy of tireless activity. The agents of Britain should be everywhere, her ambassadors like her fleets always looking for opportunities to assert themselves and advance the reputation of Queen and country. Disraeli did not think in terms of markets like Cobden or Marx, nor of colonial expansion like Joseph Chamberlain and Cecil Rhodes. Disraeli dealt in prestige, to him a solid asset. Prestige conferred authority. The steady accumulation of prestige provided for the security and well-being of the country. This process of acquiring prestige was also most enjoyable; it was what politics was all about.

Derby saw no point and some danger in all this. For him Britain was Britain, solid and respected for her solidity in an unstable world, content with her position, concerned only that it should not be threatened. Britain should wherever possible be a spectator not an actor in the European controversies which so agitated the Continental powers. Her diplomacy should prevent the emergence of a coalition which would threaten Britain or her rule in India; but that was the only effort which was needed. Intervention in the disputes of others brought no gain and could involve the country in commitments which in the end Parliament and public opinion might refuse to honour. When Disraeli declared that 'England ought to lead not follow', this was a meaningless phrase for Derby, perhaps indeed dangerous because it could lead to entanglements.[11] He did not mind being called an isolationist ... 'to me it appears that when isolated we have generally been most successful'.[12] And on another occasion, 'If foreigners can settle their affairs without us, why should we intervene?'[13] Like Palmerston, Gladstone and Disraeli (indeed that whole generation) he regarded Britain as unique; unlike them he saw this as a reason for keeping ourselves to ourselves, as far as possible outside the turmoil in which other countries chose to involve themselves.

This isolationist strand of feeling about foreigners and foreign affairs runs through British history. Usually it stays below the surface. It is the stuff of private conversation in pubs and clubs. It surfaces in blogs on the internet or in the correspondence columns of newspapers. It rarely forms part of open debate among professional politicians; it seems not quite respectable. It is associated with the view that foreigners, and especially our fellow Europeans, are in general untrustworthy and below our level. Every Member of Parliament knows from his or her constituency that this instinct survives. Some newspaper editors play on it, not so much in their leading articles (they too wish to appear respectable) as in the selection and presentation of news. It is an instinct associated with boorish prejudice and lack of education. What is remarkable about Derby, a man of high intelligence and advanced education, is that he reached the same conclusion as the bigots by a different route. Derby was neither lazy nor prejudiced. He worked diligently at his Foreign Office boxes. He was energetic in using the two main techniques through which a Foreign Secretary then operated. The first consisted of long interviews with the handful of important foreign ambassadors to the Court of St James (those of France, Germany, Austria and Russia, with Italy, the US and the Ottoman Empire in a second division). The second involved the penning of personal letters to our British ambassadors in the corresponding capitals of Europe. But idleness and inaction are not the same thing. When Derby supported inaction, as he usually did, this would be the result of hard study and clear thought. Lady Gwendolen Cecil, a biased critic, summed him up well in her biography of her father, Lord Salisbury:

> He [Derby] could recognise with unnerving sagacity the commitments which might involve such decisions [as intervention] and his fine intellectual powers were incessantly devoted to their avoidance. He was a master of the arts by which initiative in others is obstructed and definite conclusions are postponed; how to ignore inconvenient suggestions without combating them, and the use of silence in avoiding consideration of unarrived emergencies. Lord Salisbury used to declare that contending with him in council was like fighting a feather bed – and yet the obstruction was never that of stupidity or incomprehension.[14]

Pessimism combined with a deep dislike of war as cruel and wasteful provided the foundation of Derby's resolute preference for inaction. He did not bother to conceal the preference, and his lack of guile led him into trouble. Lord Clarendon, the Liberal politician who preceded him as Foreign Secretary, wrote 'I begged him ... not to proclaim our determined inaction on every opportunity that arises – the policy of not meddling is of course the right one, but it is not necessary that all mankind should be let into the secret twice a day.'[15] Clarendon, and even more Disraeli, believed in bluff as an element in foreign policy; Derby rejected bluff as dangerous and unworthy of Britain.

He had given an example of his invincible dislike of adventure during his brief period as Foreign Secretary in his father's Government in 1867. A dispute between France and Prussia over the future of the Grand Duchy of Luxembourg escalated into serious talk of war. Stanley (as he still was) allowed himself to be persuaded into holding a conference in London to resolve the matter. The conference succeeded, but only because the powers, including Britain, agreed to guarantee the neutrality of the independent Grand Duchy. This was a necessary commitment, but Stanley and his father, the Prime Minister, having given the guarantee immediately explained it away. They advised a puzzled Parliament that the guarantee was collective, and could only come into effect if all the signatories agreed. If either France or Prussia as signatories of the treaty infringed Luxembourg's neutrality then the guarantee had failed and no obligation would rest on Britain. Since only France or Prussia could conceivably threaten Luxembourg, the guarantee was thus meaningless. It would become invalid the moment it was needed. History would have been very different if Britain in 1914 had evaded by the same device her commitment to Belgium when the country was invaded by the Kaiser's army.

This was the man who returned to the Foreign Office after Disraeli's election victory in 1874. By then a formidable new player had begun to dominate the European scene. Having defeated France in war Prussia had grown into a united Germany. Her foreign policy was directed by Bismarck, who had in turn outwitted Denmark, defeated Austria and then France. During the Franco-Prussian War of 1870 most people in Britain had begun by sympathising with Germany because of their rooted suspicions of the Emperor Napoleon III; but Napoleon disappeared in defeat at Sedan, the new French republic suffered cruelly, and opinion shifted. The Prime Minister, Gladstone, grumbled at the German seizure of Alsace-Lorraine without regard for the wishes of its inhabitants. But there was never any question of British intervention. Britain was an outsider. It seemed a long time since Castlereagh and Wellington had been decisive in settling the future of Europe.

Once peace was restored between France and Germany there seemed no reason for Britain to regret the disappearance of the unpredictable Napoleon; he had combined a vague desire for principled reform with the devious pursuit of French interests in Italy, Belgium and elsewhere. In the lead now on the Continent was Germany, a Protestant German state still practising free trade and a conservative policy based on the status quo. There was no need for alarm. Derby never trusted Bismarck or believed in close co-operation with him; but he watched with well-informed detachment the beginnings of that amazing series of conjuring tricks by which Bismarck for twenty years sustained the twin objectives of the new Germany – a Europe governed on conservative principles, which denied France any opportunity to avenge her defeat and recover Alsace-Lorraine. The only visible threat to British interests was now Russia, and Bismarck was as well placed as anyone to keep Russia in check. There seemed no reason for Britain to match Bismarck's restless and ingenious energy with a forward foreign policy of her own.

By a paradox in 1875, one of Bismarck's mistakes seemed to confirm Derby's analysis. For once he placed one card too many on the house of cards which he happened to be building at the moment. He banned the export of horses from Germany and started a press campaign hinting at a German pre-emptive strike against France. This seems to have been an attempt to bully France but it misfired. The result was uproar. The press began to write of 'The War in Sight' and even the old German Emperor William was shaken. Britain and Russia for once joined in urging restraint on Bismarck, who gave the appearance of backing away from a war which he had never in fact intended. If a mild move of traditional diplomacy by Derby had achieved this striking success against the mighty new Germany, what need for a more active policy?

The following year Bismarck, who resented the Russian much more than the British intervention in 1875, made a secret approach to Britain through Odo Russell, the Ambassador in Berlin, suggesting intimate co-operation in Eastern matters. Disraeli and the Queen were attracted but Derby remained cool. What had

Britain to gain from becoming involved in one of Bismarck's schemes? He employed a technique which was, as Lady Gwendolen pointed out, one of his favourites. He sent back a polite inquiry as to what exactly was proposed. There was delay; the idea petered out.

If Disraeli as Prime Minister had not so far applied pressure to his Foreign Secretary, this was not because he had lost interest in foreign affairs. His search for fresh prestige for Britain, achieved personally by himself, soon found dramatic expression. Disraeli organised the purchase by the British Government of the Khedive of Egypt's 44 per cent holding in the shares of the Suez Canal Company. The coup had all the elements dear to Disraeli's heart – speed, secrecy and courage. The hurried Cabinet meting, the immediate agreement of Baron Rothschild to advance the necessary £4 million, the confounding of the French, the flattering of the Queen ('It is just settled: you have it, Ma'am') together made a great confection of achievement and myth. True, Rothschilds charged Disraeli a steep rate of interest. True, the Khedive's shares were mortgaged and had no voting rights until 1895. True, the French had not been confounded, but (recognising the help they had just had from Britain against Germany) the French Government refused to back a private French offer once Derby had told them it would be opposed by Britain. True, Disraeli seemed to confuse ownership of the shares of the Company with control of the Canal. (As Eden found to his cost when Nasser nationalised the Suez Canal in 1956, the two issues were separate.) Britain's vital concern was with free passage through the Canal to India. This was assured by a decree of the Khedive's suzerain the Sultan in Constantinople and later by the international convention of 1888. Disraeli's coup did not affect free passage one way or the other. But as an act of prestige the purchase was powerful and successful. It turned out to be a decent commercial investment. However illogically, but more important for Disraeli, it asserted British predominance in all Egyptian affairs and paved the way later for the British occupation of Egypt.

In Derby's mind the purchase of the Suez Canal shares fell into a rather crowded category of actions which would do neither great good nor great harm. In his diary of 29 November 1875 he wrote: 'so far as I can make out, the purchase is universally popular. I might say even more, it seems to have created a feeling of something like enthusiasm far in excess of the real importance of the transaction. It is a complete political success: yet the very fact of its being so causes me some uneasiness: for it shows the intense desire for action abroad which pervades the public mind, the impatience created by long diplomatic inactivity, and the strength of feeling which might under certain circumstances take the form of a cry for War.' He went on to grumble that if a few years back a Minister had suggested that the British Government should buy shares in a foreign company, the proposal would have been thought absurd, and the Minister ruined.[16] A few days later Derby visited Edinburgh, where he was inaugurated as Rector of the University and given the Freedom of the City. In one of his speeches in Edinburgh, he put the Suez Canal deal in perspective by saying that our aim was to prevent a great highway filled with our shipping from falling under the exclusive control of the foreign shareholders of a foreign company. The Queen complained to Disraeli that Derby was trying to pour cold water on a great success. This was just one of the first breezes which blew into a violent storm involving Queen, Prime Minister and Foreign Secretary. Derby was more interested in a charming letter which Charles Darwin wrote to his wife about the speech he had made about science during the same visit.[17]

Derby stood equally aloof from Disraeli's other prestige project, namely the Royal Titles Bill making the Queen Empress of India. This idea had been circulating at least since Lord Ellenborough as Governor General had urged it from Calcutta in Peel's time. The Queen allowed herself to be beguiled. Her Russian and German counterparts were emperors. Once old William had died her eldest daughter would become Empress of Germany and take precedence over her, which would obviously be wrong. These were royal considerations crucial for Victoria to which Disraeli added the argument, dismissed by Derby, that the change would show Russia that Britain was determined to hang on to India. Disraeli pretended to his colleagues unconvincingly that he acted under irresistible pressure from the Queen, which Derby believed he could and should have resisted. The two men even discussed whether the excited sovereign was going mad, though Derby concluded 'much of her unreasonableness is rather that of a spoilt child, arguing at finding the least difficulty in getting its own way, than of an insane person'.[18]

Meanwhile the Eastern Question moved slowly into crisis. The ramifications of the question were infinite, its essence clear enough. From the summer of 1875 into 1876 the Christian Slavs living in Bosnia and Herzegovina rose in revolt. Once again, it seemed certain that the Ottoman Empire, corrupt and cruelly ruled, lurching from one financial crisis to another, was nearing its end. Few observers in 1875 would have supposed that it would last another forty years.

The European powers reacted differently to this prospect. Russia felt a natural sympathy with the oppressed and revolting Slavs and saw an opportunity of extending her influence as far as Constantinople. Austria, herself ruling over a Slav population in Slovenia as well as millions of Hungarians and Czechs, was by definition a multinational state. She objected strongly to the idea, from her point of view thoroughly destructive, that the Balkans might dissolve into a group of national states. Bismarck had no particular German aim. He wanted if possible to maintain the Dreikaiserbund, the alliance of the three empires of Germany, Austria and Russia which offered him the best hope of keeping France isolated. He favoured the partition of the Ottoman Empire with Britain taking Egypt, thus stoking up a useful Anglo-French quarrel.

Disraeli, never a nationalist except as regards Britain herself, felt no sympathy with the insurgents but a lurking attraction for the fading Oriental empire based on Constantinople. He believed that Constantinople was the key to India, and that Russian control of the Straits would undermine our whole imperial position. Lord Salisbury had occasion to complain later that some of his colleagues used maps with too small a scale; that was certainly true of Disraeli. In reality Port Said, at the head of the Suez Canal, is nearly a thousand miles by sea from Constantinople, and much more overland. The notion that if the Russians controlled Constantinople they could make a quick grab for the Suez Canal was unreal. As his biographer Robert Blake put it, Disraeli's obsession 'stemmed from ancient habit rather than clear thought'.[19] It was true that Russian control of the Balkans and the Straits would alter the balance of power in Europe. But it was a wilder and more strictly

British fear which possessed Disraeli or, to be more precise, which he used to justify the bold forward policy which his temperament demanded.

The Austrians felt most acutely the strain created by the Balkan revolt and the danger that Russia might intervene in support of the rebels. Andrassy, their Foreign Minister, produced a plan for reforms to be implemented by the Sultan under the supervision of a joint Muslim-Christian commission. He asked all the powers to join in urging this on the Turks. It was the sort of traditional diplomatic move in which Derby saw no harm though little good, and he persuaded a reluctant Disraeli and an uninterested Cabinet to accept it.[20] When the Turks rejected the plan Bismarck turned his hand to composing something stronger. The Berlin Memorandum of May 1876 proposed similar reforms but ended with a paragraph hinting at coercion by the powers if the Turks rejected them. This time Disraeli dug in. His gout was bad. He was cross because when he asked the Foreign Office for details of the Berlin plan at lunchtime on Sunday 14 May he was told that there was no one in the office. Bad-tempered inquiries were made; it turned out the Resident Clerk had gone for a walk.[21]

Disraeli used this incident as part of his mounting campaign against what he saw as the lethargic inefficiency of professional British diplomats. By this he mainly meant their inability to share his own enthusiasm. But Disraeli's determination to reject Bismarck's plan was not based on this fit of pique. The plan had been put together by the governments of the Three Emperors before Britain had been consulted. This was intolerable. 'England has been treated as though we were Montenegro or Bosnia,' he complained to the Russian Ambassador.[22] Derby agreed and the Cabinet unanimously rejected the plan. The Queen and some qualified observers thought this might be a mistake. The British rejection confirmed most Turks in their view that they could rely on British support whatever they did. On the other hand it is hard to see how the German plan would have prospered, even with British assent, given the obstinate Turkish mood.

Derby relaxed by reading Aeschylus, the most doom-laden of Greek tragedians, 'partly to divert my thoughts, partly to see if I have forgotten my Greek'.[23] When Bismarck's plan failed Disraeli rejoiced at the discomfiture of the Dreikaiserbund. 'It was an unnatural alliance, and never would have occurred had England maintained, of late years, her just position in public affairs. I think not only peace will be maintained, but that Her Majesty will be restored to her due and natural influence in the Government of the World.'

But nothing had been settled. In June 1876 Serbia and Montenegro declared war on the Turks on behalf of their fellow Slavs. Their armies proved useless, but the escalation made Russian intervention ever more likely. Rumours began to trickle in that a rising of the Christians further south in Bulgaria had been suppressed by the Turks with great cruelty. But the British Cabinet was more concerned with a commotion of its own. Disraeli, tired, criticised for haphazard leadership, hardly able to walk when the gout attacked him, decided to give up the House of Commons but to continue as Prime Minister. He accepted the Queen's offer of an earldom and became Lord Beaconsfield.* He had talked earlier of resigning the premiership as well and of his preference that Derby should succeed him.[24] But Derby too was tired, as well as lacking in ambition. He had discussed the possibility of the premiership with his wife in May, but recognised that the Queen would be reluctant to appoint him. He concluded that he might do better to retire himself, at least temporarily, and take a rest from the Foreign Office. Disraeli probably had no serious intention of giving up the premiership at this time; but the episode at least shows that there was no serious rift in the summer of 1876 between himself and Derby. Derby summed up the relationship in his diary of 1 July, referring to 'D[israeli] being a little too anxious to excite interest, and generally to put on an appearance of greater activity than is really being shown or than there is need of. I on the other hand am supposed, perhaps with justice, to be disposed to make as little as possible of what we do. But as regard to the action to be taken we are absolutely as one; and I see no reason why we should not continue so.'[25]

Prime Minister and Foreign Secretary remained as one in face of their next challenge. The details of Turkish atrocities in Bulgaria swelled from a trickle to a torrent. The *Daily News* reported on 23

* But for the sake of clarity we continue to call him Disraeli.

June that some 25,000 men, women and children had been killed. Public opinion reacted to the reports with horror. The Liberal Opposition began to press the Government. Derby had to receive a deputation and in advance felt 'rather nervous and uncomfortable ... we have no news on which it is possible to rely'.[26]

Disraeli did not wait for reliable news one way or the other. He lacked any natural fellow feeling for the suffering rebels. He regarded such feeling in others as hypocrisy and a device to discredit his Government. When confronted with accusations of torture he turned them away with the half-jest that Orientals 'generally terminate their connexion with culprits in a more expeditious manner'.[27] Within days Disraeli became aware that a British consul, Mr Reade, had sent a dispatch from the spot giving cautious support to the accusations. Disraeli turned fiercely on Derby. 'I must again complain of the management of your office,' he wrote on 14 July: 'It is impossible to represent the F.O. in the House of Commons in these critical times without sufficient information.' The reports of consuls came through the British Ambassador in Constantinople, Sir Henry Elliot, who was strongly pro-Turkish. In one way or another, either in Constantinople or the Foreign Office, the reports were watered down. The careful scholar, Dr Temperley, later found that the published Blue Book suppressed damaging evidence which the consuls had reported.[28] This tendentious editing was the responsibility of the Permanent Under Secretary, Lord Tenterden, a particular *bête noire* of Disraeli, but Derby should have been aware of the tinkering, for which there was no justification. But even when more fully informed that some atrocities were real, Disraeli did not alter his line. His gift for the memorable phrase led him into trouble, as when he referred to further evidence of atrocities in Bulgaria as 'coffee house babble'.

Disraeli was genuinely vexed that the Turks and British public opinion between them were frustrating the Government's policy of checking Russian ambitions. His vexation overflowed into real anger when in September Gladstone, coming late but furious into the fray, published his famous pamphlet *The Bulgarian Horrors and the Question of the East*. He sold 40,000 copies in a week and 200,000 within a month. Gladstone mustered a genuine passion against mass injustice which for a few weeks swept all before it. Disraeli, incapable of such feeling himself, saw only an ambitious hypocrite seizing this device to thrust for the leadership of his Party, from which he had pretended to retire after his defeat in 1874. In his frustration, Disraeli again misjudged his response, telling Conservatives in Aylesbury on 20 September that conduct like Gladstone's 'may, I think, be fairly described as worse than any of those Bulgarian atrocities which now occupy attention'.[29]

We have seen earlier outbursts of British public opinion against foreign tyranny – and there were many more to come. Byron and Greek independence, Garibaldi and Italian unity were causes which caught fire with the public and influenced British governments. But Gladstone was the first senior politician to mobilise a growing democracy against oppression in a faraway country of which his audiences knew only what they learned from him and from the newspapers which took up his words. The power and passion of the campaign were formidable and have secured imitators and a place in history. The fire blazed as no such fire had blazed before, and then quite suddenly went out. Within months different emotions took control of opinion.

Disraeli was wrong; Gladstone was no hypocrite. He tried throughout his later life to apply the principles of an ethical liberalism in foreign policy. But he was continually frustrated by events. The man who denounced the Bulgarian atrocities and all Disraeli's imperial adventures became the Prime Minister who bombarded Alexandria and allowed Gordon to go fatally to Khartoum.

Disraeli worried that Derby would start bending policy to accommodate the public agitation against the atrocities. This was unnecessary. Derby was on principle even less likely than Disraeli to yield to clamour. As regards this particular clamour, the two men agreed in September that 'all that is not faction in it is froth'.[30] The summer had been trying for Derby, partly because the extreme heat kept him from the long walks which he loved. He reflected on his fiftieth birthday with typical and carefully calibrated melancholy. 'In regard of healthy domestic happiness and outward circumstances I have nothing to complain of, except that the wear and tear of office is sometimes oppressive; but the loss of this spring [the death of his mother] can not be repaired and has tended to lower spirits which are never very high.'[31] He spent a good deal of time fending off Disraeli's criticism of the Foreign Office and Sir Henry Elliot. 'I cannot see that D. has been either misled by false information or inadequately supplied: the truth is he has got into some trouble with the House by making so light of the affair in the first instance, and lays on his information the blame of his own careless way of talking.'[32] Derby adopted one of his customary tactics, answering criticism by silence. He commented privately that Disraeli would really like to change back to the old (now, of course, the American) system by which ambassadors were political appointments and changed with every change of government.

As the autumn of 1876 advanced, the threat of Russian intervention against Turkey grew. As this became apparent public opinion began to shift. As early as 14 September Derby recorded that the agitation on Turkish affairs had subsided; a month later he noted that since the Russians had shown their hand, public opinion had changed in a singular way.[33] The shift in events saved Disraeli from his own mistakes. The Government hung on to the Buckinghamshire seat in the by-election caused by his elevation to the Lords. The public would never come to love the Turks, but fear and dislike of Russia began to overlay the stories of Turkish cruelty.

From now on Disraeli talked often in Cabinet about the need for bold measures, in particular British occupation of Constantinople or at least of the Dardanelles Straits. These were reflections, not precise proposals: they were designed to prepare the ground and test the opinion of others. But once again Disraeli's map was small-scale. He imagined that the Russians, still deployed in their own territory north of Romania, might suddenly seize Constantinople within a couple of days. Disraeli even bypassed the Foreign Office and instructed George Hunt, First Lord of the Admiralty, to send the British fleet up to Constantinople if any Russian vessel passed through the Straits. Hunt consulted Derby, who blocked the move, attributing it to the Prime Minister's 'odd excited state'. Derby for the first time foresaw

the probability or at least the chance of a breach between us: not that as yet we have differed materially in regard to anything that has been done, but that our points of view and objects are different. To the Premier the main thing is to please and surprise the public by bold strokes and unexpected moves; he would rather run serious national risks than hear his policy called feeble or commonplace; to me the first object is to keep England out of trouble, so long as it can be done consistently with honour and good faith. We have agreed in resisting the agitation got up by Gladstone: but if war with Russia becomes popular, as it may, we are not unlikely to be on different sides.[34]

For the moment the two men still moved together. Proposals for an armistice to avert a war between Russia and Turkey developed into a plan for a conference in Constantinople. Derby was persuaded to sponsor this once his soundings showed general agreement. Disraeli, after securing Derby's agreement, asked Lord Salisbury to represent Britain at Constantinople. Salisbury was not keen: 'an awful nuisance – not at all in my line – involving sea-sickness, much French and failure'.[35] The third main actor in this particular drama of British foreign policy had stepped on to the stage – the one who gained most strikingly from its outcome.

Derby had no difficulty in welcoming Salisbury's appointment. The two men were related, Derby having married Salisbury's step-mother.* More important, they held similar grand positions at the top of British society, each being the head of a great family. Neither behaved like a typical aristocrat, but they knew the same people and talked the same language.

Two main differences between them were apparent in 1876. The first concerned their attitudes towards Disraeli. As we have seen, the alliance between Disraeli and Derby went back a long way. Though it was beginning to feel strain, there was much history to hold them together. Derby wrote in his diary as late as December 1876, 'Personal ties in politics I have none, except to Disraeli, whom I will not desert so long as he continues a Minister.'[36] In January 1877 Disraeli asked a personal favour of his old colleague: 'What do you think of intro-ducing me to the House of Lords? I know it would bore you, and

---

* Family connections can be treacherous. There was a story that Derby had slept with his future wife when her husband, Salisbury's father, was alive. Nothing was proved and the dealings between the two men over the years, though cool and once angry, do not smack of deep-seated personal enmity.

I always try to save you from being bored, but one has a feeling that it would be the proper thing.' Derby replied the same day: 'I should have felt sorry . . . if you had applied to anyone but me. Considering that we have pulled together for nearly 30 years I think that office of friendship is mine by right.'[37]

Salisbury's position was different. He had quarrelled bitterly with Disraeli at what he believed to be Disraeli's underhand tactics in passing the Reform Bill of 1867. In early life Salisbury had earned his reputation and living as a journalist; those years had sharpened his pen and widened his vocabulary of abuse. On one occasion Disraeli called him 'a great master of jibes and flouts and jeers'. It had been against Disraeli that Salisbury after 1867 directed much of his sarcasm. Derby too had suffered from his criticisms; but Disraeli had been his main aversion. The idea that he should serve in Disraeli's Government of 1874 filled him with genuine dismay. He regarded Disraeli as arrogant and untrustworthy; he went so far as to urge Derby to challenge him for the premiership. He acknowledged that if he refused to serve in the Cabinet of 1874 he might commit political suicide; but inside the Cabinet he might be a slave under a dictator. Ironically in view of what was to happen, his doubts were, if not removed, at least smoothed down in negotiations conducted by his stepmother Lady Derby, and he accepted office as Secretary of State for India. 'The prospect of having to serve with this man again is a nightmare,' he wrote to his wife.[38] But serve he did, not least because a fearful famine in Bengal needed urgent handling and he did not feel he could shirk the responsibility offered him.

The second difference between Salisbury and Derby concerned religion, at a time when religious differences could not be confined in a private compartment but often overflowed into general politics. Salisbury was a determined Anglican, more inclined than either Derby or Disraeli to sympathise with the suffering Christian subjects of the Sultan and indeed with the Russian desire to rescue them from their Turkish oppressors.

Both Derby and Disraeli pressed Salisbury to represent Britain at the conference in Constantinople. The Prince of Wales, like the Queen enthusiastic for a more active foreign policy, suggested that on his way to the conference Salisbury should meet the masters of policy-making in Paris, Berlin, Vienna and Rome. The Foreign Office, through the Permanent Under Secretary, raised their usual doubts about an exercise which cut across the traditional channels of diplomacy. Disraeli disagreed in significant terms:

> I think on these matters HRH is a better counsellor than Lord Tenterden. The Prince of Wales is a thorough man of the world and knows all the individuals personally. You must remember that we suffer from a feeble and formal diplomacy and that there has been little real interchange of thought between the English Government and foreign powers. I agree with the Prince and think it highly desirable that at this moment our comunications with the Powers should be lifted out of the slough of despondency they have so long grovelled in ... Consider this matter for yourself ... only don't concede your own convictions on the subject to Tenterdenism – which is a dusty affair, and not suited to the times and things we have to grapple with.

Disraeli did not yet directly criticise Derby, only the machine over which Derby presided. Over the years Prime Ministers, tired of being warned by the Foreign Office of the world's complexities and dangers, have often expressed similar impatience. In this letter to Salisbury Disraeli added a personal hint of unmistakable significance: 'Also personally for yourself, I wish it. This is a momentous period in your life and career. If all goes well you will have achieved a European reputation and position which will immensely assist and strengthen your future course. You should personally know the men who are governing the world.'[39] Disraeli was not a man to write carelessly on such a matter. The clear hint that Salisbury might before long be Foreign Secretary or even Prime Minister must have remained lodged in Salisbury's mind through the tortuous months which followed. He accepted the position, promising Derby to 'take his part in the comedy with all due solemnity'.[40]

Salisbury left London on 20 November accompanied by his wife, on whose participation Derby expressed himself with unusual force: 'Ly S. very noisy and violent about the arrangements: it is unlucky that she goes. She will certain quarrel with the staff, and say and do the most imprudent things; having great cleverness, great energy and not a particle of tact.'[41]

Salisbury's most important conversation on the journey was with Bismarck in Berlin. The German Chancellor argued that the Ottoman Empire was rotten to the core, but that Russia would not have the energy to sustain a war against it for long. Britain need do nothing in a hurry, but should pick up Egypt when the Ottoman Empire disintegrated. Bismarck need not have worried. Derby had made sure that Salisbury's instructions committed Britain to nothing. Before long Disraeli and Derby together became anxious that at the conference Salisbury was being lured by the subtle Russian negotiator Ignatiev into agreeing a plan for reforms which stood no chance of Turkish acceptance. Disraeli wrote to Derby: 'Sal. seems most prejudiced and not to be aware that his principal object in being sent to Const. is to keep the Russians out of Turkey, not to create an ideal existence for the Turkish Xtians. He is more Russian than Ignatiev.'[42] Disraeli was also cross with Salisbury for asking the Cabinet to stay in London unnecessarily over Christmas, and even more for authorising the withdrawal of the British fleet from Besika Bay, not far from the Dardanelles.

As a result Derby had a difficult conversation with the Prime Minister on Boxing Day. He put the best gloss on Salisbury's decisions, and came away with the uneasy feeling that Disraeli wanted the fleet to be on hand to make possible a sudden British swoop on Constantinople. Not for the first time he patiently explained to the Prime Minister that the Russians, still at peace and behind their own distant borders, were two months away from Constantinople, whereas the British fleet based in Athens could be there within three days. Salisbury's scathing comments to Derby showed none of the Prime Minister's lurking sympathy for the Turks. He wrote on Boxing Day that he would not shake their belief that Britain would in the end help them however badly they behaved, 'an army of European advisers made up of fanatics, oddities and all the declared scoundrels of Europe, who hope to feed on war ... Convincing the Turks is about as easy as making a donkey canter.'[43]

The Turks refused the reform plans agreed by Salisbury and his colleagues at the conference in Constantinople, which then collapsed. The Turks were powerfully influenced by what they rightly believed to be Disraeli's sympathy and by the fervent friendship of the British

Ambassador, Sir Henry Elliot. So long as, in the last resort, they would have British support they were prepared to defy the Russians. Salisbury angrily pressed for Elliot's recall. 'It is very unfortunate that Elliot is still here,' he wrote to Lord Carnarvon on 5 January. 'All the rascally Levantines who stir up the Porte to hold out cluster round the Embassy. My power of negotiation with the Turks is almost nil so long as he stays.'[44]

Disraeli had no admiration for Elliot, who had been so sluggish in keeping him informed of the Bulgarian atrocities; but he had even less enthusiasm for sacking an ambassador under what would appear to be Russian pressure. Elliot withdrew from Constantinople as agreed with the other European ambassadors in protest against the Turkish rejection of the conference plan, and was promoted to be Her Majesty's Ambassador in Vienna.

Salisbury returned from the conference with a passion for foreign affairs which never left him, and with a first-hand knowledge of leading European statesmen and (equally important) of the way his colleagues in Cabinet thought and operated. He possessed a mind which formed its opinions through argument, often conducted within himself. He was not always consistent in his statements as an argument took gradual shape in his brain. But from Constantinople he gained two conclusions which stayed with him.

Salisbury believed, like Bismarck, that the British policy of the Crimean War, namely full support for Turkey, was doomed because the Ottoman Empire was doomed. He applied to it his general thesis that 'the commonest error in politics lies in sticking to the carcases of dead politics . . . we cling to the shreds of an old policy after it has been torn to pieces; and to the shadow of a shred after the rag itself has been torn away'.[45] Whatever Disraeli and the British public might think, whatever it might be convenient from time to time to pretend, Constantinople was not the gateway to India. 'The Conference', he wrote to Lord Carnarvon on 11 January 1877, 'has done good. It has, I hope, made it impossible that we should spend any more blood in sustaining the Turkish Empire. And I hope it will make English statesmen buckle to the task of devising some other means of securing the road to India.'[46]

With that much Lord Derby would have agreed, though he would have added a qualifying clause that we should not allow considerations of prestige to exaggerate the threat to India. But Salisbury from this point began to diverge from Derby. He became vehement in his criticism of the vacillation and inactivity of current British diplomacy. In this he followed the lead he had privately received from Disraeli at the time of his appointment. He must also have been influenced by Disraeli's hint at that time of a shining future for him in this field. Salisbury on his way up never lacked personal ambition; but that was not his only driving force. He was not fuelled like Disraeli by a passion for prestige, nor like Gladstone by a passion for moral justice. In both respects he resembled Derby. But his intellect and conscience, unlike Derby's, were active agents. As a Christian he hated the waste of war; but in a clear-sighted and sometimes brutal way he believed that the interests of Britain needed protection by a vigilant and hard-headed diplomacy.

Back at the India Office after the Constantinople conference Salisbury continued to take an active part in Cabinet discussions. These became increasingly unhappy and confused. Czar Alexander II hesitated on the edge of war against Turkey. Disraeli pressed at meeting after meeting for action to forestall the Russians. His suggestions varied but basically he wanted to send a land force to occupy the Dardanelles, backed by the fleet. In a letter to Derby on 9 February 1877 he laid bare his belief in action for action's sake. 'You must pardon the roughness of this communication but I am in the gout which is fatal to finished composition and penmanship. The position of affairs is that critical and requires decision ... I don't fancy the country will stand laissez-faire but they will back us, I believe, in whatever we do, provided we are doing.'[47]

That part of the British public which had denounced Turkish atrocities in 1876 fell silent in 1877. Gladstone's second pamphlet on the atrocities, published in January, was a flop; there was again a noisy agitation but this time against the Russians, not the Turks. The fury was supported by the Queen. While Albert lived she had learned to function in a disciplined way, patiently reading long memoranda, working on the whole in harmony with the machinery of her own Government and well informed about events in Europe. The distaste of Victoria and Albert for Palmerston was inflamed precisely because he had enjoyed acting outside orthodoxy and in defiance of the

Courts of Europe. But Albert had died in 1861. Now the Queen thrashed about without any intellectual discipline, ignoring Ponsonby, her senior Private Secretary, swayed by personal likes and dislikes, but also by a natural empathy with the feelings of the noisiest part of her subjects. Disraeli assured others that he was doing his best to restrain her, but his flattery often had the opposite effect. The Queen was often distracted by purely personal concerns. For example on 22 January Derby was summoned to Windsor. He expected to be challenged about the Constantinople conference, which had just broken down. Instead he had to spend half a day discussing with the Queen whether her grandson, one day to be the Kaiser Wilhelm II, should receive the Order of the Garter or only the Bath.[48]

Derby brooded over personal problems that winter. He and his wife were a gloomy couple, particularly when they discussed their anxieties together. He detected in her 'the growth of a fixed and chronic melancholy'. Watching the decay of Disraeli's health, he wondered how he would answer if he was offered the premiership. He decided he would decline; his wife would be against it. He himself would not relish London life, or the duties of keeping the Queen in good humour, distributing patronage, particularly ecclesiastical, and supervising the work of departments of which he knew nothing.[49]

Diplomacy continued to fail. Ignatiev, the Russian envoy who had charmed Salisbury at Constantinople, visited England and stayed with Salisbury at Hatfield, but his protestations of goodwill failed to convince. Derby paid more attention to his own conversations with Shuvalov, the Russian Ambassador in London. Shuvalov made Derby laugh, not an easy accomplishment, and was genuinely using his influence for peace in St Petersburg – genuinely, but unsuccessfully, for on 24 April 1877 Russia declared war on Turkey.

Three days earlier another prolonged discussion in Cabinet ended with Derby and most of his colleagues blocking a decision on any pre-emptive military or naval action to secure Constantinople. He took the unheroic view that if war broke out, 'the first thing to do was to ascertain the views of the other Powers'.[50] Salisbury and the Colonial Secretary, Carnarvon, were even more emphatic against helping Turkey in any way. Derby saw himself as keeping the balance inside Cabinet; this was becoming more difficult as feeling 'out-of-doors' became more anti-Russian.[51]

The day after Russia declared war, the Cabinet held yet another discussion, again without conclusion. Derby again analysed Disraeli's attitude, which he found 'bouncing and excited' . . . 'his state of mind makes me uneasy: he evidently thinks that for England to look on at a war, without interfering even for a limited time, is a humiliating position: and of the injury to finance and industry which would be caused by taking an active part he either does not care to think, or considers that such sacrifices are a less evil than playing a secondary part. In this view of things he has the Court with him, the army and navy of course, and a section of the public but that section though noisy is small.' Derby added that he was coming into 'a sort of antagonism to the Premier, with whom I have hitherto acted in the closest union'.[52]

To Disraeli he wrote firmly, but still with some deference: 'You have been so often right when others were wrong that I hardly like to express dissent; but I am quite sure that in the middle class at least the feeling is so strong against a war that you would lose more support by asking money for an expedition than you could gain by the seizure of an important military position.'[53]

Through the summer of 1877 the crisis showed faint signs of easing. The British Cabinet summoned up enough unity to authorise Derby to warn the Russians in May that Britain had vital interests which would be put at risk by military action which threatened the Gulf, Egypt, the Suez Canal Straits or Constantinople: 'Her Majesty's Government are not prepared to witness with indifference that passing into other hands than those of its present possessors of a capital holding so peculiar and commanding a position.'[54] Disraeli's fertile mind led him to manoeuvre for an alliance with Austria to block the Russian advance in the Balkans. But Russian diplomacy had forestalled him; in return for a promise of neutrality the Russians agreed that Austria should occupy the whole of Bosnia and Herzegovina.

Britain had again failed to find a Continental ally. But, contrary to the expectation of the British military authorities and just about everyone else, the Turks themselves held up the Russian advance.

In Britain lingering concerns about Turkish atrocities in Bulgaria were now finally brushed aside by the fame of the Turkish General, Osman Pasha, who for five months gallantly defended the fortress of Plevna against the attacks of the Grand Duke Nicholas. But this could only be a temporary pause. Both the warring countries were administratively weak and quickly exhausted: eventually the Russians managed to resume their advance and the respite for Derby and the British Cabinet was over.

Disraeli continued to bombard his Foreign Secretary with prophecies of doom for the Government if it continued inactive. 'They [the Opposition] will probably turn us out in this Parliament or they will force us to a dissolution under the influence of a disastrous defeat abroad ... A Government can only die once; it is better to die with glory than vanish in an ignominious end.' He was scathing about Salisbury. 'It is quite evident to me that Lord Salisbury wishes the Russians to enter and indefinitely occupy Constantinople ... It is the Conference over again in which unquestionably he much compromised us, though you and myself then treated him with generous Magnanimity, which was thrown away in his sacerdotal convictions. The Ministry will not be weakened by his secession.'[55]

Disraeli, unable to defeat Derby by frontal argument, turned on the diplomats. On 13 September he wrote approving one particular appointment, but adding 'I wish we could get rid of the whole lot. They seem to me quite useless. It is difficult to control events, but none of them try to. I think Odo Russell the worst of all [in Berlin]. He contents himself with reporting all Bismarck's cynical bravado which he evidently listens to in an ecstasy of sycophantic wonder.' This splendid barrage of letters, written in Disraeli's sprawling hand on small sheets of notepaper thickly lined with mourning black in memory of his wife, should rank in any anthology of prime ministerial exhortation.

Derby continued to muse in his diary on the way in which his disagreement was pulling apart his long-standing alliance with Disraeli: 'The Premier sincerely and really believes that it will be better for us to risk a great war, and to spend £100,000,000 on it than not to appear to have had a large share in the decisions come to when peace is made ... I do not think prestige is worth buying so dear and

Above: Castlereagh and Canning fought their famous duel at dawn on 21 September 1809. It was a ramshackle contest; both men survived.

Left: Castlereagh and Canning lounge alongside other members of Portland's administration in 1808, dreaming of victory against Napoleon while drunk on Portugese wine. Note the 'secret correspondence' poking out of Canning's pocket – a reference to the bombardment of Copenhagen in 1807.

Canning. His speeches tended to be more powerful than his policies.

Castlereagh. A detached, calm, sensible and often melancholy man.

Top and above: Two visions of the Congress of Vienna, 1814–5. The Russian bear dances a victory jig over Poland and Saxony while Castlereagh, Metternich and Talleyrand discuss the future of Europe after two decades of war.

Right: Emily Castlereagh caused confusion and amusement in Vienna by wearing her husband's Order of the Garter as a decoration in her hair.

Aberdeen as a young
man. His life was broken
by bereavement. His
first wife, Catherine
(above), his second wife,
Harriet *(below)*, and all
his daughters *(below left)*
predeceased him.

A teenage Palmerston looking precocious and sly. His good looks and immense self-confidence made him a hit with women. *Below from left to right:* Lady Cowper, Princess Lieven and Lady Jersey all fell victim to 'Lord Cupid'.

Left: Palmerston in his prime. He liked to give the impression of being carefree and casual. Behind the surface there was a disciplined, industrious and highly ambitious man.

Below left: Aberdeen in old age. He believed in peace, he worked for peace, but found himself leading the country into the Crimean War.

Below: Mr Punch urges Aberdeen to stop the brawl between Russia and the Ottoman Empire.

ABERDEEN ON DUTY.

A—b—n. "I SHAN'T INTERFERE TILL THEY CALL MURDER!"

Right: Edward Stanley, 15th Earl of Derby: 'If foreigners can settle their affairs without us, why should we intervene?'

Below: Derby and Disraeli saw the signs but failed to spot danger. The argument between Prime Minister and Foreign Secretary created a crisis and destroyed a friendship.

AUGURS AT FAULT.

Derbeius. "CAN YOU READ THE SIGNS OF THE BIRDS?"   Disraelius. "I WISH I COULD!!!"

The Congress of Berlin, 1878. Disraeli said that he and Lord Salisbury had brought back 'peace with honour', but behind that phrase lay a certain emptiness.

Lord Salisbury. His cool temperament prevented him from being a great Prime Minister; for clarity of thought and action as Foreign Secretary he was unmatched.

I feel sure that the majority are on that side.'[56] Derby pinned his faith on the solid good sense of the British middle class. The Queen disagreed, and her denunciation to Disraeli of her Foreign Secretary became passionate with exclamation marks and underlinings. He was rash enough to argue with her about the Crimean War. The Queen looked back on it with pride, Derby with revulsion. She was enraged that British warnings to Russia against any occupation of Constantinople were diluted and made useless as they passed through the Foreign Office machine: 'Russia goes on! It maddens the Queen to feel that all our efforts are being destroyed by the Ministers who ought to carry them out. The Queen must say that she can't stand it!'[57]

The Queen wrote against a background of growing public enthusiasm for a showdown with the Russians. A new word entered the English language in a music hall song:

> We don't want to fight,
> But by jingo if we do
> We've got the ships, we've got the men
> We've got the money too

Through the autumn, Disraeli kept up a friendly relationship with his Foreign Secretary. Despite the strains Derby admired Disraeli's speech at the Mansion House on 9 November for its caution and tact. 'Ill or well his pluck never fails, and he had his reward in an enthusiastic audience.'[58] But Derby was conscious that Disraeli was constantly shifting his ground in conversation. In truth Disraeli, though anxious to keep Derby, could not conceal his unchanged appetite for a different and much bolder policy. By 27 November Derby was doubting whether the two of them could get through the winter together.[59] The real question was whether the Prime Minister could find a way of breaking the firm majority which Derby could still muster in the Cabinet for caution and peace. Disraeli had his own contacts and correspondents on the side but he could not act as he, the Queen and much of the press wished so long as Derby could control the formal machinery of decision-taking.

On 14 December Disraeli launched his next offensive in Cabinet. He urged that Parliament be recalled as soon as possible; that a large extra sum should be voted for the Army and Navy, and that we should peremptorily put ourselves forward to mediate between the Turks and Russians. Derby's counter-arguments were now weaker because of events on the ground. The Russian army was no longer hundreds of miles away within Russia itself; it was crawling, slowly and ineptly but now irresistibly, in thick snow through the mountains towards Constantinople. Derby had to fall back on the judgement derived from his conversations with the Russian Ambassador Shuvalov that the Czar had no intention of permanently occupying the city or the Straits – unless provoked by British action. Even so, and despite a formidable speech by Disraeli to Cabinet on 17 December, Derby managed to draw the teeth of the Prime Minister's proposal and the Cabinet parted for the holiday uneasy but still in one piece. In achieving this Derby had summoned the middle-class Ministers as reinforcements. 'We can hardly make a change of proceeding without consulting such men as Cross and Northcote – who will have to bear the chief burden of defending [in the Commons] whatever we do.'[60]

Derby spent Christmas at Knowsley, working on office papers 'of which I have a vast heap ... my spirits were never quite equal to a noisy Christmas party and the anxieties of the last two years have made them less so than before. So I am best in my room.'[61] He had just sent Salisbury a long, frank letter – in effect, a final appeal to those prejudices which he supposed that, as British aristocrats, the two men shared. Derby had worked closely with Disraeli as a political friend for many years, but this crisis had opened up the feeling that somehow Disraeli was different. After analysing the background he wrote of Disraeli: 'He believes thoroughly in "prestige", as all foreigners do, and would think it (quite sincerely) in the interests of the country to spend 200 millions on a war if the result was to make foreign states think more highly of us as a military power ... These ideas are intelligible but they are not mine or yours, and their being sincerely held does not make them less dangerous ... We are in real danger, and it is impossible to be too careful.'[62]

But Salisbury was on the move in the opposite direction. It is hard to believe that personal ambition played no part in that move, but there was also intellectual justification. Salisbury had in his own mind rejected as out of date the traditional British policy of helping Turkey to which Disraeli still clung, but Turkey was now beyond help. The British interest now lay in tough diplomacy which would prevent Russia from gathering the spoils to herself. But tough diplomacy was something that Derby, with all his intelligence, was temperamentally unable to provide.

Derby achieved his last defensive success in Cabinet on 12 January, but this time from a minority position. He and the Colonial Secretary, Lord Carnarvon, resisted a proposal for an expedition to seize Gallipoli and hold it as a guarantee for the security of the Dardanelles. 'For nearly an hour I thought I had ceased to be a Minister.' He hung on and as a compromise it was agreed simply to investigate the possibility.

The strain of these continuing arguments began to tell. Derby spent the next day in bed and for several days was more or less out of action, suffering from agonising cramps in much of his body. His one surviving ally in Cabinet was also in trouble; Carnarvon made an unwise speech, was ticked off by Disraeli and resigned in a huff. Derby was not personally close to Carnarvon, whom he regarded as 'weak vain and funny in his personal relations'. But he needed him in the argument, and encouraged him to withdraw his resignation.

Disraeli returned to the empty idea of an alliance with Austria, but when frustrated on this told the Cabinet on 23 January 1878 that their reputation would be ruined if they did not at once agree to send the fleet to Constantinople and provide £10 million as a supplementary estimate for the Army and Navy. Salisbury had by now turned full circle and became fierce in supporting Disraeli. Derby, for once overruled in Cabinet, wrote his letter of resignation but kept it overnight. Next day the situation changed. The Sultan of Turkey had been negotiating with the Russians and now accepted their terms. The case for sending the fleet collapsed and the order was countermanded. Britain could hardly be more Turkish than the Sultan. Derby's resignation had not been announced, and he was urged to withdraw it. After a day of thought he agreed. 'I am a check on the Prime Minister, and though I do not put much faith on them I have the assurances of several of my colleagues that they will support me in resisting a war-policy.'[63]

But his position was now fatally undermined; colleagues who had supported him had flaked away despite their assurances, and Disraeli increasingly took foreign policy into his own hands. The Prime Minister had his own particular confidant in St Petersburg, the British Military Attaché Frederick Wellesley. Professor Vincent describes the Colonel as 'a classic Victorian scoundrel ... a young rogue, a Disraelian young man'. The previous summer he had been accused by Salisbury of corruption, and two years later he ruined his career by capturing a lady called Kate Vaughan, who was not only a dancer and actress but the mistress of a member of White's Club.[64] In 1878, however, Wellesley was still well connected at Court as an ADC of the Queen as well as with the Prime Minister. Rumours originating with the Colonel suggested that the Russians were kept intimately informed of Cabinet discussions either by Derby or his wife in their conversations with Shuvalov. There was even a juicy rumour that Shuvalov and Lady Derby were sleeping together. The Ambassador was certainly a friend of the Derbys, and Derby often spoke frankly to him as a known supporter of the peace party in St Petersburg. But Disraeli and other Ministers also, then as now, chatted to foreign diplomats about the political scene. No one was more naturally communicative than Disraeli. At times of hectic political turmoil it was natural that the principal ambassadors at the Court of St James should collect and relay stories of what was happening in Cabinet, and there is no reliable evidence that the Derbys were particularly at fault in helping them. Indeed, Derby complained in his diary and to Disraeli of leaks from the Cabinet, which he would hardly have done if he was the main culprit.[65] But the Queen and those sympathetic to her increasingly looked on the Derbys as halfway to being traitors, and Disraeli did nothing to counter this view. By now he had abandoned the effort to keep on board the Foreign Secretary, who had consistently and successfully blocked his ambition for an adventurous foreign policy.

Events now closed in on Derby. The Turks signed with Russia the Treaty of San Stefano, which gave the Russians and their friends sweeping gains in the Balkans. Derby saw Disraeli on 11 February and 'found him excited and inclined to swagger, saying war was unavoidable; it would last three years; it would be a glorious and successful war for England ... I dissented but said little; being in truth disgusted with his reckless way of talking.'[66]

The Russians agreed not to enter Constantinople, and there was vague talk of a European conference to assess the Treaty of San Stefano. But a new and for Derby more threatening proposal entered the discussion. Disraeli, Salisbury and the majority of Ministers began to argue that Britain should insist on acquiring from Turkey an island – it might be Mytilene, or Cyprus, or Lemnos – or somewhere in the area which could serve as a base for our Army and Navy. This proposal marked a move from Disraeli's policy to Salisbury's, from helping the Turks to joining in pillaging them. Derby, now near the end of his tether, objected strongly on the grounds that such a seizure would be illegal and unnecessary. On 27 March he received no support from any colleague. The Cabinet recognised that this was the end of that particular road. Next day he walked with his wife in Green Park, discussing how they should use their newly recovered freedom. At five in the afternoon he made a short resignation statement in the Lords, to which Disraeli replied cordially and with dignity. 'Home: quiet, and a very happy evening.'[67] Salisbury was at once appointed Foreign Secretary. There was no break in the narrative of the Eastern Question; what changed was the style and vigour of its British components.

So ended a long and remarkable confrontation between Ministers on the essential principles of British foreign policy. To the general public then and since, Disraeli appeared in these closing years of his career as a serene elder statesman, resolute against the Russian Bear, presiding with wit and style over a patriotic and energetic foreign policy. The reality was different. Two concepts of foreign policy, the active with the risk of war versus the passive with the emphasis on peace, had explicitly opposed each other month after month in Cabinet. The prudent policy had prevailed, despite all the efforts of the Prime Minister, until the moment when in practice the risk of war had disappeared. Britain at last opted for boldness when boldness was no longer necessary. There was little left to be bold about. The Russians had with difficulty managed to beat the Turks but were incapable of further fighting. The window for energetic diplomacy suddenly opened wide. But Derby had neither the will nor the temperament to take that opportunity. The Prime Minister remained, subtle and eloquent as ever; the new Foreign Secretary dominated the action.

CHAPTER IV

SALISBURY

'Far called our navies melt away
On dune and headland sinks the fire,
Lo all our strength of yesterday
Is one with Nineveh and Tyre'
Kipling, 'Recessional'

The new Foreign Secretary was poised for quick action, clear in his mind, confident in the support of the Prime Minister and the Cabinet. Throughout his career Salisbury emphasised the importance of style and process. Of course the substance of policy had to be right, but a wise policy would founder if idly or pretentiously conducted. In March 1878 Salisbury had not worked out in detail how the Eastern Question should be handled, but the outline was clear. The Russians must be dragged back from Constantinople into the arena of European diplomacy, where change was negotiated by Ministers and diplomats and incorporated in multilateral treaties. She could not be allowed to hold on to the advantage which Turkey had conceded in military defeat. But to Salisbury the technique was almost as important as the objective. He later remarked modestly that he was 'only picking up the china that Derby had broken'.[1] An odd remark on the face of it, since the real complaint against Derby was not that he had broken china by rash action; rather he had insisted on keeping it locked in the cupboard as too precious for use. In Salisbury's eyes Derby's offence was not so much in the substance of policy, with which he had until recently agreed, but in the remote and passive way in which it had been conducted. Salisbury took over the Foreign Office at a moment of crisis. There was to be no more drifting, no more leisurely elaboration of intelligent arguments for doing nothing.

On 21 March 1878 Salisbury took his wife to an evening party. He returned at eleven and wrote alone at his desk until three in the morning. The Cabinet accepted the resulting document without amendment the next day and a circular dispatch of 1 April was sent out to British diplomatic posts. It became famous in British diplomatic history. Salisbury's dispatch did not go into detail about the objectionable Treaty of San Stefano which the Russians had imposed on Turkey, but concentrated on its general effect. This was 'to depress almost to the point of entire subjection, the political independence of the Government of Constantinople'. It was unacceptable to Britain that Turkey 'should be so closely pressed by the political force of a greatly superior power that its independent actions, and even existence, is almost impossible'.[2] Britain would only join in a congress which was able to examine the Treaty of San Stefano as a whole to remedy this defect.

The next few weeks were crucial. If Derby had remained in charge he would have allowed matters to develop at their own pace, relying on Bismarck to restrain the Russians and anyway not persuaded that they intended Britain any serious harm. If Disraeli had been in sole charge he would have relied on fleet movements and defiant public speeches designed to catch the anti-Russian mood, without any particular anxiety about war. By contrast Salisbury embarked on one of the most energetic and impressive enterprises in British diplomatic history, designed to check the Russians without war. He worked to resolve in advance by secret diplomacy the main issues which would make or break the proposed congress at Berlin. He acted with the benevolent understanding of Bismarck, who had already established himself as the chief arbiter of European affairs but was content to stand aside from an active role in advance of the congress. The great Chancellor was suffering painfully from shingles, and he was happy to see the Russians checked in the Balkans so long as this was done without infuriating the Czar and without a war in which Germany might have to take sides.

Within a month Salisbury reached in private three interlocking agreements with the three governments most closely involved. With the Russian Ambassador Shuvalov he agreed a complicated rearrangement of boundaries in the Balkans. The new pro-Russian state of Bulgaria would not, as in the Treaty of San Stefano, stretch south beyond the Balkans mountain range. A province south of the mountains would remain under Turkish sovereignty. In return the Russians would be allowed to keep their conquests in Asia, notably Kars and Batoum.

In real life, private diplomacy is sometimes accompanied by deafening public noise. As he negotiated Salisbury was bombarded with advice and anxieties expressed from every quarter. Public opinion in Britain was still dominated by the 'jingo' theme. The Queen as usual reflected the public mood. The royal telegrams delivered by the Post Office to Salisbury's house at Hatfield were in cipher, but the royal view was hardly a secret. In successive messages she thought she was being deceived by the Russians; she asked what was being done to warn the fleet; she worried that the Russians would play off Austria against England; she urged firm insistence on the withdrawal of Russian troops.[3] On the other side of the fence, Salisbury had to worry about the staying power of his Russian interlocutor, Ambassador Shuvalov. Whatever Salisbury chose to believe about the Ambassador's dealings a few weeks earlier with Lady Derby, he did not doubt Shuvalov's desire for peace. The question was whether he would be able to carry Czar Alexander with him against the vehement war party in St Petersburg. Nor were dealings easier with the Sultan in Constantinople, whose interests Salisbury rather reluctantly found himself protecting. The Sultan lived in an atmosphere of confused conspiracies, fearing for his throne and his life. On one matter he was clear: he was desperately short of money, and needed £4 million urgently so that he could include meat in his soldiers' rations.[4]

At the crucial moment a badly paid copyist at the Foreign Office leaked the draft Anglo-Russian agreement to the *Globe* newspaper, before all the other pieces on the board were in place. Salisbury denied the report, which was largely accurate. By nature given to frankness, even to indiscretion, he nevertheless would have thought it pedantic to allow literal truth to put his enterprise in danger.

His negotiation with Austria was not difficult. Britain at this time tried to breathe some self-confidence into the Hapsburg Empire because of its important role as a barrier to Russian ambition. But a mixture of greed and self-doubt held back Andrassy, the Austrian Foreign Minister, from any display of decisiveness. Instead he earned a reputation for 'indefatigable shiftiness'.[5] Andrassy was active in proposing transient schemes for the better ordering of the Balkans and reform of the Ottoman Empire; but in 1878 his main concern was to secure Bosnia-Herzegovina as Austria's share of the spoils without prejudicing her dignity as a Great Power by appearing to ask for it. Salisbury agreed that Austria should occupy the province without formally annexing it.

More difficult was the crucial arrangement with the Turks. Salisbury could tell the Turks that he was rescuing for them a slice of southern Bulgaria which they did not now particularly want. But he was conceding the Russian gains in Asia and was, moreover, determined to take Cyprus from the Ottoman Empire for Britain and to supervise reforms in Turkish Asia through a series of British consulates. This was a tough line from a country which Turkey had hitherto believed was its only effective protector. Salisbury had none of the sentimental sympathy for the Ottoman Empire and its tawdry but exotic splendour which lurked at the back of Disraeli's mind. Salisbury's aim was not to save Turkish rule in Europe but to bring it to an end over time in a way which did not upset the balance of power. He allowed the Sultan only forty-eight hours to consider the proposed secret convention. The time limit expired on the day of the Queen's birthday party in the new Foreign Office building. It was a tense evening. If the Turks had turned down the plan Salisbury's energetic diplomacy would have failed, just as surely as Derby's lassitude. At the party the Foreign Secretary received the news of the Turkish acceptance without emotion. He was establishing a tradition of cool reaction to events which fitted well alongside his occasional bursts of energy.

The way was now clear for the carefully planned Congress of Berlin. The essential work had already been done. Bismarck thoroughly enjoyed his role as its host and chairman, and claimed all credit for its success. Bismarck was perfecting the art of supporting Austria and deterring the Russians without driving them into alliance with France. In these manoeuvres Britain was useful, and Bismarck greatly preferred Disraeli and Salisbury to the moralising of Gladstone. But he misjudged the balance between the two British delegates. He flattered Disraeli, whose French was poor, by encouraging him to address the Congress in English on the grounds that it would be a privilege to listen to such a master of the language. He praised the Prime Minister in the celebrated phrase 'Der Alte Jude, das ist der Mann' while in another language dismissing Salisbury as 'ce clergyman laïque, obstiné et maladroit'.[6] But Salisbury, acting independently, had done the spadework for the success claimed by Bismarck and Disraeli.

Disraeli played a stylish rather than a masterful role in Berlin. He never gripped the detail of the different sections of negotiation. Salisbury wrote of 'the Chief': 'he is not really false; but has such a perfect disregard for facts that it is almost impossible for him to run true'. And again, because of 'Bismarck's extraordinary mode of speech, Disraeli has the dimmest idea of what is going on – understands everything crossways – and imagines a perpetual conspiracy'.[7] The Prime Minister was seventy-three and ailing, but his appetite for manoeuvre and intrigue had not weakened, and he thoroughly enjoyed his first and last international conference. The classless but class-conscious novelist relished the company of chancellors and princes, with the head of the house of Cecil at his side. He gaily dismissed some cautious reservations which reached him from Cabinet colleagues in London: 'they are all middle class men and I have always observed through life that middle class men are afraid of responsibility'. His combination with Salisbury worked well. After nearly fifteen years of relative inaction Britain was back at the centre of European affairs, and the Russians had been dramatically halted short of Constantinople. That was, anyway, how British public opinion saw it. Charing Cross station was decked with flowers to greet the two returning statesmen, notably a huge display supplied by the Queen's florist Mr John Wills of South Kensington, the whole amounting to 10,000 plants.[8] Disraeli left the train on Salisbury's arm, and the two men drove in an open barouche to 10 Downing Street, where Disraeli read a letter of congratulation from the Queen and told the cheering crowd: 'Lord Salisbury and I have brought you back peace, but peace with honour.' This was the kind of exuberance from which Salisbury himself recoiled. He was well aware of the realities of power both in Britain and in Europe.

Disraeli's reputation helped to defuse the criticism of 'jingoes', who were indignant that Russia had been able to avoid total humiliation in Asia and keep Batoum and Kars. A more valid criticism was passed by the historian A.J.P. Taylor almost a hundred years later in this pithy epitaph on the Congress:

> Great Britain won a bloodless victory with a music hall song, a navy of museum pieces and no land forces at all, except the 7,000 troops sent demonstratively to Malta ... The resounding achievement of 1878 weakened the effectiveness of British policy in the long run; for it led the British public to believe that they could play a great role without expense or exertion – without reforming their navy, without creating an army, without finding an ally.[9]

Salisbury kept to the minimum the deceit which he practised on others, and rarely deceived himself. He would have agreed that there had been an element of bluff in the British success, and bluff was a tactic which he used as seldom as possible. But the bluff worked through his own shrewd and forceful diplomacy. The substance in terms of power might be shaky, but the process had been brilliant.

So the new Foreign Secretary brought to an end the crisis which had dislodged his predecessor. But who was this newcomer? There is no doubt about his importance in the story of British foreign policy. What mix of temperament and ideas worked in this man to produce the exceptional dominance which he achieved? To those who knew him from a distance, the Marquess of Salisbury in his last years represented everything that was certain and respectable in an age when these were prime virtues. His stately figure, solid but not fat, his high brow and abundant beard conveyed authority; they might have belonged to an eminent Victorian poet, scientist or bishop. The passing years worked in his favour until his health failed. Like the Queen herself, he went on and on; he seemed always to have been there, outwardly serene and for years virtually unchallenged. By the turn of the century it became as hard to imagine a young Lord Salisbury as a young Queen Victoria; hard also to imagine an England without them. Only a certain sharpness of phrase and occasional indiscretion suggested that behind the impressive façade there had once been turmoil and uncertainty.

Salisbury's authority over himself and others was achieved as well as inherited. Born as Robert Cecil in 1830, he was the third son of the 2nd Marquess, with no expectation of succeeding to the title and the huge estate. His mother died before he was ten, and he had no siblings close to him in age. He grew up with an appetite for solitude which never left him. Eton and Christ Church, Oxford were natural staging posts for a boy of his background, but neither suited him. He was bullied at Eton and disliked the place, until the time came to send his children there. At Oxford and for years after he suffered what he called 'nerve storms'[10] which involved depression and weariness. Unusually, he was sent for the sake of his health on a tour of the Cape, Australia and New Zealand, which lasted almost two years. He returned in better health but unenthusiastic about the various choices of career open to him. 'All modes of life are equally uninviting,' he wrote to his father from abroad.[11] The immediate problem was solved in August 1853 when he was elected to the House of Commons as Conservative Member for Stamford. More important was his marriage four years later to the strong-minded daughter of a judge. Georgina Alderson brought with her no fortune but a sympathy with her shy and serious husband's intellectual and political interests. She raised his spirits and sustained him during a happy marriage of forty-two years. The first result of this partnership, however, was a breach with his father; the 2nd Marquess did not believe that a Cecil should marry into the professional classes. The estrangement meant that Robert Cecil had to work for his living; his choice of journalism alongside his unpaid career in the Commons provided him with intellectual stimulus as well as a necessary income. The strong, sometimes savage, tone of his articles in the Tory *Quarterly Review* attracted plenty of attention. They resemble Macaulay's more famous essays in the powerful and practical thrust of each argument; both writers hammer home their point with a force which can topple into overstatement.

Cecil's elder brother was in desperate health, and Cecil's unworthy marriage was forgiven once it was clear that he would soon be his father's heir. The reconciliation eased his finances and edged forward his career in the Commons. In 1866 he became Secretary of State for

India in Lord Derby's final, short-lived Conservative Government. But further progress was blighted by a bitter political quarrel in 1867 over the Reform Bill. Cecil had been willing to accept a reform which would give the vote to a substantial number of householders in the towns and cities. But the Bill which Disraeli triumphantly carried went further than Cecil and two of his Cabinet colleagues thought had been agreed, and they resigned. To Cecil, Disraeli's manoeuvre was proof of trickery. He had long suspected Disraeli as an unprincipled adventurer, and for seven years the breach between them was complete. But in 1874 Disraeli won his first and only clear election victory. Because of his ability, Salisbury (he succeeded to the title in 1868) was an obvious candidate for high office. For Salisbury, as for most politicians of integrity, the attraction of politics was not fame but the opportunity to take decisions. From this point of view the twenty-one years he had spent almost entirely in Opposition had been fruitless. The opportunity for office might not come again. As we have seen, though his dislike of Disraeli was still strong he entered the Government, first as Secretary of State for India, then as Foreign Secretary.

The opinions of most of us are largely shaped by events, and therefore change as the world changes. That was less true of Salisbury than of most Foreign Secretaries. The views of the aged Prime Minister who retired in 1902 were not precisely the same as those of the energetic new Foreign Secretary of 1878 or indeed of the slashing journalist of the 1860s. But the underlying tone and philosophy did not change. Salisbury throughout spoke and acted as a realist who did not intend to share or be deceived by the enthusiasms of the moment, even as he took account of them. His background, intellect and character gave him a position detached by several paces from those enthusiasms, whatever they might be. Irony was his natural idiom. He felt no passion for office when out of government, or for popularity when a Minister. He was not blind to the importance of these motives in the lives of others, but he did not feel obliged to share them. This did not mean that he lacked any moving spirit or that his mind was simply a machine, calculating without emotion the realities of each day of political life. Two underlying convictions, or rather characteristics, shaped his thoughts and decisions.

First, he was a Christian. Unlike Disraeli or Derby, he felt personally involved in the religious issues which played a much larger part in the politics of his day than is conceivable now. A firm Anglican throughout his life, Salisbury had been strongly attracted at Oxford to the Tractarian movement. The Tractarians exalted the position of the Church of England as a true descendant of the old medieval Church and showed affection for ritual, vestments, Gothic architecture and the sacrament rather than the sermon. The Tractarians were harassed from both sides, by the defection to Rome of some of their most ardent supporters, notably Newman, and by a hostile Protestant reaction within the Church of England. After 1874 Salisbury spent many hours arguing in Cabinet criticising the Public Worship Regulation Bill, which sought to restrain by law what the Protestants decried as Romish practices. But apart from such matters religion was for Salisbury essentially a private matter. He worshipped every day in the private chapel at Hatfield and went to church twice on Sundays; but he rarely talked about his faith. His personal belief fitted his preference for solitude. Faith was a holy mystery, at the heart of which was God. There was not a great deal more which could be said on the subject in public by a gentleman.[12] He recoiled from the notion that Christianity could be used for everyday political purposes, let alone paraded as an argument in public speeches or party manifestos. He rejected as vulgar and hypocritical the Christian element in Gladstone's denunciation of the Bulgarian atrocities or his exaltation of the right to life among the Afghan snows. Salisbury did not believe that the rules of personal conduct could be applied without modification to dealings between nations. Quietly and behind the scenes, Salisbury did what he could to relieve the plight of the Sultan of Turkey's Christian subjects; but Disraeli exaggerated when in his temporary exasperation in the spring of 1877 he told the Queen that Salisbury 'is thinking more of raising the Cross on the cupola of St Sophia than of the power of England'.[13] Salisbury would have thought this a disreputable as well as an unrealistic ambition for a British government. He was never on any subject a crusader.

Indeed, as a Christian, he had a thorough dislike of war, and did his utmost to avoid it. The last major European conflict, the Crimean War between 1854 and 1856, had been in his view botched and unnecessary; he dreaded a repetition. He was not a pacifist, and more than once the threat that Britain might go to war in Europe lay at the back of his diplomacy. This was true, for example, before the Congress of Berlin in 1878, and again, as we shall see, during the Fashoda crisis with France in 1898. But on each occasion the stakes were important and on each occasion Salisbury's diplomacy was carefully organised to make war unlikely. True, being a man of his century, he drew a distinction in his mind between a European war and lesser colonial conflicts in Asia or Africa. The second kind of war should be avoided if possible, but did not for him amount to the same catastrophe as a war between the Great Powers in Europe. It was lucky for Britain that her foreign policy in the last and potentially dangerous quarter of the nineteenth century was in the hands of Lord Salisbury rather than of a man like Disraeli or Gladstone, both of whom, for quite opposite motives (the one for national prestige, the other for an ethical crusade), might have stumbled into a major war without wanting it.

'Our first duty is towards the people of this country,' Salisbury once declared when Prime Minister, 'to maintain their interests and their rights; our second is to all humanity.'[14] That was the order in which he addressed every issue; but the second duty was not neglected because it came second. There was a substratum of morality in Salisbury's search for as peaceful and stable a world as possible, no less real because, unlike Gladstone, he never displayed or gloried in it.

Salisbury's other fundamental characteristic was his conservatism, which was profound and particularly English. He did not, like Metternich, suppose that change could or should always be resisted. The subtlety and intelligence of the Austrian Chancellor between 1814 and 1848 were devoted to propping up the fortunes of traditional Europe, stopping the leaks and keeping the flood waters at bay, suppressing a revolt here, annulling a constitution there. This became the tradition of Continental conservatism, and is one reason why, on the whole, Continental conservative parties have not prospered. Salisbury believed that change was inevitable – but also that it would be for the worse. He had none of the underlying optimism of more typical Victorians like Peel or Prince Albert, let alone Cobden or Bright. The duty of a statesman in his view was not to resist the flood, but to postpone and mitigate its impact by finding the least harmful channel into which it could flow.

This was particularly true for him of the British constitutional scene. Salisbury was not a democrat, though he constantly emphasised the power of public opinion. Change was necessary to avoid revolution, but he believed that the pace of political change should be as slow as possible. He quarrelled with Disraeli over the 1867 Reform Bill because he believed that Disraeli, while pretending to be a Conservative, was pressing on the accelerator for short-term political gain. His main domestic argument against Gladstone was that, as the aged Liberal leader tried to mobilise the masses for a radical programme, he risked sparking off a vicious class war. At home, Salisbury presided over a period of intense social change, but change inspired by individuals and groups rather than by his Government. With the important exception of local government, he provided a long pause between the reforming energy of Peel and Gladstone, and the fresh burst of change under Asquith and Lloyd George.

Salisbury applied his conservative instincts particularly to foreign affairs. This was his favourite field long before he had any practical responsibility for it. Two anonymous articles in the *Quarterly Review* showed how his mind was forming in his early years. They are written in the combative style which he later allowed to mellow, but never entirely shook off.

The first article, on foreign policy in general, was written in 1864 as part of an attack on the failures of Palmerston's Government in foreign policy during his last years. He drew a contrast between the dim reputation of Britain as he wrote and the great days of the Congress of Vienna, when 'whatever the language in which they were couched, whatever the wisdom of the statesman from whom they came, Foreign Ministers never forgot that they were backed up, in case of need, by the fleet that had baffled Napoleon, and the army that had fought at Waterloo'. By 1864, however, we were 'without a single ally and without a shred of influence'. 'Our courage is not only disbelieved but it is ridiculed as an impostor that has been found out.' Palmerston was practising 'a portentous mixture of bounce and baseness'. His Government was ruthless in bullying a small country like Brazil over a trivial incident, but had failed to stand up to Russia when she suppressed the Polish revolt of 1863 or to Prussia when she went to war with Denmark over Schleswig-Holstein. Salisbury argued that we were free to intervene in such cases, or not as we wished, but we had an obligation to make up our minds, and in this we had failed. In each of these cases Britain had hinted at intervention and then drawn back. Salisbury was particularly scathing about Palmerston's rash and well-known speech in which he had said that if anyone attacked Denmark 'it would not be with Denmark alone' that they would have to contend. Now Britain's 'pledges and her threats are gone with last year's snow, and she is content to watch with cynical philosophy the destruction of those who trusted to the one and the triumph of those who were wise enough to spurn the other'.[15]

This was good rollicking Macaulayesque denunciation; but there was another statesman whom Salisbury was ready to follow. Indeed, he had two years earlier set out in another essay for the *Quarterly Review* his reasons for admiring Castlereagh. This was the man who really understood diplomacy. He analysed Castlereagh's part in the Congress of Vienna of 1814. 'There is nothing dramatic in the success of a diplomatist. His victories are made up of a series of microscopic advantages; of a judicious suggestion here, of an opportune civility there; of a wise concern at one moment, and a far sighted persistence at another; of sleepless tact, immovable calmness, and patience that no folly, no provocation, no blunders can shake.'[16] Castlereagh, he argued, was not operating on a blank sheet of paper. He had to sustain the coalition against Napoleon and that meant honouring previous pledges, however unwise. The eventual settlement offended against the principle of nationality, but that was inevitable. Nationality was too fleeting a principle to be of much practical use. In Salisbury's analysis, Castlereagh possessed a serene, impassive intelligence free from enthusiastic passion, and this was 'an affront and an offence to the literary class'. He was not a reactionary like Metternich, but believed that great questions like the future of Italy should follow their natural course without interference from outside. Castlereagh was no orator, being made of 'the gold that does not glitter', and, unlike Canning, he left behind no devoted school of disciples, being 'honoured only by the silent witness of events'.

Events had weakened the British hand between Castlereagh's Congress of Vienna and Salisbury's Congress of Berlin. The army which fought at Waterloo had disappeared and Salisbury believed that it had gone for good; conscription in peacetime was universal among the Continental powers, but inconceivable in Britain. The coalition which had beaten Napoleon had likewise vanished. So, in Salisbury's view, had any realistic hope of collective decisions by a group of European powers. Special congresses could be held to wind up a major war or occasionally to prevent one, as at Berlin in 1878; but he dismissed as unreal Gladstone's lofty concept of a Concert of Europe handing down moral decisions to settle disputes between nations. As the tool of his diplomacy, Salisbury was left with the cool balancing and rebalancing of interests, preserving for Britain the flexibility which she needed as the world changed.

There was no need for the lies and deceits which were the hallmark of that other notable realist, Count Bismarck. Bismarck gave firm but contradictory secret assurances to preserve the peace in Europe after he had got what he wanted in war. Salisbury worked for the same end by giving no assurances at all. Until the last years of his premiership he used successfully a constitutional argument to resist all suggestions of a formal British alliance with another power. For example, when an alliance with Germany was discussed in 1901 he was clear that, for constitutional reasons, this would involve making promises which we would not keep:

> I do not see how, in common honesty, we could invite other nations to rely upon our aid in a struggle, which must be formidable and probably supreme, when we have no means whatever of knowing what may be the humour of our people in circumstances which cannot be foreseen ... The course of the English Government in such a crisis [a possible Franco-German war] must depend on the view taken by public opinion in this country, and public opinion would be largely, if not exclusively, governed by the nature of the casus belli.[17]

In a democratic age, most politicians would have gone on to praise the underlying wisdom of the people, accepting not only that politicians had to follow public opinion but also that public opinion got it right. Salisbury would have regarded this as humbug. He served his apprenticeship in foreign affairs at a time when public opinion appeared to veer within months from backing Gladstone's passionate denunciation of the Bulgarian atrocities committed by Turkey, to equally passionate clamour that Britain should defend Turkey against Russian attack, and then back to rejection in the general election of the Conservative Government which had successfully done exactly that. Part of the problem was, of course, the difficulty of measuring opinion. Were by-elections the best test, or press articles, or attendance at the increasing number of mass meetings? The problem has not been solved, only complicated, in the age of television, the internet and opinion polls. But Salisbury's critique was more fundamental, as expressed in a letter to Lord Lytton in 1876 about popular feeling: 'They wake up for a moment from time to time, when you least look for it – roused by some panic or wounded sentiment, or some sharp suffering which they lay at the door of the wrong person and the wrong law. But for the most part they are politically asleep; and must never be counted upon to resist their real enemies or sustain their real friends, at the right moment.'[18] Two years later he was making the same point to his Ambassador in Constantinople. 'This country is popularly governed and cannot therefore be counted on to act on any uniform or consistent system of policy.'[19]

Nevertheless, it was this unreliable power of public opinion which Salisbury constantly cited when resisting suggestions that Britain should enter into an alliance based on a promise to go to war in particular circumstances. In truth, Salisbury used this argument because it saved him from having to expound his real reasons for avoiding any firm alliance. He saw a world of constantly shifting elements, some of which could be dangerous for Britain. There was no fundamental clash of political creeds in that world, no natural ally or special relationship, no axis of evil. There were individuals who rose and fell, nations in different phases of prosperity or decline, in different modes of benevolence or malevolence towards Britain; there were accidents in faraway places which could produce unforeseen consequences.

Salisbury was by nature sceptical of experts or anyone who claimed to foretell the future with any exactness. Britain had nothing to demand of the world except the right to hold what she possessed and to trade and invest as freely and live as comfortably with other countries as was practicable. 'My definition of foreign policy', he once said, 'is that we ought to behave as any gentleman would – who wishes to get on with his neighbours.'[20] The metaphor of the country gentleman is rather too bland for the reality of Salisbury's diplomacy. He was acutely conscious of the dangers of Britain's position. He judged that it was not compatible with British interests to line Britain up with one or two of his neighbours in rivalry with the rest.

Those interests were already scattered widely round the world, but when it came to the crunch only two really mattered, the security of the British Isles, and India. To the Victorians, India was different from any of the other territories under British rule. Her value to Britain as a market and outlet for investment went alongside the ability of the Indian Army to contribute troops for British purposes anywhere in the world. These practical advantages may have been exaggerated, but by the late nineteenth century they were being sublimated into a sense of the uniqueness of the Raj. The Mutiny of 1857 had dissolved any illusion that the leaders of India would (as Macaulay had hoped) settle down submissively to the process of becoming Asian Englishmen steeped in the English language and happy tales of Magna Carta and Agincourt. Disraeli's promotion of the Queen to Empress of India was in practical terms an empty gesture, but it conveyed the impression of amazing power, of millions of Asians ruled by a handful of Englishmen, benevolently and under the rule of law, in an enterprise which no other European power came anywhere near matching.

But by its nature the Indian enterprise was fragile, vulnerable to internal revolt and foreign invasion from across the mountains to the north. Equally important were the lines of communication between Britain and India, originally round the Cape but, since the 1860s, through the Suez Canal. Egypt and the Cape thus became essential British concerns derived from the supreme concern with India; each bred an array of subordinate interests and ambitions which took up much of Salisbury's time. This nexus of interests was more important strategically than the other regions which were coloured red on the map, including the areas settled by emigrants from Britain. Towards the end of his career, he had to wrestle and come to terms with the advocates of the new imperialism. But he never came near to believing that the future white dominions weighed heavy in the balance of British interests as compared with India and the approaches to India.

The British Empire expanded rapidly during the quarter-century of Salisbury's influence. One phrase, 'splendid isolation', gained such wide currency that we are tempted to believe that British policy had launched itself into the open seas and no longer felt any close concern with the intrigues and alliances of Continental Europe. The truth is different. Salisbury refused any Continental alliances, but throughout his career he concentrated over-whelmingly on shifting events and relationships in Europe. He believed in a 'good natured, good humoured effort to keep well with your neighbours' and contrasted this with 'that spirit of haughty and sullen isolation which has been dignified with the name of non-intervention. We are part of the community of Europe, and we must do our duty as such.'[21]

This conclusion rested not just on neighbourly feelings but also on cool analysis. Britain's main strategic asset was the Royal Navy. The Navy protected the British Isles and projected British policy to every corner of the world. It was crucial to keep the Navy supreme on the seas, and Salisbury took sharp action when it became clear that this supremacy was faltering. But she had no army worth mentioning in the same sentence as the big Continental armies. Bismarck jested in his brutal way that if the British Army invaded the German coast he would send the local police to round them up. There was a limit in practice to what the Indian Army could be asked to do for Britain and, until the Boer War, conscription was thought to be inconceivable in peacetime Britain. This did not prevent some politicians pretending otherwise. 'Curzon always wants me to talk to Russia as if I had 500,000 men at my back, and I have not,' Salisbury complained.[22] There was also a limit to what the Navy could do. When in 1895 public opinion was inflamed against Turkish atrocities, Salisbury observed that the Royal Navy could not surmount the Taurus Mountains to rescue the Armenians.[23] Britain was in effect one-armed. In 1870, the British standing Army was 100,000-strong compared with the Russian Army of one and a half million and the new Germany Army of over a million. Salisbury summed up the position towards the end of his life with his usual irony. 'The fact that Providence is generally on the side of the big battalions is a nuisance for the only country whose institutions do not allow her to possess that luxury.'[24]*

During Salisbury's first years as Foreign Secretary, Bismarck was putting into place the intricate mechanisms with which he hoped to secure Germany's position as the leading European power. At the heart of his system was the alliance with Austria. The old rivalry between Austria and Prussia had ended in the defeat of Austria and the transformation of Prussia into a united Germany. Austria evolved into the Austro-Hungarian Empire, whose main concern was its own integrity in an age of growing nationalism. Italy, eager to play a leading part in a game for which she was not qualified, was allowed to join and this resulted in the Triple Alliance. Its architect, Bismarck, while wishing by this means to hold Russia in check in the Balkans, did not want to antagonise her to the point where she would make an alliance with France. The weak point of Bismarck's system was the harsh settlement imposed on France in 1871 after the Franco-Prussian War, and in particular the seizure of Alsace-Lorraine. Since reconciliation with France proved impossible, she had to be kept isolated. This involved the secret Reinsurance Treaty with Russia, and the public coming together in the conservative Dreikaiserbund of the Emperors of Austria, Germany and Russia.

Bismarck's activities in Europe seemed to pose no particular threat to Britain. Salisbury's main anxieties in those early years were elsewhere. He was not instinctively anti-Russian, but there seemed no doubt that Russia constituted the main threat to India. She was gradually expanding eastwards, and many believed there was a real danger of a Russian invasion through Afghanistan, bypassing the mountains of the Hindu Kush. Opinion among successive Viceroys of India and their advisers was divided. Salisbury believed we must establish a substantial mission in Afghanistan. 'We cannot conquer it; we cannot leave it alone. We can only spare it our utmost vigilance.'[25]

More attention had to be given to Russian ambitions in the Balkans, not because the Balkans themselves were crucial to Britain, but because Russia's control of the Balkans meant control of Con-

---

* That letter was written to General Roberts, the man who later proclaimed the need of conscription in Britain after the reverses of the Boer War. The argument only prevailed in the overwhelming necessities of the Great War in 1916.

stantinople. This would mean a powerful Russian influence in the Mediterranean, which was supposed to pose a threat to the vital link with India through the Suez Canal. Russia's main rival in the Balkans was Austria, and German backing for Austria was thus seen as helpful to Britain. The logic was questionable, but the assumptions were shared by almost all.

Salisbury's other anxiety was France. Personally, he enjoyed France, and spent much time in his homes there, the first a hideous Gothic building called the Chalet Cecil near Dieppe, replaced by a warmer villa on the Riviera. But he was a close student of the French Revolution and believed there were lessons there which the volatile French had not fully absorbed. The savagery of the Paris Commune in 1871 was followed by its ruthless repression, and then by a succession of insecure governments. From time to time there was a suspicion that a Napoleonic figure might emerge. Rivalry between Britain and France persisted in several parts of the world, and was most dangerous in Egypt (once again) because of the relevance to Britain's link with India. Salisbury never seriously contemplated a firm alliance with such a volatile country as France, but he kept the Anglo-French disagreements within bounds. As A.J.P. Taylor put it, the 'Anglo-French disputes, though fierce, were family quarrels between two nations with a common situation and common liberalism; they were conducted with all the bitterness, but also within the limits of a parliamentary debate'.[26]

Against this analysis of the European scene, without foreknowledge of what Germany would become, there was a case for Britain moving closer to Bismarck. It was put urgently as early as 1879 to Salisbury by his Ambassador in Berlin, Odo Russell:

I cannot but think that the friendship of a European statesman is worth cultivating who can mobilise a million men in ten days, whose power is irresponsible, and who can reckon with certainty on the sanction of his sovereign and the support of his nation. Bismarck's weakness is vanity. He likes to be connected. If we neglect him he will drift back into the already open arms of Russia — to keep France out of them. Our relations with Germany are excellent, and could be more intimate and useful if Her Majesty's Government cared to try the experiment.[27]

Salisbury consistently declined the experiment. He respected Bismarck's importance and intelligence and was happy to do business with him. But he avoided a closer embrace for good reasons. He distrusted the man, and was strongly backed in this by Queen Victoria. Fear rather than trust was the currency in which Bismarck preferred to deal. Salisbury felt no particular fear of Bismarck's million men, no wish to push France into a corner and no desire to enter into formal alliance with any European power or combination. His policy, as he wrote, was 'to lean to the Triple Alliance without belonging to it'.[28] He maintained an active, even intrusive policy in all European matters, the very reverse of isolation, because he was sure that the keys to Britain's security, including her rule of India, were kept within her own Continent. It was only in the last few years of his life that the performance of the United States and Japan became so consistently forceful as to propel both powers on to the world stage and to change dramatically the rules of the game of which Salisbury up to then had been master.

The Eastern Question had made Salisbury Foreign Secretary; the Eastern Question absorbed most of his attention in his first years in the job. It had certainly not been answered definitively by the Congress of Berlin; nor did Salisbury believe that such an answer was available. He wrote characteristically to the Ambassador in St Petersburg on 4 February 1880, it 'is a fallacy to assume that within our lifetime any stable arrangement can be arrived at in the East. The utmost we can do is to provide halting places where the process of change may rest awhile.'[29]

Where, from the British point of view, was the best halting place for the 1880s? Here Salisbury encountered within his own mind and in his dealings with others the dangerous difficulties which a fixed idea can create, even for intelligent human beings. Sometimes faulty ideas blow up in the faces of those who hold them. This was true in 1956 of Eden's obsession about Nasser at the time of Suez, and of the obsession of Bush and Blair in 2003 about Iraq's weapons of mass destruction. Sometimes such ideas linger on for decades; when they are challenged their proponents dig ever deeper trenches to defend them, so that the task of dislodging them becomes even more difficult. Such was the domino theory, which diplomats in Washington drew from the failure of appeasement in the 1930s and then applied rigidly during the Cold War, culminating in the tragic miscalculation that if Vietnam became Communist the other states of South-East Asia were bound to go the same way. Less damaging but equally misguided was the persistence with which Disraeli and many others believed that Constantinople was the gateway to India, so that it was a prime British interest to secure the city against Russian attack. Constantinople became the touchstone of British courage. It was of Constantinople that the music hall crowd thought when they sang the jingo song; it was Constantinople that haunted Queen Victoria when she talked of abdication at the heat of the crisis with Lord Derby; the safety of Constantinople became for Disraeli the test of British power and prestige.

The logic of this argument was not clear. Not even Disraeli admired the Turkish system of rule on its own merits. The rules about use of the Straits by shipping were endlessly negotiated and redefined; but the Russians then had no Black Sea fleet and the practical question was whether British warships could enter the Black Sea, not whether a Russian fleet could descend on Egypt and the Suez Canal. Disraeli's fear was that the Russian army, once in sight of Constantinople and the Straits, would swoop through Syria and Palestine on to the Canal. Yet it had taken a Russian army almost a year in 1877 to battle southwards from the Romanian frontier and arrive exhausted at the gates of Constantinople. Cairo was a great deal further on. The idea of a quick Russian swoop on Egypt was unreal.

The link between the essential interests of Britain and the survival of the Ottoman Empire based on Constantinople died hard. Salisbury had a strong general view about the danger of ancient arguments. This particularly applied to the Eastern Question. 'I feel convinced that the old policy – wise in its time – of defending English interests by sustaining the Ottoman dynasty has become impracticable, and I think that the time has come for defending English interests in a more bold way by some territorial rearrangement. But these are dreams. English policy is to float lazily downstream, occasionally putting out a diplomatic boathook to avoid collision.'[30]

That letter was written when Derby was still in charge of the boat and the boathook. It was ironical that Salisbury's burst of energy when he took charge served to revive the old policy which he had in private described as dead. The most dramatic outcome of the

Congress of Berlin was indeed to support the Turks and keep the Russians away from the gates of Constantinople. Salisbury found that he could not so easily cut away from the past and its pre-occupation with Constantinople. He wrote years later that he pitied the political party which held office when the Russians occupied Constantinople. They would share the fate of Lord North's party, which lost America.[31] This was simply to recognise a political reality at home, outdated but still strong. In private in 1886 he admitted that all along we had been backing the wrong horse.[32] By then Salisbury had to acknowledge that we could no longer control the Straits or influence the future of Constantinople; but by that time, thanks to his own foresight and the unpredictable turn of events, a more realistic policy for defending our communications with India was in place.

In the Anglo-Turkish Convention which Salisbury negotiated in advance of the Congress of Berlin, the first elements of this new policy were set out. Part of the final argument with Derby had been whether Britain needed a *place d'armes* in the eastern Mediterranean. By this was meant a base nearer to the Canal than Malta where British ships and regiments from Britain or India could congregate and prepare for any operation that might be needed. Cyprus was selected for this purpose, and the Sultan persuaded to cede the island in return for a British guarantee of Turkey's Asian borders. But such a guarantee depended in practice on a reasonable standard of Turkish administration of their Asian subjects, particularly those who were Christian. Salisbury devised and the Turks accepted a system of British or other European advisers posted as consuls across their territories. The parallel, though not one explained to the Sultan, was with the system in the Indian princely states, or with the consuls being established with their privileges in the Treaty Ports of China. This would be an example of influence exerted on the spot and veering towards indirect rule, a system which Salisbury and most of his generation greatly preferred as less expensive and less trouble-some than outright annexation. 'Good government in Asia', he wrote, 'means government by good men', and Britain had plenty of these. Unfortunately the Cabinet refused to sanction a loan to Turkey which could have financed the administrative reforms.[33] In any case the experiment was not given time to establish itself.

The annexation of Cyprus, and indeed the whole Berlin settlement, was denounced by Gladstone in the Midlothian campaign which ended in his triumphant election victory in 1880. But Gladstone found it much easier to denounce Disraeli's view than to replace it. The new Liberal Government decided reluctantly to hang on to Cyprus, but they swept away the new system of advisers in Turkey's Asian territories before it could get going.* The paradox of liberalism ran through these decisions. Gladstone wanted to see a decent standard of living in Asia, but was uneasy about dictating those values through intervention. The advisers might have deterred future atrocities, but their presence in a foreign sovereign state was unpalatable to the man who had criticised Palmerston for behaving like 'a gallant knight at a tournament'.

By accident and very much against his will, Gladstone's Liberal Government provided Britain with a more definite means of defending the link to India. The actual occupation of Egypt by a British army would provide better security for the Suez Canal than a fleet defending Constantinople or the possession of Cyprus. If that point had been put to Salisbury when he first became Foreign Secretary in 1878 he would have rejected it as impracticable. Cyprus could be annexed by agreement with the Sultan in Constantinople; but the Sultan would never consent to give up his sovereignty over Egypt in the same way. The Egyptian population would be hostile. Above all, the French would never agree, and the French were the dominant European power in Egypt. They had built the Suez Canal. They had played the largest part in the process which had fastened informal European control on Egypt, namely the financing of the inexhaustible debts of the Khedive who ruled the country under Turkish sovereignty. Disraeli's purchase of the Khedive's shares in the Suez Canal Company had shifted the balance somewhat in Britain's favour, but that was an enjoyable *coup de théâtre*, not a shift in policy. A system of dual Anglo-French control had evolved in Egypt which Salisbury had no intention of upsetting.

But events destroyed a system which both Britain and France were keen to preserve. In 1881, a year after Gladstone became Prime

* Ironically Cyprus, having passed eighty not particularly glorious years as a British colony, now once again provides a *place d'armes* for Britain in the Sovereign Base Area.

Minister, an Egyptian nationalist revolt under Colonel Arabi threatened the Khedive and all European interests. The French and British fleets gathered to react at Alexandria, but the French pulled out at the last minute. The British alone bombarded Alexandria, and the British alone followed up by routing the nationalist forces on shore at the Battle of Tel-el-Kebir. Gladstone had been compelled to act as if he were Disraeli, to the indignation of the French and the amusement of the Conservatives whose similar actions in the Transvaal and Afghanistan he had denounced with such passion. So Salisbury, returning to power in 1885, this time as Prime Minister as well as Foreign Secretary, found his country in sole occupation of Egypt. For the rest of his period in office his diplomatic stance remained virtually unchanged. Britain was in 'temporary' occupation of Egypt. Attempts were made to negotiate with the Sultan an arrangement for British withdrawal after five years, with a right of re-entry in case of invasion by someone else. These negotiations failed. Britain was always, in theory, ready to withdraw, but the time was never ripe. Salisbury and others argued that it would not be right to hand the Egyptian people back to anarchy and misrule. As A.J.P. Taylor observed, the British 'have always been anxious to show that in defending their own interests they are serving the interests of everyone else'.[34]

The French were wholly unpersuaded. They had accepted the British annexation of Cyprus, once Salisbury had pointed them in the direction of Tunis (another Turkish dominion), which became a French protectorate in 1881.* But Egypt was different. This was much the most important matter in dispute between Britain and France, and for many years held up an understanding between the two to which most other factors pointed.

The British tried to combine a military occupation which was crucial to them strategically with an effort to cleanse the Egyptian administration and improve the lot of the Egyptian peasant. Evelyn Baring, later elevated by Salisbury to become Lord Cromer, directed the process of reform, particularly in the fields of justice and finance, as British Agent and Consul General accredited to the Khedive. His

* Salisbury's actual advice to the French Foreign Minister was 'Prenez Tunis, Carthage ne doit pas rester aux barbares' – see Andrew Roberts, *Salisbury* (London: Weidenfeld & Nicolson, 1999), p. 203.

integrity was undoubted, and his authority could not be questioned. The arrangement was temporary, and endured. As the historians Robinson and Gallagher put it: 'The native authority could hardly revive while Baring ruled. Yet Baring had to rule until the native authority revived.'[35]

Gladstone's Ministry had left a further shadow over this scene. The Sudan was crucial to Egypt because the Nile flowed through it. But when the British public thought of the Sudan in 1885 they did not worry about Egypt's water supply. They saw a lonely heroic figure, British and Christian, standing at the top of the steps of the palace in Khartoum, facing death from a hundred spears because of the indecision and incompetence of the British Government. Salisbury, taking office a few months later, was well aware of this but the avenging of General Gordon could wait. The fanatical Muslims who had killed Gordon and controlled the Sudan did not have the technical competence to interrupt the flow of the Nile. Should another ruler, particularly a European power, move towards control of these upper waters, then the time would come for Gordon to be avenged.

Salisbury never forgot the Balkans. Randolph Churchill, Chancellor of the Exchequer in his Government of 1886, argued that Britain should take no further interest in the Balkan tangle and simply concentrate on Asia. But Salisbury was not yet ready for this. 'The question is', he wrote to Churchill on 1 October 1886, 'where we should draw the line. I draw it at Constantinople. My belief is that the main strength of the Tory Party both in the richer and poorer classes has an association with the honour of the country. I am afraid you are prepared to give up Constantinople; and foreign powers will be quick to find that divergence out.'[36] This was Disraeli's old argument, using the word 'honour' rather than 'prestige'. It was the argument consistently banged out by the Queen in her many missives. For Salisbury, it was a political requirement of public opinion, no longer a serious argument about the security of Britain or India. But as a result Salisbury involved himself energetically in the long-running Bulgarian crisis.

The thinking behind the settlement at the Congress of Berlin was that Bulgaria would be in effect a Russian satellite, and must therefore be confined north of the Balkan Mountains so as to give the Turks a defensible northern frontier. Under the rule of Prince Alexander of Battenberg, young, handsome and a favourite of Queen Victoria, Bulgaria turned out differently. He asserted himself against Russian influence, gained control over the southern province which had been in dispute at Berlin, and defeated the Serbs when they attempted to interfere. Salisbury, who had argued against a greater Bulgaria at Berlin, now acknowledged that the Bulgaria which had actually come to birth was a more effective barrier to Russian advance than the demoralised Turks would ever be. There is no need to relate in detail the different episodes of the Bulgarian crisis. It bubbled angrily, but thanks to the diplomacy of Bismarck and Salisbury never came as near to boiling over into a major war as had the crisis of 1877–8.

Against this background and with the encouragement of Bismarck, Salisbury concluded secret Mediterranean agreements with Austria and Italy. The three powers agreed on the need to maintain the Sultan in his rights, though reserving the right to intervene if he took illegal action – which meant yielding too much to Russian pressure. As Salisbury emphasised to the Queen, these agreements were not a commitment to go to war, but a statement of shared diplomatic objectives. This was as far as Salisbury was prepared to go in joining a European alliance. He wrote to the Queen – 'It is as close an alliance as the parliamentary character of our institutions will permit.' He argued, rather speciously, that if Britain remained in isolation the other powers might resolve their differences by trying to divide up the British Empire between them. 'Though England could defend herself, it would be at fearful risk and cost.'[37] He had once again asserted Britain's position by a bout of energetic diplomacy.

In 1890, when he reached the age of sixty, Salisbury stood at the peak of his career. His influence was to remain great, and usually decisive, for twelve more years; but new personalities and concepts began to crowd in on him and, towards the end, undermine his control of policy. Of course this came as no surprise to him. His whole philosophy was tied to the certainty of change, to the likelihood that change would be for the worse, and to the duty of a conservative statesman to delay and soften these bad effects to the extent that this proved possible. Against this background Salisbury was never given to feelings of self-satisfaction. But by 1890 he was entitled to reflect on the solid authority which he had established for himself at home, and for his country abroad.

Since 1887 he had been Prime Minister as well as Foreign Secretary; he was to continue in both roles for most of the 1890s. This combination has been rare in British history. It could be criticised as concentrating too much power in the hands of one individual. But Salisbury was not so much a Prime Minister who ran the Foreign Office as a Foreign Secretary who happened to be head of Government. There was no suggestion that he neglected his duties as Prime Minister; but he did not interpret them as meaning the same control over the work of departments and the detail of legislation as seemed inescapable for, say, Gladstone or Margaret Thatcher. During the years when Britain was the leading nation in the world the Prime Minister's workload was much less than it is now. Our power as a nation has declined, but the instinct of Government to regulate and improve our individual lives has vastly increased the duties which a Prime Minister believes to be vital.

Salisbury was able to organise his daily life to accommodate not just the work of two great offices of State, but also his private position as an individual with strong personal interests, and as head of one of the great families of the land. He worked not from 10 Downing Street but from the more spacious and elegant office devised for the Foreign Secretary on the first floor of the new Foreign Office building which had opened in 1868. He was at his desk there only in the afternoon. Before lunch and in the evenings he tackled his boxes in his private home in Arlington Street just off Piccadilly, at Hatfield or at the House of Lords.

The nature of the work of the Foreign Secretary has hugely changed. The international meetings which now crowd his diary then occurred very rarely, perhaps to end a war once in a generation. The flurry of official visits abroad and foreign visits to London, now continuous, was then insignificant. This was the age of ambassadors, and they were a tiny band. In Salisbury's time Britain deployed nine ambassadors overseas; in 1997 the total was 149.[38] The substance of Salisbury's correspondence was with these nine ambassadors; the essence of his afternoon work was conversation with the foreign ambassadors to the Court of St James in London. Today the Foreign Secretary sees foreign ambassadors rarely; he transacts business direct with other Foreign Ministers who are his counterparts overseas or through British ambassadors accredited to foreign capitals or international institutions. In Salisbury's time the foreign ambassadors were hugely important; their varying qualities of intelligence and integrity were carefully weighed. The Russian, Shuvalov, with whom Salisbury negotiated the preliminaries of the Congress of Berlin; Waddington, the Frenchman with the English background who later became Foreign Minister; Hatzfeldt, the German at the centre of the confused discussion of an Anglo-German alliance – these were men of substance who became the real interlocutors of the Foreign Secretary, knowing more of Salisbury's views in their own particular sector than did his own officials or his Cabinet colleagues.

Salisbury operated an intensely personal system of diplomacy, which fitted his own strong preference for solitude. He carried British foreign policy in his own head; outside it existed in his occasional statements and letters, but nowhere else. He liked to think alone, and would go to considerable trouble to avoid the company even of officials who existed to help him. He was invariably polite, and appeared at all times to listen carefully to what he was being told, for example by foreign ambassadors. To guard against the inevitable tedium of some of these afternoons, Salisbury equipped himself with a paperknife in the form of a wooden dagger, with which he jabbed his thigh under the table to keep himself awake. He kept records of many of these conversations in the form of letters to his own ambassadors overseas. These letters are kept in a private Foreign Office file at Hatfield, rather than with the rest of the Foreign Office papers at the National Archives; they are filled with various notes and comments in the red ink which became (and remains) the means by which the Foreign Secretary expresses himself on paper.

The clear forceful prose which Salisbury wrote has full play in these letters. His style contrasts sharply with the convoluted sentences of Gladstone or Peel. The person whom he kept in his closest confidence was the Queen. He had learned from Disraeli how important and how difficult was this task. The Queen had her own system of correspondence in Europe, which increased its range as her children made dynastic marriages. As the Queen aged, she lost little of the tendency to wayward emotion which had complicated Salisbury's task before the Congress of Berlin. The kidnapping of her favourite princeling, Alexander of Bulgaria, in 1886 called forth a flood of execration. 'Russian fiends . . . the stepping stone to getting to Constantinople . . . intriguing right and left . . . a slap in our face . . . sickening treachery . . . Russia must be unmasked . . . Russian villains . . . not one minute must be lost . . . Russia must not triumph.'[39] Salisbury mopped up the flood with patience, earning her trust and respect. The only practical alternative to him was still Gladstone, whom she continued to fear and detest. Salisbury enciphered personally his own replies to the Queen before they were taken to the Post Office; the cipher figures are clearly in his hand.

Salisbury did not care much about his appearance; he disliked parade of any kind and did not seek popularity. He must have been aware that gradually he was building a reputation as a solid and reliable leader, intelligent but not rash like Disraeli, virtuous but not a preacher like Gladstone, loyal to the Queen but with a steadier judgement. Yet behind this reputation for steadiness there occasionally appeared traces of an individuality which bordered on the eccentric. It showed in his enthusiasm for science; by 1874 Hatfield possessed a somewhat insecure system of electric light and by 1877 a telephone. It showed in his determination to achieve as fast as possible the journey in a brougham from the Foreign Office to King's Cross station for the Hatfield train, the record time being seventeen minutes. It showed in the liberal upbringing of his exceptionally gifted children. 'Their appearance, punctuality or even cleanliness hardly mattered a jot, but their Christianity, intelligence, conversation, honesty and sense of humour were all-important.' Above all it showed in the sense of irony which dominated his whole approach to life, a quality which sometimes confused foreign ambassadors, which was unknown to the Queen and most of his colleagues, but which gave to his conduct of affairs and the records he left behind in particular a refreshing flavour not matched until the days of Winston Churchill.

Salisbury was not naturally fascinated by military or naval matters. His private interests were intellectual and scientific; his public concerns were focused on diplomacy and domestic politics. Moreover he had acquired a sceptical attitude towards the kind of advice with which generals and admirals are apt to bombard their political masters. 'No lesson seems to be so deeply inculcated by the experience of life', he wrote to Lytton on 15 June 1877, 'as that you should never trust experts. If you believe the doctors, nothing is wholesome; if you believe the theologians nothing is innocent; if you believe the soldiers, nothing is safe. They all require to have their strong wine diluted by a very large admixture of insipid common sense.'[40] Nevertheless he knew that the foundation of his foreign policy was British naval supremacy. Along the crucial eastern shores of the Mediterranean the Navy could beat the Turks at Navarino, later protect the Turks at Constantinople, threaten the Greeks at Athens on behalf of a sleazy British subject, Don Pacifico, bombard Acre in one generation and Alexandria in the next. It was the Navy which had drummed slavery off the seas once Britain had decided that slavery was wrong. Above all, the Navy safeguarded the free flow of trade which was Britain's main overseas interest.

But other countries had navies and ambitions which might cut across the British interest. Other countries might even combine against Britain. By the late 1880s Salisbury was convinced that Britain was in danger of falling behind. As usual he laid his plans carefully. He persuaded his Cabinet colleagues to hold back on their favoured expenditure projects. Public finances were adjusted to make room for the massive naval armament programme authorised by the Naval Defence Act of 1889. This was based on a two-power standard, by which the Royal Navy was to be maintained at a strength equivalent to that of the next two biggest navies in the world. This meant building over the next four years after 1889 ten new battleships, thirty-eight cruisers, eighteen torpedo boats and four fast gunboats.[41] Never before in peacetime had Britain undertaken so great a naval expansion.

The Act and the speeches of Ministers politely refrained from naming the potential enemies against whom this great new armament might serve. But in their secret papers the Lords of the Admiralty did not hold back. The crucial table of new warships was headed 'Proposed Building Programme . . . with a view of providing thoroughly against a combination of France and Russia against this country without allies'.[42] No formal alliance between France and Russia had yet been signed, but the experts could read the omens. They had just lived through the last of a long line of scares about a French invasion, ignited by the possibility that the militarist General

Boulanger might take power. Even the cool-headed Salisbury showed alarm; he minuted on Boulanger, his tongue partly in his cheek: 'His principal difficulty will be to find any policy which will unite in his favour a majority of his countrymen and the destruction of London would probably recommend him to them very strongly.'[43] As for Russia, Salisbury saw her as a large blundering nation rather than a malevolent conspirator, but her blunders across the maps of Europe and Asia could cause Britain great difficulty, as had happened in 1854 with the Crimean War and in 1877–8 before the Congress of Berlin.

The experts were right to predict a Franco-Russian alliance, but wrong to deduce that this was where the future danger to Britain lay. Hardly had construction of the new British fleet begun when the young Kaiser Wilhelm II succeeded to the throne of Germany, and dismissed Bismarck. The devious, brutal but intelligent policy of the old Chancellor was replaced, not so much with a new policy, as with a sequence of dramatic poses. They were not at first specifically anti-British, but they certainly included a new German fleet as one of the necessary attributes of a Great Power.

The other warship-building nation was the United States of America. As a journalist, Salisbury, while opposing slavery, had strongly attacked the North for seeking to impose its will by force on the South during the American Civil War. At no time in his life did he show any personal warmth towards the United States. He certainly did not believe in a 'special relationship' based on a common language or devotion to democracy, which in any case was not for Salisbury a term of praise. But the facts of power were becoming inescapable. Any arithmetic which required Britain to take account of American shipbuilding as that of a potential enemy was going to prove ruinously and unrealistically expensive. But if America was to be excluded for ever from the list of possible enemies that meant a substantial adjustment of British foreign policy. It meant listening without protest to noisy American interpretations of the Monroe Doctrine which would formerly have been contested. It meant tacitly excluding from British naval superiority the waters of the Caribbean and Latin America. It meant cool patience and an understanding of the ups and downs of American domestic politics. In short, it meant putting the United States in a subtly different category from any other foreign power. The rhetoric of Anglo-American friendship came later. Under Salisbury's guidance a sort of relationship came to birth, born not out of a desire of either nation to embrace the other, but out of a recognition by Britain of a new imperative for foreign policy – that a collision with the United States had to be avoided.

The going was not easy. In 1887 trouble broke out between Canada and the United States over fishing limits. Salisbury sent Joseph Chamberlain, the Colonial Secretary, to negotiate an agreement. Salisbury had to deal in 1890 with a parallel dispute about sealing in the Bering Sea. Salisbury summoned up a cruiser squadron from the China station and the American sealers disappeared. The episode showed that the United States still had no strength to challenge the Royal Navy in any serious way; but no one who looked into the future could believe that this would stay true. Salisbury had no illusions. The United States Senate rejected Chamberlain's agreement on fisheries, and the Administration expelled the British Minister, Lord Sackville, who had chatted unwisely to journalists about internal American politics. Salisbury refused to take offence.

As the United States gained fresh strength the temptation there grew, particularly among candidates for office, to assert American authority over the whole continent. Canada was too hard a nut to crack, but in 1895 the Secretary of State, Richard Olney, thought he had found a smaller, softer target. The boundary between Guiana, a British colony, and Venezuela had never been clearly defined and a dispute had simmered slowly for several years. Olney published a dispatch inviting the parties to go to arbitration, but homing in on the thought that the very existence of the British colony was 'unnatural and inexpedient'.[44] Salisbury rejected this strange upgrading of the Monroe Doctrine. The Americans had devised the Doctrine to take advantage of Canning's decision to use the Royal Navy to prevent any further European incursions across the Atlantic. But that was seventy years ago, and the eagle felt itself full-grown. President Cleveland summoned Congress on 17 December 1895 to hear his demand that the United States should arbitrate the dispute between Britain and Venezuela and enforce her findings. The tone was warlike; but Cleveland's strength was not enough. The American press and Congress were in uproar against Britain. But the New York Stock Exchange took fright, and in the New Year the British Minister in Washington, Sir Julian Pauncefote, reported that a 'wave of reason is passing over this country ... The commonsense of the country will continue to manifest itself against the jingo crusaders.'[45]

Salisbury decided to wait until the atmosphere cooled. The messages from the American side during 1896 continued somewhat crude, and on 23 June the Minister felt obliged to apologise for forwarding one 'in such bad taste and such bad form. It was probably written by the President sitting in his short sleeves between two bottles of whiskey.' And later, 'it is surprising that few public men can carry on a discussion like a gentleman. They write like rival attorneys or newspaper editors.' Eventually an award was agreed which gave Venezuela a swathe of territory which had not been settled in any substantial way. Salisbury had drawn back, though not any great distance, and Sir Julian congratulated him. 'Had you not been at the helm at the stormiest periods the good ship peace would certainly have foundered ... the eagle will [now] have to screech at other Powers and let the British Lion nurse his tail.'[46]

During the Venezuela crisis Salisbury did not ignore the possibility of a war with America; indeed, after this episode he told Hicks Beach, Chancellor of the Exchequer, on 2 January 1896 that 'a war with America – not this year but in the not too distant future – has become something more than a possibility'. He believed it more likely than a conflict with the Franco-Russian alliance, let alone with Germany. Salisbury made no effort to please the Americans, but his calm handling of the issues between the two countries helped to make the Venezuela crisis of 1895 the last of its kind. The United States went to war with Spain three years later and chased the Spaniards out of Cuba and the Philippines. Salisbury discouraged the Continental powers from any display of European solidarity with Spain, and Britain remained strictly neutral.

In May 1898 Salisbury made a speech in which the speculations of a keen journalistic mind peeped out from behind the sober intellectual apparatus of an elderly Prime Minister. He divided the nations of the world into the living and the dying. Better organisation and military power would ensure that 'the living nations will gradually encroach on the territory of the dying, and the seeds and causes of conflict among civilised nations will appear'. Salisbury did not push too far this excursion into Darwinist determinism but the 'dying nations', of which Spain was the most obvious, were quick to wear the cap which he had devised, and they protested loudly. Among the 'living nations' the United States was clearly eminent. The Prime Minister did not define the place of his own country in this equation.[47] Britain was actually on the cusp, at the height of her power but poised for decline; and in some moods Salisbury knew it.

During Salisbury's years in authority the British Empire rapidly expanded in Africa, while other European powers founded empires of their own in that continent. But for Salisbury the scramble for Africa over which he presided was not a central part of British foreign policy. He was very conscious that the British expansion in Africa, together with the maturing of Australia, Canada and New Zealand, gave birth to a new emotion in British hearts. The British Empire became a cause in itself. The concept of an imperial federation of the colonies settled from Britain (later known as the White Dominions) gained strength. More vaguely, patriotism became defined for many in a new way as loyalty to an entity unique in the history of the world, scattered across the globe, each territory coloured red on the map, the whole comprising countless races united under one Queen-Empress. Kipling fashioned the rousing words and great myths of the Empire, though he foresaw more clearly than most that its sun would one day set. Kipling developed his enthusiasm in India; yet the possession of India had never, except briefly at the time of the Mutiny, aroused in Britain the popular emotions for Empire which became commonplace in the 1880s and 1890s. No Viceroy of India achieved the celebrity of Gordon, Livingstone or Rhodes.

Salisbury presided over and humoured these emotions, but did not share them. For him the British Isles, India and the communication between them were the essential treasures which had to be defended; he was sure that their safety depended on how Britain carried herself in Europe. Maps of Africa might replace maps of the Balkans on his walls at Hatfield House; but he would have agreed with Bismarck, who said that the real map of Africa was in Europe.

The lines of communication with India lay through the Suez Canal and round the Cape. Each of these strategic points developed an imperial dynamic of its own. The men on the spot responsible for their safety urged at intervals that this safety depended on enlarging the territory under direct British control. Thus the Cape extended to Natal, and then from Natal to the Transvaal; Egypt, because of its dependence on the Nile, induced the British up the river into the Sudan, Kenya and Uganda. Salisbury was interested in control, which was not necessarily the same as annexation. He waved no flags and preached no imperial doctrine. But when he saw practical British interests at stake he was prepared to exert his own brand of energetic diplomacy, backed when necessary by force to advance these interests and check the ambitions of others.

But before analysing these forward moves southwards and northwards into the heart of Africa we have to take leave of one of the most powerful and venerated doctrines of British foreign policy. Constantinople, it was discovered, was no longer the gateway to India. Salisbury had known this for many years but, as we have seen, he believed that public opinion would deal harshly with the Foreign Secretary who was in office when Constantinople fell to the Russians. From time to time he played with and talked about the thought of an orderly partition of the Ottoman Empire. Although he bemused foreign governments by hinting at this possibility more than once, he never produced a definite proposal. Salisbury's ambiguity was finally brought to an end by his humiliation in 1895 over the Armenian question.

By temperament Salisbury was cool when confronted with the sufferings of distant peoples. He believed that Gladstone was foolish and hypocritical in rousing the country in 1876 against the Bulgarian atrocities. He did not believe in the right of self-determination any more than he believed in the pursuit of democracy regardless of circumstances; both causes could lead to chaos and war. But Salisbury believed in the importance of public opinion as strongly as he sometimes disapproved of its consequences. In 1895 the Turkish Government set about massacring large numbers of Armenian subjects, both in Armenia and in Constantinople. Gladstone, at the age of eighty-seven, roused himself for his last great public speech. He called in Liverpool for armed British intervention and argued that to stay inactive for fear of European reactions would be 'a mistake almost more deplorable than almost any committed in the history of diplomacy'.[48] Salisbury knew that Gladstone spoke for many in weeping for the Armenians. 'Here the sympathy for them, though the area over which it extends is not very large, where the feeling exists approaches to frenzy in its intensity.' But on the Continent, it was different. 'I do not believe that from Archangel to Cadiz there is a soul who cares whether the Armenians are exterminated or not.'[49]

Against this background Salisbury tried but failed to put together a European consensus. He then put to the Cabinet a plan for unilateral action by the British fleet. The Navy might not be able to rescue the Armenians by scaling the Taurus Mountains, but it could coerce the Sultan in his seat of government in Constantinople. Or so Salisbury argued; but the Cabinet refused. For the first time in his premiership Salisbury failed to carry his colleagues. The reason was straightforward. The experts whom Salisbury despised carried the day.

Three years earlier the Admiralty had warned that the time-honoured practice of sending the British fleet into the Dardanelles had become dangerous. As France and Russia grew closer together the British ships would be in grave danger if the French fleet came out of Toulon and attacked them in the rear or slipped through the Straits of Gibraltar and became a threat to Britain itself. Salisbury had fiercely contested the argument. If the experts were right, there seemed little point in keeping a fleet in the Mediterranean at all, and British policy had been a policy of false pretences. 'If persisted in, it will involve discomfiture to all who trust in us, and infinite discredit to ourselves.'[50]

The question had gone to sleep during the Liberal Government of 1892–5. But here it was again, resurrected in a practical and painful form during the crisis over Armenia. The First Sea Lord, Admiral Sir Frederick Richards, actually walked out of a ministerial meeting rather than agree to put his ships at risk. He was supported by his political superior, George Goschen, First Lord of the Admiralty. Salisbury's failure was masked by the Gladstonian language in which he himself had begun to denounce the atrocities as 'horrors to the like of which Europe has not listened since the days of Genghis Khan and Tamerlane'.[51] In his humiliation Salisbury reacted angrily against the victorious Admirals. 'If our ships are always to be kept wrapped in silver paper for fear of their paint being scratched', he wrote to the Queen, 'I shall find it difficult to go on defending the Naval Estimates in Parliament.'[52] The incident showed the defect in the naval rearmament policy of 1889. It was no good calculating strength in terms of a global two-power standard of total ship numbers if in particular situations Britain could not cope with a Franco-Russian alliance.

But the other consequence was equally far-reaching. In September 1896 Salisbury had an audience with young Czar Nicholas II at Balmoral. He made a statement to the Czar which would have horrified Palmerston or Disraeli. Speaking of the Straits, he said: 'I thought that the interest of England in the matter was not as large as that of others, and was purely maritime. I admitted that the theory that Turkish rule at Constantinople was a bulwark to our Indian Empire could not be maintained.'[53] So that was that. The Eastern Question had not actually been solved; but Britain was no longer going to ask it.

Confirming this in a letter to Currie, his Ambassador in Constantinople, on 19 October 1897, Salisbury added: 'we have really no hold on and no interest in any of the Sultan's territories except Egypt. On the other hand our interest in Egypt is growing stronger.' The policy must be 'to strengthen our position on the Nile (to its source) and to withdraw as much as possible from all responsibilities at Constantinople'.[54]

Egypt was a pawn, perhaps even a knight or bishop, in the European game. So long as Britain occupied Egypt, French resentment against Britain would be strong, and there would be a chance that Britain might move closer to, or even join, the Triple Alliance of Germany, Austria and Italy. But Egypt was a higher piece on the secondary board where European politicians played for the future of Africa. Salisbury had never himself sought the British occupation of Egypt, but Gladstone's reluctant adventure had put Britain in possession, just at the time when Egypt was replacing Constantinople in British strategic thinking as the key to India.

The British position in Egypt needed fortifying, both internally and diplomatically. Baring worked hard to direct the Khedive's government out of debt and to bring forward reforms which would benefit the wretched Egyptian peasant. But Egyptian nationalism never had a direct link with the poverty of most Egyptians. Nothing Baring could do would make British occupation acceptable. This internal stalemate made it even more important to limit the risk that other powers would make trouble for the British position. In the absence of an agreement with the Sultan on the legal sovereignty of

Egypt, Britain was vulnerable to the pressures of other powers on a matter now thought to be crucial for its security.

This fact influenced Salisbury in his approach to other rivalries in Africa. Because it was first in the field and because of the relative strength of the Royal Navy, Britain had a head start in dividing up Africa; but Salisbury did not propose to press this advantage too far. He wanted to win, but not to take all. This led him to a series of agreements with competing powers, designed to achieve acceptable results on the ground without upsetting the precarious but essential balance of power in Europe. Ironically, the most difficult of these relationships, and the one which came closest to a total breakdown, was with France, which within a few years was to become Britain's closest ally.

But the first crucial agreement was with Germany. Bismarck, even more than Salisbury, regarded African questions as a competition played out on a side table alongside the all-important diplomatic manoeuvres within Europe. He encouraged German colonial adventures, but within limits. Immediately after Bismarck's dismissal in 1890, Salisbury took advantage of the inexperience of the new government under the young Kaiser to propose an agreement. Britain would obtain a sole protectorate over the Sultan of Zanzibar in East Africa, where British and German business interests had been feuding. In return, Britain would cede to Germany the tiny island of Heligoland at the mouth of the Kiel Canal. The German Government accepted. It was a good deal for Britain. Heligoland was indefensible and therefore of no real strategic use to Britain. The German concession on Zanzibar, both the island and the Sultan's coastal possessions, put a stop to increasing German incursions inland towards Uganda and the precious waters of the Upper Nile. The Queen objected, on the rather modern grounds that the 2,200 Heligolanders had not been consulted. She feared we would next give Gibraltar to Spain, and anyway, on a more traditional argument, 'giving up what one has is always a bad thing'.[55]

Other criticism was muted. Salisbury did well to move fast. Once fully in the saddle, the Kaiser proclaimed his world ambitions and would have been much harder to shift. Salisbury put the matter to the Queen in its European context. 'Any indefinite postponement of a settlement in Africa would render it very difficult to maintain terms of amity with Germany, and would force us to change our systems of alliances in Europe. The alliance of France instead of the alliance of Germany must necessarily involve the early evacuation of Egypt under very unfavourable conditions.'[56] He also reached an agreement with Germany about how Portuguese territories in Africa might be divided if, as at one time seemed likely, the bankrupt Lisbon Government had to dispose of them.

The colonial relationship with France was more tricky. France, unlike Germany, was in a state of grievance – robbed by Bismarck of Alsace-Lorraine and, more recently, as she saw it, manoeuvred out of Egypt by the hypocrite Gladstone and the Machiavellian Salisbury. The internal political scene in Paris was feverish and volatile; colonial interests were strongly represented in the Chamber, and colonial issues could make or break French governments.

Salisbury's energetic Colonial Secretary, Joseph Chamberlain, believed that a great new market was available for Britain in West Africa. He backed Sir George Goldie, an entrepreneur who led the Royal Niger Company in its expansionary plans. But Salisbury commented: 'there is no loot to get except in Goldie's dreams'.[57] An agreement was signed with France in June 1898 which secured northern Nigeria for Britain; but as a result of this and earlier agreements France secured vast areas in West and Central Africa. To those who simply looked at the map, France had secured the lion's share of Africa. But, as Salisbury observed, the 'constant study of maps is apt to disturb men's reasoning powers'.[58] He took the Lords into his confidence, in the tone of a man discussing rural transactions with fellow landlords at the county assizes. 'Anyone who looks at this map and merely measures the degrees will perhaps be of the opinion that France has laid claim to a considerable stretch of country. But it is necessary to judge land not merely by its extent but by its value. This land is what agriculturalists would call very light land, that is the desert of the Sahara.'[59] Waddington, the French Ambassador, and a friend of Salisbury, was sitting in the gallery; he complained mildly to Salisbury that he might have left the French to discover this fact for themselves.

But the French remained restless, and their attention turned east towards the Upper Nile. The Sudan remained under the rule of what the Victorians called the Dervishes and we would now call Muslim fundamentalists, the men who had killed Gordon and forced the Anglo-Egyptian forces out of their country. It was a cruel and repulsive regime under the rule of a Khalifa who depended heavily on slavery, but neither Salisbury in London nor Baring in Cairo hurried to avenge Gordon by overthrowing it. They were well aware that this policy of waiting might have to be rethought if the French began to move east in that direction. But the first British move back into the Sudan was induced not by a French advance but by an Italian disaster.

Crispi, the energetic Italian Prime Minister, thought, like Mussolini after him, that the greatness of his country depended on acquiring an empire. In May 1888 he proclaimed his ambition to the Chamber. 'Italy needs colonies for her future and for her trade and this bourgeois habit of always counting the costs is unpatriotic; there is something greater than material interests of civilisation ... You have always said that now we are in Rome [which had become the capital of Italy in 1870] we must create a new world.'[60] Or, as A.J.P. Taylor unkindly put it, Crispi 'made Italy run in the hope that this would teach her to walk'.[61] His predecessors had hoped that they could begin this brave new Italian world by acquiring Tunis, but the French got there first. Their ambition turned to East Africa, where the Italians established themselves in what is now Eritrea and approached Kassala, an eastern province of the Sudan. Italy was in all but form an ally of Britain, useful to check French ambitions in the Mediterranean. Salisbury had no particular sympathy with Crispi and did not want to see even a friendly Italy established on the Upper Nile.

But more dangerous than Italian success was Italian disaster. The Italian army was routed at Adowa on 1 March 1896 by a Muslim force allied to the Khalifa and the Dervishes who controlled Khartoum. The Italians appealed for help, fearing the collapse of their whole position in East Africa. After a short pause Salisbury authorised the advance of an Anglo-Egyptian army southwards along the Nile as far as Dongola. His aim was to draw Dervish forces away from the Italians to defend Khartoum. Baring disapproved, and argued strongly against any further advance. He worried about money and Egyptian politics but warned Salisbury as he had done in October 1897: 'You will have a great onslaught from the soldiers on this subject. They will all tell you that we must go on – which means an English [as opposed to Egyptian] expedition. My opinion is quite clear, that no sufficiently important English interest is involved to justify the loss of life and money which would be invested in the capture of Khartoum.'[62] In November 1897 the Cabinet agreed and the army stopped at Dongola.

Rather suddenly in January 1898, Salisbury changed course; he sent Kitchener the fresh troops he needed and authorised further advance up the Nile. The reason was clear – news of French ambitions had become more definite. Captain Marchand and a small group of French soldiers and scientists were on the move into an area where their presence, once established, was bound to cause serious trouble. Baring had argued that Britain need not worry about the French because Britain could always get to Khartoum first. But Salisbury preferred a small Anglo-French crisis in 1898 to a later and larger argument involving bigger forces.

The aim of the Sudan campaign was essentially strategic but Salisbury, like Blair after him when invading Iraq, borrowed some Gladstonian phrases to add a moral flavour to his war. He spoke of 'our desire to extirpate from the earth one of the vilest despotisms ... ever seen ... compared with which the worst performances of the worst minion of the Palace at Constantinople are bright and saintly deeds'.[63]

Kitchener's war-making was precise and mechanical. In September at Omdurman, for the loss of fifty-two men, his army, which included the young Winston Churchill, killed about 16,000 Dervishes and destroyed the Khalifa's regime. Gordon was avenged. Salisbury took no pleasure in what he called the 'ghastly butcher's bill' but commented that 'a slaughter of sixteen thousand ought to satisfy the jingoes for at least six months'.[64]

There remained a small mud brick fort in the far south of the Sudan occupied by Captain Marchand and his tiny team of soldiers and scientists, who carried with them a quantity of champagne and claret, a mechanical piano and the honour of France. If by some amazing reversal Kitchener had lost at Omdurman, Marchand would have been attacked and slaughtered within days by the Dervishes. As it was, Kitchener and Marchand met and exchanged careful courtesies. They were rivals, but the disproportion of force was overwhelming. Kitchener returned to Khartoum, leaving behind 600 men to invest Marchand's position and guard the British and Egyptian flags which he had hoisted over Fashoda, not far from the French tricolour. The flags and the troops reminded Marchand of the realities of power.

Salisbury had the double gift, rare even among Foreign Secretaries, of both foreseeing events in time to provide for them, and of handling the unforeseen firmly without fluster. He could not have foretold that at the critical point of Anglo-French rivalry in Africa, French political opinion would be convulsed by the twists and turns of the Dreyfus case, in which the honour of the French Army was brutally challenged. Nor can he have been sure in advance of the completeness of Kitchener's victory at Omdurman. But he had thought it likely that there would be a test of will with France somewhere in the region of the Upper Nile. He had worked to head off the danger that in such a crisis France might be helped by her new ally, Russia. In China and, as we have seen, in his dealings with the Czar over Constantinople, Salisbury went out of his way to show Russia that the old instinctive British hostility had evaporated. When the crisis came and the French were swept by patriotic fervour against Britain, the Russians did nothing.

British opinion was also roused. It wanted the French humiliation to be complete. Salisbury was accused of weakness and passivity while he waited for the French climbdown. In the Cabinet Chamberlain pressed for an ultimatum to France. Salisbury refused, and remained impassive. He held the strong cards. The situation was under control. He had mobilised overwhelming force at the right time. Salisbury was willing to go to war with France over the Nile. This was not a matter of dubious commercial prospects, as in West Africa three years earlier; in this case the security of Britain's link with India was at risk. But he did not think that the crisis would end in war. Unusually, the Queen was worried that her Government might be too assertive; this time she hoped for compromise. The correspondence in the Hatfield archive between Salisbury and Sir Edmund Manson, British Ambassador in Paris, is full of the latter's dark predictions of the likely French reaction to the insult to their honour. Delcassé, the French Foreign Minister, might find himself forced by public opinion into a war he did not want. Salisbury allowed this flow of gloom to pass over him. When he was told that Manson was 'dreadfully upset' at not hearing from him, he commented: 'what a plague his susceptibilities are! Writing to Ambassadors generally does harm. However I will try to put some verbiage together for tomorrow.'[65]

Salisbury was not willing to give the French any substantial concession. But neither was he going to act in the Sudan in a way which would upset his diplomacy in Europe. He wanted France out of the Nile Valley, but he did not want France so angry that it would be impossible to deal constructively with her in other continents. Salisbury sat still at the height of the crisis. But his inaction was not like that of Lord Derby, which had been a matter of temperament and a distrust of rash action. Salisbury remained quiet because he had done what was needed. On 4 November he was able to announce at the Mansion House that Marchand had been recalled. The French subsided. Salisbury paid tribute to the great judgement and common sense of the French Government. Six years later Britain and France reached an entente which became an alliance and has lasted ever since.

The older and equally important link between Britain and India passed round the Cape. Here, as with Egypt, the argument for protecting the route led Britain, decade by decade, into involvement further and further from the sea. Here, as with Egypt, the process generated its own political dynamic on the spot, reflecting the ambitions of local British leaders, as well as memories of undignified defeats which had to be reversed. For Salisbury and his contemporaries, South Africa was of the two the more difficult to handle. On the face of it, this was surprising. South Africa was much further removed from the turmoil of European power politics which was throughout the main concern of British Foreign Secretaries. The Royal Navy saw to it that no European armies or fleets could intervene in South Africa as they might in Constantinople or Egypt. Give or take the occasional supply of weapons, European interest in South Africa, however noisy, could only be expressed in diplomatic terms. For none of them would South Africa ever be worth a general war.

The difficulty for Salisbury was a different one. The favourable climate of southern Africa made it attractive for European settlement, unlike Egypt or indeed India. Before Salisbury's time two races, the

British and the Dutch, had begun to settle in substantial numbers. The British gradually became dominant in the Cape Colony itself, and then in the neighbouring colony of Natal. The Dutch Boers trekked north and established themselves in the Transvaal and what became the Orange Free State. For the first time since the future of Canada was settled in 1763, people of two European nations were pitched against each other outside Europe. In 1881 at Majuba Hill the Boers had decisively reversed a British advance, and obtained from Gladstone's Government an agreement that the Transvaal should be a self-governing republic with a vague provision for British suzerainty, particularly in dealings with other countries.

In the decade which followed the problem was immensely complicated by the discovery of gold on the Rand. What had been a slow-moving rivalry for agricultural land became a rapid struggle for authority over the fantastic wealth now giving birth to Johannesburg and the surrounding area. The newcomers, mostly British, threatened to outnumber the Boers in the Transvaal, who reacted by denying them the rights of citizenship, in particular the vote.

The sharp difference between the Egyptian and the South African problems was illustrated in the leading characters on the British side. Baring, in Egypt, was a public servant of the British Crown. Authoritative by nature, he nevertheless recognised that his instruction came from London, and in particular from the Prime Minister. He was on easy terms of social equality with Salisbury, in an age when aristocratic and banking families had begun to mix easily. The two men recognised each other's intelligence and integrity; their views of the world and of British interests were similar. As a result they corresponded with each other frankly, and when they disagreed, for example over the advance to Dongola in 1897, each expressed his opinions clearly, knowing that the eventual decision of Prime Minister and Cabinet settled the question.

Salisbury would never have achieved or wished to achieve such a straightforward relationship with Cecil Rhodes. Rhodes shared none of his background. Rhodes was not a Crown servant but a local politician, the elected Premier of Cape Colony, with roots in South African soil. He was a businessman on the make, interested in money for his own pocket, and also as the means by which the British race could establish its supremacy in Africa. Salisbury sympathised with much of this analysis. The resources of Africa badly needed capital, which could best come from London. But for Salisbury British capital did not necessarily mean British rule, with all the expense and political risk which that involved. If Rhodes could organise the investment by means of his proposed Chartered Company, then that would suit everyone – except of course the Boers, who would find themselves surrounded by British interests, apart from a precarious outlet through Portuguese East Africa. The Queen granted Rhodes the Charter of the British South Africa Company in October 1889, nearly 300 years after Queen Elizabeth I had done the same for the East India Company.

Rhodes was closer in temperament and ambition to Clive and Warren Hastings than he was to their Victorian successors as Viceroys of India. Trade and investment were the spur, not territorial conquest. But, just as in India, the Company eventually mutated into the British Raj, so Salisbury found that the flag came inevitably to follow trade for its protection, whatever the initial disinterest in London. Salisbury separated himself from Rhodes in the phrase he used: 'a gentleman with some considerable force of character'. He described Rhodes's project of a Cape to Cairo railway running all the way through British territory as 'a curious idea which had lately become prevalent'.[66] But the difference between them became one of temperament rather than policy. Salisbury hoped that over time the Boers would find themselves outgunned, not by the British Army but by the relentless advance of British enterprise; their independence would slip into oblivion without its loss being noticed. This hope was unrealistic. Its chance of success was dramatically frustrated, not just by Rhodes, but by the emergence of three other powerful characters, Paul Kruger, Alfred Milner and Joseph Chamberlain, all strangers to Salisbury's qualities of patience, readiness to compromise and respect for the slow tide of events.

Kruger, as President and undisputed leader of the Transvaal since 1853, saw clearly that the threat to Boer independence came from the inflow of British entrepreneurs and adventurers to exploit the new mineral wealth of his country. He was not prepared to allow the weight of their numbers to upset Boer authority; this meant denying them the ordinary rights of a citizen and in particular the right to vote on an equal basis with the Boer. The newcomers, known as

Uitlanders, became restless and some of them planned an uprising in Johannesburg in December 1895. The Colonial Secretary, Joseph Chamberlain, warned Salisbury that this might happen. But Chamberlain did not tell his Prime Minister that Rhodes was organising a small-scale invasion of the Transvaal by troops under the command of Rhodes's right-hand man in the British South Africa Company, Doctor Jameson. The Uitlander rising never happened, but Jameson rode into the Transvaal at the head of 500 men; he was defeated and captured by a Boer force three times the size. Rhodes at once resigned as Premier of Cape Colony. Chamberlain dissociated himself from the whole affair. Salisbury took the news calmly: 'fortunately no harm seems to have been done in the Transvaal – except to Rhodes' reputation. If filibustering fails it is always "disreputable".'[67] He noted that before Jameson's 'criminal blunder' the Uitlanders were said to be pouring into the Transvaal at the rate of 500 males a week. This meant that, given time, the Transvaal would become a British colony or a British republic. In this instance, Salisbury trusted time to do good work.[68]

His immediate concern was with the possible German reaction, given German sympathy and vague feeling of kinship with the Boers. Indeed the Kaiser, two days later, loosed off a famous telegram to Kruger, congratulating him on his success in defending his country from attack. Salisbury, who had done his best to conciliate the Germans through his contacts with the German Ambassador in London, commented only that 'the German's only idea of a diplomatic approach is to stamp heavily on your toes'.[69] The Kaiser acted on impulse without a considered plan. The telegram enraged public opinion in Britain; Salisbury's response was to send a squadron of ships to the Portuguese port of Delagoa Bay just in case the Kaiser followed up with another foolish gesture. The episode created a new distrust of German intentions among the British public, growing in scope and intensity as the nineteenth century came to a close.

1897 was a year of pause in southern Africa. It was the year of the Queen's Diamond Jubilee; the public glowed at the displayed strength and immensity of her Empire. Salisbury waved no flag and disliked public emotion. In three months he made two major speeches, remarkable as an echo of the same melancholy which had touched the mind of Kipling, the high priest of Empire, when in the same year he wrote 'Recessional'.

'Far called our navies melt away
On dune and headland sinks the fire,
Lo all our strength of yesterday
Is one with Nineveh and Tyre'

That was Kipling; this is Salisbury on the Queen's speech in February 1898:

I have a strong belief that there is a danger of the public opinion of this country believing that it is our duty to take everything we can, to fight everybody and to make a quarrel of every dispute. That seems to me a very dangerous doctrine . . . However strong you may be, whether you're a man or a nation, there is a point beyond which your strength will not go. It is madness, it ends in ruin if you allow yourself to pass beyond it.[70]

A few weeks earlier he had warned at the Guildhall of the danger of accumulating armaments and therefore of a war fatal to Christian civilisation, unless the powers could learn to act together to solve disputes and eventually form some international constitution to ensure unfettered trade and continuing peace. These sounded more like the musings of a wise but distant observer than proclamations of policy from a masterful Prime Minister. Outwardly Salisbury seemed at the height of his power, poised between two election victories in 1895 and 1900, but there were already signs of a slackening of personal authority in face of challenge. Just as the Empire which he controlled began to feel its first spasms of self-doubt, Salisbury's dramatic success at Fashoda reasserted his strength for the time being, but after that the note of detached melancholy began to sound again.

For the lull in South Africa did not last long. In March 1899 a British subject named Edgar was shot dead in the Transvaal by a Boer policeman who was not brought to justice. The British High Commissioner in Cape Town was now Alfred Milner, who shared none of Salisbury's misgivings about imperial expansion. On 4 May Milner wrote a deliberately sensational dispatch comparing the plight of the Uitlanders in the Transvaal to helots, the slaves of classical Greece. In the months that follow the helot dispatch Milner professed that he was only seeking a fair deal for the Uitlanders. In fact he was using the unfairness of their treatment as a lever to force such concessions from the Boers as would fatally compromise Boer independence. He and Chamberlain took charge of the negotiations. The Boers were willing to offer the vote to Uitlanders after five or seven years of residence. Negotiations dragged on through the summer and autumn of 1899, but the British pressed for more. At this stage Chamberlain thought that tough diplomacy and the threat of force had done the trick. He wrote to Salisbury on 18 July: 'I really am sanguine that the crisis is over. If my expectations are justified by official confirmation tomorrow the result will be a triumph of moral pressure – accompanied by special officers and three batteries of artillery.' But six weeks later his mood had changed. 'I have no doubt that it is the fact that Kruger, who might have yielded gracefully at Bloemfontein or even later, will now only yield, if at all, to the fear of force and with the determination of repudiating his obligation whenever he thinks it safe to do so.'[71]

In a private letter to Lord Lansdowne on 30 August, Salisbury had criticised Milner's view as 'too heated'. He prophesied that it might involve Government in 'the necessity for considerable military effort – and all for people whom we despise and for territory which will bring no profit and no power to England'.[72] But in practice Salisbury did nothing to rein back his subordinates. He believed wrongly that Kruger was likely to yield in the end to the slowly tightening screw of pressure. He was concerned with the importance of public opinion in Britain, as usual stressing that importance while giving it no credit for wisdom. He was concerned with timing and presentation at home, as well as with the exasperatingly slow build-up of military strength on the ground. Public opinion had to be prepared and educated into the truth about the argument with Kruger. Milner was never a skilful politician; it was unreal to compare the greedy and unsympathetic Uitlanders to Greek slaves. Salisbury shifted the public argument away from the grievances of these unpromising victims to the iniquities of Gladstone's settlement with the Boers in 1881. That climbdown had called into question the primacy of Britain's position in Africa.

Salisbury did not disagree with the views which Chamberlain

expressed to the Cabinet on 6 September. 'What is now at stake is the position of Great Britain in South Africa – and with it the estimate formed of our power and influence in our Colonies and throughout the world . . . it depends upon the action of the British Government now whether the supremacy which we have claimed so long and so seldom exerted, is to be finally established and recognised or for ever abandoned.'[73] Here, in a new form in 1899, was Disraeli's doctrine of national prestige, which had so annoyed Derby in 1877, which Salisbury had embraced in a more prosaic form in 1878, and from which he never resiled. True, Salisbury thought in traditional terms of trade and investment, of the security of the British Isles and of India. He did not share Chamberlain's vision of a worldwide imperial federation; but Kruger's obstinacy was an obstacle to Britain's interests under either definition of the national interest.

Salisbury once again, as over Fashoda a year earlier, made sure that none of the European powers would step in. He had just signed a fresh colonial agreement with Germany. He played a passive part among the powers in the Boxer Rebellion which was unfolding in China. He restrained Curzon from the forward policy on which the young, ambitious Viceroy of India was set; this was no time for a challenge to Russia's position in Asia. To some extent these prudent precautions were unnecessary. The ability of the big European powers to put millions of men in the field, however relevant to Constantinople or even Egypt, was not plausible in the context of South Africa. The continuing supremacy of the Royal Navy, despite the timidity of its admirals, meant that if war came Britain and the Boers would fight it out alone. But no one who remembered the victory of the Zulus at Isandhlwana or of the Boers at Majuba Hill would suppose that this fact would guarantee quick success.

Armed with such memories, the Boers planned a short war. They could not afford to wait while the troop ships brought more and more men from England to Cape Town. Ten thousand extra men were dispatched following a long Cabinet meeting in Salisbury's rooms in the Foreign Office on 8 September. These movements could not be concealed; indeed, part of their purpose was to add to the diplomatic pressure on Kruger. But Kruger saw the opportunity of a quick thrust which would demoralise the British before the troop ships docked. On 9 October the Boer Governor issued an ultimatum to Milner requiring him to withdraw all troops from the borders of the Transvaal and to order home the troop ships now at sea. When this ultimatum was rejected, the mounted Boer farmers invaded the Crown Colony of Natal, and the Boer War began.

Salisbury found himself the leader of a nation at war and, much worse, a nation which, to the delight of most of the world, began that war by stumbling from defeat to defeat. The series of military disasters reached their climax in the Black Week of December 1899. The British army failed to relieve the beleaguered towns of Lady-smith and Kimberley, and suffered much greater losses than they inflicted. Despite their huge preponderance of men the British were losing the war.

Salisbury neither claimed nor showed any aptitude as an active war leader. He had never taken any close interest in Army affairs. The generals, like the admirals before them, took their place in the catalogue of inefficient, negative-minded experts for whose advice he had little respect. But this did not lead him, as it did Lloyd George and Churchill in the twentieth century, to try to seize the reins himself. Temperamentally he was less of a warrior than these two successors as wartime Prime Ministers. It was simply not his style to devise bold new initiatives or spend hectic hours poring over maps of battlefields. After the Black Week of disasters the British Com-mander, Sir Redvers Buller, had to go. Salisbury appointed Field Marshal Roberts in his place, with Kitchener as his Chief of Staff. These were the most able men available. It would not have occurred to Salisbury to send for them and lecture them through the night in Churchillian style on strategy, let alone tactics. However slowly and inefficiently, the British, with the help of Australians and New Zealanders, were building up a huge preponderance of force in South Africa. Salisbury, as usual taking the long view, knew that in the end victory was certain. At the darkest moment the Queen famously told Salisbury's nephew, Arthur Balfour: 'Please understand that there is no one depressed in this house; we are not interested in the possibilities of defeat; they do not exist.' That was a statement of fact with which Salisbury agreed. Feverish activity on his part would bring victory no faster.

Nor did he see it as his duty to rouse the nation with heroic oratory. He regarded the Boers as unsatisfactory but not hateful people, and made no attempt to drum up hostility against them. He was entirely firm in sustaining the agreed policy. He had said as early as July, 'we have put our hands to the plough, and we do not intend to withdraw them from it'.[74] He held to that principle throughout. On 17 October he defined Britain's war aims in the House of Lords. 'There must be no doubt that the Sovereign of England is paramount; there must be no doubt that the white races will be put upon an equality, and that due precaution will be taken for the philanthropic and kindly and improving treatment of those countless indigenous races of whose destiny, I fear, we have been too forgetful.'[75]

Of these objections the paramountcy of England was of course in his mind the key: the Uitlanders had to be included because of their role in the preliminary bouts of diplomacy; the native races were included as a bow to the future. It would be absurd to argue on Salisbury's behalf that he foresaw a time of black majority rule. His adjectives are those of a benevolent master acknowledging the duty to improve the lot of a servant. The British in South Africa were more kindly disposed to the black race than were the Boers. This was partly because they did not share the severe Boer vision of an Old Testament society founded on a chosen people – but also because in their daily lives they felt less at risk than the Boers from the black majority which surrounded them. During the war the blacks were enlisted to help the British in many capacities but cautiously, in the knowledge that this would make the Boers even less likely to make peace.

Salisbury was not a democrat in British terms, let alone in terms of the whole world. He did not believe in the equality of races, except in the eyes of God. To him, the huge inequality between the achievements of whites and blacks was so manifest that there could be no purpose in equating their political or social status. The native population was entitled to decent treatment and to the possibility of progress; to argue for more would be unreal and therefore hypocritical. It is exact to define this attitude as racist if the word has any meaning except as an adjective of abuse;* but to dismiss Salisbury and the thoughtful Christians of his generation as morally worthless is to misplace his generation and confuse it with our own.

* Although racialist might be a more accurate description.

Salisbury went on to dismiss the argument that Britain was simply after South African gold. At the Guildhall he argued that 'England as a whole would have no advantage from the possession of gold mines, except so far as her Government conferred the blessings of good government upon those who had the prosecution of that industry. But that is the limit of our interest . . . we seek no goldfields. We seek no territory. What we desire is equal rights for men and all races and security for our fellow subjects and for the Empire.'[76]

Salisbury was capable of discussing the British setbacks in the war in the tone of a detached commentator rather than a Prime Minister supposedly in charge of events. To the House of Lords on 30 January 1900 he pointed out that four times in the nineteenth century the British had sent out expeditionary forces which had fared badly. During Castlereagh's Walcheren mission in 1809, during the Peninsular War, the Crimea and lastly in South Africa, the Government and the Army had been fiercely criticised, when the real defect was the British Constitution which was badly adapted to waging war. He forgot to mention that in the middle of the Walcheren mission the Government had collapsed and Castlereagh and Canning had fought a duel, and that Lord Aberdeen had been forced to resign during the Crimean debacle. But there was no pressure on Salisbury to resign at this moment. However distant and laidback his attitude to the war, Salisbury possessed personal authority which no one seriously challenged. The fact that the country was divided, the fact that Chamberlain, though forceful and dedicated, clearly lacked the calm judgement in which Salisbury excelled, the fact that Salisbury had long exhausted any personal ambition, all combined to make his position impregnable so long as he wished to keep it. When Salisbury went to the country in September 1900, his Government was re-elected with a majority almost as large as in 1895. This was christened the Khaki Election, and was held after the military situation had been reversed and Kruger chased out of the Transvaal. The Liberals were divided on the war, and the electorate was invited to return the patriotic and united Conservative Government. Salisbury hardly campaigned at all during the election; Chamberlain was left to bang the drum and argue that 'Every seat lost to the Government is a seat gained to the Boers'.[77]

The strange and passionate climax of the war came on the night of

17 May 1900, when the news arrived that the tiny besieged town of Mafeking had been relieved. Millions of very happy people poured on to the streets: the writer Rebecca West believed that the celebrations that night were greater than either of Armistice Day in 1918 or VE Day in 1945, all three of which she witnessed. Salisbury, by nature wholly averse to what briefly became known as 'mafficking', was caught up in the emotion because his son Edward had been serving on the staff of Colonel Baden-Powell, the commander of the Mafeking garrison. There were special celebrations at Hatfield, a short speech by the Prime Minister from the steps of the house, and a huge bonfire lit by his grandson George.[78]

But the war and the underlying argument went on. Joseph Chamberlain was not only a rigorous Colonial Secretary in charge of South African policy. He had also set about undermining in public and private the foundations of Salisbury's foreign policy. He favoured an alliance. He did not contradict but simply ignored Salisbury's often repeated argument that it was not constitutionally proper for Britain to enter into formal alliances involving a commitment to war because no government could commit Parliament in advance of a particular crisis.

As early as December 1897, he suggested an understanding with the Japanese; he wrote to Salisbury on 3 December: 'Talking of allies, have you considered whether we might not draw closer to Japan. It seems to me that they are rapidly increasing their means of offence and defence, and in many contingencies they could be valuable allies. They are at the moment much inclined to us and being very sensitive would appreciate any advance made to them ... I do not suppose that a Treaty of Alliance would be admirable, but I should hope that an understanding might be aimed at which would be very useful.' He went on to suggest that the Japanese Legation in London might be elevated to an Embassy. This would signal an unwritten alliance without commitment. 'It would flatter the Japanese, and be worth more than the Garter to the Mikado.'[79]

But Chamberlain soon moved after bigger game than the Japanese. In March 1898 the German Ambassador, Count Hatzfeldt, came to see him, and they discussed the possibility of an alliance on the basis of a statement by Chamberlain that 'it seemed to me that in these greater issues the interests of Germany were really identical to our own'. Chamberlain said that he thought Britain's policy of non-entanglement in alliances might be changed by circumstances too strong to resist. Chamberlain reported that 'the following suggestion was evolved. That an alliance might be established by Treaty or Agreement between Germany and Great Britain for a term of years. But it should be of a defensive character based upon a mutual understanding as to policy in China and elsewhere.'[80] Chamberlain explained his thinking in a private letter to Salisbury which is preserved at Hatfield. 'Recent experience seems to me to show that we are powerless to resist the ultimate control of China by Russia, and that we are at a great disadvantage in negotiating with France as long as we maintain our present isolation, and I think the country would support us in a Treaty with Germany providing for reciprocal defence. I think such a treaty would make for peace and might be negotiated at the present time. But it is for you to say whether the matter should be pursued or allowed to drop.'[81]

Salisbury had his own conversation with Count Hatzfeldt six weeks later. It was a confused talk which gave rise to the story that Salisbury had proposed the partition of the Ottoman Empire. The record does not substantiate this. On the question of an alliance between Britain and Germany, Salisbury said obscurely that there was much to be said for it so long as it dealt with general European interests.[82] In fact Salisbury had no intention of changing his fundamental analysis. He was still inclined to lean towards the Triple Alliance of Germany, Austria and Italy, but not to the extent of committing Britain to military action or of permanently antagonising France. It was one thing to stand up firmly to France at Fashoda, quite another to turn her into a settled enemy. Nor did Salisbury trust the Kaiser any more than he had trusted Bismarck. Bismarck had at least been entitled to respect for his cool judgement, which had certainly not been earned by the author of the Kruger telegram.

Chamberlain, showing more courage than prudence, at once set out his idea in a public speech. His clearest recommendation was that Britain should draw all parts of the Empire together, and 'maintain bonds of permanent amity' with the Americans. But the meat of the speech was his critique of what he misleadingly called 'strict isolation', which meant that 'we have had no allies, I am afraid we have had no friends ... We must not allow jingoes to drive us into a quarrel with all the world at the same time, and we must not reject the idea of an alliance with those Powers whose interests must nearly approximate to our own.'[83]

The philosophical argument died down in the heat of the Fashoda crisis and then the Boer War. By the time it revived, the political scene in Britain and the personal position of Salisbury had radically changed. Lady Salisbury died in November 1899, condemning him to a sad loneliness which even his talented children could not cure. His health began to fail, and his nephew Arthur Balfour became more and more influential in the daily handling of events. In October 1900 there was an embarrassed agreement between his main colleagues and the Queen that Salisbury should not continue as both Prime Minister and Foreign Secretary, the embarrassment consisting in the unwillingness of any of them to tell him. It turned out that, though sad at giving up his favourite office, he was willing to make the change and Lord Lansdowne replaced him as Foreign Secretary. Three months later the Queen herself died; Salisbury remained a senior survivor of an age which had already passed into history.

The question of an alliance came to the fore again in 1902 in the form which Chamberlain had originally suggested five years earlier. Salisbury was in his last months as Prime Minister. Balfour, Lansdowne and Chamberlain believed strongly in the virtues of an Anglo-Japanese alliance. The growing Japanese navy provided the key argument. The British could not realistically keep in Chinese waters a naval force able to face down the forces of Russia and France, by now firm allies. The policy of the open door in China to which Britain was devoted would be at risk unless Britain could find an ally. The Americans were not yet strong or active enough outside their own continent, even after they took the Philippines from Spain in 1898. If an alliance with Germany was excluded, as Salisbury steadily insisted, then an alliance with the willing Japanese was highly desirable. The Prime Minister continued to object, bringing to bear the arguments which had been persuasive for a quarter of a century. On one draft he commented: 'there is no limit: and no escape. We are pledged to war, though the conduct of our ally may have been followed in spite of our strongest remonstrances, and may be assuredly regarded by us with clear disapprobation. I feel sure that such a pledge will not be sanctioned by Parliament and I think that in the interests of the Empire it ought not to be taken.'[84] But after this stout protest his minute fell away into concern with detail. He still had the power to veto the Anglo-Japanese Treaty, but he did not use it. The Treaty was signed at the end of January 1902, and Salisbury passed quietly into retirement in July.

Salisbury does not fit into any category. He is not like any other Foreign Secretary. His high intelligence and sardonic wit make his comments and speeches more attractive to read than any other Foreign Secretary except Canning. With Canning one is never sure whether thrusting personal ambition or a genuine liberal instinct was fuelling his intellect. In Salisbury both passions were absent. With the exception of the few months in 1877 when he was man-ocuvring to replace Derby, he was content with his own position as a Cecil and a Cabinet Minister. Liberal instincts he despised. He was a patriot who despised jubilees and, except on rare occasions, imperial rhetoric. He was a sincere Christian who disliked preaching and theological dispute. Unlike most of those who believe that change is likely to be for the worse, he nevertheless did not despair; in the field of foreign affairs he was confident that energetic diplomacy and the occasional threat of force could preserve Britain and her trade from disaster. His cool temperament prevented him from being a great Prime Minister, a description he would never have sought; for clarity of thought and action as Foreign Secretary he was unmatched.

It can be argued that this ability fell short of true greatness. Salisbury's skill was more than tactical. Throughout his life he was at home in the world of changing ideas. His philosophical speeches are among his best and, as we have seen, he constantly emphasised the sad reality of change. But he did not seriously challenge the orthodoxies of his day. Others offered alternative approaches to Britain's problems in the last quarter of the nineteenth century. Although his practice fell far short, Gladstone believed in an ethical foreign policy based on the Concert of Europe. A wide group of politicians and observers believed in an imperial federation between Britain and the White Dominions. Alternatively or in addition, Chamberlain argued for an alliance either with the US or Germany as well as Japan. Agreements with France and Russia might also have been more effective as instruments of peace if concluded in the last decade of the nineteenth century rather than in the first decade of the twentieth. These are all theories whose usefulness cannot now be tested; Salisbury at the time evaded rather than refuted them. He was not trying to build a new international system fit for a new world. Rather, like Bismarck but with more humanity, he was working to make the existing system work as effectively as possible for his country. In this limited but not contemptible aim he was successful. He preserved the dignity of his country and kept alive its young men, but both survived for only a little more than a decade after his death.

CHAPTER V

GREY

'War would be so criminal, so absurd a thing that even Europe,
perversely armed to the very teeth ... no longer dares to
provoke it'

Norman Angell, *The Great Illusion,* 1910

No one was delighted, no one appalled when Sir Edward Grey was
appointed Foreign Secretary in December 1905 after the Conservative
Government under Balfour fell to pieces. Only later, after the catastrophe, came the close and hostile scrutiny of Grey's character and
qualifications.

In 1905 Grey was an active and leading member of the Liberal
Party, had already served as a junior Minister in the Foreign Office
under Lord Rosebery, and had recently made several thoughtful
speeches on foreign affairs. True, he had not travelled widely, had
no fluency in French and no pronounced interest in the habits or
culture of any country except his own. But such insularity was
hardly exceptional among British Foreign Secretaries, who were
expected to keep a decent distance from the foreigners with whom
it was their duty to deal.

A baronet aged forty-nine from Northumberland, grandson of a
Whig Home Secretary, indirectly descended from the Prime Minister
Lord Grey, the author of the great Reform Bill, educated at Winchester, then at Balliol College Oxford – this was a distinguished
rather than dramatic background. The handsome profile with strong

nose and chin fitted Grey's Whig principles, just as predictably as his unfailing courtesy flowed from a Wykehamist education. His first steps into politics were also orthodox. At the age of twenty-three in 1885 Edward Grey challenged Lord Percy, son of the Duke of Northumberland, for one of the county seats which seemed almost as firm a part of the Percy inheritance as Alnwick Castle and the 150,000 acres which went with it. The young Whig squire campaigned vigorously against Percy, but interrupted his speaking and canvassing to marry the daughter of another local landowner. He won the election handsomely and then celebrated his victory by going fishing with his opponent.[1] All this could have come from one of Trollope's political novels. Grey entered the House of Commons as its youngest Member, the latest example of an old tradition.

Few individuals, once closely examined, continue to fit a stereo-type with any exactness. There were already oddities about Grey. There had been, for example, the strange lapse into idleness at the age of twenty-two. He had had to leave Oxford on grounds clearly explained in the Balliol minutes book for January 1884: 'Sir Edward Grey, having been repeatedly admonished for idleness, and having shown himself entirely ignorant of the work set him in vacations as a condition of residence, was sent down, but allowed to come up to pass his examination in June.' He duly limped back to Oxford for the exam and achieved a humiliating Third in Jurisprudence.[2] His father and grandfather being dead, there was no one to rebuke him, and he showed no sign of penitence. He had enjoyed the social and sporting opportunities of Winchester and Oxford; but had also discovered his true love, namely the rivers and wildlife of North-umberland.

Grey's marriage proved to be another oddity. Political wives could at that time be divided into two categories: those who joined their husbands as hostesses in his hunt for political prizes, and those who stayed at home and bred his children. Dorothy Grey rejected both choices. After their honeymoon she told her husband that she dis-liked physical sex, so that was that. She felt no greater appetite for the pains and pleasures of politics. She avoided most of the many social gatherings which were open to her in London and North-umberland. She and Grey lived together as brother and sister, devoted to each other and to the exploration of thought, books, and nature which they conducted, happily though prosaically, in the spirit of William and Dorothy Wordsworth in the Lake District two generations before.

Edward nursed his Dorothy through the black moods which can afflict naturally solitary people. Fallodon in Northumberland remained their base, but it was a long way away. The simple cottage which they acquired on the River Itchen in Hampshire became for both of them a haven verging on paradise, in which they spent as many days as possible, and for which they longed at all other times. Birds, fish, trees and the passing seasons became more real and much more attractive to the Greys than the bad-tempered and unpredictable vagaries of politics. It is usual for politicians from time to time to profess a distaste for politics. For most this is part of their stock in trade, a device by which they cope with fatigue or misfortune. The feeling is not usually invented or insincere; but before long it fades and the political appetite returns. The politician would be taken aback if in the meantime his profession of distaste had been taken seriously. Of all the Foreign Secretaries we have sketched, Grey is the only one whose dislike of the political life was deeply rooted. For Grey, country tastes and pursuits were never relegated to the background; they often dominated his thoughts. They tempted him to escape from London, the centre of his professional life, of which he wrote one summer in his book on fly fishing, 'There is the aggressive stiffness of the buildings, the brutal hardness of the pavement, the glare of the light all day striking upon hard substances, and the stuffiness of the heat from which there is no relief at night.'[3]

In this preference he was powerfully supported by Dorothy. She was the stronger character, devoted to him and to their private friendship, the more precious because of the barriers which they erected against the outside world. She was killed in 1906 when the horse of the carriage which she was driving bolted and threw her on to the road. Edward had only been Foreign Secretary for a few months, but long before that the pattern had been set. So far as he could he maintained the way of life which they had shared, to which he added sadness as a tribute to his love.

These characteristics made Grey a difficult Minister. He did not shirk his work, and at that work he was no lightweight. Through ten years he was kept going by a stern sense of duty. Nor was he stupid; he read and thought widely. Nor did he confine himself to foreign affairs; on domestic matters he held with natural courtesy firm and surprisingly radical views. He favoured a largely elected House of Lords, votes for women, and Lloyd George's taxes on land. He was not a man to shirk responsibilities. But a sense of responsibility by itself lacks something as a driving force.

Grey seemed to gain neither enjoyment nor entertainment from his choice of career. There was in him no trace of the sometimes reckless excitement which drove Canning and Disraeli forward, or the sardonic and highly intellectual amusement which sustained Lord Salisbury through hours of tedious diplomacy. Because Grey gained no particular pleasure from office he was always ready to think of leaving it; this made for an awkward colleague. He could afford to be touchy about his own honour because he was ready at the stroke of a pen to protect it by resignation. His sensitivity went beyond matters of honour. Before and after taking office in 1905 he worked out a set of conditions about British foreign policy to which he held steadfastly through many storms. The need to apply and justify these convictions served as a substitute for the driving personal ambition which impelled Churchill or Lloyd George. His lack of drive did not mean that Grey was content to be out-argued or overruled by more dramatic colleagues. On the contrary, he was a stubborn man, always conscious with foreigners of his dignity as an Englishman, and with Englishmen of his equal dignity as a Member of Parliament, an educated gentleman, a Liberal and a Grey.

Although Grey's qualifications for appointment as Foreign Secretary were well established by 1905, it did not follow that he would get the job. There was one strong reason why he might not: he was on poor, even hostile terms with Henry Campbell-Bannerman, the new Prime Minister and leader of the Liberal Party. In the first years of the twentieth century the two main political parties were both split on an issue which stirred deep passions. The Conservatives quarrelled among themselves over free trade versus protection, the Liberals over the Boer War. The more radical Liberals, including Campbell-Bannerman and Lloyd George, opposed the war in principle; the others, including Rosebery, Asquith and Grey, accepted the war but criticised its conduct. Rosebery, still in his prime and a former Prime Minister, seemed the natural head of these Liberal Imperialists. A born leader by reason of eloquence, intelligence, wealth and good looks, he did not know how to lead. As the years passed his charm and intelligence became absorbed into a weary egotism. At isolated intervals he made great speeches but there was no follow-up. The man who in his youth had organised Gladstone's triumphant Midlothian campaign had lost the art of listening or working with others. More serious for Grey, Rosebery's ideas on foreign policy had markedly diverged from his own. Even within the Liberal Imperialists, there was a division.

Luckily for the Liberal Party, the British finally, after much tribulation, won the Boer War. The split in the Liberal Party, unlike its equivalent among the Tories, began to heal. It remained to make sure at a lower level that those Liberals who had supported the Boer War were not left out of office when its critic Campbell-Bannerman eventually formed a Government. Three friends, Asquith, Grey and Haldane, formed the Relugas Compact (named after a fishing lodge they rented in Sutherland) to ensure their own futures by solidarity with one another. These three principled colleagues grievously mishandled their tactics when the moment came. Grey in particular worked himself into a high-minded muddle. Vexed by Grey's reluctance, Campbell-Bannerman actually telegraphed to Cairo offering the Foreign Office to the veteran imperialist Lord Cromer, who at once declined. Eventually the pieces fell into a more natural pattern and Grey entered the Foreign Office.

Since the last years of Lord Salisbury's reign, British foreign policy had been in ferment. As we have seen, even Salisbury had been forced to agree that the security and prosperity of Britain could no longer be assured by relying on naval superiority and agile diplomacy, shunning any foreign commitments or alliances. But once the opposition to all alliances died away, the argument about the choice of ally dragged on for years. When Joseph Chamberlain announced that 'we are the most hated nation of the world and also the best loved', his advice was that we should rely on our 'kinsfolk', whoever they might be.[4] At different times he put the stress on the three possible components of this group –

the British colonies (by which he meant those who were or could be settled by white men), the United States and, in earlier versions of his ideas, Germany, thus stretching the vague concept of kinship beyond history to race. Salisbury himself, while firmly rejecting an alliance with Germany, had manoeuvred Britain into a position in European diplomacy more favourable to the Triple Alliance of Germany, Austria and Italy than to the rival alliance between France and Russia. The Kaiser's hostility to British policy in southern Africa led Chamberlain to strike out Germany as a possible ally; but to Grey's dismay, Rosebery continued to show, as he had done in the 1890s, considerable sympathy for a closer Anglo-German understanding.

Although, or because, he had visited some of these on a parliamentary commission, Grey did not believe that the colonies of the British Empire could be welded into a coherent political whole. He had supported the Boer War but was not seduced by the imperial dream of Chamberlain or Kipling. As regards the Americans, Grey moved British policy a long way forward. Salisbury had studiously avoided a quarrel with the United States, but his disdain for their loud-mouthed diplomacy was always apparent. He never accepted the American interpretation of the Monroe Doctrine. Salisbury held portentously in 1895 that 'the Government of the United States is not entitled to affirm as a universal proposition, with reference to a number of independent states for whose conduct it assumes no responsibility, that its interests are necessarily concerned in whatever may befall those states, simply because they are situated in the Western Hemisphere'.[5] Grey gave up that argument six years later. 'I have always felt that it was folly for us to argue about the Monroe Doctrine. The Monroe Doctrine is whatever the United States says it is, and what we have to consider is how far we can meet it.' But it was one thing to accept the American doctrine in America's backyard, another to treat the United States as a major actor on the world stage. For Grey in 1905 this stage was still dominated by European actors. During his years as Foreign Secretary, Grey travelled much further down the road of Anglo-American friendship, helped by a fruitful personal friendship with Theodore Roosevelt. As we shall see, the Great War transformed his idea of the role of the United States in the world; he was one of the first statesmen to see how that country could help to prevent another catastrophe. But in the various crises which led to that war, the United States still seemed a long way away.

Grey found the answer to the problem of alliances in the files of the Foreign Office and the policy of his Conservative predecessor, Lord Lansdowne. In general he favoured continuity and saw no merit in changing foreign policy simply because the party label of the Government had changed. In 1904 Lansdowne had concluded the famous agreement with France, using as its title the phrase *entente cordiale* which had originated in the agreement made by Queen Victoria, Peel and Aberdeen sixty years earlier. The 1904 agreement did not constitute a military alliance. It did not even include an undertaking to work together diplomatically. The two Governments simply settled a number of colonial disputes which had vexed their relationship for many years. It was only six years since one of these disputes had brought the two nations into passionate argument over Fashoda. The most important of the provisions of the 1904 agreement ended the long contest for dominance in Egypt. By accident rather than design, the British had acquired that dominance in Gladstone's time and had since discovered many reasons why they should not abandon it. In return for acknowledging a fact which they were powerless to alter, the French received acknowledgement of a superior special interest in Morocco which they had not yet asserted.

The existence of the 1904 agreement rather than its content was important for Grey. In October 1905 Grey was not yet Foreign Secretary; the Conservative Government was tottering towards a certain fall. Grey set out in a speech in the City the principles on which a Liberal Government would conduct its foreign policy. There would be no abrupt change; continuity was a virtue, but it was continuity with a difference. Without intellectual pretensions, without official advice or extensive study, Grey set out in Opposition the line which he then followed in office with remarkable consistency. He had grasped one fundamental point. The structure of treaties and official declarations governing relations between states may remain unaltered for years; but within those structures there is constant change. Each day the river in front of you may look the same, but it is different. Understandings such as the Anglo-French entente have, in the words of one scholar, 'an internal logic that develops as circumstances change'.[6] In his City speech, after arguing that the Anglo-French entente was a cardinal point in our foreign policy, Grey argued that the spirit of the agreement was more important than the letter. His audience may have taken this as a platitude, but the consequences of that remark would have stunned his listeners if they could have guessed them.

The entente created a dynamic which led in ten years from the settlement of distant disputes between two colonial powers to the dispatch of a British army to fight in France. Neither Grey nor anyone else foresaw how this dynamic would work: there was no far-sighted secret conspiracy. But the concept of a flexible, evolving entente suited Grey and his colleagues well. It fitted the British instinct for pragmatism much better than it suited the French. The French found themselves caught in a vague love affair with many words but no consummation. Their frustration was intense. Throughout Grey's peacetime tenure of office the French urged for a definite British commitment to come to the help of France if she was attacked. Even in the last desperate hours of peace in August 1914, Grey refused the French Ambassador the assurance he wanted.

This ambiguity which had crept into British diplomacy suited Grey and his colleagues well. It stemmed partly from Salisbury's old doctrine that no British government could commit itself in advance of a crisis because it could not pre-judge what Parliament would accept in that crisis. It was more immediately a necessary device for preserving unity in a liberal Cabinet which would have been bitterly divided if the issues had been put clearly before them. Grey was able over and over again to say to anxious colleagues and backbenchers that Britain was not committed to take sides in a European war. But, more fundamentally, the vagueness of the entente marked the continued high ambitions of British foreign policy.

Grey was no disciple of Disraeli; he avoided the intoxicating rhetoric of national prestige. Nor did he preach freedom and what we now call human rights across the world as Gladstone had done. But he and the British Establishment in general wished their country to hold a different position from any other European power. They wanted to hold the balance, not throw their weight irrevocably into one scale. They were ready to support France with diplomacy on specific occasions; that was the point to which the entente had evolved by 1905. Over the years it gradually evolved further, but never to the point where Britain was prevented from negotiating separately with Germany, from presiding over European discussions in a neutral spirit, from criticising the French when they appeared to go astray, or from truthfully telling the House of Commons that Britain's hands were free. These were the fruits of an honest ambiguity.

The element of studied uncertainty in Grey's policy exasperated both the French and the Germans, and latterly Grey's own officials. Clear, well-trained minds usually aim for certainty; less educated minds live more easily with ambiguity, which can sometimes be an advantage. This was not for Grey just a tactic to fit the domestic political scene. He saw it as a positive virtue because of the restraint it imposed on the behaviour of both France and Germany. Its critics later argued, with some justice, that clarity might have prevented war. Grey's bias in favour of France was apparent at each turn of events; but he believed that the carefully preserved doubt about Britain's intentions could be used to curb rashness by either side, and that it actually had this effect until overwhelming German ambition made diplomacy useless.[7]

The development of the Anglo-French entente into an alliance was so slow and ambiguous that never before 1914 did it provoke clear-cut debate. Joseph Chamberlain, with his tough vocabulary and straightforward advocacy of alliances, suffered a major stroke in 1906 and disappeared from the political scene. Neither the politicians nor the public relished open discussion of this fundamental change in British foreign policy.

As we have seen, the concept of a peacetime alliance was alien to Foreign Secretaries before Lansdowne and Grey. Some of them, like Castlereagh and Aberdeen, had believed in the usefulness of a general Concert of Europe. Others, like Canning, Palmerston and, as Prime Minister, Disraeli, relied principally on the free-standing power and prestige of Britain. Most, like Salisbury, combined a skilful balance of both concepts, tilting one way or the other in response to circumstances. But Grey, despite all his disavowals, manufactured a Continental alliance with France as a result of which Britain entered the most destructive war in her history. Two factors worked to explain and justify this slow revolution. The first was a recognition of Britain's declining relative power. This could be measured in terms of different kinds of wealth or the share of trade. The measurement which preoccupied Britain's leaders was naval armament. Salisbury's naval building programme of 1889 was a step, but an inadequate step, to bolster a declining supremacy. The first peacetime alliance, with Japan fourteen years later, was overwhelmingly naval in purpose and justification.

Of the dominant powers facing Britain, two were old enemies and two were newcomers. It was necessary, and proved possible, to accommodate and humour one of the newcomers, despite its occasional outbursts of hyperbole; out of this accommodation would later be born the modern Anglo-American relationship. The other newcomer staked its claims in a louder and more threatening way. When in 1901 the Kaiser proclaimed Germany's rightful place in the sun, his rhetoric was not all that different from Theodore Roosevelt's boast of carrying a big stick. Both were expressed in the noisy vocabulary of a youthful giant. But because of geography and history, the implications for Britain were rightly seen as wholly different. Efforts were made to humour the Germans as well as the American newcomer, but their success was only partial in America's case, and non-existent in Germany's.

It proved easier to achieve with the two old enemies, France and Russia, the reconciliation needed to compensate for declining relative strength; and reconciliation evolved crisis by crisis into alliances. Thucydides would have recognised the process and the spirit of rivalry which inspired these developments. The rising power of one state generated fear in another; fear generated alliances; alliances led to disputes in faraway places; disputes led to the Peloponnesian War, the defeat of Athens and the reordering of the Greek world.

In his City speech, Grey was remarkably conciliatory towards Russia. If Russia accepted that Britain intended to maintain her position in Asia, then Britain would do nothing to thwart Russian policy in Europe. 'On the contrary it is urgently desirable that Russia's position and influence should be re-established in the Councils of Europe.'[8] There were risks in this line of thought. Grey counted on bipartisan support from the Conservatives, who were traditionally suspicious of Russia as a powerful threat to British rule in India. Many in the Liberal Party detested the reactionary Czarist regime, which was in 1905 violently repressing the first serious attempt at a Russian revolution. In office, Grey did not immediately follow up this part of his City speech. He allowed the thought about Russia to mature. But he knew the facts of the situation had changed drastically since Disraeli and Salisbury hacked away at Russian ambitions at the Congress of Berlin. Britain no longer believed that Constantinople was the key to India. Moreover, the Russians had been defeated and humiliated by Japan, and Japan had been Britain's ally since 1902. The danger from Russian strength in Asia had virtually disappeared; the danger from Russian weakness in Europe was apparent. The Germans worked on Czar Nicholas II to revive in some form Bismarck's League of the Three Emperors (Russia, Germany, Austria-Hungary) and leave France isolated. Although Grey refused to join the Franco-Russian alliance, it was crucial to the balance of power in Europe that this alliance should not disintegrate.

As soon as he took office Grey found himself at the heart of a crisis which tested and illustrated his ideas. German diplomacy under the Chancellor, von Bülow, had become more flamboyant and less calculating. The Anglo-French entente had been a setback for Germany; it contained an agreement on Morocco which, without any consultation with Germany, gave France what amounted to a free hand. Germany had no particular interest in Morocco; the issue was one of prestige. The Kaiser arrived in Tangier in March 1905 and announced that Morocco was an independent state.[9] Neither he nor anyone else had thought through what should happen next. The result was uproar, talk of war, and the summoning of a diplomatic conference at Algeciras. The Germans believed they would be in a strong position. Of France's two friends, Russia was demoralised by defeat at the hands of Japan and in London the Conservative Government was disintegrating. They miscalculated. The Conservative Foreign Secretary, Lord Lansdowne, warned the German Ambassador that if Germany attacked France public opinion would not allow the Government to remain neutral.[10] Grey, on taking office, repeated the warning to the Ambassador on 3 January 1906. Two days earlier he had written to the British Ambassador in Berlin. 'The danger of speaking civil words in Berlin is that they may be used or interpreted in France as implying that we shall be lukewarm in our support of the Entente at the Conference. I think it is essential that we guard against this danger, even at the risk of sending a little shudder through a German audience.'[11] A pattern was thus established. Grey in his first crisis showed the Germans that they could not split him from the French. The Germans found themselves outmanoeuvred at the conference; they accepted a compromise which defined the French role in Morocco in ample terms, giving them control over the police. The entente had survived its first challenge.

But the French were not told how strongly Grey, or indeed Lansdowne, had spoken to the Germans. The ambiguity had to be preserved. A little shudder was to be administered to the Germans, but no corresponding thrill of enthusiastic comradeship to the French. When the French asked for clarity, both Lansdowne and then Grey told them to be content with what they got, which Grey described as 'benevolent neutrality'.[12] As a result, Britain emerged in the dual role which she had evolved for herself – as a friend of France, but also as a wise arbiter, the linchpin of European diplomacy.

Except that in the margins of the Algeciras conference the evolution of the Anglo-French entente took a significant but secret step forward. There is still doubt about the exact origin of the staff talks between the British and French military. Some discussions had apparently begun under Lansdowne, but they were not structured and the French were anxious for more. Towards the close of the Algeciras crisis, Grey specifically authorised military staff talks with the French. The Prime Minister, Campbell-Bannerman, and King Edward were told, but neither the Cabinet nor Parliament. As the French Ambassador, Cambon, reported to Paris on 31 January 1906, 'certain ministers would be astonished at the opening of such talks: it was better to keep silent and continue preparations discreetly'.[13]

These crucial staff talks continued intermittently until war broke out in 1914. The logic of Grey's position was clear. He refused to commit Britain to fight a war alongside France. He certainly believed, and indeed told the Germans, that in certain circumstances this could happen. But a sudden declaration of war without any previous military planning would be futile and dangerous. Both sides needed to know how they could fight together, in particular whether and how many British troops would be sent to France. This planning could in theory take place on a hypothetical basis, without any commitment. Grey kept himself entirely away from the talks, and professed ignorance of their content. He had indeed no personal interest in military matters, but that hardly explains his remoteness from discussions so heavy with weight for his country. But Grey needed to persuade himself and others that the die had not been cast, that he had preserved complete freedom for Cabinet and Parliament if the dreaded moment of choice should come. This was true enough, but an uneasy truth. Grey made it more possible to live with the danger by removing himself from the military talks and concentrating on the diplomacy which, if successful, would make the talks unnecessary.

During the Algeciras crisis, Grey made on his own terms a great personal sacrifice. He stayed in London. 'There are a few days in the first part of May when the beech trees in young leaf give an aspect of light and tender beauty to the English countryside which is well known but indescribable. The days are very few; the colour of the leaves soon darkens. I had now to wait another twelve months to see the great beech wood as I knew it in its greater beauty.'[14]

During his first years in office Grey became more strongly convinced that Germany was becoming fundamentally hostile to Britain. He was not influenced by French pleading or by any particular affection for France. Unlike Austen Chamberlain or Eden after him, he drew nothing from his personal tastes or upbringing which attracted him to France, or indeed to any foreign country. He was an exclusively English Englishman. But he judged that German policy was consistently opposed to his country's interests. He remembered what he believed was deliberate German mischief-making during his earlier period at the Foreign Office in the 1890s. There was a paradox here, as Niall Ferguson points out in *The Pity of War*. Britain's antagonists across the world during that period had been Russia in Asia and France in Africa. Germany was on the sidelines, making mischief certainly, keen to keep those antagonisms going, but not an active enemy. Yet in the end, the settlement of these disputes brought France and Britain together, and eventually Russia and Britain. 'The quarrels of lovers are the building of love.' It was the mischief-making of Germany, not the more serious rivalry with France and Russia, which stayed in Grey's mind.[15] Salisbury had tilted British diplomacy a few degrees towards Germany and the Triple Alliance. Joseph Chamberlain had advocated an actual alliance with Germany. The Admiralty had done its calculations on the assumption that France and Russia were Britain's likely enemies. As late as July 1905 Rosebery told Grey that, as Germany had 'four millions of soldiers and the second best navy in the world', an entente with France was 'like leaning on an aspen'. Grey disagreed: 'I think now more and more that Rosebery is wrong about Germany,' he wrote, 'and I feel it so strongly that if any government drags us back into the German net I will oppose it openly at all costs.'[16]

In that view, given six months before he took office, Grey was at once powerfully reinforced by the opinion of his senior officials whom he found at the Foreign Office. There too the memories of German mischief-making were clear. In January 1907, after the Algeciras crisis, one of the most influential of Grey's advisers wrote a memorandum which became famous. Drawing on the past, Sir Eyre Crowe argued in this memorandum, and more forcefully in later minutes, that Germany was consciously aiming at hegemony in Europe. A firm and consistent British policy of containment was therefore required. We had nothing to fear from a successful and competitive Germany, but if she sought to undermine our interests, the worst course was to continue on 'a road paved with peaceful British concessions, which had led to the almost perpetual state of tension existing between the two countries'. On the contrary, it had been shown in the Algeciras crisis that, when met with firm diplomacy, Germany calmed down.[17] But even Crowe as late as 1911 did not put too much weight on the Anglo-French entente, which was 'nothing more than a frame of mind, a view of general policy which is shared by the government of two countries'.[18] Forty years later, in an equally authoritative paper, George Kennan, after a somewhat similar analysis of Soviet intentions, also preached the doctrine of far-sighted containment. The methods were different but the message was clear: here was a country bent on domination, and new thinking was required to counter it.

It is important at this moment in our story, when, for the first time, the influence of Foreign Office officials powerfully affected policy, to consider how this came about and where it has led. During the first part of our period the influence of officials was negligible. Castlereagh took a handful of officials with him to Vienna in 1814. These were essentially clerks, who copied the diplomatic proposals and records of conversations and made sure that messages were properly conveyed. Through the nineteenth century, as the steamship, the railway and the telegraph transformed international communications, the quantity of correspondence and the number of clerks required increased steadily. A hierarchy began to grow, but even senior officials, now called Under Secretaries, were confined to routine tasks. As one of them wrote, 'Lord Palmerston, you know, never consults an Under Secretary. He merely sends out questions to be answered or papers to be copied when he is here in the evenings and our only business is to obtain from the clerks the information that he wanted.'

This highly personal system continued beyond its normal span because of the remarkable characteristics of Palmerston and Salisbury. Both men combined aristocratic self-confidence with a disguised capacity for intense hard work. Towards the end of his time Lord Salisbury increasingly relied on two successive Permanent Under Secretaries, Sir Philip Currie and Thomas Sanderson; but even they only tendered advice when asked. Sanderson was described as 'the last of the great super clerks'. By this time competitive examinations for the Overseas Diplomatic Service and for the Foreign Office had been introduced, but Salisbury kept a close eye on the outcome. As late as the 1890s it was observed that 'men from families totally unknown to Lord Salisbury or his Private Secretary need not apply'.[19]

A big change occurred in the first decade of the twentieth century. Under Grey's Conservative predecessor, Lord Lansdowne, the work of the Foreign Office was reorganised. For the first time important papers were conserved and registered, so that the past was always readily available to jog the memories of those handling the present. The new structure freed the time of senior officials, who developed the habit of tendering advice whether or not they were specifically asked for it. Senior officials had high profiles both socially and professionally. Charles Hardinge was a friend of

King Edward and went on to become Viceroy of India before returning to the Foreign Office for a second spell as Permanent Under Secretary. This progress would have been inconceivable in Palmerston's time.

Grey was not lacking in self-confidence and was by no means in the hands of his officials. But as the first Foreign Secretary since 1868 who served in the Commons, his burden of work was heavy and he was stubbornly reluctant to solve the problem by cutting back on the time spent in Northumberland watching birds or on the Itchen fishing for trout. Senior officials began to hold interviews with foreign ambassadors which Palmerston or Salisbury would have handled themselves.

These bureaucratic changes were masked from the public and to some extent even from the Cabinet by the general sense of unease which grew through the first years of the twentieth century. One issue above all brought together different irritations and bad memories into a growing antagonism between Britain and Germany. As early as 1902, Lord Selborne, the Conservative First Lord of the Admiralty, circulated a paper concluding, 'The result of my study is that I am convinced that the new German navy is being carefully built up from the point of view of a war with us.'[20] He appended an opinion of the British Ambassador in Berlin, Sir Frank Lascelles, who did not believe that the German Emperor or Government were really unfriendly, but 'we cannot safely ignore the malignant hatred of the German people or the manifest design of the German Navy'. It is not necessary to analyse in detail the naval building race which developed between the two countries. The Liberal Government was divided. Churchill and Lloyd George, who became in the next decade the fiercest of Britain's war leaders, were in the early days of the Liberal Government the fiercest opponents of naval expansion. Grey himself was temperamentally reluctant, and spoke in the Commons in August 1907 of 'the pathetic helplessness of mankind under the burden of armaments'.[21] But he supported the various decisions which led to the building of the Dreadnought battleships and kept Britain ahead in the naval arms race.

For their part, the Germans refused to accept that the British had any right to complain when Germany was simply following the British example. Liberal Ministers insisted that repeated efforts be made to reach a naval agreement with Germany to save both countries the expense of their naval programmes. The German Chancellor agreed to negotiate, but required in return for any limitations in the German programme an assurance of British neutrality in a European war. Negotiations in 1912 finally broke down on the phrasing of this clause.[22] Grey was not prepared to take any risk with Britain's ability to come to the help of France if (but of course only if) she decided to do so at the moment of crisis. Asquith, Grey and Haldane put the essential point in a polite, roundabout way at lunch with the German Ambassador on 26 June 1912:

> We said that in judging British public opinion allowance must be made for the peculiar position of Germany; she had the largest and strongest army in the world and she now had the second strongest fleet. This was an unprecedented situation. Admitting that Germany had nothing but good intentions towards us at the present moment, it was nevertheless natural to people to ask, not as regards this year or the immediate future, but as regards a few years hence, what use might be put to such power concentrated in the hands of one Government.[23]

That was the heart of the matter. Grey was not easy in talking in public about the balance of power, which meant different things to different people. But in private he wrote plainly about the Germans: 'we know that the phrase "balance of power" stinks in their nostrils. They want the hegemony of Europe, and to neutralise the only thing that has prevented them from getting it viz England's naval strength. They want an understanding which would have that effect.'[24] The hard truth in the background was obvious. A Liberal Government could never bring in conscription in peacetime. This meant that Britain would continue to have a small Army compared to the main European powers. As a result she would have to maintain her naval superiority, and reluctantly outbuild any country which challenged it.

So the antagonism flowed on, fed by a thousand tributaries of rumour and gossip. In the long years before opinion polls politicians relied on casual anecdote to gauge opinion. In the nineteenth and twentieth centuries the station master, as later the taxi driver, could play a chance but important part in assessing opinion and shaping policy. Grey relayed to his Ambassador in Berlin the story of an English lady who had been told by an Austrian officer of the great hostility towards England he had found everywhere in Germany.[25] In another letter the same year he referred to reports 'that a great number of German officers spend their holidays in this country at various points along the east and south coasts from the Humber to Portsmouth: places where they can be for no reason except that of making strategical notes as to our coasts. Friends of mine are constantly meeting in such places unexpected German officers who are known to be active, energetic and in good repute in Germany, and by no means discarded or retired.'[26] Out of such excitements emerged a crowd of best-selling novels, following the lead of *The Riddle of the Sands* by Erskine Childers in 1903. An even more exciting outcome in real life was the creation of MI5 and the Official Secrets Act of 1911.

In 1907 Grey achieved the entente with Russia which he had advocated two years earlier. The agreement followed the Anglo-French model of 1904: outstanding issues were settled without any formal alliance or undertakings for the future. In this way the ambiguities beloved by Britain were preserved, but a pattern of co-operation established which might (or might not) develop into something more formidable. The agreement, when compared for example with Salisbury's agreements with Germany, showed some signs of accepting that the world had moved into a new and less imperial century. There were no annexations, but instead spheres of influence. Russia was to keep out of Tibet and Afghanistan, both of which were to be buffer states. Persia, also in theory independent, was to be divided in three, a Russian, British and a neutral sphere of influence. Grey had trouble with the Conservative Opposition, led in the Lords by the former Viceroy Lord Curzon, who dissected the agreement for an hour and a quarter in a speech acknowledged to be powerful but too patronising to convince their lordships.[27] Crucial to Grey was the attitude of his Cabinet colleague John Morley, who might have been expected to oppose the agreement both as Secretary of State for India and as a firm Gladstonian liberal opposed to Czarist despotism. Grey's success in winning Morley round stemmed from his growing reputation for trustworthiness and sound judgement.

The Anglo-Russian entente proved a rickety affair. Both sides dabbled in Persian politics and came close to a clash. The Russians indulged in a round of diplomatic bargaining in the Balkans; this was aimed at strengthening their position in the Straits but ended only in their conniving in 1908 at the annexation of Bosnia by Austria-Hungary. Within the Foreign Office the need to sustain the Anglo-Russian entente despite these hazards was consistently argued by Sir Arthur Nicolson who became Permanent Under Secretary in 1910 after a period as Ambassador in St Petersburg.[28]

The Germans, having helped Austria outwit the Russians in the Balkans, turned their attention back to Morocco. Though the Kaiser himself was reluctant, his Ministers itched to retrieve the humiliation they had endured from Britain and France at the Algeciras conference. In early 1911 the French moved troops into Fez, going beyond what had been agreed at the conference. The Germans denounced the move and sent the gunboat *Panther* into the Moroccan Atlantic harbour of Agadir. There was immediately a crisis. The Germans demanded the cession to them of the French Congo in compensation for allowing the French their way in Morocco. Negotiations between France and Germany stalled. The British Cabinet was divided. The Admiralty did not greatly worry about a German naval presence at Agadir. Ministers refused to send a British warship as a counter to the *Panther*, and no one seriously supposed that Britain would go to war in defence of French policy in Morocco. But Grey and his advisers were alarmed that if Britain did nothing France might be forced to back down. This would put at risk both Grey's main objectives. France would blame Britain for lack of support and the entente would be undermined; Britain would lose her role as the arbiter and linchpin of European diplomacy. As Arthur Nicolson put it, 'we should have a triumphant Germany, and an unfriendly France and Russia, and our policy since 1904 of preserving the equilibrium and consequently the peace of Europe would be wrecked'.[29]

To retrieve the situation, after discussion with Grey, the Chancellor of the Exchequer, David Lloyd George, made a rousing speech at the Mansion House on 21 July. The Chancellor proclaimed in public what Grey the same day had told the German Ambassador, that Britain would not be ignored and would not accept a settlement reached without her participation. Britain was not to be treated 'as if she were of no account in the Cabinet of Nations . . . that price would be a humiliation intolerable for a great country like ours to endure'.[30] Lloyd George made no attempt to discuss the merits of the dispute in Morocco. Historians argue whether his speech was meant as a warning to France or to Germany; probably it was aimed at both. But the effect was dramatic and one-sided; the Germans took huge offence. The Agadir dispute became for a few weeks more of a row between Britain and Germany than between Germany and France. But, as happens, the quarrel subsided without further drama. The Germans drew back from demanding the whole of the French Congo and were content with two smallish slices. The *Panther* sailed from Agadir: the crisis passed; the British Lion had roared, but only once; the structure of European ententes and alliances was unchanged. Grey would not have been a British Liberal if he had not used his firmness on the entente to apply Gladstonian standards of dis-approval to French behaviour in Morocco. 'We can have nothing to do with any use [of power] that is mean and dishonourable. We have got to keep France straight in this matter or part company with her.'[31]

There were two important consequences of the Agadir crisis for Grey. During the crisis, the Cabinet learned for the first time of the military staff talks with France. The more radical members were appalled; the Lord Chancellor, Lord Loreburn, threatened to resign. Asquith, as Prime Minister, helped Grey to calm colleagues down, but he had to agree formally that no communications between staffs should directly or indirectly commit Britain to military or naval intervention. Cabinet colleagues who were temperamentally opposed to a collision with Germany began to be suspicious of Grey. If the military talks with France had been concealed for five years, what else might be going on behind their backs? Grey was walking a tightrope in a high wind. The political rationale behind his ambiguity was evident. He had set it out once again in a letter to Francis Bertie, the British Ambassador in Paris, commenting on one of his parliamentary answers. 'There would be a row in Parliament if I had used words which implied the possibility of a secret engagement unknown to Parliament all these years committing us to a European war . . . I purposely worded the answer so as not to convey that the engagement of 1904 might not in certain circumstances be construed to have larger consequences than its strict letter.'[32] Grey was not by nature a devious man; but the double negative became a tool of his policy. It was for professional diplomats to wrestle with the complications. But in the same letter Grey made it clear that if the Germans had pressed too hard at Algeciras, public opinion might have supported a war in support of France. In his mind the same was true of Agadir, and of any crisis thereafter.

In this analysis he now had two new powerful allies who had previously disagreed. Lloyd George, the radical pro-Boer Welshman, and Winston Churchill as Home Secretary had hitherto opposed naval rearmament. From now on Lloyd George had a reputation to preserve as the voice of the British Lion. More important, Churchill was now First Lord of the Admiralty. The crisis had reached its peak during a particularly hot August. Grey, to his disgust, had once again been pinned to London. Churchill kept him company, as Grey put it, 'for love of the crisis'.[33] Churchill regularly took the Foreign Secretary to swim at the Royal Automobile Club in Pall Mall and asked him to be godfather to his offspring, young Randolph. Two entirely different characters were brought together by need and trust.

This proved a crucial partnership. In 1912 naval staff talks began with the French. The logic for these talks was even clearer than for the military counterpart. Military planning was important, but in the minds of some not essential. There were both French and German experts who doubted whether the arrival of a predictably small British expeditionary force would be decisive one way or the other in a Franco-German war. The naval equation was different, and naval planning essential. In any war in which Britain and France were allies the French would obviously focus on the Mediterranean; their fleet based in Toulon would cope with any Italian or Austro-Hungarian enemies. The British would look after the Channel ports of each country, and deal with the German High Seas Fleet based at Kiel. It was the natural division of effort. But how could the French leave their Channel ports unguarded unless they had a clear commitment from the Royal Navy? The ambiguities of Grey's position, essential for political and desirable for diplomatic reasons, began to bump awkwardly against operational reality.

No period of diplomatic history has been so minutely studied as the five weeks between the assassination of the Austrian crown prince Franz Ferdinand in Sarajevo on 28 June 1914 and Britain's declaration of war on Germany on 4 August. In her book on the women in Lloyd George's life, Ffion Hague records how on 29 June Frances Stevenson brought the Chancellor a red box from the Foreign Office containing a report of the assassination. 'Lloyd George studied the message, and looked up. "This means war"', he said.'[34] Assuming that this was real foresight (rather than wisdom awarded later by an adoring mistress), the remark showed surprising prescience. For most observers another Balkan tragedy was just that – sad, but paltry. The Balkans had been in turmoil for more than two years as small states quarrelled and fought with the Turks and then among themselves over the carcass of the Ottoman Empire. Slowly and savagely the Eastern Question found its answer. Each time a limb fell away from the rotting body, a noisy squabble broke out among the flock of small Balkan predators, watched from nearby perches by their backers among the Great Powers.

Grey had added notably to his own reputation by organising in 1913 a conference of ambassadors in London supported by all the Great Powers, which achieved a temporary agreement. One outcome had been a sharpening of antagonism between Serbia and Austria, which saw the smaller state as a rallying point for dissident Slavs living within their Hapsburg Empire. The Austrians hesitated before deciding how to make use of the alleged connection between Serbia and the man who had assassinated Franz Ferdinand. The Germans for their own reasons urged Austria to lose no time in punishing Serbia. Austria, conscious of declining power and prestige, decided to gamble. As A.J.P. Taylor put it, 'The Hapsburg monarchy brought on its mortal crisis to prove that it was still alive.'[35] They drafted a tough ultimatum to Serbia, but in a final hesitation delayed another four days before delivering it on 23 July, requiring an answer within forty-eight hours. The Serbs replied within the deadline, more or less accepting nine of the ten Austrian demands, refusing only to agree that Austrian officials should join in the murder investigation. The Kaiser's first reaction was that the grounds for war had been removed, but there was by now no holding the Austrians, who declared war on Serbia on 28 July and bombarded Belgrade the next day.

Grey had tried to dissuade the Austrians, and proposed once again a conference of the powers. But this was a dog-eared card, inadequate for the occasion. The German Chancellor, Bethmann Hollweg, hesitated, and hoped the Austrians would consider Grey's plan. But more powerful German voices had assured Austria of full German support. The Russians made it clear that they would not leave Serbia to resist Austria alone. In Russia, Germany and France, the military wheels began to turn and engage each other in the downhill drive to the Great War.

At this point, the rigidity of the alliance system in Europe proved disastrous. Czar Nicholas was advised that Russia could not mobilise for a war against Austria alone; the mobilisation plan had to cover also the Russian frontier with Germany. In parallel, the German High Command insisted that if Germany went to war with Russia, she must begin by attacking France under the Schlieffen Plan: Russia's ally must be knocked out so that the German Army could be concentrated in the east.[36]

After launching his proposal for a conference, Grey retired to his cottage on the Itchen for a shortened weekend of reflection. He returned to London on 26 July in gloomy mood. He continued until the last moment his efforts at conciliation in Europe; but his energy was increasingly drawn into handling discussions, not in Berlin or Paris, but in the British Cabinet.

His own mind was clear. Britain could not go to war because Austria had attacked Serbia, nor because Austria and Russia were shaping up to fight each other. The moment France became involved, even as a result of the Franco-Russian alliance to which Britain was not a party, his attitude changed. His whole policy had been based on the entente with France. He had consistently declined to turn this into an alliance of formal obligation, but with equal consistency had warned the Germans that if the crunch came Britain was likely to intervene to help France. He had not followed the military staff talks closely, and was himself thinking in terms of British naval action rather than an expeditionary force. But the idea of British neutrality and a Germany triumphing over the collapse of the Anglo-France entente amounted in his eyes to Britain's abdication as a Great Power. He was helped by the brutal nature of the German ultimatum to France, but he would have felt the same about any war between

France and Germany except one in which France had been the aggressor.

Half the Cabinet disagreed. At a series of meetings between 21 July and 2 August a divided Cabinet refused to take a decision on intervention. Even Lloyd George showed signs of reverting from his forthright stance during the Agadir crisis. Asquith, the Prime Minister, could not be sure how many Ministers would resign if Britain went to war; he could be fairly sure that Grey and Churchill would resign if she did not. It was the fiercest Cabinet tussle on foreign affairs since Derby and Disraeli had argued over the Treaty of San Stefano; this time, the stakes were much higher.

In this situation, Grey held the last of what must have seemed an endless series of conversations with successive French and German Ambassadors in London – the last in peacetime, and the most extraordinary. Usually the temptation for Ministers and diplomats is to say to an interlocutor as much as possible of what the interlocutor wants to hear. But on 31 July and 1 August 1914, as the Austrians bombarded Serbia and the German, Russian and French troop trains carried armies to war, Grey emphasised to the German and the Frenchman the opposite of what each hoped. To the German on 31 July he hinted that Britain would be drawn in on France's side. To Cambon, the long-suffering French Ambassador, he denied on 1 August that Britain had any obligation to help France, who must make her own decisions. The next day he was authorised by the Cabinet to tell Cambon that the German fleet would not be allowed to attack the French Channel ports; no wider undertaking was possible.

The senior officials of the Foreign Office shared to the full the French frustration, and were driven to despair. Nicolson told Grey to his face that by refusing to support France 'you will render us a byword among nations'. A junior official recorded 'going to [Sir E] Crowe's room for an outlet of pent emotions; I found the dry man dissolved; tears glistened down the furrows of his face, and all that he could say was "the poor French"'. Another official remembers Crowe criticising Grey as 'not qualified by upbringing or study to understand what was going on in the sinister depths of the German mind'.[37] What Sir Eyre Crowe and others had to accept, despite their own upbringing and studies, was that in Britain in the last resort policy is made, not by professionals, but by a Cabinet responsible to Parliament.

If the argument had rested there, Britain would probably have gone to war, but with a split Government and a split nation. Ten of the twenty Cabinet Ministers, including Lloyd George, would probably have resigned. Indeed, the Liberal Government might have dissolved, with Asquith, Grey and Churchill joining the Conservatives to achieve a majority in the Commons to lead the nation into war. But it would have been a different nation and a different war.

The German Army saved the British Liberal Government and ensured that an overwhelmingly united Britain declared war on Germany on 4 August. The Schlieffen Plan for the German attack on France included a wide sweep through Belgium. Confronted with an ultimatum on 2 August, the Belgians decided to fight. The integrity of Belgium had been guaranteed by the powers, including by Palmerston and Britain, in 1839. When examined this guarantee was not entirely straightforward. A similar guarantee to Luxembourg had been defined away into nothing by Derby in 1867. Was the guarantee to Belgium equally meaningless unless all governments observed it? Was it affected by what Gladstone had said during the Franco-Prussian War of 1870? The Cabinet began to wrestle with these questions, but there was no time for the lawyers to take charge. The Cabinet decided that the decision on Belgium should be taken on political rather than legal grounds. The supreme politician Lloyd George ended his hesitation. Public opinion was for the first time stirred. It was inconceivable that Britain should allow the Germans to obliterate Belgium without intervening. On 3 August the Cabinet agreed on an ultimatum to Berlin requiring the withdrawal of German troops from Belgium.

That afternoon Grey stood up in the House of Commons to make the most important speech of his life. The task fell personally to Grey, to an extent inconceivable today. As Prime Minister, Asquith fully supported his Foreign Secretary but totally neglected what would normally be regarded as the Prime Minister's task, namely explaining to the public the new crisis which was about to engulf them. Until the last few days Asquith was much more concerned with the crisis in Ulster. Nothing Grey said on 3 August, neither analysis nor conclusion, can have surprised anyone who had followed events. But then few people had followed these events. A huge task of explanation was needed to a Parliament and a public opinion which had only just begun to turn its attention away from Ascot, cricket and the Suffragettes. The crisis in Ireland was even more compelling as the Ulster Unionists, backed by the Conservative Party, carried their opposition to Home Rule to the brink of civil war.

Grey's oration on 3 August does not read as a great speech, but its effect was great. Asquith wrote: 'Grey made a most remarkable speech about an hour long – for the most part almost conversational in tone and with some of his usual ragged ends: but extraordinarily well reasoned and tactful and really cogent – so much so that our extreme peace lovers were for the moment reduced to silence.'[38] Grey was staking his own reputation for good sense, firm character and trustworthiness. He set out in clear, pedestrian prose the policy which we have described. No one in his audience could have believed they were listening to a conspirator or warmonger. Grey that afternoon happened to speak with the voice of England. He could not have achieved the eloquence of Churchill in May and June 1940, and it would have been a mistake to try. His job was to be clear and persuasive, and in this he succeeded. There had been no time for elaborate preparation or revision, and perhaps this was as well. As Grey himself wrote: 'In a great crisis a man who has to act or speak stands bare and stripped of choice. He has to do what it is in him to do; just this is what he will do and must do, and he can do no other.'[39]

Only two Ministers resigned. Britain went to war with excitement, even enthusiasm. Queues of volunteers formed to join the Army, as memorably celebrated in Larkin's poem 'MCMXIV.' We do not know the name of the friend to whom Grey remarked, probably on the evening of 3 August, as they watched the gas lamps being lit on the edge of St James's Park beneath his window at the Foreign Office, 'the lamps are going out all over Europe: we shall not see them lit again in our life time'. That remark, rather than his speech to the Commons that afternoon, marks Grey's page in history.[40]

The Great War wrecked one European generation and shaped the next. The suffering and destruction created huge waves of anger, while seeking individuals on whom to fix guilt. Grey, who hated war and took no personal interest in military matters, bore the brunt of accusation in Britain. None of the arguments he had used, none of his decisions, none of the disputes with which he had wrestled seemed in retrospect to be of the same dimension as what followed. On this analysis he failed to provide even a fragment of justification when set in the balance against the Somme, Passchendaele or Verdun.* In his speech on 3 August Grey had argued that 'if we are engaged in war, we shall suffer but little more than we shall suffer even if we stand aside'.[41] He went on to argue that even if we stood aside at the outset, we would probably be forced into war in worse circumstances. But with hindsight his statement seemed unreal. When the war was finally over the only gainers were those who took no part in the original decisions in 1914, namely the United States and the new Communist rulers of Russia. All other participants ended at worst in anarchy, at best gravely weakened.

But this cannot be the only calculation. The judgement on Grey should begin with the question: did he behave wisely and honourably with the knowledge which he at the time possessed? The most damaging answer to this question came not from opponents of the war but from the man who became Britain's war leader, David Lloyd George. Lloyd George in his war memoirs, published in 1933, the year of Grey's death, devoted a whole chapter to denigrating his former colleague. By this time Grey had differed sharply from Lloyd George over his leadership of the Liberal Party, and Lloyd George exacted a price.[42] He wrote that Grey had 'high intelligence, but of a more commonplace texture'. His speeches were 'clear correct and orderly, but are characterised by no distinction of phrase or thought'. He produced 'a serene flow of unexceptionable diction which is apt to be reckoned as statesmanship until a crisis comes to put these

---

* Palmerston's biographer, Jasper Ridley, tells us that when Palmerston was Secretary at War in 1815, he sat down after Waterloo and calculated the total British fatalities sustained since the outbreak of the French Wars in 1793. In total, Palmerston worked out that 920 officers and 15,214 soldiers from other ranks had been killed across a span of twenty-one years; total naval fatalities amounted to 3,662. If Palmerston's calculations were correct – and there are valid grounds for questioning them – then, as Jasper Ridley has suggested, almost as many British soldiers died on the first day of the Battle of the Somme in 1916 as had died in the British Army and Navy during the entire Revolutionary and Napoleonic Wars. See Ridley, *Lord Palmerston* (London: Constable, 1970), p. 52.

urbanities to the test'. He looked imperturbable, a strong, silent man, but 'the strongest men of history have never been silent'. Lloyd George criticised Grey's failure to tell the Germans plainly that Britain would go to war if they invaded Belgium, arguing that if he had done so, they would have altered 'their dust-laden plans'.[43] This does not seem to have been the case. We now know that the German General Staff accepted that the Schlieffen Plan might lead to war with Britain, but judged that the arrival in France of a small British expeditionary force would not alter the fundamental military calculation.[44]

Because Lloyd George was a Cabinet colleague at the time he could not criticise, as many did, Grey's general conduct of diplomacy and in particular the military staff talks with France. For the Labour leader, Ramsay MacDonald, as for the American President, Woodrow Wilson, this secrecy was the heart of the problem: they argued that public opinion would not have tolerated what was being done in their name if they had known of it. This is far from self-evident. But from a Conservative viewpoint in December 1914, Austen Chamberlain made a measured comment of the same kind:

There had been nothing beforehand in official speeches or official publications to make known ... the danger that we ran to prepare them for the discharge of our responsibilities and the defence of our interests. Those who knew most were silent; those who undertook to instruct the mass of the public were ignorant, and our democracy with its decisive voice on the conduct of public affairs was left without guidance by those who could have directed it properly, and was misled by those who constituted themselves its guides.[45]

It is certainly true that neither Grey nor Asquith saw himself as a public educator, with a duty to muse aloud on the state of the world as Disraeli and Salisbury had done before them, and Churchill was to do in future. Public statements were to them part of the machinery of diplomacy, another part of which had to be conducted in secrecy.

Grey's policy, as we have seen, in particular the primacy which he gave to the Anglo-French entente, was based not on any particular affection for France, but on a belief that Germany was aiming at a form of hegemony in Europe which was unsafe for Britain. The counter-argument, put forward by the Germans at the time, and after the war by the war's many opponents, was that Germany felt encircled and threatened by the Franco-Russian alliance. She needed to neutralise this threat, but this did not involve any threat to Britain or her possessions. If Britain would declare herself neutral, then Germany would not need to build up her Navy, and Britain need not worry about what happened in the Continent of Europe.

Of course there were different German voices at different times and historians will never reach an agreed conclusion. Some even argue that the kind of Europe which would have emerged as a result of such an Anglo-German arrangement would not have been all that different from the European Union today, in which Germany is the strongest economic power. Others consider that the closest comparison is with Hitler's ambitions, which were accompanied by the same kind of peaceful overtures to Britain. The work of the German historian Fritz Fischer, and in particular his delving into the official German archives, has tilted the balance in favour of his conclusion that there was no general drift into war in 1914, but that Germany was alone determined to use the Balkan crisis as a way of asserting its own supremacy in Europe. The Germans were concerned that Russia was recovering fast from her defeat by Japan, building railways with French money, developing into a formidable military and industrial power. At the same time, Germany's only secure ally, Austria-Hungary, was weakening. Before these processes went too far Germany needed a quick and early war to secure her prime position in Europe. Because the German military were not interested in naval or colonial matters, they dismissed the importance of British intervention, even though they thought it likely. They were afraid of delay. The assassination of the Archduke gave them the opportunity. As Grey himself put it: 'Germany was not afraid, because she believed her army to be invulnerable, but she was afraid that in a few years hence she might be afraid ... Germany was afraid of the future.'[46]

If this analysis is right then Grey cannot be faulted in his general approach as he steered over nearly nine years between domestic and foreign considerations. He was caught in a diplomatic system with no accepted governing principle, and no international institutions of any validity. Castlereagh had tried and failed to build up a continuing

Concert of Europe; Gladstone had made speeches about it; but the concept had evaporated. In each national capital calculations were constantly adjusted, as those concerned weighed up factors of national military and financial power, prestige, loyalty to commitments and domestic pressures. These calculations were inevitably imperfect and subjective. Peace depended on the leaders in each country being able to guess and indeed manipulate the calculations of others. Bismarck was a master of this process, Salisbury in his detached way another. But such mastery was a matter of luck as well as skill, and luck ran out in the twentieth century. The Germans calculated that they could achieve the hegemony they thought they needed, either in peace or in a quick war. No one had the imagination or what Lloyd George called 'that high courage, bordering on audacity', which would be needed to manage the system successfully or create a new one. Although it is hard to give the last word to such an erratic buccaneer as Lloyd George, he was not wrong when he summarised the European leaders before 1914 as 'all able, experienced, conscientious and respectable mariners, but distinctly lacking in the force, vision, imagination and resource which alone could have saved the situation. They were all handy men in a well behaved sea, but helpless in a typhoon.'[47]

Grey himself took no pride in the achievement of persuading Cabinet, Commons and the nation to support his policy. He had no military instinct. He would go out of his way to avoid the sight of recruits marching to war down a cheering street.[48] He had failed to keep the peace and took no pleasure in war. He lingered on as Foreign Secretary until the fall of the Government in 1916, and Asquith's replacement by Lloyd George. These were the miserable years of his life. He was lonely. Dorothy had been his only intimate friend. His cottage on the Itchen burned to the ground. Worse, his eyesight began to fail. He disliked the wartime role of the Foreign Secretary, with good reason. He was no longer at the centre of policy-making. He had to supervise the deal which brought Italy into the war with a promise of territory and later the Sykes-Picot Agreement, by which Britain and France carved up in advance much of the Middle East. In his anxiety to keep the Russians an effective ally, he agreed to let them have their way over the future of Constantinople and the Straits. To the irritation of Churchill and Lloyd George, he was

passive and pessimistic about Greece and schemes of a Balkan federation. Most of these manoeuvres were defensible as part of the
desperate effort to win the war, but they generated no enthusiasm
in Grey.

There will never be an end to the argument whether Britain should
have stayed out of the Great War of 1914. Little such argument
surrounds the war of 1939. The wickedness of Hitler and the trans-
parency of his design reduced the argument to a secondary one:
should we have moved to stop him before 1939? The question about
the earlier war is more desperate. Could Britain, in particular Grey,
have reached acceptable accommodation with a German hegemony
on the Continent of Europe, which would have been the certain
result of British neutrality in 1914? We think not. We believe, though
no one can prove, that in the end we would have faced German
attacks on the independent existence of Britain which we would
then have been much less able to resist. The assassination of the
Archduke would probably not have produced a great European war
if exceptional men such as Bismarck or Salisbury had been in charge
of their countries. By audacity or subterfuge they would have found
a way. But by his lesser light, and in his more dangerous time, Grey
acted reasonably and in good faith. If he was culpable, it was in not
attempting to explain to the entire Cabinet earlier than 1914 why an
alliance with France was necessary. Had he done so, he might have
given himself more scope for a firmer, and more public, commitment
to France. This in turn may have had a deterrent effect on Germany,
instead of contributing to the general climate of suspicion and fear.
In this sense, Grey chose the wrong weapons, but picked the right
friends.

That verdict, whether true or flawed, only takes us so far. Sir
Norman Angell in his book *The Great Illusion*, published in 1910,
argued that the integration of the economies of the world had grown
to such an extent that war between them would be futile and therefore unthinkable. He was right about the futility, wrong to suppose
that what was futile could not happen. But it is not the wrecking
of the world's economy that we still meet to commemorate each
Remembrance Day. The slaughter of the Great War went beyond
anything that Angell or Grey could have conceived. The attribution
of war guilt to Germany, though attempted at Versailles and largely

justified, proved sterile. The only adequate response was, and remains, the attempt to find a better way of organising the world. To that task Grey returned.

His chief interest focused on his dealings with the United States before her entry into the war in 1917. The relationship was made prickly by repeated arguments over the Royal Navy's enforcement of the wartime blockade on American ships. Grey did not think it sensible to urge the Americans to join the war; they would make their own decisions. But he became intensely interested in the concept of a League of Nations, which President Wilson and his close adviser Colonel House had begun to elaborate. To the Colonel's disappointment, Grey did not see this as the way to a negotiated peace with Germany. Allied success in the field would have to come first. Lloyd George found no place for Grey in the Government which he formed at the end of 1916. Once out of office, Grey joined actively in promoting the League, and in August 1919 even accepted from Lloyd George the position of a special Ambassador to Washington with agreement on the League as his main objective. This did not work well. President Wilson could not persuade Congress to join the League; in January 1920 Grey made matters worse in a public letter explaining and appearing to accept this American reluctance. Back in London he continued with Lord Robert Cecil to support the League enthusiastically, but never again took office.

The reason for his enthusiasm for the League was clear. Grey never joined in the general denunciation of secret diplomacy, alliances and pacts. He never repented his own part – indeed in his last years he made a good job of justifying it in his two volumes of essays, *Twenty-Five Years*. But he never doubted that he had failed or that the system which he had tried to manage was inadequate. Here in the League was a set of governing principles and machinery for settling disputes which had not existed, and which the world badly needed.

After the misery of the war, Grey's last years were relatively serene. He lived to see the dimming of the new international light which he had hoped would guide an era better than his own. Such matters became less important to him. He married again and lived until 1933. But the failure of his eyesight deprived him of what had been his main interests. As his relative and biographer

Trevelyan wrote, 'when the long-hoped for hour of release came he returned to his birds, but he could no longer see them; to his books but he could no longer read them ... The trend of the world's affairs after the war baffled his hopes for the free and peaceful future of mankind.'[49]

CHAPTER VI

RAMSAY MACDONALD AND
AUSTEN CHAMBERLAIN

'And covenants, without the sword, are but words and of no
strength to secure a man at all'

Thomas Hobbes, *Leviathan*

On 22 January 1924, Ramsay MacDonald kissed the King's hands at
Buckingham Palace as Prime Minister. He had a long talk with George
V, who referred to Russia. 'Hoped I would do nothing to compel him
to shake hands with the murderers of his relatives. King plays the
game straight, though I feel he is apprehensive. It would be a miracle
were he not.'[1]

The arrival of the first Labour Government in British history
was bound to cause the weak-willed to tremble and the strong to
exaggerate. Winston Churchill, just defeated as Liberal candidate for
Leicester West, had warned that a Labour Government would be 'a
national misfortune such as has usually befallen a great state only on
the morrow of defeat in war'.[2] These fears never developed into a
nightmare. For this the King was in a minor way responsible because
of the courteous, straightforward relationship which he at once
developed with MacDonald. So was Stanley Baldwin, the defeated
Conservative leader, who still commanded more votes than Labour
in the House of Commons, but made no prolonged attempt to keep
Labour out of power.

The main reason for calm was the new Prime Minister himself. MacDonald now became a familiar figure to the nation as a whole. Not that he was by nature calm; on the contrary, he lived in an inner world of strong emotions, in which genuine idealism wrestled with a romantic, self-centred melancholy. These were not revolutionary emotions; neither Robespierre nor Lenin would have found him a kindred spirit. One of MacDonald's more awkward innovations in his first weeks in office was to decide that his entire correspondence at Downing Street should be delivered unopened for his personal attention. This raised eyebrows, but it was hardly the first spark of an incendiary regime.

MacDonald was not English, but the English had little difficulty in accommodating yet another Scot. His appearance was mildly eccentric, but not fearsome. The British Ambassador in Berlin, Lord D'Abernon, unable to avoid a patronising note, was nevertheless pleased to observe that in appearance he was 'more distinguished than most of his predecessors in office; in intelligence and personality he had none of the defects anticipated. A long fore-and-aft finely modelled head, deep seated eyes, well cut features; a tired reflective air, suggestive of an exhausted aristocratic strain; no aggression, no stridency, but in their place disillusionment, calm and resignation.'[3] The Cabinet Secretary, Maurice Hankey, calling on MacDonald for the first time in his house off Belsize Park in north London, found him 'gaunt and thin and wearing a very ancient and threadbare "sporting" coat'.[4] In this way the sports jacket arrived at the summit of British politics – a novel development no doubt, but no reason for deep concern.

MacDonald was born illegitimate in 1866 at Lossiemouth, a small fishing port to the east of Inverness. He was educated in the Scottish parish system, which he warmly praised. 'The machinery', he wrote of his school, 'was as old as Knox; the education was the best ever given to the sons and daughters of men.' The political flavour of this upbringing was immediately apparent. 'The whole of my part of Scotland was radical,' he wrote, 'and we seemed to have been born with the democratic spirit strongly developed in us.'[5]

After a few months in Bristol, MacDonald moved to London at the age of twenty. He kept a home in Lossiemouth to which he could retreat in search of rest, but from then on his life was centred on political activity in London. He earned a frugal living in clerical jobs and took an increasing part in the steady, though tortuous, movement of the British Labour movement away from the Liberal Party. In 1900 he became the Secretary of the Labour Representation Committee, the forerunner of the British Labour Party. Six years later he was elected Labour Member of Parliament for Leicester.

His personal ambition and intellectual energy were driven by his marriage in 1896 to Margaret Gladstone, namesake but no relation of the Grand Old Man. She was a steadfast companion in arms as well as a loving wife; her death in 1911 drove happiness out of his life. He kept for a time his physical and intellectual energy, but a mournful note crept into his thoughts and writings. He felt, for example, remarkably little personal exhilaration when he arrived at 10 Downing Street in 1924 – only an absorbing sense of his own emotional losses. 'Times of sad reflections and gloomy thoughts,' he wrote. 'The people of my heart are dead, their faces on my walls; they do not share with me. Had much difficulty in returning. How vain is honour now.'

MacDonald became well known to the public at large through his opposition to the Great War. The Labour Party agonised over the war, unwilling to share but unable to ignore the torrent of patriotic feeling which at first flowed through the country. Some Labour leaders helped the Government recruiting campaign, and in 1916 Lloyd George cajoled two Labour Ministers into his Coalition Government. MacDonald was not a pacifist; he believed that Britain should not have gone to war, but once the war had begun he detested the thought of a German victory. This was compatible with condemnation of Grey's policy as symbolising the whole system of secret diplomacy and the fatal build-up of armaments which he hated. He held steadily to this view, and as the horror of the trenches increased more people began to share it.

In denouncing the war he unleashed the torrential power of the Scottish oratory for which he became famous. At a meeting at Briton Ferry in south Wales, MacDonald's opponents had sabotaged the electric light in the hall. Speaking in candlelight, he linked opposition to the war with his general socialism. 'Who is entitled to mourn and weep over the sorrows of martyred Belgium? Not the men who have outraged the people of the Welsh villages by huddling them together in houses that were not fit for pigs. The people who are entitled to mourn and weep are the people who mourned and wept with you, and led you in a holy crusade before the war began.' He ended that speech with a peroration off the peg which, with variations, served him for the next twenty years. 'We shall go as and when the fair weather comes again, we shall confront the world with faces unashamed, and shall say to posterity "We await your verdict". And the verdict will be: "Blessed is the peacemaker, for he shall be called the child of God."'[6] Unlike his fellow Celt, Lloyd George, MacDonald did not craft his oratory coolly to beguile his audience; he beguiled himself first. The evident sincerity made his reputation, until it was undermined by the increasing intellectual emptiness of much of what he said.

MacDonald's opposition to the Great War led him to imagine a future in which dealings between nations were transformed. In a pamphlet of January 1917 called *National Defence* he wrote: 'Foreign affairs in some mysterious way have been withdrawn from the light of the world. They are transacted in rooms with blinds drawn, with backstairs entrances and secret doors and waiting chambers . . . the whole corrupting system should be swept away.'[7] Two new arrivals on the international scene thought much the same. MacDonald was delighted by the first stage of the Russian Revolution in February 1917 and carried his approval forward to the Bolshevik seizure of power in October. He was slow, however, to realise how wide the gap was between British democratic socialism and the Russia of Lenin and Trotsky. Given his standpoint, he warmly welcomed the Communist decision to expose the secret agreements by which Britain and France tried to ensure their post-war pre-eminence and sustain the war effort of their allies by rewarding their greed. He hoped, but in vain, that instead of making a separate peace with Germany, the Bolsheviks would somehow insist on a just peace for the whole of Europe.

Likewise he welcomed President Wilson's vehement denunciation of secret diplomacy. He hesitated, however, before the President's remedy. If the proposed League of Nations was a league of governments established by a treaty between governments, it would not solve the main problem. A lack of democracy had led to the pile-up of armaments; the pile-up of armaments had led to the war. The key

243

to a peaceful future was world disarmament imposed by democratic insistence, since so long as there were armies, there would be wars. A League of Nations, if it was not to be just a distraction, should be composed of democratic parliaments, not governments. Buried inside these arguments was the old assumption that if artificial impediments were removed, man's sense of reason would flourish, leading inexorably to harmony across the world.

These ideas, which became widely fashionable in the 1920s and early 1930s, earned MacDonald fierce unpopularity while the war was still going on. The Seamen's Union refused to carry him to revolutionary Russia with a fraternal message in June 1918. More important, he lost his seat at Leicester in the general election which Lloyd George called in December 1918 as soon as the war was over. He did not return to the Commons until 1922. Inside the Labour Party the dispute about the war faded away. The Party came together to oppose British intervention in the Russian Civil War. MacDonald's long experience of the Labour movement, combined with persistent eloquence, carried him to the chairmanship of the Party in 1922. As a result of the general election that year, Labour became the second largest party in Parliament after the Conservatives. MacDonald was thus Leader of the Opposition, and therefore the natural successor to Baldwin as Prime Minister when the Conservatives failed to win a mandate for economic protection in the next election at the end of 1923.

Cabinet-making brought out in MacDonald the strand of bewildered naïveté which was both an attraction and a disadvantage. 'I feel like an executioner, I knock so many heads into my basket. After this, every man will be my enemy.'[8] On one point he was clear: he would act as Foreign Secretary as well as Prime Minister. There was no one else who was in his confidence and acceptable to the Labour Party as a whole. Moreover, his diary shows that his mind was to a surprising extent absorbed in foreign affairs. There was a press of domestic problems – unemployment, wages, industrial relations – but these hardly featured in his private jottings during 1924. Quite apart from his personal interest, he believed that success in foreign affairs could prove that Labour was capable of providing serious and effective government.

Nevertheless, it did not seem likely that his minority Labour

Government would last more than a few months. He would not have to carry for years the double burden of the premiership and the Foreign Office. He found that the hard work which resulted helped him to keep his deep-seated melancholy within bounds. He trusted the senior officials at the Foreign Office. They in turn, whatever their inner doubts about the course which MacDonald would set, welcomed a change from the imperious methods of the outgoing Foreign Secretary, Lord Curzon. It was possible, indeed obligatory, to admire Curzon but he was never easy to work with. Because of his passion for detail Curzon had found it almost impossible to delegate, whereas a Foreign Secretary who was also Prime Minister was bound to put greater authority in the hands of Foreign Office officials. They welcomed this development; in the end it contributed to his downfall.

The Europe which MacDonald found when entering the Foreign Office in January 1924 was very different from the Europe of which he had dreamed in his wartime pamphlet or in the heady discussions of the Socialist International. In the interval, the Treaty of Versailles and a flotilla of lesser agreements had created a second European settlement which in turn involved a new Middle East and a changed Africa. The long negotiations were different in character from those which had led to the first settlement at Vienna in 1814–15. In the background of Castlereagh's work lurked, as we have seen, important differences of principle about how Europe might be kept stable; but the essence of the settlement consisted of practical compromises on frontiers, colonies and dynasties. At Versailles and in the years that followed, these practical matters were also thrashed out, but this time the clash of ideas was in the forefront.

The onrush of new ideas was led by President Wilson. For the first time, an American President ventured abroad, to be greeted almost as a Messiah by huge welcoming crowds in the capitals of Europe. Ideas which had been hidden in the shadows, or mocked as fit only for hopeless dreamers like MacDonald, were suddenly the official policy of the country which had gained most from the war. Democracy, disarmament, self-determination, open covenants openly arrived at – the phrases were on all lips. A League of Nations sustained by invincible public opinion seemed within the grasp of a world determined that the slaughter should not be repeated. Once the crowds dispersed and the negotiations began, Wilson and his supporters found that they had to reconcile the new principles with certain old facts which refused to go away. Of these the central and most stubborn was the security of France. Nothing had altered the fact that France was embedded in Europe alongside a German people who had become her committed and more powerful enemy. France had just fought a huge war, mostly on her own soil, and suffered immense casualties to prevent German hegemony. She was, but only fleetingly, in a position to use victory to alter economic and demographic facts. She thus sought to provide herself with security alongside a Germany whose weakness had to be made permanent. This meant occupation of German territory, a disarmament agreement which was not general but directed at Germany, and crippling financial penalties imposed as punishment. President Wilson, and men like MacDonald, told the French that these were out of date, even immoral ideas. A new world, they argued, could be created in which French fears would be meaningless. No French Minister in 1923 or 1924 believed this. To borrow Professor David Marquand's telling phrase, 'The French did not believe in the possibility of better weather: what they wanted was a more reliable raincoat.'[9]

The outcome at Versailles of this clash between different concepts of world order satisfied no one. The League of Nations came into existence; the Austro-Hungarian and Ottoman Empires were dismantled; a nod was made in the direction of disarmament, another towards self-determination. The British and French carved up between them the heart of the Middle East but, in a bow to the new correctness, described their new acquisitions there and in Africa as mandates of the League, not colonies.

On her side of the equation, France obtained a demilitarised Rhineland; Germany, deprived of any heavy armaments, was burdened with a huge load of reparations and humiliated by the enforced admission of war guilt. There was a balance here between old and new, at least in theory. But the scales were never in operation.

The balance of the settlement was destroyed by the refusal of the United States Senate to accept the initiative of its own President. America stayed out of the new League. Bolshevik Russia was neither willing nor invited to join. Despite these formidable absences the League took shape, anchored itself in Geneva, and began in an unpretentious way to tackle some minor uncertainties and inequities left by the Treaty makers. When summoned from minor matters in the 1930s to confront real threats to world peace, it faltered, then failed.

During most of the years between the Armistice of 1918 and the Labour Government of 1924 Britain was governed by a Liberal Prime Minister of outstanding cleverness and two Conservative Foreign Secretaries of ability above the average. But Lloyd George was too intrigued by his own tactical cleverness to form a strategic vision; Balfour was by then idle in everything except tennis and philosophy; and Curzon's gifts, which had been brilliantly suited to governing India under Edward VII, could not be adapted to serving under Lloyd George or coping with the ruthlessness of Continental politicians. The Middle East settlement was favourable to Britain, though it contained the lethal delayed explosive device of a Jewish home in Palestine. Once the United States refused to join the League, Lloyd George had no faith in it as an overriding instrument of world order. He preferred to rely on high-level, but in the end insignificant, European meetings at which he could display his charm and prowess and gain a fortnight's prestige.

British foreign policy was also now constrained by a fresh complication. The Great War had given the Dominions a greater claim to have a say in the running of imperial policies. This meant that all major foreign policy initiatives now had to be approved by each Dominion in turn. In Lloyd George's last months in power the system had crashed when the Dominions refused to support his policy during the Chanak crisis.* Throughout his nine months as Prime Minister MacDonald saw the need for tact and attention, but was irritated by the wrangling which went on. 'This is a matter that calls for most careful handling or we shall have a paralysis in F.O. initiative on the one hand or a destruction of Imperial unity on the other,' he wrote in July. 'These are anarchist times when the power to go one's own way is more valued than that of going with other people.'[10]

Meanwhile, the central problem of European security remained

---

* Lloyd George, always strongly pro-Greek, confronted the new Turkish leader, Kemal Atatürk, who, having chased the Greeks out of Asia Minor, threatened the rest of Europe – or so the British Cabinet thought. The Dominions declined to send troops to help. The crisis petered out.

unsolved. The French had by no means obtained what they thought necessary. They had accepted a demilitarised rather than an independent Rhineland; in return they had been promised an Anglo-American guarantee of their frontiers. The prospect of any American guarantee collapsed along with American membership of the League. There was no way in which Lloyd George would offer France a unilateral British guarantee; that would have smacked too much of Sir Edward Grey and the old system. Lloyd George's own diplomatic manoeuvres were less principled than those of Grey, and had little to do with the ideas of Woodrow Wilson or of Ramsay MacDonald; but he liked to give them a modern post-war flavour. For British Ministers were acutely conscious of a shift in public opinion. In British eyes France was no longer the forlorn country which had been bullied by the Kaiser, nor the ally which had suffered at Verdun as the British had suffered on the Somme or at Passchendaele. France seemed to be back in its earlier role as the European bully, unable to think of any interest except its own, preoccupied with degrading Germany to avert a threat which in reality had dissolved with the armies of Ludendorff and Hindenburg.* In these circumstances Britain seemed happy to revert to its late Victorian role, proud, risk-free and inexpensive, as an independent arbiter, ready with advice if nothing else, refusing anything so vulgar as a firm commitment or formal alliance. Except that in reality this role for Britain no longer existed. The Britain of Lord Salisbury had been pre-eminently rich and powerful; the Britain of Lloyd George was weaker and much less sure of itself.

The French Government of Poincaré, in power when MacDonald entered the Foreign Office in January 1924, was doing its best to undermine the underlying justice of its own case. When the Germans had a year earlier fallen into arrears on the payment of reparations, French and Belgian troops had marched into the Ruhr and grasped the essential strong points of the German economy. Coal was seized, industries paralysed and separatist movements in Germany encouraged. The French were using the severity of the reparation terms to carry the weakening of Germany beyond even what had been agreed

---

* The next threat was at this moment still only an insignificant and scruffy ex-corporal plotting violence in Munich.

at Versailles. Seeing this, British opinion turned strongly against the French. Poincaré, who demanded a British security guarantee as a right, acted in a way that made impossible what was already highly improbable.

MacDonald had to reckon with these realities, but he would not abandon the idealism into which he had educated himself. His approach to European problems continued to be a mixture of dreaminess and subtlety. These were not the admired qualities of Lord Curzon; but surprise can sometimes be an asset in politics. The novice began to take tricks which had eluded the veteran.

His approach was essentially that of the reasonable umpire. He was driven to despair by the French: 'France as near to being impossible as it well can be. The country seems to have been taught nothing and still runs after will of the wisps in assured power, tricky diplomacy, stupid economics, a vile press – the vilest in the world.'[11] The Germans, by contrast, were merely awkward. 'If clumsiness is of the devil, the Germans are supreme as his tools. Yet charity compels us to recognise how badly they have been tassled.'[12] But MacDonald had already decided that 'France must have another chance. I offer co-operation but she must be reasonable and cease her policy of selfish vanity.'[13] He was helped in this task by the disappearance of Poincaré and his replacement by the quieter, more moderate Herriot, who spent a weekend with MacDonald at Chequers in June. MacDonald was far from understanding the depth of France's vulnerability, as the French saw it. For example, at one stage he tried to comfort Herriot with the assurance that Britain wanted with France 'the closest of alliances, that which is not written on paper'.[14] This was the kind of remark which had driven Ambassador Cambon to despair when uttered by Grey in the years, even in the days, before the Great War. But at least in those days there had been Anglo-French staff talks to give hope that Britain's maddening ambiguity did not amount to perfidy. Despite all the lessons which they had been given in the new morality, France perversely continued to calculate safety in terms of British tanks and regiments crossing the Channel. But in 1924 it would have been inconceivable for MacDonald to offer the French staff talks; nor would he personally have thought of discussing Britain's relationship with France in such out-of-date terms.

The French occupation of the Ruhr was crippling the Germans without in any real way benefiting France. As an exercise in coercion it was a failure. Yet the doors to a European settlement seemed locked. MacDonald, in need of a key, found it across the Atlantic. The American politicians might have retired from active diplomacy in Europe, but this did not mean that American businessmen and bankers were indifferent. Germany was too big a market for American goods and American capital to be allowed to wither away. The American General Charles Dawes chaired a committee of experts on German reparations which reported in April 1924. They gave MacDonald his key. The report concluded that Germany could not meet her debts without a stable currency and a balanced budget. Once these were achieved reparation payments could gradually resume on a rising scale. But a return to prosperity required first a loan of £40 million and, second, no interference by foreign troops in economic matters, which meant in effect French withdrawal from the Ruhr. MacDonald discussed with Herriot how this plan could be carried out. Even after Herriot replaced Poincaré, the French continued to dig in their heels on the timing of evacuation of the Ruhr, and on the sanctions which would be applied to Germany if she again defaulted. Inevitably the French again asked for a security guarantee from Britain. MacDonald used all his skills through the summer to fashion with the French a realistic proposal to put to the Germans. Herriot faced severe political difficulties at home. MacDonald had a difficulty at his side in the form of his Chancellor of the Exchequer, Philip Snowden. The Chancellor used his sharp intellect and sharper tongue to support every criticism from the banking community of the proposed arrangement. Reparations were wrong, a loan was wrong; the French were always wrong; by implication his own Prime Minister was wrong too. The French, deeply alarmed, had to be told that Snowden was an independent chap who could in the end be overruled.

Finally the time came for the Germans to join the talks on reparations in London. This was a momentous occasion. For the first time since the war the Germans were not summoned to receive a diktat from victorious allies, but invited to negotiate an agreement. This was hard for the French because it meant a crucial switch from coercion to conciliation. MacDonald watched the German delegation arrive. 'They are so German in appearance that dread entered my heart, so much did they suggest long speeches and meticulous points. Moments of strain ... Herriot looked as though he were having a tooth drawn.'[15] This was MacDonald's high point. For the first and last time he was able to harness successfully his sincerity and his gift of personal intuition to achieve practical agreement in a major negotiation. The buzz among his officials was positive. He became known for long skilful silences which could coax concessions out of an interlocutor. 'Time after time I am told', wrote D'Abernon, 'RM has surmounted or turned extreme difficulties. His power of work is astounding everyone at the conference; he starts early in the morning and works hard throughout the day.'[16]

The first fortnight of August was tense. The German Foreign Minister, Gustav Stresemann, argued about the loans they would need in the first year of the Dawes Plan, about the circumstances in which sanctions could be invoked against them, about the timing of French and Belgian evacuation of the Ruhr. The French agonised; Snowden continued to obstruct. MacDonald took an evening off to watch Sybil Thorndike play Saint Joan in Shaw's masterpiece. 'Telephone messages were coming in all the time ... Evidently much excitement among the French and Germans. Whilst Joan was being condemned I agree to see Stresemann at midnight', at which point the German 'poured out his soul', arguing that all would be lost if the French insisted on staying in the Ruhr for another twelve months.[17]

MacDonald manoeuvred the different pieces into position and agreements were signed on 16 August. MacDonald, in his farewell speech, was justified in claiming that this was 'the first really negotiated agreement since the war ... we have signed it with a feeling that we have turned our backs on the terrible years of war and war mentality'.[18] The four agreements carried out the Dawes Plan and set out the sanctions to be applied if Germany defaulted. It had been agreed separately that the French and Belgians would leave the Ruhr within twelve months, evacuating Dortmund at once as a proof of good faith.

After the failure of French coercion in the Ruhr the policy of conciliating Germany was in place. Stresemann, though he never accepted the justice of the Versailles settlement, worked to soften it by negotiation within the traditional diplomatic framework. The fault, in which MacDonald later participated, was to prolong the policy of conciliation or appeasement into dealings with Fascist dictators who wished to smash the traditional framework, not improve it. This does not invalidate MacDonald's achievement. A.J.P. Taylor justly remarks that, though MacDonald is now despised and his very existence ignored, he 'should be the patron-saint of every contemporary Western politician who favours co-operation with Germany'.[19]

We should note here that the driving force of this agreement was economic – namely the consequences of the reparations imposed on Germany. The political outcome flowed from the economic dilemma. Marxists and others argue that economics lie at the heart of almost all political decisions, that for example the Great War was a clash of powers competing for markets, and that the wars against Iraq in 1991 and 2003 were inspired by appetite for Iraq's oil. Neither the evidence of research nor practical experience supports this conclusion. Of course, political leaders live and work in a set of particular economic circumstances of which they are well aware; but the Foreign Secretaries whom we describe were not primarily interested in economic arguments or influenced by industrialists or financial entrepreneurs. Left-wing or right-wing, they lived in a different world. We have seen the distance which Salisbury kept from Rhodes and, before that, the scepticism with which Palmerston handled Cobden's idea of free trade diplomacy. At the other end of the spectrum, Ramsay MacDonald and Ernest Bevin were, at home, committed socialists; but neither allowed his socialist faith to dominate his thinking on foreign policy. One could argue that this remoteness was a mistake, that British foreign policy would have been wiser if it had been more clearly linked to the huge economic changes which were taking place – for example the rise and fall of the gold standard, the shift of industrial production away from Britain to America and Russia. But the fact is that our Foreign Secretaries hardly ever placed economic factors at the front of their thinking.

The negotiation in 1924 on the Dawes Plan was an exception; so were the many discussions on the post-1945 settlement which began with Keynes's negotiations in Washington for a loan for Britain, and culminated in the Marshall Plan. In both episodes, 1924 and 1945–8, the Americans were the moving force. After 1945 Britain's economic weakness pushed money to the front of the mind of British Ministers, even those like Eden who were temperamentally uninterested. Margaret Thatcher's reforms removed the fear of an economic crisis from the forefront of British foreign policy – until 2008. Then British Ministers had to wrestle again with the financial fears which were familiar to Eden and Bevin but would have made no sense to Palmerston, Salisbury or Grey.

In 1924 MacDonald knew that he had to press on. The London Agreements sorted the immediate problems of reparation and the occupation of the Ruhr, but the French continued to feel insecure. They were trying to remedy this by alliances with Poland and Czechoslovakia, but this was no real substitute for the solid British guarantee for which they had always yearned. MacDonald could not give such a guarantee. He had to come up with a modern alternative. On 4 September he composed an eloquent speech to the Assembly of the League in Geneva. After criticising the concept of military alliances, he sang the praises of arbitration. Arbitration was the key to security. Objective arbitration of a dispute anywhere in the world would identify an aggressor or potential aggressor, who would then be publicly paraded and, if they persisted, would incur sanctions. Characteristically, MacDonald gave arbitration a mystical glamour: 'A system of arbitration is a system of watching the clouds ... of warning when a cloud, just the size of a man's hand, appears above the horizon, and the taking of steps at once, not of a military kind, but of a rational and judicial kind, to charm it out of existence.' He asked in his best prophetic style why anyone should be afraid of arbitration. With each new clause his rhetoric expanded until arbitration became something of a metaphysical quest. 'The test is, will you expose your commitments? Are you afraid of the world? Are you afraid of daylight, a lover of darkness and timorous lest the world should know what is in your mind?' The speech was a performance rather than a plan. Herriot, worried by news that the Germans might repudiate the war guilt clause of Versailles, argued in his own speech that arbitration was no substitute for security. He insisted that a reference to sanctions be included and in that form an Anglo-French proposal for arbitration was approved by the League Assembly, and christened the Geneva Protocol.

But MacDonald had flown too high. The French, though not satisfied, had to swallow anything they were given. The criticism came from the other side of the Channel. The Geneva Protocol, though immensely vague, could be read as implying vast commitments for Britain if an aggressor were identified. The Dominions objected; the British Service chiefs were hostile; the Conservative Party, now once again approaching power, became alarmed. The Geneva Protocol was stillborn, but the process of thought which conceived it produced a successor.

MacDonald had no time to pursue other ideas which caught his imagination. In July he had chaired a meeting at which the Service chiefs rejected the idea of a Channel Tunnel. 'Amazed at military mind. It has got itself and the country as well in a rut where neither fresh air nor new ideas blow. Like old woman who seals doors and windows to keep her from shivering. My burdens so heavy and so many that I cannot take up the Tunnel at present, but it must be taken up.'[20]

MacDonald's Government was running out of time. Its main mishaps were personal rather than collective. He was wounded in public opinion by his approval of a baronetcy for his friend Alexander Grant, who had lent him a Daimler and £40,000 worth of shares in the biscuit firm McVitie and Price. Grant was a noted philanthropist who had given Scotland a precious collection of legal books known as the Advocates Library. MacDonald was an innocent in such matters, but Lloyd George, by no means an innocent, had recently been exposed for his systematic abuse of the honours system. There could be no excuse for MacDonald's extraordinary foolishness in exposing his much healthier reputation to the same charge.

Worse was to come. MacDonald's policy towards France and Germany continued the general line of previous governments, though with greater verve and commitment. But towards the Soviet Union he had set himself on a controversial, much more conciliatory path, in spite of George V's earlier concern about meeting the Communist leaders who had murdered his relatives. He left the detailed negotiations to his deputy at the Foreign Office, Arthur Ponsonby, but the outline of a new treaty soon emerged under his general guidance. It would provide for an expansion of trade with Russia, compensation for holders of Czarist bonds (essential for the City) and a loan (essential for the Soviet Union). The draft treaty, in particular the loan, was denounced by the Conservatives, and when the Liberals joined them in the attack it was clear that Parliament would never approve it. Against this background of controversy, MacDonald's handling of every issue connected with Communism came under close scrutiny, and two such episodes hugely damaged him.

In a book on foreign policy it is not necessary to penetrate the murk of the Campbell case. John Ross Campbell, the acting editor of the Communist *Workers' Weekly*, published on 25 July 1924 an article calling on British soldiers to let it be known that they would never fire on their fellow workers. The Attorney General, Sir Patrick Hastings, mounted a prosecution on grounds of incitement to mutiny. There was an outcry within the Labour Party, the Cabinet discussed the matter under MacDonald's chairmanship and the prosecution was dropped. This produced an uproar against political interference in a judicial matter. In the House of Commons, Mac-Donald declared that he had not been involved either in starting the prosecution or in dropping it. This was untrue. The falsehood was exposed by the Conservative Opposition. When, in a debate on 8 October, the Liberals and the Conservatives voted together for a Select Committee to examine the matter, the Government was heavily defeated and MacDonald advised the King to dissolve Parliament.

Another mine exploded under the Government during the election campaign which followed. Grigori Zinoviev was an inveterate plotter. This was indeed his job as President of the Comintern, the organisation created by the Soviet Union to mobilise the workers of the world. Zinoviev was intriguing hard in Germany in 1923. He had written several letters of fraternal guidance to the Communist Party of Great Britain. On the whole these reflected the orthodox Moscow view that Communists should work alongside other radical forces in a united front. This was the advice which Zinoviev actually sent to the British Communists on 10 October.

A few days later Sir Eyre Crowe, Permanent Under Secretary at the Foreign Office, sent MacDonald the text of quite a different letter which Zinoviev had apparently sent a month earlier to the British Communists. This famous letter called for the establishment of subversive cells in all units of the British Army and in munitions factories. These cells would be prepared to paralyse any preparations for war by the British Government. The letter had been obtained by the Riga station of the British Secret Service (SIS) from (they later said) an agent who had copied it from a file in Moscow.[21] Latvia, like the other newly independent Baltic states, was swarming with White Russians, and the constant buzz of rumour and intrigue in which, as exiles, they excelled. On 9 October the SIS circulated the letter to the Foreign Office and other interested departments in London, observing that it contained strong incitement to armed revolution and evidence of intention to contaminate the Armed Forces, in flagrant violation of the Anglo-Russian Treaty which had just been signed. The SIS added that the authenticity of the document was undoubted.

Despite this assurance, the Foreign Office checked for authenticity and were told, on grounds that on examination seem flimsy, that the genuineness of the letter was corroborated by a report from an agent inside the British Communist Party to which the letter was addressed. The senior officials at the Foreign Office decided that immediate action was needed. This should consist of a formal note of protest to Mr Rakovsky, the Soviet Chargé d'Affaires in London, which would immediately be released to the press.

A general election campaign was now in full swing following the Labour Government's defeat over the Campbell case. Officials would have been well aware of the high sensitivity of the whole subject of Communist interference in British affairs. Obviously the action proposed needed the approval of the Foreign Secretary, who happened to be Prime Minister and was fully occupied with leading the Labour election campaign outside London.

MacDonald was receiving boxes on the campaign trail and read the Zinoviev letter. He commented that the Government needed to be certain of its authenticity, but asked that a draft letter to Rakovsky be prepared for him to look at. Officials considered that they had already checked authenticity, and nothing further was done on that front. A draft note of protest was prepared and sent to MacDonald campaigning in south Wales. MacDonald substantially altered the draft, not changing the substance, but making it more general and less formal in tone. On the morning of Friday 24 October Eyre Crowe held a meeting with senior officials. In front of them was the draft

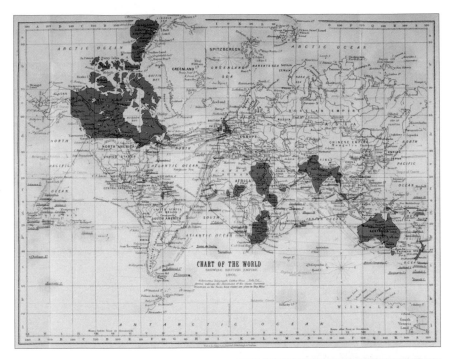

CHART OF THE WORLD
SHOWING BRITISH EMPIRE
1905

Above: By the early twentieth century, the British Empire had begun its slow decline. British Foreign Secretaries could no longer rely on either overwhelming naval superiority or an old-fashioned balance of power to provide security for the British Isles.

Right: Sir Edward Grey, Foreign Secretary from 1905 to 1916 (pictured left), attempted to chart a new course for Britain by leaning toward alliances with Russia and France. But he concealed the full extent of this policy from his colleagues in the Cabinet, including Churchill (centre).

Opposite: Bird-watching and country pursuits were much more than a pastime for Grey and his wife Dorothy; they formed the focus of their married life.

Eight years of complicated and subtle diplomacy fell to pieces in the
summer of 1914. Many later blamed Grey (centre, looking sideways)
and his foreign policy for causing the Great War, though the failure was
shared by Asquith (seated right) and the entire Cabinet.

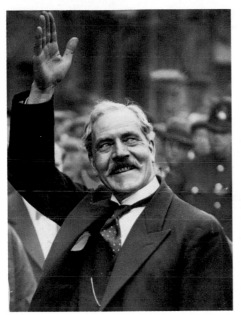

Below: MacDonald's marriage to Margaret Gladstone was a source of great happiness until her early death in 1911.

Above: Ramsay MacDonald, the first Labour Prime Minister and Foreign Secretary.

Right: The Chamberlain family became the most powerful political dynasty of the early twentieth century. But both Austen (centre) and Neville (left) fell short of the greatness their father Joseph (right) had hoped for from them.

Left: Austen Chamberlain and his wife Ivy in 1932. Despite his failure as Conservative Party Leader, Austen rebuilt his reputation as a Nobel Peace Prize-winning Foreign Secretary.

Ramsay MacDonald walking through a London crowd in October 1924.

Austen Chamberlain at a coffee table with his European colleagues, Stresemann and Briand, in 1928.

Left: Ernest Bevin, patriot and anti-appeaser.

Below: Anthony Eden after resigning as Foreign Secretary in February 1938.

Eden and Churchill
at Yalta in February
1945 . . .

. . . and at Potsdam
in July 1945 . . .

. . . followed by Bevin and Attlee at Potsdam in August 1945, alongside Truman
(seated centre), Stalin (seated right), Molotov (standing right) and Byrnes
(standing centre).

Some people worried that a new Labour Government in 1945 would cosy up to the Soviets. But with Bevin as Foreign Secretary and Attlee as Prime Minister, Britain took a tougher line on Stalin even than the Americans. For several months, Anglo-American relations became frosty, even hostile. But Bevin worked hard to win Secretary of State Marshall's (*below*) respect and trust.

Anthony Eden and his second wife Clarissa. Eden returned to the Foreign Office for the third time in the Conservative Government of 1951–5, and reached the peak of his career in 1954, resolving crises in Europe and South-East Asia.

Foreign policy is to a great extent determined by a series of inherited myths. When Disraeli purchased shares in the Suez Canal in 1876 the idea that Suez held the key to India – and therefore to British greatness – was just about plausible. By the time Eden became Prime Minister in 1955 the idea was well past its sell-by date. Each new Foreign Secretary should look again at every accepted doctrine of diplomacy and, if necessary, be prepared to puncture any inherited myths.

"MOSÉ IN EGITTO!!!"

"O, WHITHER HAST THOU LED ME, EGYPT?"

note with MacDonald's changes. MacDonald had not initialled the draft, which was and is in Foreign Office practice the formal proof of approval. The question before Crowe and his colleagues was whether the note should be put into final form with MacDonald's amendments and taken round at once to Rakovsky. Alternatively, should it be sent back to MacDonald once more for formal approval? Crowe insisted that it be presented that afternoon. There were good arguments for this. He had just been told by the SIS that a copy of the Zinoviev letter was in the hands of the *Daily Mail*. If he delayed action, MacDonald and the Foreign Office could be accused of a cover-up. The flaw in this defence is, of course, the telephone – although it may not have played much part in the daily life of Crowe. He could have consulted MacDonald in Wales. As it was, he did not even inform him that the protest note had been delivered that afternoon.

At his political meeting on Friday evening, MacDonald was asked a question about the Zinoviev letter by a journalist from the *Daily Mail* which he could not answer. The letter provided a feverish climax to an election which the Labour Government would probably have lost anyway. MacDonald was in a hopeless position. If the letter was genuine, as the Foreign Office protest indicated, then the Government was gullible in negotiating with a Bolshevik regime intent on overthrowing Britain. If the letter was forged, then MacDonald was incompetent in his management of the Foreign Office. He wrote, 'I felt like a man sewn in a sack and thrown into the sea.'[22]

No one knows who wrote the Zinoviev letter. It was certainly a forgery. The Russians took as much interest as anyone in discovering its origin. The best guess is that it originated from a White Russian ring in Berlin which specialised in this kind of forgery. It is most unlikely that either the Foreign Office or the SIS were responsible for concocting the letter. Nonetheless, the zeal with which they handled the issue cannot be separated from their hostility and suspicion towards the Soviet Union. As it happens, the Russians wanted MacDonald to win the general election of 1924, not lose it, so the tactics prescribed in the letter were out of phase. But the general strategy of subversion was undoubted and was reflected in a mass of Communist literature distributed across the world.

Eyre Crowe was bitterly remorseful as the consequences of his action became clear. He broke down in tears when he saw MacDonald afterwards. He was ill, indeed dying. MacDonald never questioned his loyalty, only his judgement. Crowe toiled for twelve hours a day, seven days a week. He was a man driven by work and killed by overwork. Being Prime Minister as well as Foreign Secretary, MacDonald had to delegate more authority to his Foreign Office officials than had been usual. Crowe assumed the extra load with a final burst of zeal. As was apparent in his famous paper of 1907, and as he had shown to Grey in August 1914, he concealed strong emotion behind a normally rigid devotion to the rules and protocol of his Service. The Foreign Office historian concludes that he was 'carrying dedication to duty to the point where both words and actions – and perhaps judgement – seem almost unbalanced'.[23]

After the election, the autopsy into the Zinoviev letter continued, but now without urgency. The political message in the election was clear – Baldwin's Conservatives had won a huge majority and the overriding need was to restore calm. A cool operator was needed at the Foreign Office. There was some talk of Lord Curzon, but he was thought to be erratic and anti-French. Baldwin turned to a more cautious and settled conservative. 'I am Secretary of State for Foreign Affairs,' Austen Chamberlain wrote to one of his sisters, 'my garden will go to ruin.'[24]

Austen Chamberlain had been an MP for thirty-two years, inspiring few, irritating several, always avoiding the overtaking lane. He had served twice as Chancellor of Exchequer, first under Balfour and later under Lloyd George. During the war, he had served as Secretary of State for India until brought down by the failures of the Mesopotamia campaign. Between 1921 and 1922 he had led the Conservative Party as part of the Lloyd George Coalition. These were respectable pinnacles in any career; they were not proof of a soaring mind.

People tended to say the same sorts of thing about Austen: he was mediocre, average, with an 'efficient humdrum mind'.[25] Perhaps Austen would restore some dignity and politeness to the Foreign Office. There would be no more grubby exchanges like the Zinoviev affair. Most people thought that he would be nicer to the French, but nobody expected adventurous jaunts or new ideas. Throughout his career Austen's chief attribute had been his family and the proud Chamberlain brand.*

The Chamberlains had by the late 1920s promoted themselves to the premier league of politics. Joseph Chamberlain's progress from Birmingham businessman to Colonial Secretary under Salisbury had fuelled the engine for his two sons, Austen and Neville, who now both sat in the Cabinet under Baldwin.

Joseph had always been more ambitious for Austen than for his half-brother, Neville, but of the two, Austen is the less remembered today. Neville's story, with moustache and umbrella, is a cautionary tale well known to all of us. The unfortunate Austen is now famous only by his failure to succeed. Rugby, Cambridge, Sciences Po in Paris, rounded off by a swift election into Parliament – the ingredients of greatness had been carefully prepared. Birmingham would be the launch-pad for Austen's operations; the final destination would be 10 Downing Street. But somewhere along the way Austen missed the turn. Uniquely (almost) in the twentieth century, he led the Conservative Party but never became Prime Minister.† His leadership was brought to an end one evening in 1922 at the Carlton Club when the Party decided to break with Lloyd George's Coalition and fight the forthcoming election alone and under a new leader, Bonar Law. Physical problems had played a part in this. Austen was weaker than his father; sleep seems to have been very important to him. From an early age he was afflicted with medical complaints, namely sciatica and lumbago. But the physical defects were always secondary to the psychological concern. George Dangerfield, journalist and historian, diagnosed the disease as 'a father-haunted mind'.[26]

Until Austen was forty-one he lived at home with his father. His first move away was when he became Chancellor of the Exchequer in January 1904. On his first night in that job he wrote to Joseph: 'I do not think there are many fathers who have been and are to their sons all that you have been to me; and my prayer tonight is that the perfect confidence which I have enjoyed for so long may continue

---

* To save confusion between the three Chamberlains, we will refer to Austen by his Christian name in this chapter.
† William Hague was elected leader of the Conservative Party in 1997 but has not yet become Prime Minister.

unimpaired by our separation.' Those same feelings – debt, devotion, an element of pressure – continued after Joseph had faded from the Westminster scene. 'I think more and more of what I owe to Father,' Austen wrote in 1911. 'He has made me in every sense of the word and, if I accomplish anything in my career, it will be due to his teaching and his example.'[27] Throughout the 1920s the symptoms persisted, sometimes in worrying about a biography of his father, sometimes in anxious comments about whether Joseph would approve of Austen's own career. From time to time the disease went into remission; it would never be cured.

Austen inherited Joseph's politics, the outer garments rather than the genes. He was recruited into Joseph's campaign to tighten the Empire through tariff reform. As it gathered speed, the campaign became a crusade pursued with religious devotion, irrespective of cost or chance of success. In 1906 Joseph's stroke had removed him from the front line. In a trying and unsuccessful decade, Austen found himself leading a campaign which he only half believed in, alongside diehard colleagues with whom he was never at ease.

In truth Austen was different. Joseph had been a shifting, restless figure, always on the make, never satisfied; Austen, by contrast, was square. For one thing, he looked square. With square jaw, firm face, neatly parted hair and a monocle he resembled his father, but there was something missing: he lacked the physical charm and debonair flourish. He had square tastes. Not for Austen the sharp tactics and quick manoeuvres of his father; not for Austen the reputation of 'Pushful Joe'. He was pernickety to excess about honour and good form. In Parliament, he used the vocabulary of the nineteenth century and kept up its modes. He continued the tradition of wearing a silk top hat in the Commons, raising it whenever he was mentioned, long after most other Members had left it behind.[28]

He lacked drive. Thus, on becoming Party leader, he commented 'it is useless to lament'. Again, in 1924, on his ambition: 'never very strong ... now ... non-existent'.[29] On his appointment as Foreign Secretary he hid any sense of excitement behind a natural pessimism. 'I feel no elation, but only a sobering sense of the great difficulties in my path.'[30] He had taken up gardening and devoted his attention to it in a way his father never would have done. 'I will pick primroses and forget politics for a week ... Did he ever want to forget politics?

I doubt it, but I constantly do.'[31] In 1919 he bought an expensive house in Sussex unpromisingly called Twitt's Ghyll for himself and his wife Ivy, where he spent long hours building an alpine rock garden. Throughout his time as Foreign Secretary, foreigners would have to compete with plants for his attention: 'I was born to be a gardener, not a foreign minister,' Austen wrote in 1926. 'Have I made that observation before?'[32]

There are shades here of Aberdeen, the 15th Earl of Derby, also of Edward Grey. Austen had no feel for the pell-mell of politics. He regarded self-promotion as distasteful, even wrong. In a conventional, unexcited sort of way Austen wanted to be Prime Minister. But he had no appetite for campaigning and was unable to compensate with any natural charisma or charm. There is a good story that at some point near the end of Balfour's long life, the old man sat with Baldwin and talked about politics. The conversation came to Austen; they wondered why he never made it to the top. Balfour turned to Baldwin, his eyes widening, 'Don't you think it is because he is a bore?'[33] But being boring has certain advantages. It is usually accompanied by level-headedness; and it leads to a certain pragmatism. There was a certain stability about Austen, a sense of perspective, balance and a seriousness which had been absent from the Foreign Office since 1919. Here was a thoughtful man who despised ideology; a sceptic who nonetheless had his own beliefs. Unlike others in that period and later, Austen was prepared to question the assumptions which others accepted blindly. He was no radical, but he thought things through.

Of course, Austen was by instinct and by intellect a strong domestic conservative. After the war, he had worried tirelessly about socialism and believed that the Labour Party was 'a serious menace to the nation'.[34] More interesting, though, was the way he had translated these ideas into foreign affairs. He had never had any patience for Woodrow Wilson and kept no real interest in the League. 'I was never among the President's admirers. He seemed to me to be the dupe of his own words.' He was sceptical also about the international spread of democracy — 'it would be idle to assume in the face of history that democracy provides a guarantee of peace'. In letters to his sisters, Hilda and Ida, Austen expressed his approval for the way MacDonald had handled the Dawes Report, but complained sourly about MacDonald's faith in arbitration. 'I read the PM's speech at Geneva and thought it indescribably bad – the prolix talk of a tired man.'[35] In one respect he set himself apart from most of his contemporaries. Twice, at crucial moments in his career, he would complain about the excessive faith in what he called 'logic' – the idea that reason, rather than instinct, governed the affairs of the world.

He had studied history at Cambridge in the 1880s and, on foreign policy, historical characters became his compass. Thus on Canning – 'He always interests me. I am quite unable to deny his greatness or the mark he left on the world, but I must admit that he is to me a kind of Dr Fell.'* On Disraeli, while reading Monypenny and Buckle's *Life* – 'The man and almost everything about him repels me, but his insight and foresight were extraordinary.' In 1927, he reviewed the great Foreign Secretaries of the nineteenth century when deciding whose paintings to hang in the Foreign Office. 'I don't much care for Palmerston; Canning inspires the same kind of mistrust in me that he did in his contemporaries; and Salisbury in his later years was, I think, weakly temporizing and without initiative to meet the new conditions of a rapidly changing world.'[36] Instead, he found himself in Castlereagh. To him, Castlereagh's policy was to be admired and followed, his respect for Great Power diplomacy and the Concert system held a key to solving Europe's crisis. Like Castlereagh, he shared by instinct a respect for caution and moderation. Like Castlereagh, he thought peace could be preserved by regular personal diplomacy between the leaders of the main European states.

After MacDonald a period of steady sailing was needed, with a sensible chart and calm captain. But the Cabinet which Austen joined in 1924 divided three ways on foreign policy, producing as many charts and even more claims to take the wheel. These problems did not come from the Prime Minister, Stanley Baldwin, who was uninterested in foreign policy. Austen suffered none of the turbulence which had disrupted Derby's relations with Disraeli. After a year in office, Austen wrote rather limply of his dealings with Baldwin – 'On the whole it works well tho' sometimes I wish that he

---

* The allusion is to the rhyme – 'I do not like thee, Doctor Fell / The reason why I cannot tell / But this I know, and know full well / I do not like thee, Doctor Fell'.

showed a little more interest and gave a more active support.'[37]

More difficult for Austen were the claims lodged by the internationalist, Robert Cecil, one of Salisbury's several sons who, as Chancellor of the Duchy of Lancaster, had a seat in Cabinet. The internationalist wing of the Conservative Party was less zealous, more circumspect than in the Labour Party, but that did not hold Robert Cecil back. He was passionate for the League of Nations. As the Minister responsible for League matters, Cecil felt entitled to ask the Prime Minister for access to all Foreign Office papers. This Chamberlain firmly and successfully resisted. 'I must make it clear that there is only one foreign policy and only one authorized exponent of it.'[38]

No sooner had Austen cleared this hurdle than a new obstacle appeared. It was obvious to Austen and most members of the Cabinet that the Geneva Protocol prepared by MacDonald had to go. Less clear was whether something else should take its place. Here the Cabinet split on old-fashioned lines. Winston Churchill, Leo Amery and Lord Birkenhead put forward the isolationist position. Backed by a powerful Beaverbrook press campaign, they argued, as Disraeli had, that Britain was an imperial rather than European power. They saw no real point in involving Britain in the acidic disputes between Germany and France.

Austen led the European counter-argument. His sense of perspective played a part in this. Just as he distrusted the Protocol with its worldwide commitments and strange geography, so he saw that British security depended on a safe Europe and, in particular, on peace in the West. 'I am much more of an "European" than most of my countrymen, for I have a clearer perception than they of the inextricable way in which our interests are bound up with every possibility of the European situation.'[39] Soon after taking charge at the Foreign Office, he defined more closely the sphere on which British safety depended. 'I would say broadly that in Western Europe we are a partner; that comparatively speaking in eastern Europe our role should be that of a disinterested amicus curiae. Our safety in certain circumstances is bound up with that of France or Belgium or Holland. If this be secured I do not believe that it is bound up with Roumania for example.'[40]

It is worth pausing to consider these arguments. In many ways, the European analysis seems obvious, even irrefutable. It certainly had a long history, reaching back to Wolsey and Bolingbroke. 'We must remember that we are not part of the Continent, but we must never forget that we are neighbours to it,' Bolingbroke wrote.[41] We have seen how the same spirit inspired Castlereagh, first in his focus on the Low Countries, later in his letters about the Congress system. In new form, the arguments are recycled today – thus, Tony Blair in his speech to the US Congress in 2003: 'You know, people ask me after the past months when, let's say, things were a trifle strained in Europe, "Why do you persist in wanting Britain at the center of Europe?" And I say, "Well, maybe if the UK were a group of islands 20 miles off Manhattan, I might feel differently. But actually, we're 20 miles off Calais and joined by a tunnel."'[42] But intelligent people before Austen and after argued powerfully that Britain could be safe by staying out of Continental affairs. According to this thesis, Britain was secure enough behind the Channel to ignore what goes on over there. This argument in various forms was deployed throughout the nineteenth century, usually buttressed by the argument that there was in Europe that vague thing – a balance of power. In more extreme form, some historians have applied the doctrine to the Great War, suggesting that Britain could have successfully stayed out irrespective of the imbalance of power. Politicians and defeatists before and during the Second World War clung to the same lines when calling for negotiations with Hitler; they believed that Britain's best hope lay in withdrawing from Europe and leaving Germany in control.

That intelligent people have occupied both aisles of this argument suggests more clearly than any essay the limits of reason in foreign policy. Background influences – culture, education, even a recent book choice – play the decisive part and govern the decisions which shape the fate of nations. In the end, intelligence has only a supporting role.

Austen was interested in Europe because he knew it from his travels there after leaving university. The Continent attracted him in a way which neither the Empire nor America ever did. America was for Austen a shallow place of high inconsistency; Europe had a rich culture and interesting plants. This attraction was compatible with having particular national preferences. He is supposed to have told people that he loved France 'like a woman, for her defects as well as her qualities'.[43] Where many in Britain by now blamed France for Europe's difficulties, Austen was always clear that Germany was the source of trouble. We can trace Austen's fear of Germany back to the 1880s, when he spent over a year there after finishing at Cambridge. During that time, he dined with Bismarck and attended Heinrich von Treitschke's lectures at the Humboldt University. Unfortunately, the lectures rather than the Iron Chancellor had the more lasting impact. 'Treitschke has opened up to me a new side of the German character,' Austen wrote in a letter in 1887, 'a narrow-minded, proud, intolerant Prussian chauvinism. And the worst of it is that he is forming a school.'[44] These feelings, not unjustified, simmered inside him and surfaced prophetically at the end of his life.

Austen aimed at a bilateral pact with France. As we have seen, this was what the French themselves longed for. He had promoted this policy since before the London conference; in July he had advised the House of Commons to make 'the maintenance of the Entente with France the cardinal object of our policy'. Early in 1925 the Cabinet discussed the proposal in two separate meetings. Each time it was gunned down.[45] Churchill and the isolationists were too powerful for Austen. Their devotion to Britain as an imperial power was supported by their pessimism about the League and their distaste for French policy. Austen went back to the drawing board, working towards a European formula more even-handed than an Anglo-French pact. On 5 March Austen let loose his feelings by speaking against the isolationists in the House of Commons. 'At periods in our history we have sought to withdraw ourselves from all European interests. There have been moments – and in the life of our nation they have only been moments – of isolation, sometimes it may have been splendid and sometimes not; but no nation can live, as we live, within twenty miles of the shores of the Continent of Europe and remain indifferent to the peace and security of the Continent.'[46]

At this time Austen began to make progress with a Note which the Germans had sent some weeks previously. By German standards, the Note had been succinct, even simple, with a clear policy – a mutual defence pact between Britain, France, Germany and Italy focused on the Rhineland. The proposal had no huge originality and had caused no deep stir. But it now developed a pragmatic appeal.

The proposal would not mean siding with any one country against any other, but would lead instead to an agreement between all the major European powers focused on one of the most contentious issues of the day. The pact would guarantee the Rhineland both from an aggressive France and from a revanchist Germany, thus removing one of the flashpoints of a future war. There was another way of looking at the proposal, set against the background of the past century. The idea of a collective security agreement between all the leading European powers, as opposed to an alliance system which divided them, was a break with the policies of Grey and a return to the European system of Castlereagh. Austen was in effect agreeing with the French that existing arrangements failed to provide them with the security to which they were entitled. But since neither his Cabinet colleagues nor British opinion would accept a remedy based on a bilateral Anglo-French guarantee, something more sophisticated had to be devised. This would be collective security in a pure and neutral form, in which an invasion by any state would be resisted by all the rest.

Austen had to execute two delicate operations before this could come about. He had to go to Geneva and sever Britain from the Protocol. On 12 March 1925 he addressed the League, driving his argument deep into the fatal flaw in the Protocol: the League was more focused on controlling the character of conflict than removing its cause.[47] 'The fresh emphasis laid upon Sanctions, the new occasions discovered for their employment, the elaboration of military procedure, insensibly suggest the idea that the vital business of the League is not so much to promote friendly co-operation and reasoned harmony in the management of international affairs as to preserve peace by organising war.'[48]

Back home, the Labour Party put up a late fight. Austen defended his decision in the House of Commons. It was a remarkable speech, not because of what it achieved, but because of what it represented. Here was one of the first serious critiques of Wilsonian internationalism as it was applied in the 1920s. 'I profoundly distrust logic when applied to politics, and all English history justifies me . . . instinct and experience alike teach us that human nature is not logical, that it is unwise to treat political institutions as instruments of logic, and that it is in wisely refraining from pressing conclusions to their logical end that the path of peaceful development and true reform is really found.'[49] Austen, without a searing intellect, had the intelligence to see the limits of reason. A few weeks later, Austen elaborated his argument in a speech in Birmingham. The problem with the Wilsonian argument was that it had forgotten that there would always be certain questions in diplomacy which were 'so vital to the honour or the necessities or even the life of the nation that they would not consent to refer them to arbitration'.[50] Neither the Protocol nor MacDonald had catered for this defect.

Meanwhile Austen was still struggling to persuade the Cabinet to consider the Rhineland scheme put forward by the Germans. The Cabinet, gripped by isolationist and anti-French feeling, had begun to manoeuvre against the initiative while Austen was in Geneva. Hard words were directed against the proposal, and by implication Austen's handling of foreign policy. For the last time, Eyre Crowe appeared on the scene to rescue the situation. Fading – a few weeks later he died – Crowe took a note of what was going on in the Cabinet and sent an early warning to Austen. Austen played the last card in his hand and did it quickly, threatening Baldwin that he might resign. Baldwin, activated by no deep feelings on either side of the argument, anxious above all for peace and quiet, gave Austen the control he required. On 20 March, the Cabinet agreed to consider the German proposal; Austen was at last able to set sail.[51]

Austen had prepared the French for the new policy. On 19 March he had discussed the scheme with the French Ambassador and informed him that any new British commitment to European security would be focused only on the disputed boundaries in the West. Britain would not commit itself to a parallel scheme covering Central and Eastern Europe.[52] Two things, however, still complicated the negotiations. There was, first, the fall of Herriot's Government, and the prospect that the harsh and stiff-necked Poincaré might again take charge. In the end, the mathematician Paul Painlevé became Prime Minister, with Aristide Briand as his Foreign Minister. Briand, with three stints as Foreign Minister and six as Prime Minister already behind him, was equipped to understand the fickleness of foreign policy. Three years earlier he had got himself into trouble with his compatriots after a game of golf at the Cannes conference, where he was photographed being taught how to handle his club by Lloyd George.[53] He now embarked on seven long years at the helm of French foreign policy, a rare icon of continuity in the French Third Republic.

Austen soon had to tackle the more fundamental issue – the scope of the guarantee. Austen's arrival at the Foreign Office had raised hopes in France that a bilateral pact might at last be forthcoming. When this did not materialise, Austen's presence at the Foreign Office continued to reassure the French. There was something in Lord D'Abernon's comment that 'France regarded Austen as a trusted lover'.[54] Because his natural sympathies were well known, it was easier for the French to believe Austen when he told them that a bilateral pact was impossible. They were inclined to trust him when he argued that the Rhineland scheme could offer France its sought-after guarantee. According to the proposals which had been sketched out, Britain would come to France's aid in an invasion, just as it would help any of the other powers who signed up for the scheme. This was wider and therefore vaguer than the French wanted, but it was all they were going to get. The contentious question became what precisely would trigger an intervention under this guarantee. The French had built for themselves a reputation for overreacting; any small spark might ignite their flame. But Austen and the British public would not be dragged into any unnecessary wars. In August, Austen set before Briand the limits of the British commitment. Britain would only intervene in the case of a flagrant violation of Rhineland security – in practice, an attempt at or preparation for invasion of France. 'I believe we can guarantee your security in the only case in which it can be seriously menaced,' Austen explained, 'but if you ask to keep your right to make war for trifles as given you by the Treaty of Versailles, my public opinion here will not allow of any guarantee.' The experts who accompanied Briand made dissenting noises; Briand silenced them and accepted Austen's narrow definition of the guarantee.[55]

With the Germans, Austen ran into a separate set of difficulties – despite the fact that they had invented the Rhineland scheme. Indeed, for a brief time after France had agreed to consider the proposals there was a real worry that Germany might draw back. The development, entirely predictable, sent Austen into a rage. He thought Germany was behaving like a woman, who 'having had a liaison is mortified to find herself giving birth to a baby and still more so when the baby loudly proclaims its maternity'.[56] But the shrewd and effective German Foreign Minister, Gustav Stresemann, was playing a subtle game. The Rhineland scheme would involve Germany accepting the Versailles Settlement, or at least those parts of it which related to the frontiers of Western Europe. This prospect came into clearer focus with the possibility of Germany joining the League. So in Germany, all the old grievances were resurrected. Across the country and in the Reichstag, the nationalists launched themselves against the scheme. Stresemann was less liberal than some of his supporters have reckoned; in the long run he appears to have aimed at returning Germany roughly to its position in Bismarck's day. But in the months which led to the signing of the Rhineland Pact, his strategy seems clear and admirable: sound like a revanchist, behave like a statesman; work hard to settle disputes peacefully.

Between April and September, the pact was chiselled into shape. Lawyers worked on the texts; a new conference was planned. At home, Austen had his own problems with a fierce Beaverbrook campaign but by the end of June he could relax. In letters to his sisters, he recited the compliments he was beginning to receive from diplomats and sycophants: 'if the policy succeeds I shall feel some title to the reputation which Houghton assures me will be mine as the true author of European peace, & in that case my long but somewhat broken public career will not have ended without one solid & complete achievement. All of which though it sounds rather boastful is in fact written with great humility but also with considerable thankfulness.'[57] Perhaps now there was a chance that his old demons could be laid to rest. 'Without me the policy would never have had a dog's chance, & I do believe that I am doing good work & I think how father & Beatrice would have felt about it.'[58]*

Austen was operating at the top of his game. He found the work exhausting and spent hours of his weekend in bed and much of the rest of it gardening. But there was a zip to his letters and a zest in his life in these months which had not been apparent before. In March, he described one weekend to his sister, Ida:

* Beatrice, Austen's elder sister, had died from influenza in 1918.

... I was worn out by the time I got to bed at 2 a.m. (as usual) on Friday night & I meant to stop in bed till dinner time tonight. I did a little work in bed on Saturday morning, but found that I simply went to sleep when I tried to study. I slept indeed till dinner time, then rose & dressed & did three hours concentrated work after dinner. Then to bed again at midnight & slept till 9.0, got up at 10 as I found that otherwise I should again sleep all day, & have since done 7 hours hard work.[59]

A few weeks later, he was absorbed by his hyacinths and polyanthus.[60] In May he was briefly distracted by the German Presidential election. 'Hindenburg's election was a surprise to me & a disagreeable one, but except for the adverse effect it has on French opinion I don't think that it is a bad thing. And I am glad to say that the French Gov't do not appear to be going to alter their policy in any way on account of it. But what do these things matter when half your cottage tulips have been eaten off by slugs?'[61] In the summer recess of 1925 Austen would spend about eight hours every day in the garden and some three or four hours working on his dispatches. The rest of the day he passed eating and sleeping. At some point he found time for history. 'Did you read Webster's Foreign Policy of Castlereagh? Very interesting. Now I have Temperley's new Canning on my table.'[62]

The conference, which was held at the Palace of Justice in the Swiss town of Locarno between 5 and 16 October 1925 to discuss the Rhineland proposal, was thought, both by participants and observers, to be a turning point in European relations. Rightly, it was believed that the seven agreements negotiated by the seven countries present at Locarno represented a new atmosphere in European relations. Rightly, it was believed that the conference could mark an end to the warring spirit which had existed since 1914 and the start of a new period, if not of friendship, then certainly of peace. Wrongly, European leaders then and later believed that this new spirit of co-operation and diplomacy could withstand any future storm.

Perhaps the proceedings of the conference were less smooth than the legend tells. There was a strong gale blowing even before the diplomats arrived. In late September the German Ambassador, Dr Sthamer, had handed Austen a copy of the declaration which the German Government were planning to publish in advance of the conference. The declaration rekindled all the old irritants – disarmament; the allied occupation of Cologne; German war guilt. Dr Sthamer, messenger rather than mechanic behind this late spanner in the works, was rewarded with a long homily from Austen about the deficiencies of his country. 'I listened to the declaration and to Herr Sthamer's explanations in silence,' Austen chronicled in a dispatch to D'Abernon, 'but when he had finished I said to him that the German Government was indeed the most difficult Government to help of any of which I had experience.' Like a nagging woman, the Germans had raised an issue entirely unconnected with the specifics of the Rhineland Pact. 'Why on earth did the German Government raise the question now? What possible useful purpose could be served by their so doing?' There were some things, Austen explained, in the Treaty of Versailles which he thought stupid, and one of them was the confession of German war guilt. This was not because he thought it untrue as a description of what had happened in 1914, but because Germany had signed it under compulsion and this rendered it meaningless. 'There it was, however. Nobody asked the German Government to repeat it; there was no occasion to refer to it, and history must be left to judge.' The German Ambassador reminded Austen 'of a little dog which knows it has done wrong, but anxiously deprecates the punishment which it feels it has deserved'.[63]

On 30 September Austen set out his views once again for D'Abernon. 'Your Germans – I use the possessive pronoun as one says to one's wife: your housemaid – are very nearly intolerable. From the first to last very nearly every obstacle to the Pact negotiations has come from them. Briand has almost taken my breath away by his liberality, his conciliatoriness, his strong and manifest desire to promote peace. The German attitude has been just the contrary – niggling, provocative, crooked.'[64] At Locarno these prejudices were hidden by the Alpine landscape and scenery; Briand and Austen both swallowed their distaste for Germany. Halfway through the conference, Austen wrote to the Permanent Under Secretary, Sir William Tyrrell, recalling the first meeting with the Germans in the conference room. Noticing the strain on the Germans' faces, Austen marched over to shake their hands. He looked over his shoulder to find Briand advancing with an expression, not of anger, 'but literally one of pain as of a man approaching to ask the surgeon what was the result of the operation just performed upon his wife'.[65]

The Germans redeployed at Locarno their tactic of detonating new and previously unexpected claims at the last minute of complex negotiations. Out of the blue, they raised in one of the final sessions of the conference the issue of the clause in the Versailles Treaty covering military inspections in Germany. The record tells of a complete silence as the discussion broke down. Patiently, the bomb was defused, but not before Austen had again become angry. 'It shows once again how difficult it is to help a German or to make him understand any argument but a bludgeon.'[66] Taken together, these were small dissonances in a rich harmony. What made Locarno remarkable was that the arguments, usually commonplace, were no more than occasional interruptions to the cordial atmosphere which prevailed. The new spirit of diplomacy which contemporaries observed and later marvelled at was no illusion; the dissonant moments were merely hints of a key change later on.

Nestling happily in neutral Switzerland, on the shore of Lake Maggiore, Locarno was a calm and attractive place for a conference between angry powers. One of the most awkward issues was settled at a party to celebrate Ivy Chamberlain's birthday on board a launch called the *Orange Blossom*. The Germans were worried that if they joined the League they would be required under the provisions of Article XVI not only to provide economic or military assistance in the case of a foreign conflict, but also to allow foreign troops to travel through their country to intervene in any future war between Poland and Soviet Russia. On the boat, enjoying the view and without their advisers, the leaders came to an agreement by which Germany's military and geographical difficulties would be taken into consideration when making such decisions.[67]

Good diplomacy depends on small details. Here Austen's natural politeness triumphed: no question of etiquette was overlooked. He seems to have spent some time trying to find a round table for the negotiations in an effort to ensure that there was no hierarchy. After failing to find any acceptable furniture, he decided to use a square one instead. In a similar fashion, he took care to leave his calling card with the Germans on arriving at the hotel, 'a civility which I believe had not been paid at any of the previous Conferences'.[68]

Hidden agreements and secret clauses in treaties were no longer acceptable in a Europe of democracies; but Austen maintained the commonsense difference between the actual products of diplomacy, which should be transparent, and the process, which could never be so without crippling the negotiations. 'You must allow us', he told the media, 'to cook the meal in the kitchen, but as soon as it is ready it shall be properly served and submitted to the approbation of Parliament, and through Parliament to the public.'[69] This is not a bad metaphor for settling one of the running arguments about diplomacy in a democracy.

Each of the three Foreign Ministers at Locarno played his part. Briand, stooping slightly, with untidy hair and a vigorous moustache; Stresemann, rather thick and bald, but perhaps more cultured and intelligent than the rest; and Austen, correct and dapper, with his monocle and square jaw. At the close, a new figure appeared on the scene. Three years earlier Benito Mussolini and his National Fascist Party had taken power in Italy. His country was involved in the negotiations over the Rhineland Pact. Towards the end of the conference, Il Duce decided to travel to Locarno himself. His visit confirmed in Austen an admiration for the dictator which he would later pass on with mixed results to his wife. 'It is not part of my business as Foreign Secretary to appreciate his action in the domestic politics of Italy, but if I ever had to choose in my own country between anarchy and dictatorship I expect I should be on the side of the dictator. In any case I thought Mussolini a strong man of singular charm and I suspected of not a little tenderness and loneliness of heart.'[70]

At 12.25 p.m. on 15 October, Austen sent a telegram to Tyrrell:

> Following from Secretary of State for Sir W. Tyrrell.
> Cock-a-doodle-do!!

Tyrrell's reply came through a few hours later; a civil servant's sense of humour shone through: 'Never imagined you could warble so sweetly but to you all things seem possible now.'[71] The Pact was initialled the following day, coinciding with Austen's sixty-second birthday. The final agreements covered seven treaties but in only one did Britain play a signatory part – the Treaty of Mutual Guarantee between Belgium, France, Germany, Italy and Britain – better known later as the Locarno Pact. It was focused on the same principle as had been suggested in the original German Note. The frontiers between Germany, France and Belgium were guaranteed, and those countries also agreed not to attack each other. In the case of a flagrant violation of the agreements covering the demilitarised zone, Britain and Italy agreed to intervene – in urgent cases, before waiting for any decision taken by the Council of the League. Through the Locarno treaties, and the linked agreement that Germany would join the League, the Germans recognised the borders of Western Europe as established at Versailles and renounced their old intentions of taking back Alsace-Lorraine.

These agreements were by no means comprehensive. Austen had decided that Britain would only commit itself to a security arrangement covering Western Europe; there could be no parallel agreement covering the frontiers in the east. Some experts had argued behind the scenes about the danger in leaving the eastern borders open to doubt. In September the Polish Foreign Minister had made late appeals urging Austen to rethink. Count Skrzynski was a prophet: concluding the Western Pact without settling the eastern frontiers would mean that 'no such settlement would ever be reached, war would break out there again, and . . . Great Britain would inevitably be involved in a conflagration which would destroy all Europe and perhaps embrace the world'.[72] But Austen could not and did not want to persuade the Cabinet to take on an eastern commitment. The 'true line of progress', he had argued in February, 'is to proceed from the particular to the general, and not, as has hitherto been embodied in Covenant and Protocol, to reverse the process and attempt to eliminate the particular by the general'. He resisted new British commitments in Eastern Europe – at least until questions closer to home were settled. In a phrase borrowed from Bismarck, he described the Polish Corridor as something 'for which no British Government ever will or ever can risk the bones of a British grenadier'.[73] It remained for his half-brother, Neville, to give the Poles the guarantee they hankered after; by the time he gave it in 1939, it was too late for the British grenadiers to be of any help.

Optimists could argue that if an agreement could be reached in the west, covering one of the most treacherous strips of land in Europe, this might open up the door to future diplomacy in the east. That this did not happen does not prove that the strategy was unworkable. Indeed, the limits which Austen set himself at Locarno were a refreshing change on what had gone on before. There was a tendency in these years when the idealists ran riot to reach for too much too quickly; difficulties would tumble from one disagreement to another and no progress was made. The focus on the Rhineland was a compromise which worked.

In later years Austen would defend Locarno on the grounds that it had satisfied Britain's ancient requirement that the Low Countries were independent and safe. It was 'because the peace and security of these islands and their immunity from attack are closely bound up with the independence and integrity of the Low Countries and France that we felt justified in giving in that sphere alone a guarantee which we refused to make general. In guaranteeing those frontiers we insured our own.'[74] The argument had held true for centuries; but whether the Low Countries were still uniquely vital in an age of aeroplanes and industrial warfare was debatable.

Locarno neutralised European relationships; that was its most powerful achievement. More clearly than at the London conference, Germany was accepted at Locarno not as an enemy but as a colleague by the old allied powers. The Rhineland Pact did not label any particular state as an enemy, but set up an impartial system which would meet aggression carried out by any power. This suited the mood of the 1920s, when the aims of most European nations were still confined to keeping the peace. No staff talks followed between Britain and France. Indeed, the Pact made any planning ludicrous: the talks would have had to be conducted with the Germans as well as the French. For a few years Locarno served its purpose. It was the first major security pact of the twentieth century to be signed by all the main Continental powers collectively.

There was another achievement, no less important for being unsaid. Locarno disrupted the odd, if half-hearted, alliance which had sprung up between Germany and Soviet Russia. This confirmed Russia's isolation in Europe; inside the British Cabinet, some still wanted to go one step further, breaking all contact and removing her from the normal processes of international discourse.

The final moments of the conference captured the spirit which it evoked across Europe, indeed all over the world. There were tears, embraces, dancing, fireworks. Austen cherished the moment and recorded how Briand had grasped Ivy and 'with tears in his eyes had spoken of my help and support, repeating again and again, *"Ah, sans lui, je ne l'aurais jamais tenté!"'* A few seconds later, Mussolini caught Ivy's hands and covered them with kisses.[75]

Back in Britain, the achievement seemed unreal. 'I am astonished & a little frightened by the completeness of my success,' Austen explained to his sister on 31 October.[76] A few weeks later came a sense of perspective. In Parliament, he talked about a new beginning – 'we regard Locarno, not as the end of the work of appeasement and reconciliation, but as its beginning'.[77] In private, there was pessimism: 'Never again will it be possible to win a like success.' Rather suddenly – perhaps he had found time to read Webster's volume again – Castlereagh crossed his mind:

> I was called to face a situation comparable to that which faced Castlereagh after the fall of Napoleon. I had to face it without having been, as he was, the representative of my country in the years which won victory for the Allies & without any of his acquired prestige & little, very little, of his personal knowledge of & intercourse with foreign rulers. I came into office with clear ideas of what must be done & with confidence that I knew how & how only it could be done. A little later Webster's 'Castlereagh's foreign policy' was published & I found that I had been talking Castlereagh (adapted to the XXth century) without knowing it. And I like to think that there is a continuity of British foreign policy; I am grateful that I can feel that I have justified my father's belief in me & repaid the care he gave to my training, & I am proud to feel that as the foreign minister of a great nation I have restored confidence in our word & won back our old influence.[78]

The Locarno treaties were to be signed formally in London on 1 December 1925, in the lavishly gilded room in the Foreign Office which now bears the name. The evening before the ceremony, Austen found that there was a blank space on one of the walls. He made inquiries. Apparently James II's portrait was being cleaned but would be returned in time for the signing. Austen decided that James II was no longer suitable. He asked Lord Londonderry if he could borrow a portrait of Castlereagh. The next day, Austen's hero was in place to supervise the signing of those treaties which he had, in a small way, inspired.[79]

The golden moment was well decorated. Austen was awarded the Garter while Ivy was granted the GBE in recognition of her work on Lake Maggiore. Later, it was announced that Austen had won the Nobel Peace Prize for 1925; the following year Briand and Stresemann shared the Prize.

History is carved up by dividing lines; academics are always on the hunt for a new way of compartmentalising great periods of time. As we have seen, after the London conference, MacDonald had talked about the start of a new era in which the old war mentality was overturned. But Locarno has a better claim to this title; many contemporaries felt that it marked the start of a new age. Austen thought that the treaties would 'mark in history as the dividing point between the era of war and the era of peace'.[80] George V noted in his diary on the day of the signing – 'This morning the Locarno Pact was signed at the Foreign Office. I pray this may mean peace for many years. Why not forever?'[81] A few weeks later Balfour wrote to Austen with a similar message: 'The Great War ended in November 1918. The Great Peace did not begin until Oct. 1925.'[82] Yet within four years, the spirit of Locarno had dissipated; in another seven, the Rhineland Pact would be renounced. If Locarno had been a dividing line, it was quickly erased.

With time, comes further perspective. Locarno was not a guarantee of plain sailing, but instead a better boat. It required decent captains, happy crews and no stormy weather to make progress. All of these ingredients disappeared during the Great Depression: the goodwill evaporated; the dictators saw and seized their chance.

Austen became sluggish in his last years at the Foreign Office, lapsing into old instincts before petering out. In private he became more vain. He was absorbed by the success of Locarno, writing papers about it and mentioning it too often.[83] He collected the compliments which were bestowed on him without much thought by courteous officials and used them to prove one of his favourite doctrines – the importance of personal diplomacy. 'Yesterday', he told his sister in January 1927, 'I had a minute from one of the Asst. Secretaries of the F.O.: – "Germany, Poland & Lithuania are all as irritable & irritating to one another as possible at this moment. The only person who can calm them is the S/S if he will speak to them at Geneva!" My bedside manner again! But there is a basis of truth for it, & I may have to try. After all it is the fact that personality counts for so much that makes this work so attractive.'[84] Quiet meetings between the leaders of the main European states; personal understanding and private concord – this was of course the stuff of Castlereagh. Austen used the technique to good effect; Neville pushed it to destruction.

Towards America, Austen felt a biting disdain. One vivid letter, of 1 February 1920, is worth quoting at length:

> The American mind is so ignorant of European conditions, so suspicious of the English intentions & so afraid of losing votes that they complicate every problem & give no help in settling any of them. If we take a Mandate, we are grabbing territory. If we ask them to do so, we are seeking to involve them in our troubles. If we help the Anti-Bolsheviks, we are militarist. If we blockade the Bolsheviks, they protest that it is illegal. They will send no more help & order the withdrawal of all their soldiers. If we withdraw our blockade, they accuse us of seeking to steal & trade advantage from them. If we withdraw our troops, they ask why we acted without first consulting them & why we & the French take decisions without their leave. If we consult them, their representatives have no instructions, can take no responsibility & record the fact. No, they really are an impossible people in their foreign relations & most impossible of all when they have elections in prospect which is of course every two years![85]

When he was Foreign Secretary the same feelings resurfaced. 'Apparently nothing will cure the Americans of the view that they are a people apart morally as well as geographically and that our policy is dictated by selfish motives and an overbearing temper which have no counterpart in the United States,' he wrote in 1927. In 1928, the same sentiments again – 'the United States has no foreign policy. The ship drifts at the mercy of every gust of public opinion.'[86] The American Secretary of State, Frank Kellogg, came in for particular venom. 'Kellogg is an old woman without a policy & trembling at every breeze which blows from the Senate.'[87]

There was a dangerous concern in these years about the balance of power between the British and American navies. Since 1922, agreements had been in place setting out limitations on certain categories of ships. In 1927 Britain, Japan and America met again to try to extend these agreements to other types of boat. No progress was made and the issue lingered on unhappily.

When, a year later, Austen announced to the House of Commons that Britain had come to an agreement with France on arms control, the news caught everyone by surprise – in Washington, but also inside the Cabinet, where permission had not been given for the new plan. The alarm turned into amazement when it became clear what the agreement entailed. The proposals went against the attempts made with Washington to limit a naval race. By including a deal about the composition of French military forces, they suggested the start of an Anglo-French pact. There was anger, irritation and worry in Germany and America; inside Britain, there were anxious discussions about a return to the old ways. The spirit of Locarno was in jeopardy.

At this moment in August 1928 Austen collapsed. Off and on throughout 1926 and 1927 he had been unwell. This time he caught pneumonia which turned into neuritis. He had to take a long cruise to recover and travelled to California for a holiday. On arriving there he weighed nine stone and his hand trembled so much that shaving was dangerous.[88] He returned to Britain in November and lurked in the background until the general election the following year, in which Baldwin and the Conservatives lost power. Austen, inattentive to his own Birmingham West constituency, only clung on by forty-three votes. A bad year in politics was made worse by personal misfortune. Austen's finances had unravelled and he had to sell Twitt's Ghyll, along with his cherished garden.

Some months later, Austen delivered an address at Chatham House reviewing his foreign policy. He took as his title and theme 'Great Britain as a European Power'. He spoke thoughtfully, talking about the difference between instinct and reason. He embellished these ideas with some advice about Britain's position in the world. Isolation ran up against the facts of geography. The policy may once have been splendid, but it was never safe; even under Lord Salisbury it was fraying: 'we were isolated only in the sense that we had no friends'. On he moved, treading carefully through international co-operation and sovereignty. In closing, he arrived at the principles under which all Foreign Secretaries should operate. Promise no more than can be delivered; exercise a moderating influence; above all, preserve union among the greater powers and prevent Europe settling down into two great camps again – 'this, as it seems to me, should still be in the twentieth century the aim of British statesmanship, as it was a hundred years ago the policy of Castlereagh'.[89]

This was one of many references to Castlereagh in Austen Chamberlain's life. The inheritance which Austen claimed from the dead statesman was not false or affected. A century earlier, Castlereagh had invented a system of collective security. All the leading powers had come together to pledge themselves to protect the Vienna Settlement and defend it against any attack. After Napoleon had been defeated, Castlereagh tried to carry this forward into a general system of security, in which no one country was treated as an enemy. Austen Chamberlain's achievement was to replicate that model on a smaller scale and apply it to the Rhineland. The Locarno Pact was a neutral agreement between neutral nations – neither France nor Germany was identified as posing a threat. So Europe was, for a time, neutralised rather than divided into rival camps.

Against this achievement, the policy put forward by Edward Grey twenty years earlier looks narrow-minded and inflammatory: he had sided with France and Russia against Germany and Austria, taking part in a rivalry which ended in the Great War. But this is too hard on Grey, judging him against a situation in the 1820s and 1920s which did not exist in 1906. By the time Grey arrived at the Foreign Office in 1906 the moment for a collective agreement had passed. The system imposed by Castlereagh after the Napoleonic Wars, and copied by Austen Chamberlain after the Great War, was only possible because the aggressor had just been defeated. In 1906 the problem was coping with the emergence of a potential new aggressor. The Kaiser was a threat to Britain and European stability; Grey was right to take sides against him. As we have seen, his error was not in his choice of friendships, but in the obscure way they evolved. An alliance against a dangerous nation only works if it is made public and the deterrent can influence the potential aggressor's plans. This did not happen in the run-up to 1914. It took another war against an even more dangerous aggressor for the lesson to be learned. Only in 1949, when it seemed as though a third world war was about to break out in Europe against a new aggressor, did diplomats apply the rules of alliance diplomacy and deterrence correctly, resulting in the North Atlantic Pact.

MacDonald returned to office as Prime Minister in 1929. The second Labour Government was mangled, split and finally destroyed by the world slump and the collapse of the financial system. MacDonald found himself presiding over a National Government which Baldwin and the Conservatives dominated and which in the general election of 1931 inflicted a devastating defeat on the Labour Party. This drama lies outside the scope of this book. MacDonald did not venture to hold the Foreign Office a second time. He retained his interest, but was not at ease with his choice as Foreign Secretary, Arthur Henderson.

During his second Government, the defects which sat uneasily alongside MacDonald's virtues increasingly gained the upper hand. His speeches, which had always relied on torrents of generous sound rather than reason, became even longer and more tortuous. One peroration followed another until there seemed no reason why the Prime Minister should ever sit down. His social life became a matter of jest as he pursued a series of dreamy infatuations with unattainable titled ladies. His harmless vanities became more obvious to more people. A Fabian Socialist, Lady Margaret Cole, described how, on a visit to Chequers, she found MacDonald playing three roles in a single afternoon. First, as the inheritor of broad acres, which actually belonged to the Chequers Trust; second, the Son of the People; third, and at greatest length, 'the Lonely Leader, grappling with problems which no one but he could understand, and burdened with inferior colleagues, not one of whom really appreciated him or inspired his confidence'.[90]

MacDonald might consort with duchesses and eventually head a Government dominated by Tories, but in foreign affairs he kept, indeed intensified, the strongest of his early beliefs. Whatever the merits of Locarno, whatever the moral force of the League, he was sure that neither of these would endure without a wide agreement between the major powers on disarmament. After much controversy in Cabinet, he presented a British disarmament plan at the beginning of 1933 as a means of keeping discussions alive.

The basic dilemma had changed its form rather than its essence.

Britain would still not give France a security guarantee; without such a guarantee France would not give Germany the same rights as any other state in armaments; without equality of rights Germany would not sign. MacDonald, his sight failing, his speech ever more ragged, persevered even after Hitler became Chancellor in April 1933. He criticised the new Chancellor, but added that Hitler 'was an interesting problem which we must understand in all its bearings and meanings if we are to steer wisely through this mess'. MacDonald could not conceivably rejoin the Labour Party, which he had driven into the wilderness; but on these matters of foreign policy his personal views were not at heart any different from those of the pacifist George Lansbury, who became the Labour leader after Arthur Henderson.

Meanwhile, Austen Chamberlain gradually slipped out of sympathy with the National Government. There was disappointment as well as vanity in the way he criticised his successors. The Marquess of Reading, Foreign Secretary under Baldwin in 1931, was 'merely an interrogation mark'; Sir John Simon, who followed him, was 'basically wrong'. Austen was also unhappy with MacDonald – 'a bit of quaking jelly'.[91] But here the unhappiness ran deeper, born out of Austen's fears of a new danger which the Government was underestimating

Austen Chamberlain was one of the first men to warn Parliament that Adolf Hitler was not 'an interesting problem' but a grave, probably unappeasable threat. On 13 April 1933 he delivered what was perhaps the first great speech of the 1930s on this theme. He had been alarmed by the way MacDonald had been talking about giving 'equality of status' to Nazi Germany. 'I understood that the promise made by the Five Powers was of equality of status, to be reached by stages. Before you can afford to disarm or to urge others to disarm, you must see a Germany whose mind is turned to peace, who will use her equality of status to secure her own safety but not to menace the safety of others; a Germany which has learnt not only how to live herself but how to let others live inside her and beside her.'

Some cynics murmured that Austen was being anti-German again. Certainly, his old doubts had come to the fore. But throughout these years his argument was objective; his description of the new spirit of German nationalism was fair. It represented the worst of the old

Prussian imperialism, 'with an added savagery, a racial pride, an exclusiveness which cannot allow to any subject not of "pure Nordic birth" equality of rights and citizenship within the nation to which he belongs'. Concessions and appeasement would not restrain Hitler; Britain had to set a new course. 'After all, we stand for something in this country. Our traditions count for our own people, for Europe, and for the world. Europe is menaced and Germany is afflicted by this narrow, exclusive, aggressive spirit, by which it is a crime to be in favour of peace and a crime to be a Jew. That is not a Germany to which we can afford to make concessions. That is not a Germany to which Europe can afford to give equality.'[92]

After that speech in April, people started to talk about what Austen had said. From all over the world, people wrote to him. Messages of support, congratulatory sonnets, money for the Treasury poured into Austen's postbag.[93] Nearly a fifth of these messages came from Jewish communities in Europe and America.[94] One letter in particular must have caught Austen's eye. A Grimsby man, remembering how he had had to 'cower with wife & little children under stairs while German bombs were dropping all around' during a coastline bombardment in the Great War, wrote to Austen to thank him. 'As sure as the Sun will rise tomorrow, so surely will Germany start a war of revenge as soon as ever she feels strong enough to do so.'[95]

Austen continued his sharp speeches throughout the next years. Two thoughts underpinned his arguments. He saw a link between repression inside Germany and the likely course of its foreign policy. 'The temper of the new German Government repels me in its domestic aspects and fills me with anxiety for its possible consequences in foreign affairs,' he explained. Sooner than most, Austen accepted that for 'a people who believe in nothing but force, force is the only answer'.[96] The second thought stands at the heart of this chapter. Indeed, it gets to the difference between Austen Chamberlain and Ramsay MacDonald. On the balance between instinct and reason Austen's views were clear. 'The fact is,' Austen explained in 1934, 'as I have always said, feelings and sentiment − not logic − govern the day to day policies of nations.'[97] By seeing the limits of reason, Austen understood why a policy of appeasement would not deter Hitler from his chosen path.

When we think about the 1930s, we think of Winston Churchill, a lonely campaigner for rearmament and a robust foreign policy. But in the first years after Hitler had taken charge in Germany, it was Austen who led the anti-appeasers. Churchill tended to alienate people by his imperial harangues; Austen, for the first time in his career, built up a small personal following made up of people like Anthony Eden. These men paid close attention to his speeches and eagerly sought out his advice. Robert Cecil, the old League of Nations man who had battled with Austen in the 1920s, explained the difference between Austen and Churchill in June 1936. 'I do not think Winston's queer manoeuvres matter one way or the other very much. He just lacks that bourgeois quality which makes Austen so formidable.'[98]*

Austen did not live to see his brother become Prime Minister; he died in March 1937. Even with his firm sense of family loyalty, it is hard to see that he would have approved of what Neville did. Anthony Eden's story of a dinner party with the two men, when Austen interrupted his brother mid-flow and said, 'Neville, you must remember you don't know anything about foreign affairs', raises endless questions.[99] But, alas, poor Austen, however perceptive, had never been quite able to hammer through his arguments when it came to the crunch. In 1935 he had had a chance to seize control of the rudder and lead a mutiny against the Government – but once again the old caution and correctness had held him back.

As we shall see, in that year the Government fell into a trough over Mussolini's invasion of Abyssinia. For a time, the crisis was so damaging that it looked as though the Government might fall; Austen's position had become pivotal for its survival. His support or criticism could have been enough to swing the vote either way. Baldwin, ruthless and skilful when clinging to power, told Austen that he wanted to talk to him about the Foreign Office as soon as the incumbent, Sam Hoare, had been deposed. With this promise in

---

* Austen also recovered some lost ground in his constituency in these later years, doing rather better in general elections than he had done in 1929. He seems to have paid more attention to his constituents and visited them every once in a while. At least one unlikely voter was won round by Austen in one of these visits to West Birmingham. Brian Walden remembers meeting a sympathetic lady when canvassing as a Labour candidate in All Saints, Birmingham in 1963, who told him that she would like to vote for him but could not do so because Austen Chamberlain had once helped her turn her mangle.

mind and other feelings in the background – the old sense of honour, dignity, good manners – Austen held back when it came to debating Abyssinia in Parliament, in effect letting the Government off the hook. But there was no happy return to the Foreign Office. Baldwin met Austen and told him that he would have loved to make him Foreign Secretary, but worried that Austen was too old. Austen was embarrassed and angry. 'He told me I was ga-ga.' From the sidelines, Churchill passed his own judgement. 'Poor man, he always plays the game and never wins it.'[100] This was the verdict which stuck.

Ramsay MacDonald and Austen Chamberlain operated in a world of rules without power.

Although on maps Britain seemed all-powerful, in reality it was on the way down. The strongest countries in the world were no longer European, and the ascendant nations – America, the Soviet Union, to some extent Japan – were not focused on European concerns. British diplomats had to make sense of the general disorder with faulty institutions – the League of Nations, the British Empire, a surplus of summit diplomacy. Occasionally, as at the London conference and particularly after Locarno, it looked as though progress was being made to create new institutions and restore some balance. But these new instruments of diplomacy required first-rate performers and a patient audience. Neither of these was forthcoming in the 1920s; in the 1930s both disappeared.

All the while, Britain was looking for inspired leadership and failing to find it. This does not mean that politicians were particularly stupid in these decades; on the contrary, Westminster was full of intelligent men. What was lacking was a certain strength of character and judgement. To give an academic parallel, it was as though Lloyd George had earned himself a First for leadership during the Great War, but had then been sent down for bad behaviour later on. Churchill, despite his huge ability, was in these years dangerously erratic and several times verged on failure. So the decade passed into the hands of second-class men.

In a vague way, Ramsay MacDonald and Austen Chamberlain flailed about looking for new paths through the uncertainty. MacDonald, a pure believer in the progress and strength of human reason, focused his faith on the power of democracy, disarmament and arbitration to resolve any dispute before a war could break out. At one point only, the London conference of 1924, he allied some of that idealism with a mastery of the facts. Austen, worrying that mankind was less civilised than MacDonald and many of his contemporaries seemed to realise, focused on calming the new antagonisms by having a proper respect for ancient instincts. At Locarno he scored a genuine success for collective security, rediscovering Castlereagh in the process and the idea of Concert diplomacy between the leaders of the main European powers.

The old disagreement between Castlereagh and Canning had mutated. The two elements of Canning's thinking, namely the pursuit of liberal causes and the need for a robust independent British policy, had passed into different hands. The internationalists, led by MacDonald and Lord Robert Cecil, had inherited the liberal urge. The insistence on a vigorous, independent and global policy had passed through Disraeli to Churchill and Leo Amery. In his heyday Austen tried to resolve this disagreement among Canningites by reinventing Castlereagh, with his emphasis on a European Concert, on flexible and courteous diplomacy, on a pessimism which stopped short of despair.

Each of these strands was caught up in the arguments about appeasement which broke out in the 1930s. As we have seen, it was Austen who had talked about Locarno as the start of a process of appeasement; it was Austen who had developed that technique of personal diplomacy which Neville deployed later on. But it was Austen who first called time on the policy as it applied to Nazi Germany.

Appeasement, properly executed, is neither immoral nor ineffective. It is, as Professor Paul Kennedy has told us, 'a positive policy, based on certain optimistic assumptions about man's inherent reasonableness'.[101] In British foreign policy it has a long history and, on the whole, a successful record. Indeed, it is the natural policy of a satisfied power. But it only works if it is applied to trustworthy people with moderate intentions. In the 1920s and 1930s British diplomats and politicians tended to assume that all people were reasonable, and that the more reasonable one's own foreign policy, the more reasonably everyone else would behave. MacDonald was the chief culprit here, the Geneva Protocol and disarmament conferences his most serious mistakes. As we will see, his successors in the Labour Party and in the National Government – George Lansbury in the first category, Neville Chamberlain in the second – fell into the same trap. But professional diplomats also played their part. 'I have no extravagant belief in anyone,' Lord D'Abernon wrote in his diary in July 1925, 'but incline to the maxim that you make many people better by treating them with consideration and confidence. The German is partly what you make of him.'[102] Partly, perhaps; but other factors came into play in Germany which no amount of British consideration or confidence could assuage.

Austen saw more clearly. It is hard to say why precisely, although his experiences in the 1880s certainly had something to do with it. An uneasy Tory feeling, deep down inside him, told him that the old passions of pride, self-interest, national prestige were more powerful than reason in governing the affairs of the world. Late in the day, and long after Locarno, he saw that the moment for appeasement had passed and he had the strength to stand up in Parliament and say so. This was a small success in the grand scheme of things; it did not result in a change of direction. But it was an early chink of light in that decade of fog and thunderstorms; it fell to others to focus the beam.

CHAPTER VII

BEVIN AND EDEN

'Till the war-drum throbbed no longer, and the battle-flags were furl'd
In the Parliament of Man, the Federation of the World . . . '

Tennyson, 'Locksley Hall'

October 1935

George Lansbury's pilgrimage had arrived at its final shrine. In the Dome at Brighton, the Labour Party conference exulted in emotion; a number of women wept. Here was the leader of the Party, the high priest of idealism, preaching the futility of war.[1]

These were difficult days for pacifists. Fascism had begun to focus people's minds. In recent months even the Labour Party had begun to sense foreign danger; their doubts had registered in small doses. At the 1934 conference the Party had overturned the decision it had taken a year earlier, to organise a strike in the event of a war. More recently, the Party's National Executive Committee had decided to support the use of economic sanctions by the League of Nations against Italy, as Mussolini prepared to conquer the African country then known as Abyssinia.[2]

This was the argument in dispute at Brighton. At no point did anybody suggest using force against Italy. The issue was whether the League should take any action at all to deter aggression. For Lansbury, the answer was no. He believed it was his duty to turn the Party away from any avenue which might eventually lead Britain to war.

Lansbury had based his leadership of the Labour Party on a clear belief in Christian Socialist values. At times, he had been almost militant in his mildness. Everyone remembered the message he had sent to the Fulham East by-election in 1933: 'I would close every recruiting station, disband the Army and disarm the Air Force. I would abolish the whole dreadful equipment of war and say to the world "do your worst".'[3] But now, standing before his wavering Party, Lansbury adopted a defeated, aged tone. He spoke sadly, alluding rather too often to the Bible. He began by suggesting that he could no longer remain leader of the Labour Party if it supported sanctions:

> It may be that I shall not meet you on this platform any more.

Tamely, the audience bleated 'NO'. Lansbury resumed his rambling; he was sustained by divine authority.

> . . . one whose life I revere and who I believe to be the greatest figure in history has put it on record that 'Those who take the sword shall perish by the sword'.

He composed an anthem of abnegation, an appeal against even self-defence:

> If mine was the only voice in the conference, I would say in the name of the faith I hold, the belief that God intended us to live peaceably and quietly with one another – if some people do not allow us to do so, I am ready to stand as the early Christians did and say 'This is my faith, this is where we stand and if necessary, this is where we will die'.[4]

Lansbury's argument bore no relation to the facts of Abyssinia's fate. This did not matter. The Labour Party responded like a sinner who had been shown the error of his ways.

As the outpouring of applause faded, so did the calm weather. Ernest Bevin waddled to the podium with a hailstorm breaking above his head. By the time he started speaking, stones of ice were battering down on the Dome.[5] Fifty-four years old, a thick rolling rhino of a man, Bevin began his slow charge. Lansbury's speech had made him angry. As founder and General Secretary of the Transport and General Workers' Union, Bevin inhabited a different world. His socialism was earthier, more rooted in the harsh reality of working-class life. He studied and feared the paths of the dictators, and had been trying to move the Left towards a firmer stance on foreign policy for some time. Now Lansbury had tried to reverse his hard work in a fit of sentimentality laced with spin.

Even so, the viciousness of Bevin's speech was surprising. His tirade was tempered by the lilt of his West Country tones. He focused on Lansbury's hint of resignation: this was emotional blackmail. 'It is placing the Executive and the Movement in an absolutely wrong position to be hawking your conscience round from body to body, asking to be told what you ought to do with it.'* Uproar followed, even booing. When the noise died down Bevin continued. 'There is one quotation from the Scriptures which George Lansbury has quoted today which I think he ought to apply to himself: "Do unto others ... ".' The shouting returned.[6]

So it went on. After dislodging Lansbury's reputation, Bevin turned on the others in the Party who opposed sanctions. He focused in particular on Sir Stafford Cripps, the leader of the Socialist League. Cripps had spoken poisonously about the League of Nations. In his scheme of things, the League was 'nothing but the tool of the imperialist powers'. This was too much for Bevin. Cripps was wrong about the League of Nations, and wrong about the real threat to the working class. It was Fascism which was destroying the trade union movement, not a capitalist conspiracy. 'It is we who are being wiped out and who will be wiped out if Fascism comes here,' he proclaimed.[7]

The following day, 2 October, the conference, dominated by the block vote of the trade unions, voted by 2,168,000 to 102,000 to give conditional support to the use of sanctions by the League; on 3 October the Italians invaded Abyssinia; on 8 October Lansbury resigned.[8] Some criticised Bevin. He did not repent. 'Lansbury has been going about dressed in saint's clothes for years waiting for martyrdom. I set fire to the faggots.'[9]

It was a small victory in a long campaign to change the way the Left thought about war. Meanwhile, the National Government was having similar problems of its own.

---

* There is a question whether Bevin said 'hawking' or 'taking'. According to the Labour Party's official record, Bevin said 'taking'. Others present at the conference thought he said 'trailing'. These are interesting arguments worth following in Alan Bullock's 'first

January 1938

Another rough day. The plane from Paris to London had been cancelled and the Foreign Secretary was forced to take the sea crossing. In the storm, the boat rammed the pier at Folkestone, doing itself £3,000 of damage.

Two sombre figures were waiting for Anthony Eden on the quayside – his own Private Secretary, Oliver Harvey, and Sir Alexander Cadogan, Permanent Secretary at the Foreign Office. Only then did Eden understand why Cadogan had insisted that he break off a short holiday near Cannes, where he had played tennis and gossiped with Winston Churchill and Lloyd George.[10]

The news which the two officials brought to Folkestone on 15 January 1938 should have been encouraging. They told him that Franklin Roosevelt, President of the United States, was ready to launch his country into the maelstrom of European diplomacy. In a secret message to the British Prime Minister, Neville Chamberlain, Roosevelt had proposed that he should suggest to the whole Diplomatic Corps in Washington that all governments should agree on the principles of international relations, including reduction of armaments, access to raw materials and the laws of warfare.[11]

This was vague stuff. But Eden and the Foreign Office badly needed a new script and a new actor on the scene. Eden had made his reputation as a League of Nations man, yet the League of Nations, never powerful, had proved its impotence over Abyssinia. Encouraged by this failure, Hitler had marched his army into the Rhineland in defiance of the clauses in the Treaties of Versailles and Locarno which forbade this. He was now preparing to absorb Austria into the German Reich, bullying the Austrian Chancellor Schuschnigg into submission. Having tested both, Eden had no illusions left about the good faith of Hitler or Mussolini; what Britain lacked was the means and the will to resist their ambitions. Eden had long hoped against the odds that the United States might come forward to provide both. Now, at last, the United States had appeared.

The woolliness of the President's proposal could be combed out, so Eden thought, by skilful diplomacy. The essential problem lay

volume of *The Life and Times of Ernest Bevin* (London: Heinemann, 1960–83), p. 568, footnote 1.

not in Washington but in Downing Street. Eden had at first been pleased when Neville Chamberlain, Austen's brother, succeeded Baldwin as Prime Minister in May 1937. The two men had worked well together as Cabinet colleagues, and there had seemed at the start no reason why they should not continue to do so now. By January 1938, however, Eden knew that he and the Prime Minister differed fundamentally.

As Chancellor of the Exchequer, Neville Chamberlain had lived at one remove from the growing effrontery of the dictators. His self-confidence had not been dented; on the contrary, he was preparing to play a decisive role in preserving peace by agreement. To Eden, President Roosevelt's letter was a welcome new move in a desperate game; to Chamberlain, it was a clumsy and unwelcome interference with his own exercise of personal diplomacy. Taking advantage of Eden's absence in France, Chamberlain had already sent Roosevelt a chilling reply.

Once he was back, Eden did his best through the Embassy in Washington to argue that the way was still open for an American initiative. He rammed home the argument in a letter to Chamberlain on 17 January. 'I truly believe that with the world as it is now it is almost impossible to overestimate the effect which an indication of US interest in European affairs may be calculated to produce ... we shall have committed the greatest mistake if as a result of any action of ours President Roosevelt is deterred from launching his appeal.'[12] Nothing worked. The American initiative petered out. Worse, the Prime Minister was planning his own diplomatic offensive.

Behind Eden's back, Chamberlain was in touch with the Italian Government through his sister-in-law, Ivy Chamberlain, Austen's widow, and the devious Italian Ambassador, Count Grandi. On 18 February, after four weeks of unhappy manoeuvring, Chamberlain and Eden saw Grandi together at 10 Downing Street. At the Prime Minister's suggestion, Grandi set out his view of Anglo-Italian relations. Chamberlain amazed Eden by nodding his head approvingly at each of Grandi's arguments. 'The more N.C. nodded the more outrageous became Grandi's account until in the end it would almost seem that we had invaded Abyssinia.'[13] In his report, Grandi sensed the dramatic heart of the occasion: 'Chamberlain and Eden were not a Prime Minister and Foreign Secretary discussing with the

Ambassador of a foreign power a delicate situation of international character. They were – and revealed themselves as such to me in defiance of all established convention – two enemies confronting each other, like two cocks in fighting posture.'[14]

As soon as Grandi left Downing Street, the argument flared up between the Prime Minister and Foreign Secretary. Chamberlain wanted to ask Grandi back that afternoon and tell him that he intended to open talks with the Italians at once. Eden refused to agree. Chamberlain strode up and down the room, criticising his colleague. 'Anthony, you have missed chance after chance. You simply cannot go on like this.' Eden insisted, as was his right, that the Cabinet be consulted. A Cabinet was hurriedly called next day, Saturday 19 February. Ministers, surprised that their weekend had been interrupted, were shocked to find themselves in the middle of an unsuspected row between Prime Minister and Foreign Secretary. Chamberlain set out his argument forcefully: a golden opportunity existed to discuss and, if possible, agree with Mussolini the means of breaking the deadlock between democracies and dictatorships in Europe. It would be wrong to miss the opportunity because of Foreign Office misgivings about timing. Eden argued that to run after Mussolini in this way would be regarded as another defeat at the hands of the dictators. Most of the Cabinet sided with Chamberlain; all were horrified when, after three hours, Eden said that in these circumstances he must resign. The Cabinet adjourned until Sunday while efforts were made to find a compromise. Sir John Simon and some of the Government Whips began to insinuate that Eden was ill.[15]

On Sunday 20 February, the majority again sided with the Prime Minister. Among his papers at Birmingham University is the card on which Eden and Chamberlain scribbled during the discussion. Eden: 'This is very painful, but it really does not help. It is what you expected.' Chamberlain (carefully worded, typical of the man): 'It is what I expected and I cannot control the weight of the representation made. The difference between us is not one of ultimate aims or principle but of outlook and method. If even now any way out can be suggested by which the painful decision can be avoided without reversing the view expressed by the majority yesterday I should welcome it most heartily.' But no compromise was possible.[16]

Eden returned to the Foreign Office to write his letter of resignation. 'It cannot be in the country's interest that those who are called upon to direct its affairs should work in an uneasy partnership, fully conscious of differences of outlook, yet hoping that they will not recur.' On Monday 21 February he explained his reasons to a packed House of Commons. It was a curiously tentative performance. 'We are in the presence of the progressive deterioration of respect for international relations ... In the light – my judgement may be wrong – of the present international situation this is a moment for the country to stand firm, not to plunge into negotiations unprepared.' He developed his point about the traditional method of diplomacy, which was to prepare carefully, not to negotiate under the threat of 'now or never'. Harold Nicolson, MP and diarist, a strong supporter of Eden, was disappointed: 'There was just a sufficient note of recrimination to spoil the dignified effect and not enough to constitute an appeal.'[17]

Eden left out the clinching argument. Neither in Cabinet, nor in his resignation letter, nor in the Commons, nor in his speech a few days later in his constituency did Eden mention except obliquely the American initiative which Chamberlain had smothered. Yet it was this action which had started the political crisis and proved crucial in his decision to resign. Historians can doubt whether anything useful might have happened if Roosevelt had intervened in Europe's diplomacy at that moment in 1938. But the way Chamberlain had dismissed Roosevelt's offer had been seriously wrong.

On the day he resigned, Eden did not know the full depth of Chamberlain's secret dealings with the Italians. Argument about the timing and conditions of talks with Mussolini might not by itself have forced Eden from office. It was Chamberlain's unprofessional reaction to the Americans which shocked Eden, the convinced professional, and convinced him that he could not continue to work with the Prime Minister. But it was precisely this same professionalism which prevented him from explaining the full truth to Parliament or public or even to his Cabinet colleagues. Roosevelt's initiative had been secret, and must remain so. Eden's reticence, maintained to his own misfortune, would be inconceivable today.

Neither then, nor a few months later after Munich, did Eden take the lead in opposing appeasement. He was too much of a diplomat to despair of diplomacy.

Eden was born in 1897, the third son of Sir William Eden, a baronet of long rather than famous ancestry who owned 8,000 acres and a beautiful house at Windlestone in County Durham. Charming, erratic, devoted to art, equipped with a furious temper, Sir William was not an easy father or husband. Eden's mother Sybil came to prefer other company – notably The Souls, a group of gifted, good-looking young men and women who moved from country house to country house in the 1880s and 1890s, eloquently enjoying each other's company and occasionally each other's beds. Eden did not dismiss out of hand the story that he was the son, not of the eccentric baronet, but of one of the most glamorous of the Souls, George Wyndham; but it turns out that Wyndham was in South Africa when Eden was conceived.[18]

Eden was not particularly close to either of his parents, but he inherited their aesthetic sense and was devoted to Windlestone. As a schoolboy at Eton, another characteristic came to the fore. Eden was not apt at team games; he preferred tennis and rowing to cricket. Unlike most Englishmen of his type, he never gathered round him a group of close male friends.

The ordinary and agreeable process of growing up as an aristocrat in aristocratic England was shattered by the outbreak of war in August 1914. His eldest brother, Jack, was killed at Ypres that October while Eden was still at Eton. Eden insisted on leaving school and joining the King's Royal Rifle Corps as soon as he turned eighteen at the end of the following summer. After training, he embarked for France in May 1916. That month his younger brother Nicholas, of whom he was particularly fond, was killed at the Battle of Jutland, just after his sixteenth birthday, while serving as midshipman on HMS *Indefatigable*. Eden's own moment of direct trial came three months later. On 14 August, as he led a party out on patrol in no man's land, one of them, Sergeant Harrop, was badly wounded. The persistence and courage which the nineteen-year-old Second Lieutenant showed in rescuing the wounded man earned Eden the Military Cross. Many years later he wrote in *Another World* about his experiences as a boy and in the war. In this simple and moving book Eden did not mention his Military Cross. To him it was just one episode in a catastrophe which had brought death to two brothers and countless acquaintances, and shaped the lives of all who survived. Sergeant Harrop was more specific. 'I owe my life to Mr Eden who as soon as he found I had not returned, at once set off back with two or three of the men and dragged me to safety. He knew just where I would be lying.'[19]

At Christ Church, Oxford Eden took up the threads which the war had suspended. In many ways he followed a conventional pattern. By 1923 he had achieved a degree and was about to marry Beatrice, the beautiful daughter of a Yorkshire landowner. He had turned down the idea of a diplomatic career, believing that he would have to wait too long for real responsibility and 'be for ever handing round teacups in Tehran'.[20] He found a safe Conservative seat at Warwick and Leamington Spa, for which he was elected in 1923. Though conventional in appearance, upbringing and manner, Eden was different. At Oxford he had studied Arabic and Persian. His leisure was devoted to French literature and to pictures. He was one of the founders of the University Uffizi Society, to which he read an enthusiastic paper on Cézanne. Behind the conventional good looks and flirtatious charm, this was a sensitive and complicated young man.

No one of sensitivity could go through what Eden called 'the death, muck and misery of war'[21] and come out believing that British society could or should be reconstructed in pre-war form. Men like Eden and Harold Macmillan were not prepared to treat trade unionists as enemies, or Edwardian capitalism as an unqualified good. Eden held close to his Party leader, Stanley Baldwin; he admired his cautious handling of the General Strike in 1926. But Baldwin operated by instinct rather than intellect. For intellectual stimulus Eden turned to a fellow backbencher. Noel Skelton's articles in *The Spectator* and his book *Constructive Conservatism* described how free enterprise could work towards greater equality through the growth of a property-owning democracy. Skelton coined this phrase, which was made famous by Eden and became the heart of the latter's not very profound thinking on domestic matters. Skelton died early of cancer before he could make a public mark.

Economics, meanwhile, had taken a more severe and direct grip on Ernest Bevin's life. He was born into heavy rural poverty in a cottage off Exmoor in the spring of 1881. Bevin's mother, Diana, left a blank space in the birth register where a father's name should have been. Shortly after Bevin's eighth birthday, a second and more serious blank appeared in his life when Diana died. Bevin's half-sister took him into her care. After an inadequate and abortive education he was shunted out of the country and into Bristol, where he tried his hand at an assortment of jobs. He delivered pies; he delivered mineral water; he worked in a butter shop, as a pageboy, and as a conductor on horse trams. He helped to run some refreshment rooms. He then settled down as a driver of mineral water wagons, with a wife called Florence Townley.

This was a chequered CV, but not untypical. Bevin's experiences of working-class life mirrored the uncertainty felt by millions as the requirements of British trade and industry shifted at the turn of the century. Like others, Bevin made sense of these changes initially through the doctrines of nonconformist worship, and then through socialism. But Bevin stood apart from the growing phalanx of Fabians by the practical manner in which he tried to put Britain to rights. The defining moment in his life came not in reading George Bernard Shaw or J.A. Hobson, but on the Avonmouth and Bristol docks in the summer of 1910. There was a strike; Bevin got involved; he found he was good at mobilising workers to lobby employers for a better deal. The following spring he left his mineral water wagons and became an organiser for the Dockers' Union, with a salary of £2 a week.[22]

From here, Bevin moved in a drab but determined direction, building up the trade union movement in Britain. The process took him through the Great War and to the mammoth achievement of 1922 when he brought together twenty-two trade unions to create the Transport and General Workers' Union, which would become the largest trade union in the world. There is something unshakeably detailed and dour about the history of the trade union movement. Even in those early days, so much trade union life was about bureaucracy and infighting. Only occasionally does the inspiration for it all shine through. But Bevin did not shift his gaze from the underlying motive. Several times in his career he found ways of transmitting his sense of working-class solidarity to otherwise uninterested crowds.

One such occasion was the Shaw Inquiry into dockers' wages between February and March 1920. Here Bevin coolly and carefully set before an industrial tribunal the arguments for raising dockers' wages to sixteen shillings a day. He faced down the precise Cambridge statistician A.L. Bowley by asking him to explain his calculations for a docker's income in terms of each item of food. In a moment of theatre and some genius, Bevin produced for the court the specified allotment of bacon, and then asked the helpless don whether he thought it represented an acceptable meal: 'I want to ask any employer, or you, or the Court, whether a Cambridge professor is a competent judge of a docker's breakfast.' The Inquiry awarded the dockers their sixteen shillings a day.[23]

Another occasion came a few months later; Bevin often referred to it later in life. In February 1919, war had broken out between Poland and Soviet Russia. By the spring of 1920, the tables had turned dangerously against Poland; it looked for a time as though the Russians would topple Warsaw. Britain, having already failed in one intervention against Bolshevik Russia, now stood poised to launch another to stem the Soviet tide.

When the London dockers refused to load a ship called the *Jolly George* with arms for Poland in May 1920, it was Bevin who rallied to their cause. 'I think we have a right to refuse to have our labour prostituted to carry on wars of this character.' Forgetting the beleaguered Poles, he rested his case against intervention on an older argument: 'Whatever may be the merits or demerits of the theory of government of Russia, that is a matter for Russia, and we have no right to determine their form of government, any more than we would tolerate Russia determining our form of government.'[24] Bevin took the debate to Downing Street. Alongside a delegation of trade unionists, he met Lloyd George and set out his view. A 'vital principle is at stake', he told the Prime Minister, 'which we want you to note especially – we feel we cannot admit the right, in the event of a revolution in a country, of every other nation using . . . their armed forces to crush out or stem a change that is being made'. After a lengthy exchange, Lloyd George accepted the thrust of Bevin's argument.[25] Britain did not intervene; the Poles successfully fought back alone.

Three pointers to the future follow from these stories. First, there is his faith in the facts. In August 1920, Bevin told the Trades Union Congress: 'In the name of the British Labour Party, I say that no one man or set of men has the right to say that the honour of a country is at stake when the country does not know the facts.'[26] This same spirit flowed through Bevin's trade union work, as he assembled evidence of wages, prices and subsistence levels. It was also the reason why he never blinded himself to the threat posed by Hitler's regime. Long after Lansbury's downfall, Bevin kept up his campaign against appeasement. 'We have had thousands of resolutions,' he warned the 1937 Labour Party conference, 'but we cannot stop Fascism by resolutions.'[27]

Second, and as a result of this first point, he came to despise Communism and Communists. Although he had defended the rights of Russia's revolution in 1920 to exist without interference, the more he saw, the more he doubted the virtues of the Soviet regime. He told the TGWU after meeting with Soviet representatives in 1922 that Russian Communism was 'contrary absolutely to our conception of democracy'.[28] This feeling grew into firm hostility in the 1930s as he fought Communist subversion within the trade unions at home.

In third place, Bevin could not stand the middle class. He would later tell one of his senior diplomats: 'I don't mind the upper class. As a matter of fact, I even rather like the upper class. They may be an abuse but they're often as like as not, intelligent and amusing. Of course I love the lower class and it's the backbone of the country. But ... I frankly can't abide the middle class. For I find them self-righteous and narrow-minded.'[29] That, of course, had been Disraeli's criticism too.

There was a touch of acid in his distrust of the bourgeoisie. Like many socialists in the early twentieth century, Bevin was captured by the notion of suspicious financiers who maliciously manipulated the market. Like some other socialists, Bevin thought these financiers tended to be Jews. One speech to the Trades Union Congress in 1931 dwelt on this image: 'It's a terrible burden this usury. You will remember that in the Old Book the prophet of Nineveh lectured the

Jews about quarrelling over money-lending, and he told them they must not lend money to each other in future but only lend it to the gentiles. The prophet's direction appears to have been carried out.'³⁰ Others better educated than Bevin shared the prejudice; with Bevin it would surface painfully later in life.

All this passed Eden by without interesting him; his enthusiasm was for foreign affairs. Advancement came quickly through the convulsions of political life between 1926 and 1935. In 1926 he became Parliamentary Private Secretary to the Foreign Secretary, Austen Chamberlain. He was made a junior Foreign Office Minister in the National coalition Government of Ramsay MacDonald in September 1931 with specific responsibility for League of Nations affairs, first outside the Cabinet, then in the Cabinet under Baldwin as Lord Privy Seal.

These were the years when the world's hope turned sour. The idealism of MacDonald was cruelly punished. Now that appeasement has become a dirty word, the League of Nations is usually dismissed as a failure doomed from the start, and universal disarmament a hopeless chimera. Yet in the 1920s and early 1930s these causes gained the enthusiastic support of millions of intelligent men and women. They depended on the belief that reason could become the guiding force in the affairs of a humanity chastened by the unspeakably awful experience of war. Eden joined Austen Chamberlain during the warm glow which followed the Treaty of Locarno. His friendship with the older man strengthened two instincts which were already implanted by his upbringing and personal tastes: a deep affection for France, with a belief in Anglo-French co-operation as a foundation stone of British foreign policy; and a respect for the courteous processes of traditional diplomacy. Because of Locarno, he believed that the European settlement was no longer a victor's peace imposed upon a humiliated Germany; in a new form it had now been freely accepted by Germany's democratic government.

In one of his first speeches as a Minister, Eden talked of the advance of reason in world affairs. It was not cowardice but a belief in reason which led him and millions of others to champion Locarno, the League and disarmament. He believed that Germany would have to be given equality of status in any agreement on armaments, thus abolishing the provision for a disarmed Germany in the Treaty of

Versailles. But because this was the most important part of the post-war settlement for France, its disappearance would have to be accompanied by a firm military guarantee by Britain to France, which would be more specific than the Pact of Locarno.

In these years, Eden steadily built his reputation with press, public and Parliament. He looked the part; he played it well. He learned the techniques of persuasion, of chairmanship, of attention to detail. Naturally there were jealousies and doubts. Two critical comments from these early days found echoes later on. Robert Vansittart later recorded his opinion at the time, that Eden 'said the right thing so often that he seemed incapable of saying anything else'.[31] Harold Laski from the Left made a similar point. 'Mr Eden is the English gentleman at his best. He is a pragmatist to his fingertips. He does not dig into foundations because he knows that it is a dangerous adventure.'[32]

In the 1930s, Eden served under two Prime Ministers and two Foreign Secretaries whom he could not respect. MacDonald sank in old age into a morass of platitude. Eden wrote in his diary: 'Ramsay creates this impression in conversation that not only do all the cares of the world rest upon his head, but that no one can ever have been Prime Minister of England before.'[33] His successor, Baldwin, was in foreign affairs 'fitful and lethargic'.[34] The two Foreign Secretaries, Sir John Simon then Sir Samuel Hoare, were awful. Calculating, narrow and ambitious, lacking the driving sincerity of either Churchill or Neville Chamberlain, they formed the heart of what became known as The Old Gang. As their junior colleague in the Foreign Office, Eden showed outward loyalty but was full of private complaints. He was particularly scornful of Simon who used his sharp analytical lawyer's mind to avoid decisions. From the flat prose of Eden's memoirs there sometimes emerges a telling phrase. Thus on Simon: 'Too penetrating a discernment and too frail a conviction encouraged confusion where there should have been a fixed intent.'[35] In later years, our foreign policy has sometimes suffered from the reverse – too many proclaimed convictions and too little real discernment.

From 1933, the shadows cast by three dictators steadily darkened the European scene. In 1934 and 1935 Eden, though not yet Foreign Secretary or even in the Cabinet, met all three. He visited Hitler in

February 1934 to present a new set of disarmament proposals . . . and was impressed. He thought Hitler was 'clearly more than a demagogue . . . and seemed to me more sincere than I had expected'.³⁶ To his wife, Eden admitted, 'I rather liked him'; and to the Prime Minister, 'I think we can trust the Chancellor not to go back on his word'.³⁷ These were early days for Hitler, and others were equally bemused. This first contact with Hitler was eased by the discovery that they had both served on the same part of the Western Front. This coincidence surfaced again when Eden accompanied Simon on another visit to Berlin in March 1935. Hitler and Eden discovered that they had actually been stationed opposite each other at Le Fère in March 1918 during Ludendorff's last offensive, Eden as a young staff officer, Hitler as a corporal. They drew a map together on the dinner card, marking in the different military positions. Afterwards, the French Ambassador asked Eden if this was true and commented: 'Et vous l'avez manqué? Vous devriez être fusillé.'³⁸

From Berlin in 1935 Eden travelled to Moscow to meet Stalin. Amazingly, he was the first Western Minister to visit Russia since the Bolshevik Revolution of 1917. He was impressed by Stalin's clear grasp of the European scene and his inner strength. At the Bolshoi, the conductor, whirling and passionate, played 'God Save the King' as if it was a revolutionary hymn. Eden had no doubt that Stalin presided over a cruel tyranny – but one with which it might be possible to do business.

Of the three dictators, Eden most disliked and distrusted Mussolini. Mussolini's table manners were offensive to Eden; moreover, 'he was a complete gangster and his pledged word meant nothing'. This dislike was reciprocated: the Duce's verdict was 'I never saw a better dressed fool'.³⁹ Eden thus separated himself from a section of British opinion with which on other points he sympathised. This group included his old chief Austen Chamberlain and the passionate Robert Vansittart, Permanent Secretary at the Foreign Office; at some moments they attracted the support of Winston Churchill. These men took Mussolini at his own valuation of himself, as a man of power who had put Italy to rights by firm government and could play a decisive part in restraining Hitler and preserving peace. The ludicrous Mussolini familiar to us later from Low's cartoons, Charlie Chaplin's film *The Great Dictator* and his own lamentable performance during the Second World War, had not yet been revealed.

Italy had joined late in the scramble for colonies over which Salisbury and Bismarck presided in the last quarter of the nineteenth century. She had to be content with apparently barren Libya and two unpromising tracts of land in East Africa, namely Eritrea and Italian Somaliland. Worse, the Italian attempt to enlarge this puny empire had met with humiliating disaster at the Battle of Adowa in 1896, when Italian troops were cut to pieces by the Abyssinians. Mussolini could not claim to have restored the dignity of Italy, let alone the glories of the Roman Empire, until this wrong had been righted. Ramshackle, independent Abyssinia, which separated the two Italian colonies in East Africa, was the obvious target. Mussolini could claim that he was not acting differently from Britain, Germany, France, Portugal and Belgium fifty years earlier. But those fifty years mattered. The world had moved on. There was now a League of Nations, of which Abyssinia was a member. There were new rules and a changed public opinion. Imperialism was out of fashion.

Mussolini dispatched more and more troops to his two colonies bordering Abyssinia. Eden was deeply concerned. He was no cynic. He believed in the League of Nations. His own growing reputation was closely linked to its success. He recognised Mussolini's deliberate challenge and wished to meet it with robust diplomacy. This meant using the League to mobilise the public opinion which was supposed to be its strength. On 24 May 1935 he achieved a unanimous vote in the Council of the League in favour of a peaceful resolution of the dispute.

Eden would not have been Eden, and Britain would not have been Britain, if they had not tried to use this precarious advantage to push for some sort of compromise. Eden worked out the details with his superior, the new Foreign Secretary, Samuel Hoare. They produced an ingenious scheme which in various forms had been kicked around Whitehall for several years. Britain would offer Abyssinia a corridor to the sea and a small seaport in British Somaliland; in return the Abyssinians would give Italy a slice of territory in the south of the country which would enlarge Italian Somaliland. Eden agreed to go to Rome, and he met Mussolini twice. He found Mussolini coherent in formal discussion but preposterous and pretentious in the presence of other Italians. Eden made no progress. He returned to London convinced that Mussolini was set on war.

But then, to Eden's surprise, Hoare delivered at Geneva on 10 September a speech of remarkable force and clarity, pledging Britain to support 'steady and collective resistance to all acts of unprovoked aggression'. The speech, which coincided with the deployment of the battle cruisers *Hood* and *Renown* in the Mediterranean, made a powerful impact for a few weeks. If it was meant to deter Mussolini it came too late; on 3 October, the Italian invasion began.

The British electorate heard many firm words about collective security and the League during the general election campaign of October and November 1935, which resulted in a renewed success for Baldwin and his largely Conservative Government. The League condemned the Italian invasion and began to consider sanctions. But French hesitations strengthened the hand of those in England who felt that Eden was pushing too hard against Mussolini. Hoare began to vacillate. Probably he had never believed in the strength of his own words at Geneva. He did not support Eden's argument in favour of supplying arms to Abyssinia. He wobbled over the most important possible sanction, namely oil. Eden was sure the League should press ahead with oil sanctions and did not believe that Mussolini would go to war against Britain and France. 'Signor Mussolini has never struck me as the kind of person who would commit suicide. He has been ill-informed about our attitude in this dispute, and while he may well be exasperated there is a considerable gap between that condition and insanity.'[40]

Hoare did not possess the intellect of Simon, the calm geniality of Baldwin or the driving meticulousness of Neville Chamberlain. It was felt that, though it meant keeping Eden waiting for a prize which would one day be his, Hoare had earned a spell as Foreign Secretary. Few would have expected from Hoare great flights of imagination or strokes of boldness; what could surely be relied on were caution and the well-informed calculation of odds. They got the opposite.

Hoare had entered the Foreign Office an exhausted man who was entitled to a break after seeing the India Bill through the Commons. He arranged a holiday in Switzerland in December 1935. It was convenient to stop over in Paris and compare notes with the French Premier Laval on Abyssinia and the situation in Europe. A thick fog delayed Hoare's arrival in Paris. He agreed to stay another day. One planned meeting with Laval became two; two meetings gave birth to a plan. Only then did he move on to his Swiss holiday. He had been accompanied to Paris by Vansittart, the Permanent Secretary at the Foreign Office. Back in London, Eden was told that Hoare and Vansittart were satisfied with the meetings in Paris. He was therefore amazed to receive details of the proposal for partitioning Abyssinia on which Hoare and Laval had agreed. Abyssinia would receive its seaport but would be required to cede to Italy huge slices of territory, amounting to about half the country. It was incredible that Hoare, flanked by Vansittart, should have thought this outcome compatible with his own speeches on collective security. Eden at once told the Prime Minister that neither Emperor Haile Selassie of Abyssinia nor the League of Nations would accept the Hoare-Laval terms. Baldwin saw there was a let-out, since the agreement was subject to Cabinet and League approval. There might have been a graceful withdrawal, but the plan leaked and there was uproar. Eden thought of resigning, but was persuaded to remain and pick up the bits. The wretched Hoare, so far from enjoying his holiday in Switzerland, broke his nose while skating. He was called back to London. On 17 December, Baldwin and Eden visited him at home. 'How do you feel?' Baldwin asked 'I wish I were dead,' Hoare replied.[41] He resigned the next day, and Baldwin told the Commons that the Hoare-Laval pact was indeed dead. Its part-author lived on to become a successful British Ambassador in Madrid during the war.

Eden was the obvious successor. It was the job at which he had long aimed, and for which he was fully qualified. But when it seemed in his grasp he hesitated. This was a moment of great public humiliation for the Cabinet. The reputation of the Foreign Office was badly damaged; the repair work was bound to be hard and might prove impossible. Eden advised Baldwin to appoint Austen Chamberlain; as we have seen, the Prime Minister said he was too old. Eden suggested Lord Halifax, but Baldwin thought that in the circumstances the Foreign Secretary must be in the Commons. There was a silence, broken by Baldwin: 'It looks as if it will have to be you.' On this unpromising note Eden entered his inheritance.

Anthony Eden's first period as Foreign Secretary lasted just over two years, from December 1935 until his resignation in February

1938. This was a drear time between great disasters. The slow drift towards war continued. As Foreign Secretary, Eden continued to work as hard as he had as Lord Privy Seal, but the cards were stacked against him.

The 1930s had become a decade of retreats for the democracies and advances for the dictators. Manchuria, Abyssinia, the Rhineland, Austria, Sudetenland, the rest of Czechoslovakia, Poland – the slide to eventual war continued past these way-marks. Of them all, Abyssinia was for the British public the most shameful retreat. It turned out that Hitler was much the more dangerous aggressor, as well as more brutal in persecuting sections of his own people. But Mussolini's aggression against Abyssinia was more brazen than anything Hitler attempted before 1939. The bombing and the use of poison gas were plainly barbarous. The aggression was undisguised; there was no complicating argument about self-determination such as Hitler deployed in his earliest exploits.

On 7 March 1936 German troops marched into the demilitarised Rhineland. Many critics later on, including Eden himself in his memoirs, held that this was the occasion when Hitler should have been called to order.[42] If the French army had moved boldly to throw the German troops out of the Rhineland, Hitler would have had to draw back. But the question was academic; there was no appetite for such boldness. The French Government was weak and hesitant. It might have acted if given firm support by Britain, but opinion in the British Cabinet and among the public was clear: whatever the legal position, Hitler could not be challenged for marching into part of his own country. Like Grey before 1914, Eden persuaded the Cabinet to agree that serious staff talks should be held with the French. The danger of war with Germany had clearly increased, but the reaction in London was to redouble efforts to reach a European security agreement which would reinforce Locarno. In one of his last conversations as Prime Minister with his Foreign Secretary, Baldwin told Eden on 20 May 1936 that he wanted '"better relations with Hitler than with Musso – we must get nearer to Germany", "How?" I asked. "I have no idea, that is your job."'[43] Eden began to urge his colleagues to speed up the pace of British naval rearmament, but he did not relax his diplomatic efforts to find an agreement with Berlin which might hold Hitler back.

The Civil War in Spain began to affect the whole of European diplomacy. The British Left worked itself into passionate enthusiasm for the Republican resistance to Franco's rebellion. Here again, Bevin was a heretic. He had by this time lost any real faith in Communism, and he felt no sympathy for either side in Spain: 'One works through the Red International and the other through the Pope.'[44] There was no serious suggestion anywhere in British politics that Britain should intervene militarily in Spain. But the barbarous bombing of Guernica by the Luftwaffe showed that both Germany and Italy were deeply involved on Franco's side. Italian submarines attacked British and other vessels in the Mediterranean. Eden and his French colleagues summoned an international conference at Nyon which in September 1937 authorised an Anglo-French Mediterranean naval patrol. This began to operate successfully, and the attacks ceased. Eden quickly built a solid relationship with the new Popular Front Government in Paris under Blum. He wrote to Churchill on 25 September 1937 that the spectacle of eighty British and French destroyers jointly patrolling the Mediterranean should have an effect on the dictators. 'There is plenty of trouble ahead and we are not yet of course anything like as strong in the military service as I would wish, but Nyon has enabled us to improve our position and gain more time.'[45]

But by now Eden was having to cope with the determination of the new Prime Minister, Neville Chamberlain, to come to an accord with the dictators. Chamberlain found great pleasure as an amateur pitted against the professional diplomats of the Foreign Office. This was his opportunity to shape the world from 10 Downing Street. 'I can look back with great satisfaction at the extraordinary relaxation of tension in Europe since I first saw Grandi. Grandi himself says that it is 90% due to me and it gives one a sense of wonderful power that the Premiership gives you.'[46] The mixture of vanity and insecurity with which Austen had been afflicted affected his brother as well.

The argument between Eden and Chamberlain was partly one of method. Eden believed in proper preparation of discussions, and the use of professional diplomatic channels. It was not just pride which led him to question the wisdom of Lord Halifax accepting an invitation from Goering to hunt wild boar in the Black Forest and have a talk with Hitler. Halifax nearly ruined the visit on arrival at

Berchtesgaden by mistaking Hitler for a footman. The discussion led nowhere. Throughout his career, Eden disliked the notion of initiatives by senior politicians outside the ordinary framework of relations between countries.

Chamberlain remained on good personal terms with Eden, but wanted to free the young Foreign Secretary from what he saw as the shifting negativeness of the Foreign Office officials, most of whom by now regarded both Hitler and Mussolini with total suspicion. Of course, there were arguments on Chamberlain's side. British rearmament was under way, but the Service chiefs agreed with Chamberlain that the country could not contemplate a simultaneous war with Germany, Italy and Japan. If, by the Prime Minister's diplomacy, Italy could be removed from the list of possible enemies, Britain would, they thought, be safer. But this assumed what Eden and most Foreign Office officials now doubted – that Mussolini could be trusted to keep an agreement.[47]

Rather worryingly, Chamberlain began to profess a concern for Eden's health. After congratulating him on Nyon, Chamberlain wrote 'don't hurry home. The FO can always refer things to me. You need a proper holiday.'[48] Two months later: 'I was very concerned this morning to see you so low-spirited and unlike yourself. You are carrying a tremendous load and it is not surprising that you should sometimes feel disheartened, especially when you have got a temperature. I suppose all of us suffer from depression at times – I know I do. But things pass and then I know that I have been exaggerating . . . Take a long weekend. Remember that you are precious to us and that your health concerns all of us as well as yourself.'[49] The longer the Foreign Secretary spent away from the Foreign Office, the freer the Prime Minister felt. Although Cabinet colleagues were surprised by the contest between Chamberlain and Eden when it broke into the open in January 1938, it had been simmering for several months.

After Eden's resignation, Chamberlain moved forward into the final phase of appeasement, culminating in the Czech crisis of September and October 1938. In those weeks, the Prime Minister reached new heights of fame and reputation. He had prevented war. Huge crowds gathered at Heston airport on the afternoon of 30 September to welcome Chamberlain home from Munich. A hundred and twenty Etonians cheered on either side of the road as he drove away from the airport.[50] Never did a Prime Minister's reputation rise and then crumble so quickly.

The policy of appeasement had powerful arguments in its favour. It had enjoyed a long and respectable history in the hands of Salisbury and, before him, of Castlereagh. Neville Chamberlain pursued the policy with integrity and determination. But the experiences of both Eden and Bevin revealed the policy's two fatal weaknesses. Eden learned, and through Eden the public learned, that it is useless to appease rulers who had no intention of keeping their word. Bevin learned, and through Bevin the public learned, that Hitler ruled Germany with a ruthless brutality towards groups of his own people – a brutality which made his regime a source of instability for Europe and the rest of the world. In both instances the lessons were learned too late to be useful. Neither Eden nor Bevin was able to stop the abuse of appeasement in time.

In May 1940 both Eden and Bevin found themselves working together to pull Britain back from Europe's abyss. Eden had come back into office under Chamberlain when war broke out in September 1939. The following year he returned to the high table of diplomacy as part of Churchill's Government, first as Secretary of State for War, and then as Foreign Secretary in the War Cabinet. More radically, Churchill recruited Bevin – still a trade unionist and not even an MP – to become his Minister of Labour and join the Cabinet. Steps were taken, a constituency was found and Bevin joined in the desperate attempt to evade Hitler's clutches.

Each man's contribution was overshadowed by Churchill's personality and prowess. Yet victory would certainly have been impossible if it had not been for Bevin. Coaxing, cajoling, occasionally coercing British men and, controversially, women to mine, build and dig for victory, Bevin achieved a level of mobilisation never reached by Hitler in Germany, or indeed by any other warring power.[51] Meanwhile, Eden acted loyally and skilfully as Churchill's lieutenant. In war, a Foreign Secretary tends to be an auxiliary rather than one of the main drivers of the effort. This had been true of Grey and his successors in the Great War, though not of Castlereagh in the final years of the struggle against Napoleon. Churchill's personal grip of the war effort included a sustained mastery of everything pertaining to foreign policy. He thoroughly enjoyed dangerous travel and dealing with difficult foreigners. It would never have occurred to Eden to challenge Churchill and question his diplomatic ventures as he had once challenged Chamberlain. But his own contribution, quiet and effective, was still critical to Britain's wartime effort.

Under Churchill's ingenious, tireless and exasperating leadership, Eden found himself wrestling in a new form with Castlereagh's twin tasks. He had to keep in running order a ramshackle alliance, constantly repairing the faults and healing the stresses created by the tugs and tears of war. As with Castlereagh, so for Eden, that task was made easier when his foe invaded Russia. But whereas in 1812 Napoleon's rash move had been enough to tilt the balance decisively in Britain's favour, in 1941 Hitler's Russian mistake was not sufficient to ensure an Allied victory. Instead, Churchill and Eden had to invoke the spirit of Canning, calling on the New World to rescue the Old.

At the same time, Eden had to prepare for the uncertainties of peace, looking to a settlement which would be tolerable for a victorious Britain and provide against yet another world war. But whereas Castlereagh had been free to operate as an independent and pre-eminent power, for Eden the task was made more difficult by the declining strength of the British Empire and its economy. The longer the war went on, the more this problem developed: for the first time since the end of the sixteenth century, British commitments outweighed resources. As a consequence of this, success in both efforts, winning the war and building the peace, came to depend on a vigorous Anglo-American alliance. As Churchill fashioned the rhetoric of the special Anglo-American relationship, he was learning painfully and as privately as possible the humbler techniques of operating as the junior partner of the United States. Eden was equally reluctant by temperament to accept the necessary subordination of the old country to the new, but his skills were needed in smoothing out difficulties with the Americans, in particular at the summit conferences of Teheran in 1943 and Yalta and Potsdam in 1945.

As before, France loomed large. Eden, like Castlereagh, had to ask how a recently defeated France would fit into the post-war world. The context was different, but both men found a successful answer. Castlereagh persuaded his victorious allies, even after the shock of

Napoleon's return from Elba, not to impose a punitive peace on France but to admit her quickly to the new arrangements for the security of Europe. On the same point, Eden, in a colourless style which Castlereagh would have recognised, wrote to Churchill in January 1945: 'I find it difficult to contemplate a future in which France will not be a factor of considerable importance ... she must be interested in almost every European question. If we do not have her co-operation she will be able – not at once perhaps – to make difficult the application of any solution which does not suit her.'[52] At San Francisco the next year, Eden helped to ensure that France was enrolled among the five permanent and veto-holding members of the new Security Council of the United Nations. Eden's understanding of France was based on a clear sense of her shared interests with Britain – but also on his love of French civilisation, literature and painting, which went back to his Oxford days.

But during these years Eden's main concern was with Russia. Here again, Castlereagh would have recognised the scenery. The ruler of Russia was ready to use the presence of a massive army in the heart of Europe to ensure Russia's long-term security, in particular by imposing Russian authority on Poland. None of the other exhausted Allies was willing to take up arms against Russia in a new war. Thus Eden, like Castlereagh, was reduced to offering futile reminders to the Russians that the war was meant to be a war of liberation, and that Russia's actions contravened their own promises.[53]

In truth, the Russian obstacle in 1945 was tougher than anything Castlereagh had known. Stalin was single-minded, experienced and entirely without scruple, whereas Czar Alexander had wavered under different influences and at heart belonged to the European culture which Stalin rejected and despised. Eden, unlike Churchill, carried no anti-Bolshevik reputation from the time of the Russian Civil War. He found it possible to establish the necessary minimum of wary understanding with the Russians which the wartime alliance required. When the bodies of up to 10,000 Polish officers were found in the Katyn forest near Smolensk in 1943, Eden did not believe the Soviet accusation that the Germans were responsible. He recognised the probability of Russian guilt and then closed his eyes. It was not, he thought, a matter which could be probed further at a time when alliance with the Soviet Union was crucial to the defeat of Germany.

This was one of several harsh choices, easy to criticise, difficult to avoid. All his predecessors and successors in office, with the possible exception of Ramsay MacDonald, would have done the same and would have been right. It is sometimes the duty of a Foreign Secretary to deal courteously with villains.

Faced with the increasing and unscrupulous assertion of Soviet authority in Europe, Churchill and Eden tried to counter with the modest means at their disposal. The best-known example was the British intervention in Greece in the winter of 1944 to prevent the Communist wing of the resistance movement taking over the country. They risked their prestige in controversial political bargaining with Greek politicians, and were rewarded with loud criticism in the British and American press. Less obvious but of greater importance was the order to Montgomery in May 1945 to seize the German coasts bordering on Denmark, and so prevent the Red Army from sweeping west to Copenhagen. This was, after 140 years, a reasonable British amends to Copenhagen for Canning's bombardment. If Denmark had followed the course of Poland and fallen under Soviet authority, the whole post-war scene in Europe would have changed disastrously.

More drastically, the British leaders had to consider, however quietly, whether an attempt could be made to check the Soviet Union by force. Churchill ordered a study of the possibility, just as Lord Liverpool and his colleagues had considered in 1814 whether the war against Napoleon might be followed by a war within the alliance to check Czar Alexander. The result of both discussions was that it could not be done. War against the Czar in 1814 was marginally more likely than war against Stalin in 1945. In both cases Britain was exhausted; neither the will nor the means existed for a new conflict. In both cases the United States was crucial; in 1814 the British troops who might in theory have been used against the Czar were fighting round New Orleans; in 1945 the United States, much the most powerful ally, did yet not share the clear pessimism of Eden about Soviet intentions.

From time to time, Churchill deluded himself that by force of his own personality he could dilute or divert Stalin's ambitions. Eden had no such illusion. He wrote to Churchill in March 1945, 'I take the gloomiest view of Russian behaviour everywhere . . . I am deeply concerned at the pattern of Russian policy, which becomes clearer as they become more brazen every day.'[54] But clear sight did not give Eden the power to change what he saw. Reading biographies of Castlereagh and Canning on the eve of the Potsdam conference at the end of the war, Eden wrote: 'I am not so conceited as to suggest that I am like Canning. He had brilliant scholarship, exceptional oratorical gifts, all the things I have not.'[55] Lacking Canning's talents, Eden found the task of winning over Americans to support British foreign policy even harder than his famous predecessor had. Confidential polls carried out in America showed that from December 1944 until the late spring of 1945, more Americans blamed Britain than Russia for the tensions in the alliance.[56] This trend was mirrored at the top level. Churchill found himself isolated from both the two new superpowers.

1945, the year of victory, was the saddest in Eden's life. He was ill for much of the summer with a duodenal ulcer. His son Simon was killed while serving as navigator in a RAF Dakota over Burma. Simon had been his father's particular friend and companion; his death completed the break-up of his parents' marriage, which had long been faltering and ended in divorce. In the midst of this, political shock added to the personal anguish. Churchill and the Conservatives were surprisingly beaten in the general election in July. The war had acted as a great stirring pot for domestic change. Just as after 1815, so in 1945, the appetite for reform, held up during the conflict, burst into the open. The Labour Party, campaigning with a radical socialist manifesto, won a decisive victory. Eden held his seat in Warwick and Leamington, but lost the Foreign Office. By the end of the summer of 1945 the main props of his existence had been knocked away – job, son and wife. For a short time he lost also the resilience which had kept him going through the years of almost constant stress.

Eden hoped that Clement Attlee, the new Prime Minister, would choose Ernest Bevin as his Foreign Secretary. He had come to know and respect Bevin during the war. But most people expected Attlee to appoint Hugh Dalton to the Foreign Office. Eden was therefore relieved when Dalton was dispatched to the Treasury, and Bevin took up where he himself had left off.

The general election had fallen in the middle of the Allied

conference at Potsdam. The watching world, already struggling to understand how a man who had just won a world war could lose an election, witnessed one Prime Minister and one Foreign Secretary leaving the Allied conference on 25 July, and another Prime Minister and Foreign Secretary replacing them on the 28th. Stalin accepted the change by commenting on Attlee's weight: 'He does not look like a greedy man.' It is unlikely that he said the same thing about the new Foreign Secretary. Bevin's body had deteriorated in the ten years since the Labour conference at Brighton. When Bevin's doctor first examined him in 1943, he claimed that there was not a functioning organ in his body apart from his feet. As one heart attack was followed by another, the doctor became a permanent appendage to the patient. Bevin would introduce him to people as follows: 'This is Alec. 'E treats me be'ind like a dartboard.'[57] Bevin had himself to blame for most of these ailments. He ate, smoked and drank too much. He also found it difficult not to talk while eating and so tended to spit his food out and about. On one occasion – a wartime dinner in honour of the Viceroy of India – Bevin twice reached into his mouth, pulled out his false teeth, examined them and reinserted them in full view of the table.[58]

For many people, these impediments were less worrying than the new Foreign Secretary's politics. A few months earlier Bevin had drawn attention to himself at the Labour Party conference. 'Left understands Left,' he had proclaimed, 'but the Right does not.'[59] In July 1945, it was easy to see in that brushstroke an alarming painting: Britain was now governed by a class-warring administration and the naïve new Foreign Secretary was a Soviet sympathiser. Except, of course, that Bevin had no sympathy for the Soviet Union; he had been talking about France, not Russia, in the conference speech. If anything, Bevin had by this time turned into a patriot figure in the mode of Joe Chamberlain. He had even adopted some of his arguments. In an article for *The Spectator* in 1938 Bevin had made the case for a new Assembly of the British Commonwealth as the 'nucleus for the establishment of a World Order'.[60]

There was also something else, a change which both Bevin and Attlee had undergone in the War Cabinet. Bevin's biographer, Alan Bullock, dwells subtly on the point in his gargantuan book. The experience of working in a wartime coalition Government which had spent two years fighting for the survival of the country had dispelled any lingering illusions about the requirements of statecraft. They had learned the importance of following the facts and balancing priorities; the need to make decisions with limited resources; the constantly changing intricacy of the world around them. For these reasons, and others, Eden told the House of Commons during the debate on the King's Speech in August that he and Bevin had had 'many discussions on foreign affairs' in the War Cabinet, 'but I cannot recall one single occasion when there was a difference between us. I hope I do not embarrass the Foreign Secretary by saying that.' Bevin responded: 'No.' Eden continued: 'There were no differences on any important issue of foreign policy. My Right Hon. Friend helped me during those critical war years, and, in the same spirit, I should like to try to help him now.'[61]

Ernest Bevin arrived at Potsdam in no doubt about what needed to be done. He got off the aeroplane and told the Chief of Staff, General Ismay: 'I'm not going to have Britain barged about.' His first meeting was with the new American President, Harry Truman, and his Secretary of State, James Byrnes. 'His manner was so aggressive that both the President and I wondered how we would get along with this new Foreign Minister,' Byrnes later recalled. Some were surprised by the way Bevin treated his foreign counterparts. But, as he explained to his Private Secretary, Nicholas Henderson, he had in the past done 'a good deal of negotiation with ships' captains of all nationalities. These people, Stalin and Truman, are just the same as all Russians and Americans; and dealing with them over foreign affairs is just the same as trying to come to a settlement about unloading a ship. Oh, yes, I can handle them.'[62]

Bevin's oddities invaded his diplomacy. Language played a key part in this. He had no patience with grammar but liked to reinterpret names. Thus the Italian Foreign Minister, Count Sforza, became 'that man Storzer'. His French colleague, Georges Bidault, could be either 'Biddle' or 'Bidet' depending on the day. Meanwhile, the Soviet Foreign Minister, Vyacheslav Molotov, was renamed 'Mowlotov' in a deliberate and successful attempt to annoy him. Bevin rejoiced in the cultural discord he believed his appointment had caused in King Charles Street. He opened his first conversation with Gladwyn Jebb, a senior diplomat responsible for the United Nations, with the comment: 'Must be kinda queer for a chap like you to see a chap like me sitting in a chair like this.' When Jebb did not take up the challenge, Bevin continued: 'Ain't never 'appened before in 'istory.' At this point, Jebb could no longer stay silent and expounded the life of Cardinal Wolsey, the butcher's boy who became Henry VIII's senior statesman. Bevin was impressed.[63]

In Bevin's hands, these oddities could become attributes; more often they ended in minor failures. During a key conference in London in 1945, a dinner was held at the French Embassy. Britain's Ambassador to France, Duff Cooper, complained afterwards that Bevin had told 'a great many stories, all more or less obscene, which made Attlee rather nervous and which were difficult to translate into French'. A few days into the same conference, Duff Cooper noted that Bevin rambled and repeated himself so much that 'the interpreter reduces the length of what he says by half'.[64]

Bevin's trump card as Foreign Secretary was his relationship with the Prime Minister. It was clear immediately that there would be a change in working patterns from those of Churchill and Eden. Attlee left Bevin to speak where Eden had been silent. 'Foreign affairs are the province of the Foreign Secretary,' Attlee explained later. 'It is in my view a mistake for the Prime Minister to intervene personally except in exceptional circumstances.' He used a slightly silly simile to develop his point: 'you don't keep a dog and bark yourself – and Ernie was a very good dog'.[65]

But barking at Britain's problems in 1945 would not make them go away. In the first place there was Germany, its present status and future fate. The natural case study for comparison was 1918. But here the analysis varied, depending on whether one thought the Versailles settlement was too stern or too soft on the Germans. Bevin had clashed with Eden on the issue in the War Cabinet. His preference was for breaking Germany up into several states. Eden, always cooler, stressed rehabilitation. In America, these arguments were exaggerated. The Treasury Secretary, Henry Morgenthau, produced a plan for de-industrialising Germany to the point where it became a society of small states and farm holdings. Both the US army and the White House remained uneasy about this policy and argued for a more moderate approach. Their case was strengthened by their concerns about Stalin. With Soviet troops still occupying much of

Germany and most of East Europe, the issue was not resolved at Potsdam. Thus, in defeat, Germany became the focus of a new argument with the USSR.

The Allies could understand why Stalin wanted to protect himself against foreign invasion: European troops had entered Moscow twice inside a century and a half. But the Allies could not understand what Stalin thought this security might involve. In September, Bevin met Molotov and explained why a peaceful European system was impossible if the Soviets did not set out their aims in full. He told Molotov that 'our relationship with the Russians ... was drifting into the same condition as that which we had found ourselves in with Hitler'.[66] In response, Molotov deployed a tactic which would become tedious in the years ahead, ignoring the question and criticising Britain at some length. Bevin's inquiries got nowhere, and were not helped by the wavering interest of the USA.

Meanwhile, Stalin was trying to disrupt the relationship between Britain and the USA. A breakdown in the Anglo-American alliance would leave him free to operate in Europe and perhaps try his hand further afield. Ideology inspired him in his strategy. He was convinced that capitalist countries could not co-operate peacefully.* In the second half of 1945 it looked as if he might be right.

Those who talk from time to time about the uniqueness of the special relationship between Britain and America should look at these months in 1945. There was, first, President Truman's announcement on 21 August that Lend-Lease was to stop immediately. This announcement was made without warning. John Maynard Keynes described it as 'a financial Dunkirk'.[67] One disaster quickly developed into a second. Keynes was sent to America to ask for a loan. The Americans dismantled his appeals systematically. A grant-in-aid would be impossible, and there was no chance of the Congress approving an interest-free loan. Keynes and the British Ambassador in Washington, Lord Halifax, were advised politely that

---

* This was a point that Kennan would emphasise in the Long Telegram in 1946, and Stalin repeated the theory in the Soviet response to Kennan in September of that year. Anglo-American co-operation was 'plagued with great internal contradictions and cannot be lasting'. Even as late as 1952, Stalin was still going on about how 'the inevitability of wars between capitalist countries remains in force'. Doubters who see in Stalin only a pragmatic Napoleon figure should read John Lewis Gaddis, *The Cold War* (Allen Lane, 2006), pp. 14, 30.

their success would depend on liberalising imperial trade. More brutally, they were told that 'arguments based on our past sacrifices and especially on comparisons between ourselves and the United States would do no good and should be advanced if at all from the American side'.[68] In the end, a loan was agreed for $3,750 million which would be repaid over fifty years at 2 per cent interest. The Lend-Lease debts were to be settled by Britain paying $620 million. Meanwhile, Britain made commitments to reduce preferences and free up its trade. Sterling would have to be made convertible within a year.[69]

The details of the deal left London in an upsurge of indignation. Jennie Lee, the wife of the Health Minister, Aneurin Bevan, told the House of Commons that the settlement was 'niggardly, barbaric and antediluvian'. The feelings were reversed across the Atlantic. Why should America provide money, one Congressman demanded, which would only go towards 'too much damned Socialism at home and too much damned Imperialism abroad'. In fact each side had looked to its own material interest in a reasonable way. The loan deal aroused so much anger in Britain because people had come to believe the illusion which they had created about an English-speaking alliance. The illusion consisted of the belief, which still surfaces today, that even if the two partners were unequal in power, intangible considerations based on history and sentiment would even the scales. Averell Harriman, American Democrat and diplomat, had a clear-eyed view of the real situation. 'England is so weak she must follow our leadership. She will do anything that we insist upon and she won't go out on a limb alone.'[70]

Bevin was infuriated by the seemingly ruthless treatment of Britain by the USA. In September he wrote a long letter to Sir Stafford Cripps, pouring out his frustration. 'When the Prime Minister made his statement in the House on Lend-Lease we were met with headlines in the United States in certain papers calling us "Cry-babies". We ignored it, but all this percolates through to the British people and while you will appreciate as I do that there are no more generous souls in the world, yet there are no more combative people if they feel they are being treated unfairly.' Bevin tried to console himself with a mixture of patriotism and pugnacity: 'I should hate any rudeness or anything undignified . . . but I do think the time has come when the world must realize that though we have paid such a terrible price in this war we are not down and out. We shall survive.'[71]

Deep down, Bevin had never been attracted by the vision which Churchill had conjured up during the war of a future Anglo-American world. One example in particular gives a vivid glimpse of this crucial difference between the two men. In November 1945 the Americans sent Bevin a list of bases which they wanted to occupy. Bevin sent the list to Churchill, asking for advice. Churchill's response to this inquiry was uplifting and evasive. 'I have not studied particular islands and bases in detail on the map.' There were more important issues at stake than a few rocks on the sea:

> ... a special and privileged relationship between Great Britain and the United States makes us both safe for ourselves and more influential as regards building up the safety of others through the international machine ... Our duties to mankind and all States and nations remain paramount, and we shall discharge them all the better hand in hand ... The future of the world depends upon the fraternal association of Great Britain and the Commonwealth with the United States ... What we may now be able to achieve is, in fact, Salvation for ourselves, and the means of procuring Salvation for the world ... You are indeed fortunate that this sublime opportunity has fallen to you, and I trust the seizing of it will ever be associated with your name. In all necessary action you should count on me, if I can be of any use.
> Yours sincerely,
> Winston S. Churchill.[72]

Bevin's response to this rhetoric was equally emblematic in its own brief way: 'I agree with you about joint bases. But the difficulty is that we have committed ourselves to the United Nations, and I must keep this aspect in mind.'[73]

Germany was stuck; America uninterested; Russia insecure and expanding. These were hefty problems even before they were added to a cracked Empire and a creaking economy. Meanwhile, the world was trying to steady itself with new institutions and with weapons which might wipe out the human race.

Many people looked at what had happened at Hiroshima and

Nagasaki and predicted a bleak future for all. Eden worried that 'the discovery of ... atomic energy science has placed us several laps ahead of the present phase of international political development'. As things stood, 'unless we catch up politically to the point we have reached in science ... we are all going to be blown to smithereens'.[74] Here, Bevin was reassuring and effective. He developed a Clausewitzian theme: 'War is not caused by the invention of weapons,' he told the House of Commons in August. 'It is policy that makes war ... the intention to go to war.' What nuclear weapons had actually done was bring about the decline of geography. We saw how in 1815 geography was the key to Britain's defence. Churchill's decision to sweep Montgomery through Denmark in 1945 showed that the Low Countries were still important to Britain, but they were no longer the primary concern. Bevin put the development into his own language: 'Science has developed to such a point that it has made boundaries look silly.'[75]

Access to the atom bomb quickly became a defining question for Britain's position in the post-war world. 'Until decisions are taken on this vital matter,' Attlee explained to Truman, 'it is difficult for any of us to plan for the future.' As the Americans hesitated then halted their wartime co-operation with Britain on nuclear weapons, Attlee took matters into his own hands. The process was hidden. There was only an amorphous group known to historians by its file name, General 75. Step by step the necessary decisions were taken. At various points the question of cost cropped up. Doubters like Dalton and Cripps wanted to stop proceedings; Bevin made sure things carried on. Arriving late for one crucial meeting in 1946 (he had fallen asleep after lunch), Bevin was told that because of finances, the programme needed to be delayed. Patriotism and pride powered Bevin forward. 'That won't do at all, we've got to have this,' he told the group. 'I don't mind for myself; but I don't want any other Foreign Secretary of this country to be talked at by a Secretary of State in the United States as I have just had in my discussions with Mr Byrnes. We have got to have this thing over here whatever it costs ... We've got to have the bloody Union Jack flying on top of it.'[76]

The nuclear dilemma affected the institutional conundrum. As in the First War, so in the Second, the Great Powers had turned their co-operation towards writing a new rule book. In 1945 the new rule book was located in a new institution, founded at San Francisco as the United Nations. Both Eden and Bevin believed in the principle which inspired this development. In November 1945 Eden surveyed history and concluded that 'we have got somehow to take the sting out of nationalism'.

> It is something more than 100 years ago that Castlereagh first conceived the idea of making progress in diplomacy by conference. He was on the right lines, but he failed. After the last war the nations tried again, by the League, to make another effort more in conformity with the developments that had taken place in the intervening period, and they failed, and during this war we at San Francisco tried again to lay the foundations of a new world order.

In the following weeks, Bevin developed this theme in his own speeches in the Commons and at the UN Preparatory Commission. He spoke about the views of the common man. 'His common interest is to live, to have a good standard of life, to be free to travel, free to exchange and to know other peoples of the world. That is the great future of the common man. Somebody once asked me when I became Foreign Secretary, what my policy really was. I said I have only one: it is to go down to Victoria Station here, take a ticket and go where the hell I like without anybody pulling me up with a passport.' Bevin thought this could be achieved with 'a world assembly with a limited objective, the objective of peace'. There would be 'a world law with a world judiciary to interpret it, with a world police to enforce it, with the decision of the people with their own ideas resting in their own hands, irrespective of race or creed, as the great world-sovereign elected authority'.[77]

But Bevin saw the problem. Even before he had delivered the speech to the Commons, he had circulated this paper to the Cabinet: 'I should be willing to pursue the policy of working in with the UN Organisation on the ground that it gives the best hope for the world, if the facts of the situation allowed us to do it. But my colleagues must be made aware of the situation that has arisen ... Instead of world co-operation we are rapidly drifting into spheres of influence or what can be better described as three great Monroes.'[78] Just as Canning had, so Bevin recognised that the new international institutions around him were faulty and inadequate when faced with the Russian threat. He began to cast about for alternative schemes.

In November 1945 Bevin broke off a speech in the House of Commons for a moment of sad reflection. 'I am sorry to be so long, I cannot help it. All the world is in trouble and I have to deal with all the troubles at once.'[79] For the rest of that year and much of 1946, he found himself dealing with many of these troubles alone.

In one place in particular Bevin was painfully isolated. Since 1920, Britain had governed Palestine under a League of Nations Mandate. The Mandate, following the Balfour Declaration by Britain in 1917, promised a Jewish homeland in the Middle East without forfeiting the rights of the resident Arabs. Since non-Jews made up 90 per cent of the population in Palestine, this promise was impossible – one side or the other was going to be let down. The situation soured in the 1930s as more and more Jews made their way to the Promised Land. As the evidence emerged about the Holocaust the Zionist quest became more urgent. Wise men had already sensed catastrophe. Churchill in his last days as Prime Minister had written to the Chiefs of Staff suggesting withdrawal: 'I don't think we should take the responsibility upon ourselves ... while the Americans sit back and criticize. Have you ever addressed yourself to the idea that we should ask them to take it over? ... Somebody else should have their turn now.'[80]

These were not propitious omens. They were further complicated by the USA. Pressed by a powerful Zionist lobby, Truman was deaf to the difficulties of Britain's position. Instead he made things worse for the fragile British administration by arguing that the immigration figure for Jews into Palestine should be raised to 100,000. It fell to Bevin to avoid the inevitable disaster. He set out thoughtfully enough: 'I want to avoid an explosion on the part of the Arabs, and to check what I regard as a positive danger, the development of Pan-Islamism.'[81] There was foresight here, but when Jewish terrorists blew up British soldiers, Bevin's attitudes hardened. The situation was rushing out of control. Bevin's policy was simply to search for a compromise, which remained, and still remains, out of reach.

On 2 November 1945 Bevin met Zionist leaders in London to discuss what was going on. 'I cannot bear English Tommies being killed,' he told them. 'They are innocent.' The Zionists reminded him that millions of Jews had just been killed in the Holocaust and many were still dying in refugee camps. Bevin was slightly moved. 'I do not want any Jews killed either, but I love the British soldiers. They belong to my class. They are working people.' He went on, rambling in the way people do when faced with a problem they do not know how to solve. 'The problem is intolerably difficult. It would have been less difficult if the Balfour Declaration had been worded more clearly, if they had not tried to ride two horses at once. It is a very difficult business, but we are honestly trying to find a way out.'[82]

It is a bad idea to set targets when dealing with international relations, particularly when discussing the Middle East. On 13 November Bevin yielded to this temptation, the first of his big mistakes. He told the House of Commons, 'I will stake my political future on solving the problem.' No one heard the disclaimer he tagged on at the end: 'but not in the limited sphere presented to me now'. Elated by the challenge he had set himself, he moved from one error to the next. He went from the Commons to a press conference. 'I am very anxious that Jews shall not in Europe over-emphasise their racial position . . . [I]f the Jews, with all their sufferings, want to get too much at the head of the queue, you have the danger of another anti-Semitic reaction through it all.' Even without the rash boast about solving the crisis, the quote about queue-jumping Jews cast a cloud which would not go away.[83]

The following year, the cloud turned into a storm. Bevin told the Labour Party conference that the reason why the Americans wanted to increase Jewish immigration into Palestine was that they 'did not want too many Jews in New York'. Older prejudices certainly played a part in his vocabulary, although to what extent they infected his analysis, it is impossible to tell.

A few weeks later, on 22 July 1946, a Jewish organisation called the Irgun blew up the King David Hotel in Jerusalem, destroying the British Secretariat and Army Headquarters, wounding forty-five people, killing ninety-one. There was by this stage no doubt that Bevin was unfit to broker any lasting deal. Churchill attacked the Government's Palestine policy in the House of Commons: it had been 'a monument of incapacity'. He repeated the option he had suggested twelve months earlier. 'I had always intended to put it to our friends in America, from the very beginning of the postwar discussions, that either they should come in and help us in this Zionist problem, about which they feel so strongly . . . or that we should resign our Mandate, as we have, of course, a perfect right to do.'[84] Lame and lost, Bevin clung on.

He was not doing better with Russia. Here, again, he was often forced to operate alone.

The United States was still wrong-headed about Soviet Russia, and Secretary Byrnes was particularly unsound. He thought that the Soviet Union was a difficult but not disastrous entity which just needed some time to settle down. Like Roosevelt and indeed Neville Chamberlain before him, he thought he could speed things along through a little personal diplomacy. He decided to arrange a new conference of Foreign Ministers – this time in Moscow – where he could negotiate directly with Stalin if things with Molotov failed. Meanwhile, in Britain the public did not understand or accept Bevin's stand-off with Russia, and blamed him for getting things wrong. One correspondent summed up London's mood as the year drew to a close: 'Mr Eden never would have made the mistakes that Mr Bevin has made and . . . the Conservatives would not have allowed ideological differences to create what has virtually amounted to breaking off relations with Russia for a month.'[85]

Bevin did his best to ensure that the Moscow conference was a funny if not felicitous event. Peter Ustinov would later tell Bevin's story of the evening the Foreign Ministers spent at the Bolshoi Ballet. When the performance ended, the Ministers applauded – only for the dancers to applaud the Ministers in return. This farce continued for some time . . . until Bevin decided to grip the situation. 'I could see no future in it,' he explained later, 'I didn't know who was applauding who. So I got up and behind Molotov's back I gave them the clenched fist salute. That brought the house down, but I got a rocket from Clem when I got back.'[86] On Christmas Eve during the conference, Stalin annoyed Byrnes and the American delegation by playing films focused entirely on the role Russia had played in the defeat of Japan, which had been negligible. After one film was over, Byrnes had had enough and made his way to leave. Bevin found the experience highly amusing, and walked Byrnes to his car. 'You know, Jimmy, it reminds me of your American film about the war in

Burma: all the fighting was done by Errol Flynn and the US Army, without an Englishman in sight.'[87]

Bevin was beginning to enjoy his lonely anti-Soviet crusade. He was at his best a few months later, defending himself against bogus Soviet arguments at the UN. 'I know when I displease the Soviet Government because all the shop stewards who are Communists send me resolutions in the exact same language ... one of those strange coincidences that occur.' He had developed a type of tabloid diplomacy, not really bothering with nuance. In Molotov he found himself a suitable sparring partner. 'Molotov was like a Communist in a local Labour Party,' he had explained to Dalton in September. 'If you treated him badly, he made the most of the grievance and, if you treated him well, he only put his price up and abused you next day.' This description became the point of departure for each future exchange. He was back on the docks with a truculent navvy. Byrnes's interpreter, Charles Bohlen, recalled one late argument between the two men which ended in disaster. 'Bevin rose to his feet, his hands knotted into fists and started towards Molotov, saying "I've had enough of this, I 'ave".' Other occasions were more restrained. At dinner one evening with Attlee and Bevin, Molotov started to ask them about Marx. He suggested they read the commentary by Rudolf Hilferding. 'You can tell Mr Molotov', Bevin told the interpreter, 'that I've read 'Ilferding and I found him tedious.' Molotov smiled. Bevin repeated himself, this time louder. The conversation on Marx came to an end.[88]

At this stage, Bevin saw Britain as striking a separate course against both the superpowers. In February 1946 he described Britain as the 'last bastion of social democracy' standing against both 'the red tooth and claw of American capitalism and the Communist dictatorship of Soviet Russia'.[89] A few months later, a new milestone was passed when Bevin signed a Cabinet memorandum which argued that the 'danger of Russia has certainly become as great as, and possibly even greater than, that of a revived Germany'.[90] Meanwhile, American diplomacy was starting to move in the same direction. Shortly after the Moscow conference, Truman had scratched a message at the end of a memorandum: 'I'm tired of babying the Soviets.'[91] In February 1946 George Kennan, the Deputy Head of the American mission in Moscow, sent his Long Telegram to Washington. Containment became the watchword, poised patient, firm and vigilant over the Soviet Union. The policy changed, and so did the players. Byrnes faded from the front line of foreign policy, and would be replaced by George Marshall early in 1947. This did not stop Stalin's advances in Europe; in November 1946 French Communists took a clear electoral lead over other French parties. But it did make coping with Communism much easier for Bevin.

Bevin began to achieve a new popularity at home. One poll published in February 1946 placed him above both Eden and Churchill – in that order – as a popular successor to Attlee.[92] Unfortunately for Bevin, this support was not replicated inside his own Party. Indeed, beginning in the summer of 1946, mutinies sprang up against him from the left wing. A lot of these focused on surface complaints. Bevin had not socialised the Foreign Office in the way many Labour activists demanded; there had been no purge of elite personnel. Sir Orme Sargent had remained Permanent Under Secretary; Duff Cooper had stayed on as Ambassador in France. All this was easy for the Foreign Secretary to fend off. 'I am not one of those who decry Eton and Harrow,' he told the conference. 'I was very glad of them in the Battle of Britain – by God! I was – these fellows paid the price in those fatal days.'[93]

More seriously, in November 1946 fifty-eight Labour MPs signed an amendment to the King's Speech criticising British foreign policy. Although the amendment was easily defeated, 130 MPs abstained from the vote. The revolt brought from Bevin a historical tantrum. 'Ain't nothing like this been heard of since the days of Castlereagh.'[94]

As Bevin's support ebbed and flowed through 1946, so his record of achievements continued to be very mixed. The Middle East was a mess which he had done his best to muddy. Western Europe, wrestling with the economic catastrophe of the Second World War, was independent but incapable. Eastern Europe had fallen within the Soviet sphere, and Central Europe looked to be going the same way. In the Mediterranean, Britain struggled to hold off Soviet advances, and British assistance had become the main barrier to the Communist onslaught in Greece and Turkey. Thousands of troops and a great deal of money propped up the Greek Government in its Civil War against Communist foes. But then, on 1 December, the Prime Minister wrote to Bevin, suggesting retreat.

'I think we have got to consider our commitments very carefully lest we try to do more than we can,' Attlee explained. 'In particular, I am rather worried about Greece.' He set out the case for retrenchment. 'While I recognise the desirability of supporting the democratic elements in S.E. Europe and while I am conscious of the strategic importance of oil, I have, as you know, always considered that the strategic importance of communications is very much overrated by our military advisers, a view that is shared by some Service authorities.' He came finally to the missing piece in the puzzle. 'There is a tendency in America to regard us as an outpost, but as an outpost that they will not have to defend. I am disturbed by the signs of America trying to make a safety zone round herself while leaving us and Europe in No Man's Land.' Bevin repelled these arguments for the time being. He was sure that Britain would rediscover its old power. 'Let us wait until our strength is restored,' he told Attlee on 9 January 1947, 'and let us meanwhile, with U.S. help as necessary, hold on to essential positions.'[95] Bevin was not the man to make a tactical retreat.

As happens, a change in the weather settled the argument.

The night of 28 January 1947 was the coldest in eighteen years. The Thames froze at Eton and Windsor. Coal stocks ran out and most British industry had to close for up to three weeks. Unemployment rocketed from 400,000 to 2.3 million – a disaster for any government, but especially for one elected on the promise of full employment.[96] The case for continuing aid to Greece and Turkey collapsed along with the economy.

The next weeks became one concert of catastrophe. Key talks in London between Arabs and Jews broke down, with the Arabs refusing Jewish self-government and the Jews insisting on an Israeli state. The Cabinet, on 18 February, took the only door left unopened and returned the Mandate to the UN. On 21 February the Government sent a message to America that all British commitments in Greece and Turkey would stop on 31 March. Accompanying these surrenders, Attlee announced to the House of Commons a few weeks later that Britain would leave India not later than June 1948. Meanwhile, Labour backbenchers were preparing another foray into foreign policy. Early in May, Richard Crossman, Michael Foot and Ian Mikardo, along with a dozen other Labour MPs, published a series of articles called *Keep Left*, criticising Bevin's foreign policy and calling for a fundamental rethink.

America moved swiftly to grip its share of Britain's crisis. Irritation at Bevin's abrupt announcement about ending Britain's Mediterranean role soon faded behind quick and creative thinking, culminating in Truman's address to Congress on 12 March. He asked for authority to assume Britain's responsibilities in Greece and Turkey, and for $400 million dollars in aid for the Mediterranean. 'I believe that it must be the policy of the US to support free peoples who are resisting attempted subjection by armed minorities or by outside pressure,' he told Congress. 'I believe that we must assist free people to work out their own destinies in their own way.'[97]

These phrases became the Truman Doctrine. They marked a new stage in American diplomacy, and a final inversion of Anglo-American power. Almost a century and a quarter previously, British power had, through Canning and the Polignac Memorandum, enabled President Monroe to set out one doctrine, claiming a sphere of freedom for the New World. Now British weakness had inspired another President to develop a new doctrine which sponsored freedom everywhere. Only Palmerston, among British Foreign Secretaries, had ever made such ambitious claims.

Radical as it was, in the short term the Truman Doctrine rescued only one part of the world.* It certainly offered no solution to Britain's economic weakness, or to the wider problems which were affecting Europe. Indeed, it was becoming clear to many Americans that the basic problem in Western Europe was not so much political as economic. War and occupation had broken the normal processes which made up Europe's trade, and, lacking dollars, Europeans were no longer able to buy necessary goods from America. Europe had thus entered a vicious cycle of economic collapse. Worried messages from across Europe were beginning to arrive on the desk of the new American Secretary of State, George Marshall. One message in particular caught this depressed mood: 'Europe is steadily deteriorating . . . Millions of people in the cities are slowly starving . . . The modern system of division of labour has almost broken down.'[98]

---

* As it turned out, British troops stayed on in Greece until the Civil War was over, continuing to train Greek forces alongside the American mission.

Many Americans rightly worried that Europeans would see Communism as the cure to these problems. Kennan was tasked with finding a solution. Together with his Policy Planning Staff, he produced a policy which all good students of strategy should read and learn from. Clear, focused and achievable, the plan was for America to provide dollar aid to kick-start Europe's economy, thus building markets for surplus American production and cutting away the well-springs of support for Communism in Europe. On one point Kennan was particularly specific: the 'formal initiative must come from Europe; the program must be evolved in Europe; and the Europeans must bear the basic responsibility for it'.[99]

On 5 June 1947 George Marshall made the policy public in a speech at Harvard's graduation ceremony. Bevin heard the news on his bedside radio. It was, he later admitted, 'like a life-line to sinking men'. He scuttled round, getting French support, preparing the way. He remained focused throughout on Marshall's galvanising phrase – *'The initiative, I think, must come from Europe'*. Perversely, the process of supplication restored Bevin's faith in British power. He told a meeting of the Foreign Press Association on 13 June: 'if anybody in the world has got it into his head that Britain is down and out, please get it out. We have our genius and science; we have our productivity, and although we have paid the price, I venture to prophesy that in a few years' time we shall have recovered our former prosperity.'[100]

The Soviet Union complicated Marshall's plan and Bevin's diplomacy. Marshall had extended his offer of aid to Stalin, but he was running a significant risk. The Soviets had no interest in the success of the policy – weak economies strengthened support for Communism. Bevin worried that if the Soviets were involved in the Marshall Plan, they would try to shackle the scheme with caveats and make it collapse. But not inviting Stalin to discuss the offer would isolate the populations of those countries already within the Soviet sphere. In Moscow, Stalin wrestled with the dilemma from the opposite angle. Not accepting the offer of generous and needed aid from America would damage his support in Europe; but joining the scheme would mean opening his empire up to American influence.

On the evening of 20 June Bevin met these uncertainties head on at the Eton College Political Society – a speaking engagement he had taken on as a favour to the son of his Private Secretary, Pierson Dixon. One boy asked Bevin whether he thought the Russians would accept the invitation to discuss Marshall's offer. Bevin hid behind history: 'The Czar Alexander still hasn't answered Castlereagh's questions', was how he replied.[101]*

Soon, everything was in place for a discussion between the Soviets, Britain and France of Marshall's offer. Stalin dispatched Molotov to test the air. By the fifth session of the negotiations, Stalin's suspicions had prevailed. Molotov accused France and Britain of seeking to extend their power over the small states of Europe through the Marshall Plan. He ended his speech by warning that the policy would be seen as a hostile act. During Molotov's monologue, Bevin turned to Dixon and said: 'This really is the birth of the Western bloc.'[102]

Within days, the organisation which would steer Marshall's policy into an aid plan had been established. Its first meeting was held in Paris on 12 July. Bevin travelled to Paris for the opening of the new conference. As usual, he stayed at the British Embassy with Duff Cooper and his glamorous wife, Diana. This time, Bevin's exuberance may have exceeded its usual limits. The night before the conference opened, Duff scribbled in his diary that when Diana had tried to show Bevin to his room Bevin had 'made violent advances to her and seriously suggested that she should sleep with him'. The following night Duff delivered his personal verdict: 'I think Bevin is rather in love with Diana.'[103]

But Bevin had more serious things to think about than jumping into bed with diplomats' wives. He was still unhappy about Britain's position in the post-war world. He had been cheered by the signs that America was living up to its responsibilities in Europe. But he certainly did not regard relying on America as a satisfactory long-term plan. Partly, this was because of his experiences with Palestine, where the violence and anger continued through 1947.

In July 1947 British authorities in Palestine discovered the booby-trapped bodies of two young British sergeants who had been hanged by the Irgun. The news provoked anti-Semitic riots

---

* Was Bevin referring to Castlereagh's letter to the Czar in 1821? One of the authors of this book attended the meeting, but is unable to shed any light on what Bevin meant. His diary entry for that evening simply records: 'Snubbed. But he very good and learned, the man for the job.'

in the UK; a synagogue was burnt.[104] Each new atrocity added to Bevin's irritation with the USA. The Americans, it seemed to him, were incapable of offering steady and impartial leadership. Lacking this, all diplomacy was bound to fail. The UN suggested partition. The US seemed to agree, but then rejected the policy. In the end, Britain had already announced a final date for departure when the State of Israel was proclaimed on 14 May 1948. Within minutes of the declaration, the USA recognised the new state. There was fighting, tenuous truces, more fighting. There is still bloodshed in Palestine today.*

If catastrophes on this scale were to be avoided closer to home, Britain had to find some new way of exerting its own influence on the world. One solution would be for Britain to act as America's mentor. Bevin had tried this out during the negotiations on the Marshall Plan. He wanted to achieve for Britain a special status in implementing the Plan. 'The British did not want to go into the programme and not do anything', was how he had put it to the Americans. This 'would sacrifice the little bit of dignity we have left'.[105] But America rebuffed the approach on the reasonable grounds that the point of having a European reconstruction policy for all Europe was that there was no special role for anyone. Bevin continued to believe that Britain had a part to play in educating America about its new responsibilities. America, Bevin explained, had 'not so much experience in foreign affairs as we had and that while she was developing a sense of responsibility remarkably well, there must occasionally be setbacks'.[106] The Americans were not overly forthcoming about seeking Bevin's advice, so he continued to scout around for alternative alliances. There were several horses in the running; Bevin straddled them all in turn.

One option was an Anglo-French union, similar in some ways to the one which Churchill had suggested in the crisis of 1940. Orme Sargent had given new wings to this initiative in the autumn of 1945

---

* The sense of confused hopelessness which enveloped Palestine can be compared to the same feeling during the Bosnian War up to autumn 1995. In both cases the diplomacy was intricate and tireless, but each time a settlement seemed possible the pause was shattered by some fresh act of bloodshed. Whichever way the policy-makers turned they found it blocked by seemingly impenetrable obstacles of blindness and bad faith.

when relations with America had entered a trough over the loan deal. He thought that Britain could strengthen its world position by becoming 'THE great European Power', collaborating with France 'with a view to our two countries establishing themselves politically as the leaders of all the Western European Powers and morally as the standard-bearers of civilization'. By the middle of 1947, this approach had been set in motion with the signing of the Treaty of Dunkirk between Britain and France. This did not go far enough for Bevin. In September, he suggested an Anglo-French union to the French Prime Minister, Ramadier. With 'their populations of 47 million and 40 million respectively and with their vast colonial possessions', Britain and France could 'be as powerful as either the Soviet Union or the United States'. Duff Cooper wrote that after the meeting Bevin had said to him: 'We've made the union of England and France this morning.' Cooper, forever Francophile, was delighted by this. 'He would certainly like to, and I believe that if it were not for other government departments he might bring it off.'[107] Other departments were one thing, nine centuries of history another. The Anglo-French union never got very far.

The second idea was more amorphous and less attractive to Bevin. For some time, Europeans including Bevin had been using vague phrases. In 1927 Bevin had spoken of the need for a united Europe in order to prevent the emergence of a dominant power. After the war, these arguments gathered pace with Churchill at the steering wheel. What was needed was a 'United States of Europe'. The Council of Europe was created as a vehicle for this purpose. But Bevin held back, wary of giving away anything, let alone sovereignty. 'If you open that Pandora's Box, you never know what Trojan 'orses will jump out', was how he expressed the concern.[108]

Bevin was not, however, opposed in principle to a new alliance between the European powers. Indeed, it had an important role in the third option on the table in 1947; an important role, but not the main one. For, oddly as it seems now, Bevin's idea of joining together Europe's empires as a third world power would depend for its success on Africa.

In July 1947 Bevin ordered an inquiry to find out where America was short of raw materials, and which of these deficiencies could be filled by Britain's imperial resources. The news came back that the

USA was short of nickel, chrome ore, tin, industrial diamonds, quartz crystals, plate graphite and long-fibre asbestos. As the report helpfully pointed out, five of these were produced by Britain's African colonies.[109] For fifteen months after this report arrived on Bevin's desk, these items became vital hinges in Bevin's plan to reorder the world. In his diary, Hugh Dalton recorded a meeting with Bevin in October 1948 dominated entirely by Bevin explaining his plan to 'reorganise the middle of the planet'. If Britain 'only pushed on and developed Africa we could have US dependent on us, and eating out of our hand, in four or five years. Two great mountains of manganese are in Sierra Leone, etc. US is very barren of essential minerals and in Africa we have them all.'[110] Behind the scenes, others had been sketching more detailed and expansive versions of the same idea.

Montgomery of Alamein, Chief of the Imperial Staff, scourge of Rommel, was not a man built for peacetime. Things moved too slowly there, and without clear objectives or lines of command. He had been bored before he began his tour of Africa in November 1947, and he was determined to find something interesting to do. Hungry for action, ready to engineer some if necessary, he decided to come up with a plan for Africa.

His plan was conceived in the high ancestry of Empire. Disraeli's Crystal Palace speech in 1872, when he decided that Britain had become an Oriental power; Joseph Chamberlain's speech in Birmingham in 1903 – 'I do not believe in a Little England' – these are prosaic trifles compared to Montgomery's African report. Arriving on the Foreign Secretary's desk on 19 December, Montgomery's memorandum orchestrated Bevin's big idea.[111] The Introduction got straight to the point.

It is impossible to tour Africa without being impressed with the following points:
(a) the immense possibilities that exist in British Africa for development.
(b) the use to which such development could be put to enable Great Britain to maintain her standard of living, and to survive.
(c) the lack of any 'grand design' for the development of British Africa and consequently the lack of a master plan in any Colony.

More important than any of this was the next conclusion: 'These lands contain everything we need.'

Montgomery decided that Britain's African colonies had to be completely reorganised, with new frontiers and political structures. These units would then implement what he referred to as 'The Grand Design: 'There must be a grand design for African development as a whole, with a master plan for each Colony or nation. In this, there must be vision; we must think big, and go for big worth-while projects. The "great opportunity" is there; the "grand design" is lacking.' A strand of racism, not unusual at the time, ran through the argument: 'There will be many people in the U.K. who will oppose such a plan on the grounds that the African will suffer in the process; there is no reason whatever why he should suffer; and in any case he is a complete savage and is quite incapable of developing the country himself.' International law was no obstacle: 'We should have no nonsense with the UNO about Tanganyika; it should be absorbed into the British bosom.' The Field Marshal closed on a characteristic note: 'Difficulties: These will be immense; so they were when we went to Normandy in 1944.'[112]

Taken as whole, this was a vivid grand strategy, well suited to Bevin's own mind. Bevin wrote to the Prime Minister a few days later: 'I have been reading the C.I.G.S.'s Report on his recent visit to Africa, of which he also sent a copy direct to you. I also discussed the Report with him this morning. I think that the issues he raises, more particularly those dealing with the development of Africa, require serious and urgent study.'[113] A meeting was arranged for early January. By this stage the professionals had been at work, unpicking each of the proposals. At some point, the Colonial Secretary stepped into the argument. Arthur Creech-Jones was a man of sour and progressive virtue. He poured cold water on the scheme:

> The imposition on the African Territories of a grand design or master plan by central control and direction from London would not be practical politics and would conflict with our declared policy of devolution in the process of building up self-government, which is based on the experience of the history of the British Commonwealth. Such a course would not secure the co-operation of the local people, without which effective development cannot take place.[114]

A ministerial meeting on 9 January put out most of Montgomery's arguments; the report was left to fizzle away.[115] But the flame was not extinguished entirely.

When it became clear that Montgomery's plans were going nowhere, Bevin merged the African concept with the European idea. In a memorandum circulated to the Cabinet called the 'The First Aim of British Foreign Policy' he developed this thought. The memorandum began with bland statements; it soon became more radical and interesting:

> ... the countries of Western Europe which despise the spiritual values of America will look to us for political and moral guidance and for assistance in building up a counter attraction to the baleful tenets of communism within their borders and in recreating a healthy society wherever it has been shaken or shattered by the war ... Provided we can organize a Western European system ... backed by the power and resources of the Commonwealth and of the Americas, it should be possible to develop our own power and influence to equal that of the United States of America and the USSR.[116]

The Cabinet discussions were favourable. There could have been no doubt about what Bevin was proposing when he told them that 'It would be necessary to mobilise the resources of Africa in support of any Western European union; and, if some such union could be created, including not only the countries of Western Europe but also their Colonial possessions in Africa and the East, this would form a bloc which, both in population and productive capacity, could stand on an equality with the western hemisphere and Soviet blocs.' The Cabinet decided to move forward with Bevin's policy and 'consolidate the forces of the Western European countries and their Colonial possessions' to create a Third World force.[117]

But events, not ideas, set the pace of diplomacy. A strategy is only as strong as its ability to manage the next event. In February 1948 events in Prague made brutally clear the inadequacy of the Cabinet's Third Force strategy, and the need for a more resilient approach.

Czechoslovakia had been gradually falling within the Soviet sphere of influence. In the summer of 1947 the Czechs were pressed by Stalin into rejecting the Marshall Plan. In February 1948 the Czech Foreign Minister fell, or was pushed, out of a high window in Prague. Czechoslovakia moved from one stage of interference to the next. Defenestration was followed by domination; Communists took control in a coup. These developments, brutal for the Czechs, were alarming for both Britain and America. If the same process was repeated in other countries within the Soviet reach – in particular, in Finland and Norway – the Iron Curtain would become a steel blanket enveloping Britain. America would find itself facing a Eurasian landmass controlled almost entirely by Soviet power.

A good strategist can change his policy when events change direction. Bevin's actions in the weeks following the Czech coup were, by this standard, momentous feats of skilful statecraft. There was no longer any time to hypothesise about Africa or about a Third Way. Something needed to happen immediately to stop Stalin. Bevin saw the facts and followed them to the only possible plan. A message was dispatched to America. It was imperative 'before Norway goes under' of concluding 'under Article 51 of the Charter of the UN a regional Atlantic Approaches Pact of Mutual Assistance, in which all the countries directly threatened by a Russian move to the Atlantic could participate, for example US, UK, Canada, Eire, Iceland, Norway, Denmark, Portugal, France (and Spain, when it has a democratic regime)'. History helped him in his analysis. 'The alternative is to repeat our experience with Hitler and to witness helplessly the slow deterioration of our position, until we are forced in much less favourable circumstances to resort to war in order to defend our lives and liberty.'

Marshall seized the message and acted straightaway. He consulted the President and wrote to the British Ambassador the following day: 'Please inform Mr Bevin that in accordance with your *aide-memoire* of 11 March, we are prepared to proceed at once in the joint discussions on the establishment of an Atlantic security system.'[118] On 17 March, the Treaty of Brussels was signed, bringing into being the Western European Union – a collective defence pact for Europe. But now this was viewed as a precursor to an Atlantic commitment involving the USA. Through the summer months, negotiations continued secretly in Washington on the plan.

Confidence flowed across Western Europe in these months. In April, Communist support, long thriving in Italy, fell away in the elections there. The Western occupiers of Germany began to merge their own zones of control in the country. The thirst for retribution was quenched by the need to protect Europe from Stalin. These initiatives reached a stumbling block when applied to Berlin. The German capital was located deep inside the Russian zone, but it was meant to be administered jointly by all the Allied powers. All around the city, across the highways and lines of communication, the Russian grip was strong. In March, the grip tightened. There were excuses about engineering works, but no doubts about the fact that Berlin was cut off from the Western world for several weeks. The RAF did its research and came up with figures for supplying the people of West Berlin by air. But then the restrictions were lifted, and the crisis seemed to have passed.

On 18 June, Russia's grip contracted again following the Western Allies' decision to institute a new currency in the Western zones of Germany. A full Soviet blockade of Berlin started. The stocks in the Western zones could not last much more than a month; without relief, the Berliners would starve.

The news reached Bevin on holiday at Sandbanks. A torpedo boat sped him back to the mainland. It was clear that the Russians were trying to force the West to choose between fighting their way to Berlin, withdrawing from Berlin, or negotiating a damaging truce on Russian terms. The idea for the airlift seems to have come from an RAF officer called Air Commodore Waite. The figures assembled by the Air Force in the spring were put forward and persuaded the Americans that it was possible. On 26 June the operation began. The airlift lasted for 324 days, keeping two and a quarter million Berliners in supply.

Meanwhile the plans for an Atlantic defence pact moved into their final stages. Bevin's African idea still occupied him from time to time. At one point during the Berlin crisis, he called the press corps together for a meeting. 'I've been thinking ... ', he began, before expanding on the importance of Africa.[119] The idea lived on but it would never be enacted. In September, the Atlantic Pact plans were completed; the following spring the North Atlantic Treaty was signed. At its heart NATO had the concept which Bevin had referred to in his message to Marshall: an attack on one would be seen as an attack on all the rest. But, unlike the United Nations, where security was limited by the Soviet veto, all the participants in NATO were willing and prepared to act.

History had provided the argument for the rules of NATO; it had also given birth to new ideas about power. 'The accusation has been made that the Atlantic Pact is an aggressive thing and that it will bring war,' Bevin told his fellow MPs when presenting the Treaty to the House. 'My answer is that the absence of the Atlantic Pact did not stop war in 1914 and 1939, and I suggest that if a pact like this had existed and the potential aggressor had known what he would have to face, those wars might have been avoided.' Preventing wars was better than trying to stop them once they had started – so the emphasis should be on deterring attacks. 'The real purpose of this pact is to act as a deterrent. Its object is to make aggression appear too risky to those who are making their calculations, for they must realise before they start their nefarious game, that defeat is their certain end.'[120]

What Bevin had realised from Hitler's success in the 1930s was that rules were not enough to deter dictators. What was needed was a physical show of power. The old system of collective security based on guarantees between countries to help one another in case of an attack would not restrain a ruthless despot like Stalin. In an age of nuclear weapons and mechanised warfare, by the time friendly countries had clubbed together to liberate an invaded nation, it might be too late. D-Day had been hard enough in 1944; it would have been even more difficult in the late 1940s – not least because Stalin was on the verge of developing the Bomb. Bevin grasped these developments and pressed them on his American colleagues in the NATO Council in May 1950. 'It would be a terrible blow to Europe to say: "Well, we shall liberate you again, but you have got to go under first and we have not organised sufficient strength to remain on the Continent",' he told the Council. 'The best insurance against war is if the aggressor knows that we shall give a good account of ourselves in the opening stages as well as later on.' The Government had already pursued this logic through to its conclusions for Britain's Armed Forces, raising spending on arms production in 1949. In 1950, Bevin pressed his European partners to make similar changes. He sent a message to British ambassadors in Western Europe, urging them to lobby for improved defences. 'Mr Bevin does not believe that the Russians will venture on aggression against Europe if the Europeans show their determination to fight. The Russian tradition is to push in when they calculate that they can obtain gains without encountering serious opposition. Moreover, their main objective would be to secure European resources intact.'[121]

In October 1949, Bevin reviewed for the Cabinet all the ideas and options he had been considering since 1945.

The general conclusion of this paper may be summarized as follows:—

(a) The Commonwealth alone cannot form a Third World Power equivalent to the United States or the Soviet Union.

(b) Commonwealth solidarity is more likely to be promoted by the consolidation of the West than by the formation of a Third World Power independent of America.

(c) A weak, neutral Western Europe is undesirable and a strong independent Western Europe is impracticable at present and could only come about, if at all, at the cost of the remilitarisation of Germany.

(d) The best hope of security for Western Europe lies in a consolidation of the West on the lines indicated by the Atlantic Pact.

(e) During the next 10–20 years, Western Europe, provided it continues on its policy of co-operation, should emerge from economic and even from military dependence on the United States but the two areas will remain interdependent.

(f) The United Kingdom will have an increasingly important part to play in the consolidation of the West, and must also seek to maintain its special relations with the United States of America.

E.B.[122]

With this dry evaluation, the Cabinet dropped any remaining ideas about Euro-African power blocs, and settled down within the orthodoxies of the Atlantic Alliance which have guided Britain ever since.

Recent critics of Bevin have seized on the African scheme as evidence of his inadequacy. He was not, these critics complain, the vigorous champion of an Atlantic Alliance. He was a man of hare-brained ideas and a new colonialism, all of which failed to take root. He stumbled into an Atlantic Alliance late in the day and without deep enthusiasm. The analysis here is accurate, the judgement unfair. Bevin had ideas on a daily basis; many of them were odd. But what matters in diplomacy is not what you think, but what you do; Bevin acted on his ideas only if the facts supported them. As Foreign Secretary, he let facts set the pace and shape the direction; ideas merged with the evidence in a highly effective way. Operating on this basis, Bevin, together with George Marshall, Dean Acheson and George Kennan, created through the Marshall Plan, NATO and the Atlantic Alliance a balance of power and rules which outlasted each of them – the high-water mark of success.

By establishing a balance of power in Europe, NATO altered the geography of the Cold War. The focus moved away from Europe to more unsettled parts of the globe. Here, Britain had a part to play by virtue of its imperial ties and past history, but these dilemmas were never quite as threatening for Britain as the European tensions had been.

For several years, alarm bells had been ringing in Asia. Bevin did his best to warn the Americans but they looked on dispassionately from afar. Alarm bells soon evolved into emergencies, first in Malaya, at that time still under British control. The challengers were Communist, but they were strong in only the Chinese part of the population; the British were able to deal with the emergency before handing over to a democratic and independent Malaysia. Then in China, Mao at last defeated the Nationalists and established a Communist regime. Bevin had to protect British trading interests there and ensure the safety of Hong Kong. He took the only option open to him and recognised the Communist regime. This act of appeasement infuriated the Americans but allowed Hong Kong to prosper for another half a century under British control. Finally, in Korea in 1950, Stalin acquiesced in the decision of the North Koreans to invade South Korea. At the United Nations, the Russian boycott of the Security Council left the other powers in a position to act under Chapter VII of the Charter, and a resolution was passed to go to the aid of South Korea according to Article 51. Troops from fifteen nations poured into a conflict which came to be dominated by the brilliance and brinkmanship of General MacArthur, and which ended in a stalemate which in a new millennium is still not resolved. In between these emergencies, Bevin did his best at the Colombo conference of Commonwealth Ministers in January 1950 to engineer a burst of diplomacy led by the Commonwealth countries in Asia. The plan for a system of alliances and development projects in Asia was Bevin's last big idea. But, beyond cordial exchanges and aid agreements, it never managed to travel very far.

Back at home, left-wing criticism of Bevin's foreign policy faded as the brutality of the Soviet regime became clear. It was replaced instead by arguments about Europe. A great deal of pressure had already been applied by the Americans, who were anxious to do all in their power to promote a United States of Europe. Now Churchill and Eden became unconvincing champions of European integration; angry exchanges took place in the House.

A key issue was whether and how Germany should join the Council of Europe. Bevin complained about the robust manner in which the new Federal Republic was dictating the terms of its accession to the Council of Europe; he compared its actions back to the 1920s and 1930s. Churchill interrupted to argue that the parallel did not work because Hitler was no longer present. Bevin responded with venom: 'The Hitler revolution did not change the German character very much. It expressed it.' Again, Churchill voiced his dissent, but Bevin continued. 'That is what it did. It was latent there right from Bismarckian days. I had to deal with them as well as the right hon. gentleman. I had to deal with them as employers, and in shipping, and in many other things where I got into close contact with these gentlemen.' Running deep was Bevin's anger and distrust of the Germans, an instinct that he never shook off. 'I tried 'ard, but I 'ates them,' he explained.[123]

Meanwhile the French developed an alternative system of European integration. Jean Monnet's idea of placing all French and German coal and steel production under an International Authority, and then inviting other European countries to participate, was in its own way as subtle and focused as the Marshall Plan. Monnet's idea moved fast from the drawing board into diplomacy. After securing agreement from the Germans, the French Foreign Minister, Robert Schuman, announced the plan to the world in April 1950. Bevin and the British Government stalled; there were suggestions about special status and non-binding decisions, but these soon fell away. Eventually, with Bevin in hospital and Attlee on holiday, the acting Prime

Minister, Herbert Morrison, decided not to take up the scheme: 'It's no good. We can't do it; the Durham miners won't wear it', was his final word.[124]

Eden and Churchill both criticised the Government for not taking up the initiative. They argued that the Government should have involved itself in the discussions while issuing a disclaimer that it might pull out. It is hard to see how this could have happened; the French were opposed to any half-hearted association. Besides, the real opposition to the scheme came from inside the Government, and to a large extent from Bevin. 'Ernie has no faith in the solidity or efficiency of France or Belgium and believes Western Europe will be a broken reed, and will not even attract the loyalty of Europeans or impress the Russians, unless it is very solidly linked to North America,' Kenneth Younger noted in his diary on 14 May. 'I think this is realistic though depressing.'[125]

Perhaps sickness played a part. Bevin's energies had swiftly diminished after NATO. The angina attacks became more painful and regular, the absences from work more lasting and frequent. Early in 1950 the Labour Party survived a general election with a reduced majority, enough to hang on in Government for slightly more than another year. Bevin should have taken this opportunity to resign. But he struggled on, living for a job he believed only he could do, but doing it worse every day. Dean Acheson, the new American Secretary of State, noticed that he dozed off during meetings. 'His staff seemed accustomed to it, though I found it disconcerting.'[126]

Eventually the decision was made for him. On 9 March 1951 the Foreign Office threw a party to celebrate their chief's seventieth birthday. Midway through the celebrations Attlee telephoned, asking to speak to Bevin. A few moments later Bevin returned and told his wife: 'I've got the sack.' Attlee appointed Herbert Morrison as his successor; Bevin was made Lord Privy Seal. He continued to attend Cabinet, but spent most meetings asleep. Dalton described one such appearance in his diary: 'EB at Cabinet today seemed quite finished. Out of harness, he'll soon drop.'[127] A month later, Bevin was dead.

In 1951, after Churchill's election victory, Eden returned for the third time to the Foreign Office. In an orderly way, the new

Conservative Ministers set about analysing their inheritance. The analysis was more powerful than the conclusions for policy. In the economic sphere, the discussion led to Chancellor of the Exchequer Rab Butler's proposal that the pound should float freely on the exchanges, a secret and revolutionary enterprise (nicknamed Robot) which his colleagues torpedoed. In June 1952, Eden put forward his share of the analysis in a memorandum on 'British Overseas Obligations'. This paper differs markedly from anything he would have produced during his earlier stints at the Foreign Office. Its significance has been rightly seized on by Professor Peter Hennessy in his book *Having it so Good*. A new and unwelcome fact could no longer be ignored. Britain was in serious and persistent economic trouble. This could no longer be treated as a temporary consequence of war, nor as something which Marshall Aid could permanently alter.

In the 1930s it had been the appeasers, and in particular Neville Chamberlain, who had stressed the importance of the British economy in deciding foreign policy. According to his logic, if we ruined our economy by spending too much too soon on rearmament, then we would be weakening Britain just as surely as if we ran down our Armed Forces. The economy was the fourth arm of defence, after the Army, Navy and Air Force. The opponents of appeasement, including Churchill and Eden, were not interested in economics and remained unconvinced by this argument. They did not so much answer as ignore it. It seemed to them irrelevant in a world where dictators were on the loose, month by month threatening military aggression.

After the war, Attlee and Bevin faced the facts of Britain's economic plight boldly, but then did their best to pass by on the other side. Tough decisions had been taken, certainly, but they had been taken with a sense of temporary expediency. Bevin always thought things would improve.

Bad news travels slowly in Whitehall. Only in 1952 did the fact of national poverty become the main factor in Cabinet debates on British foreign policy. Thus, Eden found himself refashioning Chamberlain's argument in modern form. 'The essence of a sound foreign policy', his paper argued, 'is to ensure that a country's strength is equal to its obligations.'

If this is not the case, then either the obligations must be reduced to the level at which resources are available to maintain them, or a greater share of the community's resources must be devoted to their support. It is becoming clear that vigorous maintenance of the presently accepted policies of Her Majesty's Government at home and abroad is placing a burden on the country's economy which is beyond the resources of the country to meet.

It followed that the first task of Government was to decide how Britain's external obligations could be reduced or shared 'without impairing too seriously the world position of the United Kingdom and sacrificing the vital advantages which flow from it'. If, after careful review, it was found that the required effort was still beyond our resources, then the British people would either have to accept a reduced standard of living or, 'by relaxing their grip in the outside world, see their country sink to the level of a second-class Power, with injury to their essential interests and way of life of which they can have little conception'.[128]

Many similar papers were written in later years – at least, until Britain's economic decline was halted after 1980. Professor Hennessy is right to pick out Eden's paper of 1952 as a classic statement of the dilemma. But the paper petered out when it passed from analysis to recommendation. In fact, the process of transferring responsibilities from Britain to the United States had already begun in the Balkans, and was to continue in the Middle East and elsewhere. The dismantling of the British Empire was already under way and would soon accelerate. Economic weakness was one factor in this, though only the withdrawal from the Gulf and Singapore announced in 1968 was openly the result of a desire to save money. Most of the impetus came from the rapid build-up of nationalist pressures in British colonies, together with a weakening of willingness at home to carry the burden of an imperial power in a world which defined imperialism as evil.

But Eden's paper is more than an illustration of Britain's state of mind in the 1950s. It evokes the whole concept of national prestige. He discussed, albeit in vague terms, its importance or unimportance in British foreign policy. This thread runs through our whole story, and, under Eden, returned for a final time.

Most previous Foreign Secretaries, and a good many Prime Ministers, believed that national prestige was an asset for Britain. We have seen how Disraeli harped constantly on this theme. He believed that prestige was all-important and that we would wither away unless we constantly used it. By contrast his Foreign Secretary, Derby, held that our reputation would weaken if paraded in speeches. There was no reason, he thought, for Britain to scurry about. For Derby, dignified silence, even inactivity, was evidence of strength.

Castlereagh and Canning, opposed on many matters, would have agreed that British prestige rested on three main foundations – naval, commercial and financial strength. The naval and commercial elements remained valid through the nineteenth century. But Canning, Palmerston and most strongly Gladstone introduced a new element, namely moral force. Britain, they thought, built her own prestige by her support for the freedom and well-being of others. For some decades in Salisbury's time another element was introduced: the imperial destiny. Britain was great not just because of the Royal Navy, the trade and investment figures, the victories of Trafalgar and Waterloo, and the abolition of slavery – but also because of the Empire, the amount of the world which, in properly appointed atlases, was coloured red on the map.

All these elements, naval, commercial, financial, moral and imperial, persisted into the twentieth century, but in new proportions. By the time Eden wrote in 1952, the naval dimension of relative strength had disappeared and the economic dimensions had turned to weakness. The moral dimension had been strengthened by Britain's heroic fighting role in and after 1940. The imperial dimension was fast disappearing. On balance, these changes greatly lowered our prestige. Some, including at times Churchill, refused to recognise their full extent. Eden tended to be more realistic. He did not dispute the independence of India; he himself brought about in 1954 the British military withdrawal from Egypt. But neither Eden nor most of his generation accepted that Britain had become a second-class power, if that meant that she was to be excluded from the key decision-taking processes of the modern world.

When they took the stage in the 1950s, Churchill and Eden redefined how and where Britain could use her power. The opportunities for Britain lay, according to these two leaders, in her position within three circles – Europe, the Commonwealth and the Anglo-American Alliance. Eden used this concept in his Party conference speech at Margate in 1953. Churchill illustrated the idea on the back of a menu card preserved in the German Chancellor's house at Kornhof. The three circles were of equal size. Churchill and Eden believed that geography and history gave Britain the unique advantage of operating within each.

The trouble lay in mistaking a snapshot for a long-term analysis. The three circles were changing shape and size quite rapidly. Churchill and Eden took no account of this. Eden knew the Commonwealth well, from visits as a young man and from his time as Dominions Secretary at the beginning of the war. Throughout his life, he took trouble to keep in touch with Commonwealth leaders. He liked the historic feel of the institution and its base in human relationships. He used to point out that the great bulk of letters received from overseas by his constituents in Warwick and Leamington came from Commonwealth countries. He remembered vividly how Commonwealth countries had helped to win both world wars. But the nobility of the story and the close personal and cultural links which resulted could not be translated into a political force. The very independence of mind which formed the character of both old and new Commonwealth members would frustrate any attempt to weld them together. They were not even a powerful forum for resolving disputes. In practice Eden realised this and made no such attempt; but the rhetoric lingered on because it corresponded to a sympathy which he shared with millions.

The Anglo-American Alliance had also changed in character while Eden had been in Opposition. Bevin's diplomacy with the Americans after 1945 had been different to that practised by Churchill and Eden during the war. In particular, he had learned that, whatever emotional and historic ties existed between the two countries, these did not compensate for the growing indebtedness and economic weakness of Britain. Nor did they mean that the United States would support Britain and her Empire if it was not in her clear interest to do so. These two changes did not destroy the importance of the Alliance, or prevent it remaining the most important of the three circles; but they complicated most transactions within that circle. Eden began to grasp the extent of American reserve more quickly than Churchill, but he never developed the skills of persistence and persuasion which Bevin had developed. More seriously, deep down he believed that America was incapable of understanding traditionally British parts of the planet. The National Archives at Kew have recently released the notes made by the Cabinet Secretary during meetings under Eden's chairmanship in 1955. One minute in particular gives a taste of Eden's belief that only he was equipped to understand the Middle East: 'We must realise tht. U.S. has almost always bn. wrong on M/E. They are ignorant of it and cannot steer steady course. The big interest in M/E is ours – not U.S. We are dependent on M/E oil. We must therefore do our own thinking on this.'[129]

Europe, third and for most in Britain the least important of the circles, was the one which was being most vigorously transformed. Churchill had made European integration a political issue in 1950 and 1951, but neither he nor Eden really supposed that Britain could be a full partner in Europe's new process. Eden's reluctance increased as it became clear that the arrangements for coal and steel and the plan for a European Defence Community (EDC) had a fundamental political purpose. These were to be the first steps towards a European federation led by a supranational authority, the United States of Europe long discussed.

Throughout his final stint as Foreign Secretary, Eden continued to hold back. There were sound reasons for this. Britain had won the Second World War. It could not be expected to take the medicine prescribed for those who had been occupied and defeated. Instead, in her own way, Britain would help forward the efforts towards European unity. On 5 February 1952 Eden promised the Commons that we would 'associate ourselves as closely as possible with the EDC in all stages of its political and military development and keep armed forces on the Continent for as long as was necessary'.[130] But a month earlier, in a carefully prepared lecture at Columbia University in New York, he spoke of 'frequent suggestions that the United Kingdom should join a federation on the Continent of Europe. This is something which we know, in our bones, we cannot do.'[131]

Eden knew Europe well. The whole make-up of his tastes and convictions put him in a different category from an isolationist, or from an Empire loyalist like Beaverbrook. But the Europe he knew and liked was a Europe of states and statesmen, returning after the tragic breakdown of war to discuss once more the question of European security and to solve disputes in other parts of the world in which Europe was involved. A Franco-German army co-operating with British troops on the Continent might be a reasonable updating of Locarno. But British soldiers could no more be expected to serve in an integrated European army than British coal and steel industries could be expected to subordinate themselves to European authority. What Eden felt in his bones limited the range of his eyes and his brain.

The debate on Europe in Britain moved on at a glacial pace, the debate on the Continent at a speed which caught Britain off-guard. Harold Macmillan, with his restless mind, and some of the new generation like Ted Heath, began to realise that the European process could not be confined within Churchill's circle; Britain in her own interest should be much closer to what was going on. Whitehall was divided, but most Ministers and officials, certainly including Eden, operated in a mixture of misunderstandings The new European process would probably not get very far; if it did, the result would probably not be in Britain's interest. A vague and benevolent super-vision was the right approach. The reaction of Eden's own Government in November 1955 to the Messina conference which prepared the Treaty of Rome, the European Economic Community and the Common Market was eventually the same as Bevin's reaction five years earlier to the Coal and Steel Community. This approach was in line with public opinion at the time. Whether bolder, more far-sighted leadership could have led rather than followed opinion we will never know; it could not have been expected from Eden.

Eden's last period as Foreign Secretary was dominated by his relationship with Winston Churchill. The dealings between Prime Minister and Foreign Secretary are bound to be complex when the Prime Minister takes an active interest in foreign affairs. Churchill's interest, always passionate, became poignant as he became conscious of his waning powers and the short time available to him to do great things. His overriding concern was with the threat of nuclear war. His last duty, he believed, was to use his own personal authority and prestige to secure peace through discussion at the top level with the Soviet Union. Stalin died in April 1953, and to Churchill the omens looked good. He saw no problem if his scheme meant cutting across the Foreign Office. Like his predecessors and successors, Disraeli, Lloyd George, Neville Chamberlain, Margaret Thatcher and Tony Blair, Winston Churchill in the 1950s believed that his own intervention as Prime Minister was worth an infinity of diplomatic meetings and manoeuvres. Through 1953 and 1954, Eden doggedly put the opposite view to Churchill – just as he had done in 1938 when faced with Chamberlain's Italian plan. In his own words: 'The more critical the negotiating position of a democracy, the more important it is to hold to the tested form of diplomacy, to proceed step by step, to make sure of agreement on the preliminaries before embarking on the detailed negotiations.'[132]

Behind this disagreement about method lay a personal struggle, the more painful because largely concealed. For more than a decade, Eden had been Churchill's obvious, almost anointed successor. Never in these years did a serious rival to the succession appear.* By talent, experience and popularity, Eden established himself beyond challenge. Repeatedly, Churchill intimated that he would soon retire. In 1953, 1954 and 1955 dates were discussed. Each time, Churchill pulled back. There was always one further meeting which he had to attend, one more duty which only he could perform.

These delays built up in Eden an intense frustration. His outward loyalty to Churchill was not false; genuine affection and respect lingered on. The personal relationship between the two men formed by many years of almost daily dealings was complex and volatile; it baffled them both. The relationship was reinforced when in August 1952 Eden married Churchill's niece Clarissa. Churchill was delighted, acted as principal witness and insisted that the reception be held at 10 Downing Street. When Eden was dangerously ill in April 1953, Churchill behaved like an anxious and affectionate uncle who happened to be Prime Minister. He treated the event as a major crisis. He tried to take personal command of the medical treatment. He hovered over the surgeons who performed two operations to

---

* As early as January 1945, an opinion poll put Eden top, well above both Churchill and Attlee, as the man preferred to lead the post-war Government. This trend continued after the war, although Bevin now took the lead over both Eden and Churchill. See Hadley Cantril and Mildred Strunk, *Public Opinion: 1935–1945* (Princeton University Press, 1951), p. 280.

remove gallstones from Eden's bile duct, repeatedly emphasising that nothing must be allowed to go wrong. Despite or because of this pressure neither operation succeeded; Eden's life was in danger. Churchill was reluctantly persuaded that the chances of recovery would be better if Eden were treated at a reputable clinic in Boston. He ordered that the substantial expense should be covered by the Conservative Party.

Characteristically, Churchill took firm charge of the Foreign Office in Eden's absence, even though he had himself only just recovered from his latest stroke. He used the opportunity to deliver his famous speech on 11 May 1953 in which he called for an early conference at the highest level between the leading powers, a conference which should 'not be overhung by a ponderous or rigid agenda, nor led into mazes and jungles of technical details, zealously contested by hoards of experts and officials drawn up in vast cumbrous array'. Even if no 'hard faced agreements' were reached, 'there might be a general feeling among those gathered together that they might do something better than tear the human race, including themselves, to bits'. It was great stuff, capturing the mood of optimism which characterised the Coronation summer of 1953. It was a proposal which, as Churchill well knew, his Foreign Secretary would have fiercely resisted had he not been cooped up in bed.[133]

The combination of affection, disagreement and frustration came to an explosive climax in July 1954 on the *Queen Elizabeth* liner. The two men were travelling home together from a meeting in Washington. Professor Hennessy describes this as 'the most extraordinary sea voyage in the recent history of British high politics'. The immediate issue was Churchill's determination to send Molotov* a telegram proposing that he should visit Moscow in August for talks with one of the new Soviet leaders, Georgii Malenkov. Eden disliked the idea on principle, and also because the Americans had discouraged it at the recent talks in Washington. As with Chamberlain, so with Churchill, Eden focused not on substance but on the constitutional argument that the Cabinet must be consulted before such a telegram was sent. He was not much comforted by an indication that Churchill

---

* Molotov had a knack for survival. After being sacked by Stalin, he outlived him, becoming Foreign Minister again under Khrushchev. After Khrushchev left office, Molotov lived on for several more decades, finally dying in 1986.

would retire in September. Such indications had been given before, and proved worthless.[134]

In the confined space of the *Queen Elizabeth* over a hot and muggy weekend, tempers boiled. Sir John Colville, Churchill's Private Secretary and no friend of Eden, wrote: 'They both went to bed in a combination of sorrow and anger, the PM saying that AE was totally incapable of differentiating great points and small points (a criticism that has an element of truth in it).'[135] Colville urged Eden to be amiable. 'The PM thrived on opposition and showdowns; but amiability he never could resist.' A compromise was reached: Eden agreed not to oppose Churchill's idea – provided that the Molotov telegram was shown to the Cabinet before being sent. Dinner the next night was friendly, with 'much quoting of Pope, Shakespeare and others on the PM's part and a dissertation on Persian and Arabic poets and writing by Eden ... To bed at 2am.'[136] Once ashore and back in Cabinet, the compromise fell to bits. There was a big row in which several Ministers joined. The question of a visit by Churchill to Moscow became entangled with the proposal that Britain should manufacture the hydrogen bomb. In the end the Russians solved the problem by proposing a wide meeting of European leaders, which clearly ruled out an Anglo-Soviet summit for the time being. Colville admitted later that he exaggerated, but not greatly, when he summarised: 'W. began to form a cold hatred for E. who, he repeatedly said, had done more to thwart him and prevent him from pursuing the policy he thought right than anyone else.'[137]

This spat with the Prime Minister occurred in the middle of the most successful year in Eden's political life. Having apparently recovered from his dire illness in 1953, he seemed at the height of his powers. By chance a number of crises came to a head in 1954 which required not striking phrases or imaginative strategy, but the slow grind of careful diplomacy. In such situations Eden excelled. In 1954, Eden gathered a harvest from his natural talent and twenty years of almost continuous experience.

His operating moods and methods were now well established. Eden worked hard, but kept no office hours. Charming and successful with women, Eden lacked any cohort of men friends, either political or personal. He often spent a long morning working from his bed in Carlton Gardens. Thus on 29 December 1952: 'Raining and cold.

Clarissa says this is the right way to run the F.O. Lie in bed, direct office by telephone and read Delacroix. Very good too.'[138] This method put a particular burden on the Private Secretaries who formed the link between Eden and officials. Eden treated the holders of this office as friends. They became confidants, sharing intelligence and emotions with the Foreign Secretary, asked for advice on the most delicate and embarrassing political questions about their master's political prospects. Eden did not try to conceal from them his quick temper and extreme sensitiveness to criticism, particularly in the press. He shouted, threw things, used vain and childish arguments – and then repented in affectionate apology. Nor were the Private Secretaries alone in this treatment. The young wife of one Private Secretary watched Eden in a tantrum throw a glass of sherry at the wall at Chequers and then at dinner afterwards consult her with great charm about a major naval deployment which he had been asked to authorise. 'What do you think I should do, my dear?'[139]

Eden was a highly competent communicator by the standards of his time. In particular, he had established a quiet hold on the House of Commons. He based this mastery not on wit or emotion, but on a thorough grip of the details of each situation. He was particularly adept at winding up a debate, if necessary lowering the temperature, dealing fairly and knowledgeably with each main point raised by either side. He made no attempt at eloquence. On the contrary, he would exasperate his speech writers by deliberately cutting out a striking phrase and substituting a cliché. He wanted to clinch an argument, not strike a phrase. Fine phrases can come back to dog their authors. His persuasiveness in broadcasts, in speeches in and outside the Commons and in his meetings with foreigners was built on the steady deployment of considered arguments. His listeners could not guess at the turmoil and anxiety which might have gone before the moment of delivery. His voice and words were as well measured as the clothes which he wore. His was not golden eloquence, but solid silver.

The four diplomatic crises which Eden helped to resolve in 1954 would probably not have been resolved without him. Each one bore the residue of a Bevin failure. They were not at the same level of grandeur or excitement as Churchill's ambitions for a world agreement to prevent humanity from destroying itself. But three of these crises involved the danger of war, and the fourth risked the collapse of a European security system.

Italy and Yugoslavia were still in dispute over the port of Trieste in the Adriatic – at that time governed by the Allied Military. Eden had got to know the Yugoslav dictator, Tito, and visited him in the autumn of 1952. Two years later, he succeeded in brokering an agreement signed in London on 5 October and based on territorial compromise. Eden described it in his memoirs as a 'classic example of the true function of diplomacy, an open agreement secretly arrived at'.[140] This was in the true spirit of Austen Chamberlain's kitchen cookery at Locarno.

More difficult and more important for Britain was the agreement with Egypt for the withdrawal of British forces from the Canal Zone. The huge garrison of 80,000 men authorised by the Anglo-Egyptian Treaty which Eden had signed in 1936 was under increasing siege from guerrilla attack. Bevin had failed to come to any clear agreement with the Egyptians about a lasting deal on whether or not the troops should stay. Their deployment constituted a burden which Britain could no longer afford. But the idea of withdrawal touched a raw nerve in British politics, particularly among a group of right-wing Conservative Members of Parliament and with the Prime Minister himself, who allowed his acolytes to brief against the Foreign Secretary. But the logic of withdrawal from Egypt was inexorable; the new agreement was signed in October 1954 after the Chiefs of Staff persuaded the Cabinet that in a thermonuclear age, a Soviet thrust into the Middle East would be checked by air attack rather than by the deployment of British forces out of Egypt.[141] Eden followed up this agreement with a visit in February 1955 to the new Egyptian leader, Colonel Nasser. He wanted to press Nasser to join the Baghdad Pact, the new Middle East security pact which the Americans and British were planning on the model of NATO. Accounts of Eden's dinner with Nasser at the British Embassy in Cairo vary and may be distorted by knowledge of what later went wrong. Eden greeted his guest in Arabic and probably overdid the charm until it seemed patronising. The grandiose impressiveness of the British Embassy with its stately rooms and attentive servants reminded Nasser of a subservient past. Eden certainly failed to convince Nasser of the merits of the Baghdad Pact.

On 30 August the French Assembly failed to ratify the treaty setting up the European Defence Community. Although, as we have seen, Eden always intended to keep Britain out of the EDC, he had been strongly in favour of the concept and very conscious of the danger of letting it collapse without replacement. He at once took the initiative with a plan of his own, visiting all six European capitals. The Allied occupation of Germany would end; Germany under Chancellor Adenauer would join the Western European Union and, through the WEU, NATO; Britain also promised to keep 55,000 men in Germany as the British Army of the Rhine. The long saga of German rearmament, almost as fraught in the 1950s as in the 1930s, was this time brought to an end in the friendly spirit which has endured to this day.

But the main threat to peace, and Eden's main diplomatic achievement in 1954, arose from the Far East. Here again, Bevin had tried his hand but failed to find a settlement.

In the French colony of Indochina (composed of Vietnam, Laos and Cambodia), the main challenger was the Communist leader Ho Chi Minh as leader of the Vietminh movement, supported by the Chinese Communist Government in Peking. The French were engaged in a colonial war which they were steadily losing. This was not for the French a sideshow as Malaya, Burma, even India were for post-war British public opinion. The Indochina War lay at the heart of French politics. Worse, the Americans had by now convinced themselves about the domino theory, that if Indochina fell under Communist rule other Asian countries would inevitably follow. The Americans were therefore drawn into supporting the weak French Government in a colonial war. In early 1954, they had set no limit to the nature of that intervention. At the same time they began to plan SEATO as an international security organisation in South-East Asia based on the successful model of NATO.

Britain had no direct involvement in Indochina. But Eden, like Churchill, believed that as Britain was a first-class power, she had a role in defining the world's direction. Britain had no interest in seeing France humiliated, and it was important to stop a colonial war spilling over into world conflict. This did not mean that Eden had formed a strategy for dealing with the problem. He certainly did not plan the outcome in 1954, namely the partition of Vietnam and the gradual transfer of influence in the non-Communist part of the country from France to the United States. Eden thought and acted tactically. In each turn of events and at each meeting he tried to move discussion towards agreement and away from war without sacrificing any important interests.

Churchill was not personally interested in Indochina, and content to leave his Foreign Secretary a free hand, which was denied him in dealing with the Soviet Union or Egypt. The Cabinet was fully consulted, but ready to accept his advice. Public opinion in Britain was hardly engaged except at moments of crisis. Eden, as ever, felt a natural sympathy for France, and had a clear-eyed sense of French difficulties. He was keen that disaster in Indochina should not cripple the ability of the French Government to act constructively on German rearmament and European defence. As regards the Americans, Eden was content to go along with yet another regional security organisation. But he did not accept the American domino theory as justifying military intervention in Indochina. He set out his cool reasoning in a letter to his Minister of State, Selwyn Lloyd, on 21 May:

> I do not personally agree with the people who suggest that if Indo China were to go, Siam Malaya etc. must be indefensible. They would obviously be much more difficult to defend but that is not in itself a reason for intervening in Indo China even if we could do so effectively at this stage. If something could be saved from the wreckage in that country, well and good. But we do not want to bring a greater disaster on our heads by trying to avert the immediate one.[142]

Nor was Eden hemmed in by another emotion which in 1954 still beset the Americans. The Chinese Communist success in throwing Chiang Kai-shek out of mainland China and establishing themselves in undisputed power was regarded by many Americans as a major defeat. The Chinese Communist Government should not in their view be accepted as a member of the international community, at the United Nations or elsewhere. The Chinese intervention in the Korean War and their support for the Vietnamese in Indochina made things worse. It was, therefore, thought out of the question that American representatives should sit round a table on equal terms with Chinese Communists. Britain had already set out on a different course when

355

Bevin recognised the Peking Government in 1950 and established a small mission there. Eden, who in his early days had shaken hands with Hitler, Mussolini and Stalin, was not likely to draw the line at the Chinese Foreign Minister, Chou En Lai.

In February, the Foreign Ministers of the US, France, Britain and the Soviet Union agreed that an international conference should be held in Geneva to discuss, first of all, a political settlement in Korea (to follow the ceasefire already in place), and then the restoration of peace in Indochina. To this second discussion the Chinese Communist Government would be invited. This decision was a marked setback for American policy on China. John Dulles, the American Secretary of State, gave way, not accepting the arguments from Eden or Molotov, but yielding to intense pressure from the French Foreign Minister, Bidault. The French had daringly but disastrously concentrated their army at Dien Bien Phu in the heart of Vietnam; that position was already besieged and the chances of holding it were uncertain. They continued to fight but told their allies not to expect French military victory. As often happened under the Fourth Republic, French diplomacy made the most of their weakness. They foretold defeat and disintegration unless a conference was held on Indochina; a useful conference could not be held without the Chinese.

From May to July 1954, Eden worked at Geneva to prevent war. He took the chair of the conference alongside Molotov. It is not necessary to go through the details of the negotiations, first to achieve a ceasefire, then to reach a political agreement. Eden had to coax the parties into agreement at the table, and at the same time prevent the roof falling in on them while they talked. The roof was certainly unsafe. Part of the US Administration was planning military intervention, even with nuclear weapons, to save the French; part of the French Government played secretly with the same idea. Wrestling for peace, Eden put at serious risk his reputation in Washington. It was fortunate for him that Dulles could not abide the thought of negotiating with the Chinese Reds and left the American chair to General Bedell Smith, a less complicated character. It was fortunate that a weak (and therefore dangerous) French Government under Laniel was replaced by a brisker and more definite team under Mendès-France. Eden took advantage of each development to press the negotiation.

Throughout the conference, Eden exerted himself without stint. In a circus with many performers he was the ringmaster, willing and able to communicate personally with the Western Allies, with the Commonwealth and, through Molotov and Chou En Lai, with the Vietnamese. The top Americans, like his colleagues in London and his close staff, were conscious of his occasional vanities; the rest of the world knew only the charm and patience which were the tools of his trade. He did not operate spontaneously; each move on procedure or substance required careful discussion and drafting within the British delegation. This made for hard work, but in the end for success and for Eden general praise. Evelyn Shuckburgh wrote later that the 'complexities and excitements of that Conference gave ... as much joy to Eden as anything in his life. It was an atmosphere which he really loved and in which he moved with professional assurance.'[143]

Typically, Eden's success was tactical, rather than strategic. The Geneva Agreements did not settle the future of Vietnam. Despite the arrangements for monitoring and supervision there were no elections and the country remained partitioned between Communist North and anti-Communist South. The Americans were led by the domino theory into deep and eventually ruinous involvement. The immediate merits of the Geneva Agreements were threefold: first, the killing stopped in Indochina; second, the French extricated themselves without total humiliation; third, and most important, the conference averted the danger of a wider war including the United States and possibly involving the use of nuclear weapons.

During the conference, Eden often in his own mind harked back to Locarno, the diplomatic triumph of his first mentor, Austen Chamberlain. Chamberlain had received the Order of the Garter after Locarno. In October 1954, the Queen bestowed the same Order on Eden.

In April 1955 Churchill at last stepped down; Eden became Prime Minister. As one of his last acts in office, Churchill entertained the young Queen to a celebrated dinner in Downing Street. After the Queen had left, Colville went up with the Prime Minister to his bedroom. Churchill sat on his bed, still wearing his Garter, Order of Merit and knee breeches. 'For several minutes he did not speak and I, imagining that he was sadly contemplating that this was his last night at Downing Street, was silent. Then suddenly he stared at me and said with vehemence "I don't believe Anthony can do it".[144]

The story of Eden's premiership is dominated by the failure of the Suez operation which brought it to an end. This was a tragedy for Eden personally. Perhaps it was less of a tragic turning point for Britain than is sometimes supposed. Throughout their lives Eden and Bevin directed the foreign policy of a country which was declining in narrow terms of power, measured by military or financial resources, or even by political will. There were ups as well as downs along the path downwards, but the slide began long before Suez.

The story of Suez has been told and retold so often and so recently that we see small value in going over it all again. Pedantically, we can argue that Eden was not Foreign Secretary at the time and therefore the episode falls outside the scope of the book. This excuse includes an important truth about Suez. The Foreign Secretary was Selwyn Lloyd, who had acted as Minister of State at the Foreign Office under Eden as Foreign Secretary. He was accustomed to obeying Eden as a subordinate, which is a perfectly proper role for a junior Minister. He never altered that stance, sometimes enthusiastic, sometimes sullen, always subservient, when he became Foreign Secretary. The relationship between the Foreign Secretary and the Prime Minister should be more subtle. The Prime Minister is first among equals but should treat his Foreign Secretary as a colleague. There was no hint of collegiality in Eden's attitude to Selwyn Lloyd.

That was just one illustration of the main cause of the disaster. It is sometimes thought strange that Eden came to grief in the area of foreign and military affairs in which he was most expert – just as Gordon Brown as Prime Minister stumbled on precisely those economic questions which he had directed almost unchallenged for ten years as Chancellor of the Exchequer. But the sense of mastery which experience conferred on Eden helped his undoing. Relying too exclusively on his own judgement, he ignored the warnings and expressions of dissent which were plentiful in the lower reaches of Government. The Chiefs of Staff, and in particular Lord Mountbatten, were unhappy. The Law Officers of the Crown were doubtful or negative. Almost all senior diplomats and the Intelligence community were dismayed. The Prime Minister sensed this dissent. His reaction was not genuine consultation but a determination to exclude dissenters from essential knowledge of what was going on, in particular the collusion with the French and Israelis at Sèvres. Recent studies show that the Cabinet itself was fully informed; but the Cabinet can be a poor thing if cut off from the full flow of advice from the professionals who serve it. The only safe rule of political policy-making is that decisions should flow from the facts. If the flow of facts is impeded on its way or distorted because the decision-takers prefer to hear only what they welcome, then decisions are likely to go astray. A Prime Minister, as Eden found in 1956 and Blair over Iraq in 2003, can always find advisers to praise his wisdom. The British constitutional machine, properly used, provides an antidote in the form of solid mechanisms of fact-finding, analysis and recommendation. Neither Prime Minister nor Cabinet need to be slaves to the facts laid before them; but suppression or distortion of the facts is never a recipe for success.

Eden, living day by day with the memory of the Fascist dictators of the 1930s, allowed those memories to distort his judgement. Nasser became in his imagination another Mussolini, a hollow drum of a man, dangerous only if he was not exposed and confronted. The real force and resilience of Arab nationalism thus eluded him. As a result, he decided to invade Egypt and humiliate or overthrow Nasser without any serious concept of who or what would take his place.

Both these mistakes, together with neglect of the facts available to the Government machine, also characterised Blair's decision to go to war on Iraq. Where the two decisions diverged was as regards the relationship with the United States. In 1956 memories of wartime co-operation were still strong. These memories particularly focused on President Eisenhower who, as Commander-in-Chief twelve years earlier, had masterminded the greatest possible example of such co-operation, namely the invasion of France on D-Day and the later victorious campaign. Strengthened by his diplomatic success in facing down the Americans in 1954, Eden believed that when it came to the point the Americans would again back away and allow him to follow his own policy. He was strongly supported in this by his Chancellor of the Exchequer, Harold Macmillan, in whom wartime memories were equally strong. During the crucial week of decision-taking both men were prepared to ignore the American criticisms and anxieties. When it came to the point, Macmillan realised his mistake and pressed for withdrawal. The road backwards from Suez was much more difficult for Eden.

British diplomacy during these decades was dominated by three men. Churchill was the visionary, Bevin the strategist, Eden the tactician.

Bevin had his own techniques of diplomacy, but more often than not these did not work. We saw how the Middle East was made more unmoveable by his cack-handed ways and clumsy phrases. To this was added a regular flow of minor disasters, at conferences as well as in the media. Eden never made these kinds of errors. His successes were based on superb execution, attention to detail, patience and subtle negotiating skills. Indeed, by deploying these talents so effectively for most of his career, Eden established a reputation for Britain as the world's diplomat, entitled to stand at the high altars of arbitration in Geneva and New York.

Bevin, like Churchill, believed firmly in the importance of ideas and communicating them to the public. A.J.P. Taylor evoked this characteristic in a vivid phrase. Bevin's 'mind ran over with cock-eyed ideas, and his rambling talk, if taken down, could have gone alongside Hitler's Table Talk'. Attlee had a similar opinion. He later said that he had 'never met a man in politics with as much imagination as he had, with the exception of Winston'. But, unlike Churchill, Bevin did not allow any one idea to overwhelm the evidence. Churchill spotted this and thought it was a failing. He told the House of Commons in 1949 that while Bevin had had a decent record, he lacked an overarching vision. His foreign policy 'cannot be reconciled with any integral theme of thought. It has been swayed, and at times dominated, by his personal likes and dislikes, strengthened by pride and enforced by obstinacy.'[145]

Churchill's analysis was right; his judgement was wrong. In Britain today we now argue about the special relationship with America. Churchill was the main original author of the relationship; it was Bevin who turned it into a working institution. After the war, it became clear that Churchill's vision of an English-speaking alliance between Britain and America was largely a matter of inspiring rhetoric. Bevin followed the facts through a range of complicated alternatives before in the end fastening on and inventing the North Atlantic Alliance which still protects the UK today.

It was Bevin who perfected the practice of acting as a junior partner to the USA. Of course, Bevin was by instinct unhappy with the new role. He never lost that slightly patronising sense of superiority which Eden also felt about American policy in the Middle East. But once these instincts were out of the way, Bevin did what all good allies do best – he argued. At one of the lowest points in post-war Anglo-American relations, one of Truman's senior staff noted: 'Byrnes gave it as his opinion that we could not be in the position of doubting the good faith of Britain. He said he was confident that so long as Bevin was in his post as Foreign Minister there would be no possibility of such a break ... He said that Bevin had lived up completely and wholeheartedly to his agreements – he had debated vigorously and sometimes harshly before entering into them, but having once committed himself he would carry out his contracts to the full.' It was this attribute which led Attlee to claim later that Bevin's greatest contribution as Foreign Secretary was 'standing up to the Americans'. But Bevin's task was made easier by the receptive and enlightened leaders who then conducted American diplomacy. When things became more tense than normal, there was Lew Douglas, the American Ambassador in London, warning his superiors in Washington 'against jumping to the conclusion that there is something wrong simply because the British disagree with us'.[46]

The difference between the visionary, the tactician and the strategist hinges on the way each of them sees history. The visionary appreciates history but draws from it only those lessons he wants to see; the tactician has some sense of chronology, but no idea about wider themes; the strategist has a proper sense of history and allows this to guide his own views. A proper sense of history does not mean knowing every detail and date. It means understanding causes and appreciating their effects; it means looking at the past and drawing the right conclusions about war and peace, politics and power. Eden mishandled this process. He was too focused on the procedure of each event to appreciate the wider historical forces at play. When, as Prime Minister, he could no longer rely on tactics but was forced to make judgements about the world, he was unable to draw from history the right sense of perspective.

Bevin was not an educated man but he developed a thoughtful sense of history, partly by studying the lives and careers of his predecessors in the Foreign Office. Dean Acheson captured the respect Bevin felt for them in a glorious passage: 'He read their papers; he talked of them as slightly older people whom he knew with affectionate respect . . . He conferred a single title on them all. It was "old". "Last night," he said to me, "I was reading some papers of Old Salisbury. Y'know 'e had a lot of sense." "Old Palmerston" too came in for frequent and sometimes wistful mention.'[147] Bevin's understanding of strategy also came from drawing the right lessons from the history he had himself lived through. Fifteen years and a day after his speech in the Dome at Brighton, he addressed a Labour Party conference for the last time. He took as his theme the same question that he had debated in October 1935:

> Can you lay down your arms and be safe? China had no arms and Japan walked in, Abyssinia had no arms and Mussolini walked in . . . Czechoslovakia had no arms and a coup d'etat was carried out one evening and their liberty was gone. Inside that iron curtain now stretching from the Baltic to the Black Sea, there is no freedom. Do you want that to be extended? Would you sit down and let it be extended? I could not. I could not be a member of a party that decided that was their policy, and I do not believe you could either.[148]

Bevin had made a similar argument in 1935, but this time history came down on his side. Britain has never since flirted with the idea of total disarmament; for the most part, we have kept up that sense of scepticism which was absent from our planning between the wars.

Bevin had also discovered something else about international relations. He had come to understand that the context was changeable, but many of the questions stayed the same. That the basic principles of war and peace, progress and human nature could be transferred across different periods and settings. That by looking closely at what had gone on beforehand, you can develop a better sense of where you should be going. This is surely what Dean Acheson had in mind when he said many years later that Bevin could 'lead and learn at the same time'.[149]

EPILOGUE

'Out of the crooked timber of humanity no straight thing was
ever made'

Immanuel Kant,
Idea for a Universal History with a Cosmopolitan Purpose

Two hundred years ago Castlereagh and Canning fought their duel
on Putney Heath. This was a personal feud between ambitious men
jostling against each other for power. In 1809 their rivalry had little
to do with ideas; it was about character and competence. But over
the next decade the relationship between them changed. Castlereagh
and Canning learned to live together without fighting; but as one
difference faded another took its place. Both men became successful
Foreign Secretaries; both looked behind the flow of events for the
ideas which should underlie policy. They found different answers.
The difference between them survived Castlereagh's suicide and
Canning's death five years later. It is a difference which, while
finding different channels at different times, runs through the
century and a half of British foreign policy that we have described.

Those who consciously or not have followed Castlereagh have
believed in quiet negotiation, in compromise, in co-operation with
other countries. They worked for arrangements or alliances which
could span an ideological divide, for institutions which combine
rules and power to advance peace and stability. Those who followed
Canning prefer a noisier foreign policy, with an emphasis on independent British action and national prestige, a preference for liberal
causes across the world and a willingness to intervene, sometimes
by force, to help these causes prevail.

We have traced this argument in Britain, but it knows no boundaries. The same two sets of opinion have been arrayed against each
other across the Atlantic in all recent American presidencies. They
take a particularly American form, shaped by the geographical separation of the United States from the noisy cockpit of Europe, and

by the revolution which stamped on that separateness a novel quality. To all Americans, America is unique, but the direction which that uniqueness should take was and remains disputed. Was it the destiny of the United States to spread the American virtues of freedom and democracy around the world? Canning would have recognised that call; it became a leitmotif of Woodrow Wilson's Presidency and it was trumpeted loudly by the second President Bush. Or did destiny beckon in a direction which Castlereagh would have understood, to consolidate the West of the United States, to establish through the Monroe Doctrine a supervision of the whole American continent, then to enter the wider concert of nations and share the burden of governing the world? These themes were Castlereagh's, but the rough tone in which they were sometimes expressed, for example by Theodore Roosevelt, would have grated on him. Castlereagh would have preferred the deft touch of Kennan, the cool reckoning of Nixon and Kissinger.

The personalities and the contexts are different; but the same debate occurs naturally in countries with the background which we share. It is particularly clear during the moment – for Britain the nineteenth century; for the United States now – when those countries can make choices which move the whole world. Indeed, the British story has a peculiar relevance for America today. President Obama finds himself in a position roughly comparable to that of Britain under Lord Salisbury. The United States is no longer able to dominate international discussions and decisions as it did after the collapse of the Soviet Union in the early 1990s. None of the dangers confronting the United States can be overcome by the asset in which she is still unmatched, namely the massive use of military force. Her leadership is not openly challenged by a comparable rival, but she needs patience to be effective and has to be prepared to take the long view. This will require steady judgement, careful listening and a sense of history.

It would be easy but dangerous to overstretch the parallel. Events are wayward and there are no straight lines in history. Castlereagh and Canning would have both been baffled by the very different scene which confronted David Miliband. Governments sometimes drive, are more often driven by circumstances. Prime Ministers and Foreign Secretaries find themselves seeking shelter in places far removed from the haven where they would be. They feel compelled to act in ways contrary to the principles which they have preached. Thus Palmerston, the liberal interventionist, sat idle while the Poles were brutally suppressed and the Danes bullied out of Schleswig-Holstein. Aberdeen, who hated war, led his country into a harrowing and avoidable conflict in the Crimea. Austen Chamberlain, having brought Germany back into the community of nations in 1925, became after 1933 Germany's sternest critic. Eden, the glamorous young hero of the League of Nations, ended his career by launching an aggressive war.

Nevertheless, the underlying argument remained and mattered. Sometimes it flowed underground and then resurfaced. After Castlereagh and Canning there was an even deeper division between Palmerston and Aberdeen; the quarrel flared up to an almost comical extent between Disraeli and the 15th Earl of Derby. Salisbury anaesthetised the argument with his intelligent pragmatism; for about fifteen years with Lord Salisbury at the helm the nation did not feel much need for chart or compass. But after Salisbury, Grey found himself in a hostile world of confrontational alliances which Bismarck had invented and which could only be saved from disaster by someone with Bismarck's unscrupulous genius. There were no geniuses around in the first decade of the twentieth century.

The Vienna Settlement had, with many changes, lasted a century. The Versailles Settlement after the Great War survived for only twenty-five years. The two philosophies were jammed together but failed to coexist. For a few years after 1919 liberal ideas and international institutions seemed to gain the upper hand, supported by a public opinion sick of slaughter. Ramsay MacDonald had his short day. But in the background the old diplomacy continued. The United States decided it was not as idealistic as its President and abandoned the League. Britain and France had no real faith in this foundling child left on their doorstep. Austen Chamberlain worked for a synthesis and at Locarno earned his brief moment of sunshine, but this soon gave way to a new darkness.

The third settlement, after the Second World War, achieved the best reconciliation yet between rules and power. A whole range of institutions were constructed between 1945 and 1950 – the United Nations and its many agencies, the financial institutions agreed at

Bretton Woods, the trade system now embodied in the World Trade Organisation, and finally NATO. Unlike the League of Nations, these institutions were built realistically on the power structure of the day.

That was the settlement and these are the institutions under which we live today. There they stand, like palaces on a hill, more than half a century old, still impressive when seen from afar, and in the constant bustle of their activity measured in innumerable meetings. But as one gets closer one sees the crumbling pillars, cracked steps and gaping holes in the roof through which the water pours. The weather of sixty years has done its work; none of the institutions is fit for its present purpose. In 2008 and 2009 the financial institutions were most clearly defective. But the same is true of the institutions designed to ensure peace or justice and the protection of human rights. For one modern need, the mastering of climate change, no international institution yet exists; the only worry about the future of the planet in 1945 was the atom bomb.

Looking back, we can see the missed opportunity for a fourth settlement. When the Cold War ended in 1989 there was a sense of optimism and a period of wise American leadership under the first President Bush. This could have been the moment to replace or renew the palaces on the hill, strengthening sector by sector the rules by which even the powerful agree to be governed. But there seemed no need. The world was not in ruins, as before the first three settlements. To borrow a phrase from recent domestic British controversy, when the sun is shining it is tempting to forget about fixing the roof.

So the opportunity of 1989–90 was missed, and we are drifting. For the task of international renewal American leadership is essential, but the relative power of the United States has slipped away. The dangers besetting the world have multiplied; the world's response has become more feeble and incoherent. This inadequacy is concealed to some extent by suffocating clouds of rhetoric. In a media-driven world, speech is increasingly regarded by our leaders as a substitute for thought. The proofs lie around us, too many and depressing to bear listing. We can find them in trade and finance, in the degraded environment, in the handling of nuclear proliferation, in the misnamed 'war against terror'.

We take just one example where the fog of rhetoric is perhaps thickest. From the disasters of the early 1990s in Bosnia and in Rwanda there developed a strong urge to validate the right of the international community to intervene in the internal affairs of a nation in order to protect its people from the cruelty of their rulers. The United Nations in its millennium General Assembly accepted that the international community has not just a right but a responsibility to intervene in such cases. This responsibility included, though only as a last resort, the use of force. The provision of Article 51 of the Charter against intervention in the internal affairs of member states has been set aside, or at least redefined by the new 'responsibility to protect'. The three men most prominent in bringing about this change were Kofi Annan, then Secretary General of the UN, Bernard Kouchner of France, and Tony Blair in Britain.

As Prime Minister, Blair made a speech in Chicago in 1999 in which he eloquently and intelligently set out the doctrine of humanitarian intervention. In that speech he stressed that the facts of a situation have to be clear, that all measures short of force have failed, that proper authority has been obtained, and that the prospects of achieving a successful outcome by the use of force are sound. The thoughts in his speech could be traced back clearly to the medieval doctrine of the just war based on Aquinas. Unfortunately, when it came to the point in 2003, Blair flung the argument for humanitarian intervention into the pile of words he used to justify the Anglo-American attack on Iraq, once his original pretext about weapons of mass destruction began to collapse. Weapons or not, it was argued, Iraqis had to be rescued from a vile dictator. The conditions laid down in the Chicago speech were ignored; so were the facts about the likely Iraqi reaction to a foreign invasion. The result has been on the one hand 150,000 Iraqis killed and four million refugees; on the other hand the discrediting through misuse of the doctrine of humanitarian intervention.

There is another set of circumstances more poignant even than those we have faced in Iraq. It is possible to imagine a case in which all the conditions for successful intervention listed above are fulfilled, including the prospect of a successful outcome – but where by misfortune or mismanagement the enterprise turns out wrong. The case for intervention in Afghanistan was and remains very strong. But it has been weakened by adversity and by a failure to communicate effectively the limits of our ambition. In the absence of clear leadership we have allowed the spread of exaggerated and unrealistic ideas. Belatedly we are now correcting this mistake and stressing the link which existed from the beginning, between our effort in Afghanistan and our own security.

The lesson is hard but necessary. Intervention may be morally defensible, yet it can only be justified in practice if the facts are right. To be justified in practice the conditions outlined above have to be respected and the balance of likely consequences positive. This means that some acts of wickedness will go unchecked, and some wicked men go unpunished because the costs in human suffering of righting the wrong will be too great. There is no dodging this difficulty. You may call your standards universal, but they will never be universally applicable. The practitioner of an ethical foreign policy has to lay himself open to the charge of double standards. Sometimes attempting what is right would cause more suffering than already exists. In that case, doing what is right would in fact be wrong.

This is tough, but blame goes with the job. We cannot rescue Tibet from Chinese rule any more than we could rescue the people of Zimbabwe from President Mugabe. It seems unlikely that direct intervention will save the people of Darfur. But these facts should not hold us from intervention in places such as Sierra Leone or Kosovo or from struggling year after year to keep within bounds slaughter and suffering in the Democratic Republic of Congo. We should do good where we can, but not pretend that we can do good everywhere. Rhetoric, however sincere, which disregards the facts is a corrupter of policy.

Method remains important, and the rules of method have hardly altered. To listen as carefully as you speak; to speak from a background of knowledge; to study the character, the background and motives of those with whom you deal; to form your own judgement of your interlocutor rather than accept automatically the judgement of others; to practise courtesy and patience unless you decide that harsh words and impatience will help you to your objective; to store clearly in your mind your understanding, agreed when necessary with your colleagues, of what that objective is; to calculate how much of what in that objective you can abandon in discussion in order to achieve what is essential; to explain clearly and truthfully before and after your discussion what you have done and why – these are the rules of diplomacy, obvious yet often ignored, which have not changed since the days of Canning and Castlereagh.

We can go further without running into too much controversy. To meet an adversary or a bad ruler is usually an act not of surrender but of good sense. A handshake is not an absolution. Only by such contact is it possible to separate those who can be reconciled from those who cannot.

But good methods are not enough. Eden was a master of method, but Bevin was needed for the wider thinking. Both men missed what was happening in Europe, but it was Bevin who, after playing with illusory ideas about Africa, set Britain on its post-war path.

Should British foreign policy have a moral foundation? The question cannot be shirked, and the answer must be yes. Early in its time, the previous British Government muddied the debate by talking about an ethical foreign policy as if this was something they invented in 1997. One of us, when out of office, was solemnly asked by an interviewer what proportion of his time as Foreign Secretary he had spent on ethical foreign policy. This is a silly confusion; the debate is not about a compartment of policy but about the purpose of the whole. The mistakes of our leaders, their blindness in the face of uncomfortable facts, and the abundance of false rhetoric should not push us back into moral nihilism. We cannot force other countries into democracy, free speech, free trade or good government by bullets and missiles. It does not follow that these are ideas peculiar to ourselves in Britain or in the West, and that we have no right to encourage them where they do not exist. Each country will work out its own way; but it is a general good, as true in China and Africa as in Britain or the United States, that government is best when acceptable to and chosen by its people; that human beings should be able to express their views freely and lead their lives with minimum direction from the state; and that prosperity comes, not perfectly but least imperfectly, from the free exchange of goods and services. It would be a mistake to set up a formal league of countries which accept these principles, since this would pointlessly complicate dealings with the others. Instead of a League of Democracies, we need a new concert of nations, enshrined in a fourth settlement.

The search for the fourth settlement must be led by the President of the United States. We wrote this sentence more than two years ago. During that time President Obama has lost much of his popularity. Of course, he still has time to recover before he faces re-election, but the outlook for American leadership is dimmer than it was immediately after the election of 2008. Nevertheless, what we wrote holds true in the changed circumstances. There is, in practice, no substitute for American leadership if we are to create a better and more stable world. This remains true even if the margin of American superiority has been eroded at several points.

Of course, such leadership may not be forthcoming from the Americans. In that case we shall continue to muddle along as best we can. The outlook for the world is thus even more confused than when we began to write this book. The countries of the East have continued to gain ground. They have survived the economic downturn with smaller losses than those of the West. But we should beware of dogmatic prophecy. There is nothing inevitable about the eastern surge. China in particular faces formidable social and political problems which may well impose a pause on her progress. The same is true of India and other Asian countries.

We may possibly have to abandon the traditional idea that any one country is bound to emerge as a clear winner. Instead, we may have to reconcile ourselves to a prolonged uncertainty, during which power constantly shifts between the competitors. Such uncertainty is full of danger. As Europe found a century ago, the search for a balance of power can quickly become a quagmire. Indeed there is, in our view, a serious possibility that the confusion which baffled and nearly ruined Europe between 1900 and 1914 may be repeated, this time on a global scale, affecting and impeding the whole world.

The remedy is a new set of institutions which all countries accept and respect. These institutions must cover modern problems, such as climate change, which are at present running out of control. They must cope with ancient problems which have baffled us just as they baffled our grandparents and great grandparents. We need to rework and complete those imperfect codes of international behaviour, without which we shall totter from conflict to conflict.

If we have to live in a multipolar world with no clear leadership then we must establish the conditions which will make such a world tolerable. A world of nations without a superpower is safe only if we can devise a set of rules which are respected. We have to finish the work which Eden and Bevin began with others around 1945. Either the human race will be crushed by the sheer weight of these problems or we shall summon enough ingenuity and courage to overcome them together.

In the new circumstances, Britain can still be active and effective, as she was in making the earlier settlements we have described. But we will need to be clear in our minds about how we can make the most of our strength.

It is customary at this point to recite the conventional list of our assets – the quality of our Armed Forces, our diplomatic and Intelligence services, the achievements of our universities, our language, the financial skills of the City of London, and our Parliament. The integrity of these last two has recently been called into question, though we do not doubt that with time the damage can be repaired. All of these assets are and will remain important – but they are not the main source of our strength.

It is difficult to pin down where this strength comes from precisely, although there are clues in our history – the slow evolution of our representative institutions; the absence, unique in Europe, of a violent revolution in the last three centuries; the extraordinary displays of determination during the Napoleonic Wars and the Blitz. These were not the result of any specific technical or financial ability, still less the wise achievement of any particular leader or king. They were the sign of something strong and deep in our society – a set of values, shared but not oppressive, binding but not too tight, which drew people together in moments of danger and austerity, allowing them to weather the storm.

The values and character which helped to carry Britain through these dark episodes are well known to us all. We deny they exist but like to portray and watch them in films and sitcoms. The cliché, which critics dismiss as inhibition, is both important and true – in a crisis, we are resilient. After a tragedy, we come together. We are now beset and temporarily weakened by great storms of silliness but, despite the media, our eventual response to these scandals tends to be proportionate and reasonable. Most important of all, at

371

moments of despair or intense difficulty, our society has a habit of throwing forward new leaders – men and women who lift themselves out of the morass and put forward a generous and imaginative vision of a more decent and orderly world. No country is perfect, but our society can make us great.

So if we are to regain our influence, to punch above our weight in the world, we need to understand our past. The past has formed these assets which give us that extra potential for good. This does not mean indulging in nostalgia or pining for a golden age which never was. It means forming a clear view of our history and bringing to bear on present problems the best of that inheritance. If you added together in one mind the talents of Castlereagh and Canning, resolving their differences by an intelligent middle way, you would have devised a truly great, a superb Foreign Secretary. This Foreign Secretary, who never quite existed, should be the model of his successors today.

BIBLIOGRAPHY

Manuscripts and Archives
Birmingham University Special Collections

The Avon Private Papers
The Chamberlain Papers (microfilm reproductions at Yale University)

British Library

Aberdeen Papers

Hatfield House

Robert Arthur Talbot Gascoyne-Cecil, 3rd Marquess of Salisbury
Private Foreign Office Correspondence

Liverpool Record Office

Papers of Edward Stanley, 15th Earl of Derby

The National Archives, Kew

Foreign Office Papers: France, 1910–11, FO 800/52
Foreign Office Papers: Germany, 1906–9, FO 800/61
Foreign Office Papers: Germany, 1910–14, FO 800/62

Foreign Office Papers: Africa, 1946–50, FO 800/435
Foreign Office Papers: Commonwealth and Colonial Territories, 1947 48, FO 800/444
Foreign Office Papers: North Atlantic Pact, 1948–50, FO 800/483
Foreign Office Papers: Soviet Union, 1945–6, FO 800/501
Foreign Office Papers: USA, 1945, FO 800/512

Records of the Cabinet Office: CAB 129/23: CP (48) 6
Records of the Cabinet Office: CAB 128/12: CM (48) 2
Records of the Cabinet Office: *Cabinet Secretary's Notebook*: CAB 195/14

Ramsay MacDonald, *Diary*, PRO 30/69/1753/1

West Yorkshire Archives, Leeds

Harewood Mss: Canning Papers

Published Sources

Evelyn Ashley, *The Life and Correspondence of Henry John Temple, Viscount Palmerston*
(London: Richard Bentley and Son, 1879), 2 Vols

373

Kenneth Bourne, *The Foreign Policy of Victorian England, 1830–1902* (Oxford: Clarendon Press, 1970)

George Canning, *Select Speeches of the Right Honourable George Canning*, ed. R. Walsh (Philadelphia: Key & Biddle, 1835)

Hadley Cantril and Mildred Strunk, *Public Opinion: 1935–1945* (Princeton University Press, 1951)

Viscount Castlereagh, *Correspondence, Despatches, and other papers*, ed. C. Vane (London: William Shoberl, 1852), 12 Vols

Viscount Castlereagh, *The State of the nation, at the commencement of the year 1822* (London: J. Hatchard & Son, 1822)

Austen Chamberlain, *Down the Years* (London: Cassell & Company, 1935)

Carl von Clausewitz, *On War*, ed. and trans. Michael Howard and Peter Paret (Princeton University Press, 1989)

John Colville, *The Fringes of Power: Downing Street Diaries 1939–1955* (London: Weidenfeld & Nicolson, 2004)

Duff Cooper, *Diaries: 1915–1951*, ed. John Julius Norwich (London: Phoenix, 2006)

Viscount D'Abernon, *An Ambassador of Peace: Lord D'Abernon's Diary* (London: Hodder & Stoughton, 1929–30), 3 Vols

Anthony Eden, Earl of Avon, *Facing the Dictators* (London: Cassell, 1962)

Anthony Eden, Earl of Avon, *Full Circle* (London: Cassell, 1960)

Clarissa Eden, *A Memoir* (London: Weidenfeld & Nicolson, 2007)

Viscount Grey of Fallodon, *Twenty-Five Years: 1892–1916* (London: Hodder & Stoughton, 1925), 2 Vols

Hansard, *Parliamentary Debates*

David Lloyd George, *War Memoirs* (London: I. Nicholson & Watson, 1933–6), 6 Vols

Karl Marx, 'The Story of the Life of Lord Palmerston', in Lester Hutchinson (ed.), *The Secret Diplomatic History of the 19th Century and the Story of the Life of Lord Palmerston* (London: Lawrence & Wishart, 1969)

Harold Nicolson, *Diaries 1907–1963*, ed. Nigel Nicolson (London: Weidenfeld & Nicolson, 2004)

Charles Petrie, *The Life and Letters of the Right Hon. Sir Austen Chamberlain* (London: Cassell & Co., 1940), 2 Vols

Lord Salisbury, *Essays* (London: J. Murray, 1905)

Robert C. Self (ed.), *The Austen Chamberlain Diary Letters: Correspondence of Sir Austen Chamberlain with his sisters Hilda and Ida, 1916–37*, Camden Fifth Series, Vol. 5 (Cambridge University Press, 1995)

Evelyn Shuckburgh, *Descent to Suez: Diaries, 1951–56*, ed. John Charmley (London: Weidenfeld & Nicolson, 1986)

Edward Stanley, 15th Earl of Derby, *Diaries*, ed. John Vincent (London: Royal Historical Society, 1994)

Harold Temperley and Lillian Penson (eds), *Foundations of British Foreign Policy* (New York: Cass, 1966)

Harold Temperley and Lillian Penson (eds), *A Century of Diplomatic Blue Books, 1814–1914* (London: Cass, 1966)

United States Department of State, *Foreign Relations of the United States: The British Commonwealth; Europe*, Vol. 3 (1947)

Books and Articles

Sir Roderic Barclay, *Ernest Bevin and the Foreign Office* (London, 1975)

Gill Bennett, *'A most extraordinary and mysterious business'*: *The Zinoviev Letter of 1924*, FCO History Note No. 14 (London: FCO, 1999)

Leslie Bethell, 'George Canning and the Independence of Latin America', Bicentenary Lecture, Canning House, 15 April 1970 (London: Hispanic and Luso Brazilian Councils, 1970)

Robert Blake, *Disraeli* (London: Eyre and Spottiswoode, 1966)

Philip Bobbitt, *The Shield of Achilles: War, Peace and the Course of History* (London: Penguin, 2003)

David Brown and Miles Taylor (eds), *Palmerston Studies* (University of Southampton: Hartley Institute, 2007), 2 Vols

Alan Bullock, *The Life and Times of Ernest Bevin* (London: Heinemann, 1960–83), 3 Vols

James Cable, *The Geneva Conference of 1954 on Indochina* (Basingstoke: Macmillan, 2000)

Algernon Cecil, *British Foreign Secretaries 1807–1916: Studies in Personality and Policy* (London: G. Bell and Sons, 1927)

Lady Gwendolen Cecil, *Life of Robert, Marquis of Salisbury* (London: Hodder & Stoughton, 1921–32), 2 Vols

Muriel E. Chamberlain, *Lord Aberdeen: A Political Biography* (New York: Longman, 1983)

James Chambers, *Palmerston: 'The People's Darling'* (London: John Murray, 2004)

John Charmley, *Chamberlain and the Lost Peace* (Basingstoke: Papermac, 1991)

John Charmley, *Splendid Isolation?: Britain, the balance of power and the origins of the First World War* (London: Hodder & Stoughton, 1999)

Oxford Dictionary of National Biography (Oxford University Press)

Peter Dixon, *Canning: Politician and Statesman* (London: Weidenfeld & Nicolson, 1976)

David Dutton, *Austen Chamberlain: Gentleman in Politics* (Bolton: Ross Anderson Publications, 1985)

Niall Ferguson, *The Pity of War* (London: Penguin, 1999)

Foreign and Commonwealth Office, History Note No. 3, *Locarno 1925: Spirit, suite and treaties* (Revised Edition, August 2000)

John Lewis Gaddis, *The Cold War* (London: Allen Lane, 2006)

David Gilmour, *Curzon* (London: John Murray, 1994)

Ffion Hague, *The Pain and the Privilege: The Women in Lloyd George's Life* (London: HarperPress, 2008)

Neil Hart, *The Foreign Secretary* (Lavenham: Terence Dalton, 1987)

Richard Heller, 'East Fulham Revisited', in *Journal of Contemporary History*, Vol. 6, No. 3 (1971)

Peter Hennessy, *Having it so Good: Britain in the Fifties* (London: Penguin, 2007)

Holger Herwig and Richard Hamilton (eds), *The Origins of World War I* (Cambridge University Press, 2003)

Wendy Hinde, *George Canning* (London: Collins, 1973)

Wendy Hinde, *Castlereagh* (London: Collins, 1981)

Giles Hunt, *The Duel: Castlereagh, Canning and Deadly Canning Rivalry* (London: I.B. Tauris, 2008)

Douglas Hurd, *The Arrow War: An Anglo-Chinese Confusion, 1856–60* (London: Collins, 1967)

Douglas Hurd, *Robert Peel* (London: Weidenfeld & Nicolson, 2007)

H. Montgomery Hyde, *The Strange Death of Lord Castlereagh* (London: William Heinemann, 1959)

Lucille Iremonger, *Lord Aberdeen* (London: Collins, 1978)

Roy Jenkins, *Asquith* (London: Collins, 1978)

Wilbur Devereux Jones, 'The British Conservatives and the American Civil War', *American Historical Review*, Vol. 58, No. 3 (1953): 527–43

Paul Kennedy, 'The Tradition of Appeasement in British Foreign Policy 1865–1939', in *British Journal of International Studies*, Vol. 2 (1976)

John Kent, 'Bevin's Imperialism and the Idea of Euro-Africa, 1945–49', in Michael Dockrill and John W. Young, *British Foreign Policy: 1945–56* (Basingstoke: Macmillan, 1989)

William Keylor, *The Twentieth Century World: An International History* (New York: Oxford University Press, 1992)

Henry Kissinger, *A World Restored: Metternich, Castlereagh, and the Problems of Peace 1812–22* (Boston: Houghton Mifflin, 1957)

Ione Leigh, *Castlereagh* (London: Collins, 1951)

E. Phillip LeVeen, 'A Quantitative Analysis of the Impact of British Suppression Policies on the Volume of the Nineteenth Century Atlantic Slave Trade', in S.L. Engerman and E.D. Genovese (eds), *Race and Slavery in the Western Hemisphere: Quantitative Studies* (Princeton University Press, 1975)

Elizabeth Longford, *Victoria R.I.*, (London: Weidenfeld & Nicolson, 1964)

C.J. Lowe, *The Reluctant Imperialists: British foreign policy 1878–1902* (London: Routledge and K. Paul, 1967), 2 Vols

David Marquand, *Ramsay MacDonald* (London: Richard Cohen, 1997)

Edward S. Mihalkanin (ed.), *American Statesmen: Secretaries of State from John Jay to Colin Powell* (Westport, CT: Greenwood Press, 2004)

Austen Morgan, *Ramsay MacDonald* (Manchester University Press, 1987)

John Morley, *The Life of William Ewart Gladstone* (London: Macmillan, 1903), 3 Vols

Ferdinand Mount, *Umbrella – A Pacific Tale* (London: Heinemann, 1994)

William Mulligan, 'From Case to Narrative: The Marquess of Lansdowne, Sir Edward Grey, and the Threat from Germany, 1900–1906', in *International History Review*, 30:2 (2008), pp. 273–302

Thomas Munch-Petersen, *Defying Napoleon: How Britain Bombarded Copenhagen and Seized the Danish Fleet in 1807* (Stroud: Sutton Publishing, 2007)

T.G. Otte, '"Almost a law of nature"? Sir Edward Grey, the Foreign Office, and the Balance of Power in Europe, 1905–12', in *Diplomacy & Statecraft*, Vol. 14, Issue 2 (June 2003), pp. 77–118

Robert Pearce, 'Ernest Bevin', in *History Review*, 2002

Lillian Penson, 'The Principles and Methods of Lord Salisbury's Foreign Policy', in *Cambridge Historical Journal* (1935), pp. 87–106

Bradford Perkins, *Castlereagh and Adams: England and the United States, 1812–13* (Berkeley, California: University of California Press, 1964)

A.R. Peters, *Anthony Eden at the Foreign Office, 1931–1938* (Aldershot: Gower, 1986)

David Reynolds, 'Marshall Plan Commemorative Section: the European Response: Primacy of Politics', in *Foreign Affairs*, May/June 1997

Robert Rhodes James, *Anthony Eden* (London: Papermac, 1987)

Japer Ridley, *Lord Palmerston* (London: Constable, 1970)

Keith Robbins, *Sir Edward Grey: A biography of Lord Grey of Fallodon* (London: Cassell, 1971)

Andrew Roberts, *Salisbury: Victorian Titan* (London: Weidenfeld & Nicolson, 1999)

Ronald Robinson, John Gallagher, Alice Denny, *Africa and the Victorians: The official mind of imperialism* (London: Macmillan, 1961)

Lorenzo Sabine, *Notes on Duels and Duelling: Alphabetically Arranged with a Preliminary Historical Essay* (Boston: Crosby, Nichols, and Co., 1855)

Robert Shepherd, *A Class Divided: Appeasement and the Road to Munich 1938* (London: Macmillan, 1988)

Paul Smith (ed.), *Lord Salisbury on Politics: A selection from his articles in the Quarterly Review, 1860–1883* (Cambridge University Press, 1972)

David Steele, *Lord Salisbury: A Political Biography* (London: Routledge, 2001)

Zara Steiner, *The Foreign Office and Foreign Policy, 1898–1914* (London: Cambridge University Press, 1969)

A.J.P. Taylor, *The Origins of the Second World War* (London: Penguin Books, 1961)

A.J.P. Taylor, *The Struggle for Mastery in Europe: 1848–1918* (Oxford University Press, 1971)

Harold Temperley, *Life of Canning* (London: Greenwood, 1905)

Harold Temperley, *The Foreign Policy of Canning, 1822–27: England, the Neo-Holy Alliance, and the New World* (London: Cass, 1966)

D.R. Thorpe, *Eden: The Life and Times of Anthony Eden, first Earl of Avon, 1897–1977* (London: Chatto & Windus, 2003)

George Macaulay Trevelyan, *Grey of Fallodon* (London: Longmans, Green, 1937)

Sir Charles Webster, *The Foreign Policy of Castlereagh* (London: G. Bell, 1931–4), 2 Vols

Sir Charles Webster and Harold Temperley, 'The Duel between Castlereagh and Canning in 1809', in *Cambridge Historical Journal*, Vol. 3, No. 1 (1929), pp. 83–95

Peter Weiler, *Ernest Bevin* (Manchester University Press, 1993)

Francis Williams, *Ernest Bevin: Portrait of a Great Englishman* (London: Hutchinson, 1952)

Keith Wilson, *British Foreign Secretaries and Foreign Policy: from the Crimean War to the First World War* (London: Croom Helm, 1987)

Adam Zamoyski, *Rites of Peace: The Fall of Napoleon and the Congress of Vienna* (London: HarperCollins, 2007)

NOTES

Chapter 1: Castlereagh and Canning

A great mass of material, primary and secondary, exists about Castlereagh and Canning. We cite below those works which have provided us with particular references or facts. But it would be wrong to skirt over the great wealth of research into the lives of these two men without mentioning those scholars whose work has been a particular encouragement to us.

The biographies published thirty years ago by Wendy Hinde and Peter Dixon remain authoritative and hugely readable guides to Castlereagh and Canning. We have also benefited from an injection of new energy into the history of this period, supplied by Philip Bobbitt's *The Shield of Achilles*, Adam Zamoyski's *Rites of Peace* and Thomas Munch-Petersen's recent work on the bombardment of Copenhagen.

We are also extremely grateful to Lord Harewood for allowing us access to Canning's personal papers, and for making these papers available to us over the course of a comfortable and erudite weekend at Harewood House in June 2008.

[1] Ione Leigh, *Castlereagh* (London: Collins, 1951), pp. 213–14; Wendy Hinde, *George Canning* (London: Collins, 1973), p. 227; Wendy Hinde, *Castlereagh* (London: Collins, 1981), p. 166; Giles Hunt, *The Duel: Castlereagh, Canning and Deadly Canning Rivalry* (London: I.B. Tauris, 2008), pp. xi; 137–8; Lorenzo Sabine, *Notes on Duels and Duelling: Alphabetically Arranged with a Preliminary Historical Essay* (Boston: Crosby, Nichols, and Co., 1855), p. 83

[2] Leigh, *Castlereagh*, p. 18; C.K. Webster, *The Foreign Policy of Castlereagh*, 2 Vols (London: G. Bell, 1931–4), Vol. 1, p. 5

[3] Peter Dixon, *Canning: Politician and Statesman* (London: Weidenfeld & Nicolson, 1976), p. 6; Hinde, *Canning*, p. 23; Harold Temperley, *Life of Canning* (London: Greenwood, 1905), pp. 18; 23

[4] Temperley, *Canning*, pp. 18–26

[5] Leigh, *Castlereagh*, p. 38; Hinde, *Castlereagh*, pp. 27; 30

[6] Temperley, *Canning*, pp. 31; 44

[7] Hinde, *Castlereagh*, pp. 34–5; Carl von Clausewitz, *On War*, Vol. 8, Ch. 3

[8] Hinde, *Castlereagh*, p. 173

[9] Hinde, *Castlereagh*, pp. 69; 105; 71; 42

[10] G. Canning, *Select Speeches of the Right Honourable George Canning*, ed. R. Walsh (Philadelphia: Key & Biddle, 1835), p. 23

[11] West Yorkshire Archives, Leeds: *Harewood Mss: Canning Papers:* WYL250/8/22, Correspondence with Joan Canning, fol. 97: George Canning to Joan Canning, Wednesday 25 March 1807

[12] Canning, *Select Speeches*, pp. 23–37; Temperley, *Canning*, p. 85

[13] Temperley, *Canning*, pp. 81–2

[14] Temperley, *Canning*, p. 72, Thomas Munch-Petersen, *Defying Napoleon: How Britain Bombarded Copenhagen and Seized the Danish Fleet in 1807* (Stroud: Sutton Publishing, 2007) p. 130

[15] Munch-Petersen, *Defying Napoleon*, pp. 83–4

[16] *Canning Papers*: WYL250/8/44, Diplomatic Correspondence and Papers, 1807–1809

[17] Munch-Petersen, *Defying Napoleon*, p. 100

[18] Dixon, *Canning*, p. 111

[19] *Canning Papers*. WYL250/8/44, Castlereagh to Lord Cathcart, 19 July 1807

[20] For a lively and astute portrait of the Count D'Antraigues, read Munch-Petersen, *Defying Napoleon*, pp. 117–21

[21] Munch-Petersen, *Defying Napoleon*, p. 126; Dixon, *Canning*, p. 111

[22] Munch-Petersen, *Defying Napoleon*, pp. 131–3

[23] Munch-Petersen, *Defying Napoleon*, pp. 138–41

[24] *Canning Papers*: WYL250/8/22, fol. 104, George Canning to Joan Canning, Friday Morning, 31 July 1807

[25] *Canning Papers*: WYL250/8/22, fol. 107, George Canning to Joan Canning, Saturday 1 August 1807

[26] Munch-Petersen, *Defying Napoleon*, pp. 199–202

[27] Munch-Petersen, *Defying Napoleon*, pp. 111–12; Temperley, *Canning*, p. 77; Hinde, *Canning*, p. 188

[28] See Munch-Petersen, *Defying Napoleon*

[29] *Canning Papers*: WYL250/8/22, fol. 113, George Canning to Joan Canning, 26 August 1807; Dixon, *Canning*, pp. 114–15

[30] Temperley, *Canning*, p. 81

[31] Dixon, *Canning*, p. 113

[32] Hansard, *Parliamentary Debates*, Vol. 11: 15 June 1808, cols. 890–1; Harold Temperley and Lillian Penson (eds), *Foundations of British Foreign Policy* (New York: Cass & Co., 1966), pp. 22–4; Hinde, *Canning*, p. 195

[33] Hinde, *Castlereagh*, p. 155; Hinde, *Canning*, p. 205

[34] Hinde, *Canning*, p. 218; Temperley, *Canning*, p. 89

[35] Hinde, *Canning*, pp. 218–22

[36] Hinde, *Castlereagh*, pp. 161–3

[37] Hinde, *Canning*, pp. 222–4; Hinde, *Castlereagh*, pp. 161–3

[38] Hinde, *Canning*, pp. 225–6

[39] Hinde, *Castlereagh*, pp. 165–6

[40] Dixon, *Canning*, p. 136

[41] Leigh, *Castlereagh*, p. 213

[42] Dixon, *Canning*, pp. 136–40; Hinde, *Castlereagh*, p. 168

[43] Hinde, *Castlereagh*, p. 179

[44] Hinde, *Castlereagh*, p. 183

[45] Temperley, *Canning*, p. 112

[46] Hinde, *Castlereagh*, pp. 189–90

[47] Temperley, *Canning*, p. 130

[48] Viscount Castlereagh, *Correspondence, Despatches, and other papers*, ed. C. Vane,

12 Vols (London: William Shoberl, 1852), Vol. 9, p. 41

49 Castlereagh, *Correspondence*, Vol. 9, p. 41

50 Temperley and Penson (eds), *Foundations of British Foreign Policy*, pp. 10–21

51 Henry Kissinger, *A World Restored: Metternich, Castlereagh, and the Problems of Peace 1812–22* (Boston: Houghton Mifflin, 1957), p. 40

52 Temperley and Penson (eds), *Foundations of British Foreign Policy*, pp. 18–19

53 Temperley and Penson (eds), *Foundations of British Foreign Policy*, p. 34

54 Temperley and Penson (eds), *Foundations of British Foreign Policy*, p. 30

55 Hinde, *Castlereagh*, p. 198

56 Hinde, *Castlereagh*, p. 201; Adam Zamoyski, *Rites of Peace: The Fall of Napoleon and the Congress of Vienna* (London: HarperCollins, 2007), pp. 137–8

57 Hinde, *Castlereagh*, p. 202

58 Hinde, *Castlereagh*, pp. 204–5; Webster, *The Foreign Policy of Castlereagh*, Vol. 1, pp. 206–10

59 Webster, *The Foreign Policy of Castlereagh*, Vol. 1, p. 505

60 Hinde, *Castlereagh*, pp. 205–6; Webster, *The Foreign Policy of Castlereagh*, Vol. 1, pp. 212–13

61 Hinde, *Castlereagh*, pp. 205–9; Webster, *The Foreign Policy of Castlereagh*, Vol. 1, pp. 215–27

62 Philip Bobbitt, *The Shield of Achilles: War, Peace and the Course of History* (London: Penguin, 2003), p. 161

63 Webster, *The Foreign Policy of Castlereagh*, Vol. 1, p. 509

64 Hinde, *Castlereagh*, pp. 213–15

65 Webster, *The Foreign Policy of Castlereagh*, Vol. 1, pp. 268–9

66 Webster, *The Foreign Policy of Castlereagh*, Vol. 1, p. 543

67 Hinde, *Castlereagh*, pp. 216–17

68 Webster, *The Foreign Policy of Castlereagh*, Vol. 1, p. 413

69 Hinde, *Castlereagh*, p. 219

70 Hinde, *Castlereagh*, p. 220

71 Hinde, *Castlereagh*, p. 221; Zamoyski, *Rites of Peace*, pp. 344–5

72 Hinde, *Castlereagh*, p. 222

73 *Canning Papers*: WYL250/8/69, Canning to Liverpool, 16 February 1815

74 Hinde, *Castlereagh*, pp. 223–5

75 Webster, *The Foreign Policy of Castlereagh*, Vol. 1, p. 359

76 Zamoyski, *Rites of Peace*, p. 370

77 Zamoyski, *Rites of Peace*, pp. 392–3

78 Webster, *The Foreign Policy of Castlereagh*, Vol. 1, pp. 419; 423; 424; Hinde, *Castlereagh*, p. 229

79 Hinde, *Castlereagh*, pp. 230–1; Webster, *The Foreign Policy of Castlereagh*, Vol. 1, p. 444

80 *Canning Papers*: WYL250/8/98a, Castlereagh to Canning, 12 August 1815

81 Hinde, *Castlereagh*, pp. 231–3; Webster, *The Foreign Policy of Castlereagh*, Vol. 1, p. 473

82 Hinde, *Castlereagh*, p. 233

83 Hinde, *Castlereagh*, p. 234; Temperley and Penson (eds), *Foundations of British Foreign Policy*, pp. 36–7

84 Hinde, *Castlereagh*, p. 238

85 Hinde, *Castlereagh*, p. 242
86 Temperley, *Canning*, p. 128
87 Hinde, *Canning*, p. 276
88 Dixon, *Canning*, p. 212
89 Temperley, *Canning*, p. 137
90 Temperley, *Canning*, pp. 127; 137
91 Hinde, *Castlereagh*, p. 228
92 Temperley and Penson (eds), *Foundations of British Foreign Policy*, p. 45; Castlereagh, *Correspondence*, Vol. 12, pp. 48; 311–18
93 Castlereagh, *Correspondence*, Vol. 12, pp. 53–8
94 Castlereagh, *Correspondence*, Vol. 12, p. 63
95 Castlereagh, *Correspondence*, Vol. 12, pp. 75–6
96 Hinde, *Castlereagh*, pp. 249–50
97 Hinde, *Castlereagh*, pp. 253–5
98 Castlereagh, *Correspondence*, Vol. 12, pp. 239–40; H. Montgomery Hyde, *The Strange Death of Lord Castlereagh* (London: William Heinemann, 1959), p. 139
99 Temperley and Penson (eds), *Foundations of British Foreign Policy*, p. 54
100 Harold Temperley, *The Foreign Policy of Canning, 1822–27: England, the Neo-Holy Alliance, and the New World* (London: Frank Cass & Co., 1966), p. 45
101 Hinde, *Castlereagh*, p. 259
102 Hyde, *The Strange Death of Lord Castlereagh*
103 Temperley, *Canning*, pp. 144; 146
104 Hinde, *Castlereagh*, pp. 264; 271
105 Castlereagh, *Correspondence*, Vol. 12, pp. 403–20
106 Castlereagh, *Correspondence*, Vol. 12, pp. 443–6
107 Viscount Castlereagh, *The State of the nation, at the commencement of the year 1822* (London: J. Hatchard & Son, 1822), pp. 87; 129–30
108 For more on this, see the close medical analysis in Giles Hunt's recent book, *The Duel*.
109 These passages draw on the detailed and careful detective work carried out by H. Montgomery Hyde in his remarkable essay, *The Strange Death of Lord Castlereagh* – especially pp. 5; 29; 46; 51; 51–75; 96. Also see Hinde, *Castlereagh*, pp. 277–81 for a clear account of Castlereagh's nervy last days, and Temperley, *Canning*, p. 149 for Metternich's quote.
110 Hinde, *Canning*, pp. 320–1; 324; Dixon, *Canning*, pp. 209; 211
111 Temperley, *The Foreign Policy of Canning*, p. 27
112 Temperley, *The Foreign Policy of Canning*, p. 86
113 Temperley and Penson (eds), *Foundations of British Foreign Policy*, p. 65; Canning Papers, WYL250/8/106: Canning to Bathurst, 7 December 1825
114 Castlereagh, *Correspondence*, Vol. 12, pp. 66–9; 90–1
115 Hinde, *Canning*, p. 350
116 Temperley, *The Foreign Policy of Canning*, pp. 70–6
117 Hinde, *Canning* pp. 352–3; Bradford Perkins, *Castlereagh and Adams: England and the United States, 1812–13* (Berkeley, California: University of California Press, 1964), pp. 305–6; Temperley, *The Foreign Policy of Canning*, pp. 124–5
118 Hinde, *Canning*, p. 353; Temperley, *The Foreign Policy of Canning*, p. 130
119 Hinde, *Canning*, p. 355

[120] Dixon, *Canning*, pp. 229; 232
[121] Dixon, *Canning*, pp. 234–5; Hinde, *Canning*, pp. 362–3
[122] Dixon, *Canning*, p. 233
[123] Hansard, *Parliamentary Debates*, Vol. 16: 12 December 1826, cols 396–8
[124] Leslie Bethell, 'George Canning and the Independence of Latin America', Bicentenary Lecture, Canning House, 15 April 1970 (London: Hispanic and Luso Brazilian Councils, 1970), pp. 8–9; Temperley and Penson (eds), *Foundations of British Foreign Policy*, p. 67
[125] Hinde, *Canning*, pp. 406–7; Dixon, *Canning*, pp. 242–3
[126] Canning Papers, WYL250/8/106: Canning to Bathurst, 7 December 1825
[127] Hinde, *Canning*, p. 409
[128] Hinde, *Canning*, p. 380
[129] Hansard, *Parliamentary Debates*, Vol. 16: 11 December 1826, col. 335; 12 December 1826, cols 367–9
[130] Stephen M. Lee, 'Palmerston and Canning', in David Brown and Miles Taylor (eds), *Palmerston Studies I* (University of Southampton: Hartley Institute, 2007), p. 9; Hinde, *Canning*, p. 423
[131] Hunt, *The Duel*, p. 172
[132] Hinde, *Canning*, p. 462; Hunt, *The Duel*, p. 177

Chapter 2: Aberdeen and Palmerston

Several good books are written about Palmerston every decade, but Aberdeen has faded from the historical scene; he is remembered vaguely, either as a feeble leader or mild catastrophe.

Two writers in particular have done their best to rescue Aberdeen from this oblivion – the historian Muriel Chamberlain and the novelist Ferdy Mount. Chamberlain's biography and Mount's novel, *Umbrella*, are best read consecutively, late at night, and accompanied by a good whisky.

Both Foreign Secretaries were brought alive for us in one file at the British Library. Volume 43,069 of the Aberdeen Papers contains the chain of searching and deeply thoughtful correspondence between Aberdeen and Palmerston in the run-up to the Crimean War. We are grateful to the British Library for allowing us access to it and the ensuing volume of correspondence between Gladstone and Aberdeen.

[1] *Aberdeen Papers*, British Library, Add. Mss 43,338: f. 122: Aberdeen to Lady Maria Hamilton, 22 October 1813
[2] *Aberdeen Papers*, Add. Mss 43,338: 122: Aberdeen to Lady Maria, 22 October 1813
[3] Muriel E. Chamberlain, *Lord Aberdeen: A Political Biography* (New York: Longman, 1983), p. 92
[4] Chamberlain, *Aberdeen*, p. 158
[5] Chamberlain, *Aberdeen*, p. 108
[6] Chamberlain, *Aberdeen*, pp. 106–9
[7] Kenneth Bourne, *The Foreign Policy of Victorian England, 1830–1902* (Oxford: Clarendon Press, 1970), p. 266
[8] *Aberdeen Papers*, Add. Mss 43,338; Chamberlain, *Aberdeen*, pp. 140; 139
[9] Chamberlain, *Aberdeen*, p. 131

[10] Chamberlain, *Aberdeen*, p. 167

[11] Chamberlain, *Aberdeen*, p. 8

[12] *Aberdeen Papers*, Add. Mss 43,338: f. 125: 30 October 1813

[13] Chamberlain, *Aberdeen*, pp. 175; 181

[14] Chamberlain, *Aberdeen*, p. 22

[15] Evelyn Ashley, *The Life and Correspondence of Henry John Temple, Viscount Palmerston* (London: Richard Bentley and Son, 1879), Vol. 1, pp. 5–6

[16] Neil Hart, *The Foreign Secretary* (Lavenham: Terence Dalton, 1987), p. 70

[17] Japer Ridley, *Lord Palmerston* (London: Constable, 1970), p. 117

[18] Karl Marx, 'The Story of the Life of Lord Palmerston', in Lester Hutchinson (ed.), *The Secret Diplomatic History of the 19th Century and the Story of the Life of Lord Palmerston* (London: Lawrence & Wishart, 1969), p. 167; Ridley, *Palmerston*, p. 519

[19] Bourne, *The Foreign Policy of Victorian England*, p. 251; Ridley, *Palmerston*, pp. 336; 153

[20] Chamberlain, *Aberdeen*, p. 404

[21] Stephen M. Lee, 'Palmerston and Canning', in David Brown and Miles Taylor (eds), *Palmerston Studies I* (University of Southampton: Hartley Institute, 2007), p. 13

[22] Bourne, *The Foreign Policy of Victorian England*, p. 298

[23] *Aberdeen Papers*, Add. Mss 43,070: ff. 341–3, Aberdeen to Gladstone, 11 December 1856

[24] Chamberlain, *Aberdeen*, p. 399

[25] Ridley, *Palmerston*, p. 590

[26] Ridley, *Palmerston*, p. 111

[27] Ashley, *Life and Correspondence of Viscount Palmerston*, Vol. 1, pp. 136–7

[28] Ashley, *Life and Correspondence of Viscount Palmerston*, Vol. 1, pp. 174–5

[29] Ridley, *Palmerston*, pp. 100–1

[30] Ridley, *Palmerston*, pp. 102–3

[31] Chamberlain, *Aberdeen*, pp. 260–1

[32] Ridley, *Palmerston*, p. 154

[33] Ridley, *Palmerston*, pp. 108–9

[34] Ridley, *Palmerston*, p. 156

[35] Chamberlain, *Aberdeen*, p. 272

[36] Ridley, *Palmerston*, pp. 196–7

[37] Bourne, *The Foreign Policy of Victorian England*, p. 34; Ridley, *Palmerston*, pp. 174–5

[38] E.P. LeVeen, 'A Quantitative Analysis of the Impact of British Suppression Policies on the Volume of the Nineteenth Century Atlantic Slave Trade', in S.L. Engerman and E.D. Genovese (eds), *Race and Slavery in the Western Hemisphere: Quantitative Studies* (Princeton University Press, 1975), pp. 51–81

[39] Ridley, *Palmerston*, p. 276

[40] James Chambers, *Palmerston: 'The People's Darling'* (London: John Murray, 2004), p. 159

[41] Bourne, *The Foreign Policy of Victorian England*, p. 255

[42] Ridley, *Palmerston*, p. 275

[43] Ridley, *Palmerston*, p. 248

44 Ridley, *Palmerston*, p. 255

45 Ridley, *Palmerston*, p. 257

46 Chamberlain, *Aberdeen*, p. 304

47 Chamberlain, *Aberdeen*, p. 339

48 Douglas Hurd, *Robert Peel* (London: Weidenfeld & Nicolson, 2007), p. 281

49 *Aberdeen Papers*, Add. Mss 43,070: ff. 144–5, Aberdeen to Gladstone, 27 December 1844

50 Chamberlain, *Aberdeen*, p. 386

51 Bourne, *The Foreign Policy of Victorian England*, p. 257; Ridley, *Palmerston*, p. 290

52 Bourne, *The Foreign Policy of Victorian England*, pp. 262–3

53 Bourne, *The Foreign Policy of Victorian England*, p. 292

54 Chambers, *Palmerston*, p. 255

55 Bourne, *The Foreign Policy of Victorian England*, p. 293

56 Bourne, *The Foreign Policy of Victorian England*, p. 298

57 Chamberlain, *Aberdeen*, p. 401

58 Ridley, *Palmerston*, p. 381

59 Hansard, *Parliamentary Debates*, Third Series, Vol. 111: 17 June, cols 1361–2; Ridley, *Palmerston*, p. 384

60 Ridley, *Palmerston*, p. 386; Hansard, *Parliamentary Debates*, Third Series, Vol. 112: 25 June, cols 413–14

61 Hansard, *Parliamentary Debates*, Vol. 112: 27 June, cols 583–7

62 Hansard, *Parliamentary Debates*, Vol. 112: 28 June; Hurd, *Peel*, Ch. 18

63 Chamberlain, *Aberdeen*, p. 410

64 Chambers, *Palmerston*, p. 178; Ridley, *Palmerston* p. 393

65 Bourne, *The Foreign Policy of Victorian England*, p. 316

66 These can be found at the British Library in the *Aberdeen Papers*, Add. Mss 43,069

67 *Aberdeen Papers*, Add. Mss 43,069: ff. 75–6, Palmerston to Aberdeen, 4 July 1853

68 *Aberdeen Papers*, Add. Mss 43,069: ff. 78–9, Aberdeen to Palmerston, 4 July 1853

69 *Aberdeen Papers*, Add. Mss 43,069: ff. 81–3, Memorandum by Lord Palmerston (12 July 1853)

70 *Aberdeen Papers*, Add. Mss 43,069: ff. 85–6, Memorandum by Lord Aberdeen on the Eastern Question, in answer to Lord Palmerston's Memorandum (13 July 1853)

71 *Aberdeen Papers*, Add. Mss 43,069: ff. 87–8, Palmerston to Aberdeen, 15 July 1853; *Aberdeen Papers*, Add. Mss 43,069: f. 90, Aberdeen to Palmerston, 15 July 1853

72 Chamberlain, *Aberdeen*, p. 502; *Aberdeen Papers*, Add. Mss 43,070: ff. 372–5, Gladstone to Aberdeen, 12 August 1853

73 *Aberdeen Papers*, Add. Mss 43,069: ff. 122–3, Palmerston to Aberdeen, 7 October 1853

74 *Aberdeen Papers*, Add. Mss 43,069: Aberdeen to Palmerston, 7 October 1853

75 *Aberdeen Papers*, Add. Mss 43,069: f. 143, Aberdeen to Palmerston, 31 October 1853

76 *Aberdeen Papers*, Add. Mss 43,069: ff. 144–9, Palmerston to Aberdeen, 1 November 1853

77 *Aberdeen Papers*, Add. Mss 43,069: ff. 151–4; 161–3, Aberdeen to Palmerston, 4 November 1853 (draft copy); 6 November 1853 (final version)

78 *Aberdeen Papers*, Add. Mss 43,069: ff. 168–72, Palmerston to Aberdeen, 10

December 1853; *Aberdeen Papers*, Add. Mss 43,069: ff. 180–1, Aberdeen to Palmerston, 13 December 1853

79 *Aberdeen Papers*, Add. Mss 43,069: ff. 189–90, Palmerston to Aberdeen, 23 December 1853

80 *Aberdeen Papers*, Add. Mss 43,069: f. 195, Aberdeen to Palmerston, 24 December 1853

81 Ridley, *Palmerston*, pp. 434–6; 438

82 *Aberdeen Papers*, Add. Mss 43,070: ff. 221–3, Gladstone to Aberdeen, 10 February 1855

83 *Aberdeen Papers*, Add. Mss 43,070: ff. 262–3

84 *Aberdeen Papers*, Add. Mss 43,070: ff. 333–4, Aberdeen to Gladstone, 5 December 1856; ff.341–3, Aberdeen to Gladstone, 11 December 1856

85 Chamberlain, *Aberdeen*, p. 527; Lucille Iremonger, *Lord Aberdeen* (London: Collins, 1978), p. 325; Ferdinand Mount, *Umbrella* (London: Heinemann, 1994), p. 194

86 Ridley, *Palmerston*, pp. 427; 467

87 Bourne, *The Foreign Policy of Victorian England*, p. 364

88 W.D. Jones, 'The British Conservatives and the American Civil War' in *American Historical Review*, Vol. 58, No. 3 (1953), pp. 532–3

89 Ridley, *Palmerston*, p. 569

90 Ridley, *Palmerston*, p. 217

91 Bourne, *The Foreign Policy of Victorian England*, pp. 377–9

92 Chambers, *Palmerston*, pp. 499–500

93 Ridley, *Palmerston*, p. 583; Chambers, *Palmerston*, p. 503

94 Bourne, *The Foreign Policy of Victorian England*, pp. 83; 369; 110

Chapter 3: Derby (and Disraeli)

Like his father, the 14th Earl, Edward Stanley, the 15th Earl has become almost a forgotten figure in British politics. That he has not entirely disappeared is due to the extraordinary and careful efforts made by Professor John Vincent in editing his diaries, and more recently by John Charmley and his academic followers at the University of East Anglia. These scholars have restored Derby to his proper place in the history of British conservatism and foreign policy. We have learned much from them.

We are also extremely grateful for the support we received from the present Lord Derby as we pursued this project, and also for the assistance we received from the staff of Liverpool's Record Office, who opened up for us a range of letters exchanged between Derby and Disraeli in the crucial years of 1874 and 1878.

1 Robert Blake, *Disraeli* (London: Eyre and Spottiswoode, 1966), p. 523

2 Bourne, *The Foreign Policy of Victorian England*, p. 403

3 Blake, *Disraeli*, p. 575

4 *Oxford Dictionary of National Biography:* Edward Stanley, 15th Earl of Derby, p. 2 of entry

5 Edward Stanley, 15th Earl of Derby, *Diaries*, ed. John Vincent (London: Royal Historical Society, 1994), Vol. 4, p. 6

6 Derby, *Diaries*, Vol. 4, p. 13

[7] Derby, *Diaries*, Vol. 4, p. 423

[8] Derby, *Diaries*, Vol. 4, p. 384

[9] Derby, *Diaries*, Vol. 4, p. 369

[10] Bourne, *The Foreign Policy of Victorian England*, p. 85

[11] Derby, *Diaries*, Vol. 4, p. 269

[12] Derby, *Diaries*, Vol. 4, p. 15

[13] Derby, *Diaries*, Vol. 4, p. 427

[14] Lady Gwendolen Cecil, *Life of Robert, Marquis of Salisbury* (London: Hodder & Stoughton, 1921–32), Vol. 2, p. 114

[15] Bourne, *The Foreign Policy of Victorian England*, p. 189

[16] Derby, *Diaries*, Vol. 4, p. 257

[17] Derby, *Diaries*, Vol. 4, p. 259

[18] Derby, *Diaries*, Vol. 4, p. 290

[19] Blake, *Disraeli*, p. 578

[20] Derby, *Diaries*, Vol. 4, pp. 269–79

[21] John Charmley, *Splendid Isolation?: Britain, the balance of power and the origins of the First World War* (London: Hodder & Stoughton, 1999), p. 24

[22] A.J.P. Taylor, *The Struggle for Mastery in Europe: 1848–1918* (Oxford University Press, 1971), p. 236

[23] Derby, *Diaries*, Vol. 4, p. 297

[24] Blake, *Disraeli*, p. 565

[25] Derby, *Diaries*, Vol. 4, p. 306

[26] Derby, *Diaries*, Vol. 4, p. 309

[27] Blake, *Disraeli*, p. 593

[28] Harold Temperley and Lillian Penson (eds), *A Century of Diplomatic Blue Books, 1814–1914* (London: Cass, 1966), p. 252

[29] Blake, *Disraeli*, p. 602

[30] Derby, *Diaries*, Vol. 4, p. 328

[31] Derby, *Diaries*, Vol. 4, p. 311

[32] Derby, *Diaries*, Vol. 4, p. 317

[33] Derby, *Diaries*, Vol. 4, pp. 326; 332

[34] Derby, *Diaries*, Vol. 4, p. 337

[35] Charmley, *Splendid Isolation*, p. 55

[36] Derby, *Diaries*, Vol. 4, p. 751

[37] Liverpool Record Office: *Papers of Edward Stanley, 15th Earl of Derby*, 920 Der (15) 17/2/3

[38] Andrew Roberts, *Salisbury: Victorian Titan* (London: Weidenfeld & Nicolson, 1999), p. 131

[39] Cecil, *Life of Salisbury*, Vol. 2, p. 95

[40] Derby, *Diaries*, Vol. 4, p. 841

[41] Derby, *Diaries*, Vol. 4, p. 345

[42] Blake, *Disraeli*, p. 616

[43] Liverpool Record Office: *Papers of Edward Stanley, 15th Earl of Derby*, Salisbury to Derby, 26 December 1876

[44] Cecil, *Life of Salisbury*, Vol. 2, p. 120

[45] Keith Wilson, *British Foreign Secretaries and Foreign Policy: from the Crimean War to the First World War* (London: Croom Helm, 1987), p. 18

46 Cecil, *Life of Salisbury*, Vol. 2, p. 122

47 Liverpool Record Office: *Papers of Edward Stanley, 15th Earl of Derby*, 920 Der (15) 17/2/3

48 Derby, *Diaries*, Vol. 4, p. 369

49 Derby, *Diaries*, Vol. 4, p. 369

50 Derby, *Diaries*, Vol. 4, p. 392

51 Derby, *Diaries*, Vol. 4, p. 392

52 Derby, *Diaries*, Vol. 4, p. 394

53 Liverpool Record Office: *Papers of Edward Stanley, 15th Earl of Derby*, 920 Der (15) 17/2/3, Derby to Beaconsfield, 24 May 1877

54 Bourne, *The Foreign Policy of Victorian England*, p. 408

55 Liverpool Record Office: *Papers of Edward Stanley, 15th Earl of Derby*, Der (15)

56 Derby, *Diaries*, Vol. 4, p. 432

57 Blake, *Disraeli*, p. 622

58 Derby, *Diaries*, Vol. 4, p. 452

59 Derby, *Diaries*, Vol. 4, p. 452

60 Liverpool Record Office: *Papers of Edward Stanley, 15th Earl of Derby*, Derby to Beaconsfield, 22 December 1877

61 Derby, *Diaries*, Vol. 4, p. 470

62 Blake, *Disraeli*, p. 676

63 Derby, *Diaries*, Vol. 4, p. 493

64 Derby, *Diaries*, Vol. 4, p. 25

65 Derby, *Diaries*, Vol. 4, p. 461

66 Derby, *Diaries*, Vol. 4, p. 505

67 Derby, *Diaries*, Vol. 4, p. 533

Chapter 4: Salisbury

Salisbury used to complain that his diplomats used maps with too small a scale. Students of Salisbury can easily make a similar mistake. A mass of primary material exists about the man and his career; over-zealous researchers risk being distracted by minor episodes and missing the big picture of this cool, detached, complicated man. We were warned against these errors by the work done by Andrew Roberts and Lady Gwendolen Cecil in their biographies. The present Lord Salisbury and the staff of Hatfield House were also particularly helpful and generous in granting us access to the key Foreign Office papers at Salisbury's ancestral estate.

1 Roberts, *Salisbury*, p. 91

2 Bourne, *The Foreign Policy of Victorian England*, p. 412

3 *Hatfield Papers*, FO Private, Vol. 1: 3 and 4

4 *Hatfield Papers*, FO Private, Vol. 3: 1 and 9

5 Cecil, *Life of Salisbury*, Vol. 2, p. 247

6 Lillian Penson, 'The Principles and Methods of Lord Salisbury's Foreign Policy', in *Cambridge Historical Journal* (1935), p. 87

7 Cecil, *Life of Salisbury*, Vol. 2, p. 287

8 Roberts, *Salisbury*, p. 204

9 Taylor, *Struggle for Mastery*, p. 258

[10] *Oxford Dictionary of National Biography:* Robert Cecil, 3rd Marquess of Salisbury, p. 1

[11] *Dictionary of National Biography:* Salisbury, p. 1

[12] Roberts, *Salisbury*, pp. 23–4

[13] Blake, *Disraeli*, p. 624

[14] Roberts, *Salisbury*, p. 489

[15] Lord Salisbury, *Essays* (London: J. Murray, 1905), pp. 182–231

[16] Salisbury, *Essays*, p. 12

[17] Temperley and Penson (eds), *Foundations of British Foreign Policy*, pp. 519–20

[18] Paul Smith (ed.), *Lord Salisbury on Politics: A selection from his articles in the Quarterly Review, 1860–1883* (Cambridge University Press, 1972), p. 101

[19] Penson, 'The Principles and Methods of Lord Salisbury's Foreign Policy', p. 87

[20] David Steele, *Lord Salisbury: A Political Biography* (London: Routledge, 2001), p. 244

[21] Roberts, *Salisbury*, p. 488

[22] C.J. Lowe, *The Reluctant Imperialists: British foreign policy 1878–1902* (London: Routledge & K. Paul, 1967), p. 236

[23] Roberts, *Salisbury*, p. 606

[24] Roberts, *Salisbury*, p. 741

[25] Steele, *Salisbury*, p. 104

[26] Taylor, *Struggle for Mastery*, p. 315

[27] *Hatfield Papers*, FO Private, Vol. 9, 27/12/29

[28] Lowe, *The Reluctant Imperialists*, p. 250

[29] Roberts, *Salisbury*, p. 224

[30] Cecil, *Life of Salisbury*, Vol. 2, p. 130: Salisbury to Lytton, 9/3/1877

[31] Roberts, *Salisbury*, p. 400

[32] Roberts, *Salisbury*, p. 646

[33] Lowe, *The Reluctant Imperialists*, pp. 20; 32

[34] Taylor, *Struggle for Mastery*, p. 290

[35] Ronald Robinson, John Gallagher, Alice Denny, *Africa and the Victorians: The official mind of imperialism* (London: Macmillan, 1961), p. 280

[36] Roberts, *Salisbury*, p. 400

[37] Bourne, *The Foreign Policy of Victorian England*, p. 426

[38] Roberts, *Salisbury*, p. 513

[39] Elizabeth Longford, *Victoria R.I.* (London: Weidenfeld & Nicolson, 1964), pp. 493–4

[40] Cecil, *Life of Salisbury*, Vol. 1, p. 153

[41] Roberts, *Salisbury*, pp. 539–40

[42] Lowe, *The Reluctant Imperialists*, Vol. 2, p. 82

[43] Lowe, *The Reluctant Imperialists*, Vol. 2, p. 76

[44] Steele, *Salisbury*, pp. 331 et seq.

[45] *Hatfield Papers*, FO Private, America 1895–8 A/139, pp. 13, 1333

[46] *Hatfield Papers*, FO Private, America 1895–8, 107, 148

[47] Roberts, *Salisbury*, p. 692

[48] John Morley, *The Life of William Ewart Gladstone* (London: Macmillan, 1903), Vol. 3, p. 522

[49] Lowe, *The Reluctant Imperialists*, Vol. 2, p. 104

50 Bourne, *The Foreign Policy of Victorian England*, pp. 430–1

51 Roberts, *Salisbury*, p. 610

52 Roberts, *Salisbury*, p. 608

53 Lowe, *The Reluctant Imperialists*, Vol. 2, p. 105

54 Lowe, *The Reluctant Imperialists*, Vol. 2, p. 108

55 Roberts, *Salisbury*, p. 829

56 Lowe, *The Reluctant Imperialists*, Vol. 2, p. 137

57 Steele, *Salisbury*, p. 326

58 Robinson, Gallagher, Denny, *Africa and the Victorians*, p. 296

59 Robinson, Gallagher, Denny, *Africa and the Victorians*, p. 303

60 Lowe, *The Reluctant Imperialists*, p. 140

61 Taylor, *Struggle for Mastery*, p. 320

62 Lowe, *The Reluctant Imperialists*, Vol. 2, p. 112

63 Steele, *Salisbury*, p. 345

64 Roberts, *Salisbury*, p. 697

65 *Hatfield Papers*, Vol. 119 (31)

66 Roberts, *Salisbury*, pp. 532–4

67 Roberts, *Salisbury*, p. 622

68 *Hatfield Papers*, Colonial Office, A/92

69 Roberts, *Salisbury*, p. 623

70 Roberts, *Salisbury*, p. 687

71 *Hatfield Papers*, Colonial Office, 154, 159

72 Roberts, *Salisbury*, p. 732

73 Bourne, *The Foreign Policy of Victorian England*, pp. 461–2

74 Roberts, *Salisbury*, p. 726

75 Roberts, *Salisbury*, p. 743

76 Roberts, *Salisbury*, p. 746

77 Roberts, *Salisbury*, p. 776

78 Roberts, *Salisbury*, p. 765

79 *Hatfield Papers*, Colonial Office, Chamberlain 1896–7, p. 117

80 Bourne, *The Foreign Policy of Victorian England*, pp. 453–4

81 *Hatfield Papers*, Colonial Office, Chamberlain 1898–9, p. 123

82 Bourne, *The Foreign Policy of Victorian England*, p. 455

83 Bourne, *The Foreign Policy of Victorian England*, p. 457

84 Bourne, *The Foreign Policy of Victorian England*, p. 477

Chapter 5: Grey

The fateful period leading up to the outbreak of war in 1914 has been studied in more detail and produced more argument than almost any other period in British history. In recent years the verdict has again swung away from Grey and towards the idea that Britain should have stayed out of the war on the Continent. This argument will go on for ever and the subject will always attract attention. But the judgements will depend less on new discoveries than on an author's own attitudes to peace and war.

1 Keith Robbins, *Sir Edward Grey: A biography of Lord Grey of Fallodon* (London: Cassell, 1971), p. 22

[2] Robbins, *Grey*, p. 17

[3] Robbins, *Grey*, p. 72

[4] Bourne, *The Foreign Policy of Victorian England*, p. 180

[5] Robbins, *Grey*, pp. 5–8; 130

[6] T.G. Otte, '"Almost a law of nature"? Sir Edward Grey, the Foreign Office, and the Balance of Power in Europe, 1905–12', in *Diplomacy & Statecraft*, Vol. 14, Issue 2 (June 2003), p. 80

[7] Otte, '"Almost a law of nature"?', p. 88

[8] Otte, '"Almost a law of nature"?', p. 82

[9] Taylor, *Struggle for Mastery*, p. 428

[10] Otte, '"Almost a law of nature"?', p. 82

[11] The National Archives, Kew: *Foreign Office Papers: Germany, 1906–9*, FO 800/61, ff. 12–15, E. Grey to Sir Frank Lascelles, 1 January 1906

[12] Otte, '"Almost a law of nature"?', p. 86

[13] Taylor, *Struggle for Mastery*, p. 437

[14] Viscount Grey of Fallodon, *Twenty-Five Years: 1892–1916* (London: Hodder & Stoughton, 1925), Vol. 1, pp. 127–9

[15] Otte, '"Almost a law of nature"?', p. 81

[16] William Mulligan, 'From Case to Narrative: The Marquess of Lansdowne, Sir Edward Grey, and the Threat from Germany, 1900–1906', in *International History Review*, 30:2 (2008), p. 237

[17] Bourne, *The Foreign Policy of Victorian England*, p. 482

[18] Robbins, *Grey*, p. 238

[19] Hart, *The Foreign Secretary*, pp. 110–11

[20] Bourne, *The Foreign Policy of Victorian England*, pp. 478–9

[21] Robbins, *Grey*, p. 175

[22] Niall Ferguson, *The Pity of War* (London: Penguin, 1999), p. 71

[23] *Foreign Office Papers: Germany, 1910–14*, FO 800/62, f. 270

[24] *Foreign Office Papers: Germany, 1910–14*, FO 800/62, f. 89, Grey to Nicolson, 22 October 1910

[25] *Foreign Office Papers: Germany, 1910–14*, FO 800/62, f. 305, Grey to Goschen, 9 December 1908

[26] *Foreign Office Papers: Germany, 1910–14*, FO 800/62, ff. 219–20, Grey to Lascelles, 22 February 1908

[27] David Gilmour, *Curzon* (London: John Murray, 1994), p. 377

[28] Zara Steiner, *The Foreign Office and Foreign Policy, 1898–1914* (London: Cambridge University Press, 1969), p. 121 et seq.

[29] Otte, '"Almost a law of nature"?', p. 104

[30] Robbins, *Grey*, p. 242

[31] *Foreign Office Papers: France, 1910–11*, FO 800/52/370, Grey to Sir F. Bertie, 8 November 1908

[32] *Foreign Office Papers: France, 1910–11*, FO 800/52/208, Grey to Bertie, 10 April 1904

[33] Robbins, *Grey*, p. 243

[34] Ffion Hague, *The Pain and the Privilege: The Women in Lloyd George's Life* (London: HarperPress, 2008), p. 255

[35] Taylor, *Struggle for Mastery*, p. 521

36 William Keylor, *The Twentieth Century World: An International History* (New York: Oxford University Press, 1992), p. 50

37 Steiner, *Foreign Office*, p. 162

38 Roy Jenkins, *Asquith* (London: Collins, 1978), p. 329

39 Grey, *Twenty-Five Years*, Vol. 2, p. 14

40 Grey, *Twenty-Five Years*, Vol. 2, p. 70

41 Grey, *Twenty-Five Years*, Vol. 2, p. 306

42 Robbins, *Grey*, p. 370

43 David Lloyd George, *War Memoirs* (London: I. Nicholson & Watson, 1933–6), Vol. 1, pp. 89–99

44 Taylor, *Struggle for Mastery*, p. 525

45 Ferguson, *Pity of War*, p. 165

46 Ferguson, *Pity of War*, p. 152

47 Lloyd George, *War Memoirs*, Vol. 1, p. 57

48 Hall, *The Foreign Secretary*, p. 136

49 George Macaulay Trevelyan, *Grey of Fallodon* (London: Longmans, Green, 1937), p. vi

Chapter 6: Ramsay MacDonald and Austen Chamberlain

David Marquand's comprehensive biography is the compulsory starting place for any student of Ramsay MacDonald. We paid close attention to his scholarship and also to his epistolary advice. Through his work, we discovered MacDonald's Diary at the National Archives at Kew. This was a great source of treasure, although a note on the front cover cautioned us against excessive use: the jottings were 'meant as notes to guide and revive memory' rather than a strict account of events.

There is no set reading list for people who want to learn about Austen Chamberlain. David Dutton's 1985 biography was an isolated companion in our research. Instead, we launched ourselves with the help of Birmingham University Special Collections at the wealth of primary material held in the Chamberlain archive – in particular, Austen's letters to his sisters and the documents surrounding the run-up to Locarno.

1 The National Archives, Kew: Ramsay MacDonald, *Diary*, PRO 30/69/1753/1/180

2 David Marquand, *Ramsay MacDonald* (London: Richard Cohen, 1997), p. 297

3 Viscount D'Abernon, *An Ambassador of Peace: Lord D'Abernon's Diary* (London: Hodder & Stoughton, 1929–30), Vol. 3, p. 29

4 Hankey, *Memoirs*, p. 353

5 Austen Morgan, *Ramsay MacDonald* (Manchester University Press, 1987), pp. 6; 7

6 Marquand, *MacDonald*, p. 185

7 Marquand, *MacDonald*, pp. 203–5

8 MacDonald, *Diary*, PRO 30/69/1753/1/128, 19 January 1925

9 Marquand, *MacDonald*, p. 333

10 MacDonald, *Diary*, PRO 30/69/1753/1/188–9

11 MacDonald, *Diary*, PRO 30/69/1753/1/189, 23 July 1924

12 MacDonald, *Diary*, PRO 30/69/1753/1/189, 2 August 1924

13 MacDonald, *Diary*, PRO 30/69/1753/1/180, 3 February 1924

14 Marquand, *MacDonald*, p. 341

[15] MacDonald, *Diary*, PRO 30/69/1753/1/190, 5 August 1924

[16] *D'Abernon's Diary*, Vol. 3, p. 90

[17] Marquand, *MacDonald*, p. 349

[18] Marquand, *MacDonald*, p. 351

[19] A.J.P. Taylor, *The Origins of the Second World War* (London: Penguin Books, 1961), p. 79

[20] MacDonald, *Diary*, PRO 30/69/1753/1/186, 1 July 1924

[21] This account is based on the excellent study carried out in 1999 by Gill Bennett, Chief Historian of the Foreign and Commonwealth Office – '*A most extraordinary and mysterious business': The Zinoviev Letter of 1924*, FCO History Note No.14 (London: FCO, 1999)

[22] FCO History Note, *The Zinoviev Letter*, p. 73

[23] FCO History Note, *The Zinoviev Letter*, p. 54

[24] *The Chamberlain Papers* (Birmingham University Special Collections/Microfilm Reproductions at Yale University), AC5/1/329: Austen to Hilda, 9 November 1924

[25] David Dutton, *Austen Chamberlain: Gentleman in Politics* (Bolton: Ross Anderson Publications, 1985), p. 156

[26] Robert C. Self (ed.), *The Austen Chamberlain Diary Letters: Correspondence of Sir Austen Chamberlain with his sisters Hilda and Ida, 1916–37*, Camden Fifth Series, Vol. 5 (Cambridge University Press, 1995), p. 5

[27] *Austen Chamberlain Diary Letters*, pp. 3–4

[28] *Austen Chamberlain Diary Letters*, pp. 5; 12

[29] Dutton, *Austen Chamberlain*, p. 6

[30] *Chamberlain Papers*, AC5/1/329: Austen to Hilda, 9 November 1924

[31] Dutton, *Austen Chamberlain*, p. 91

[32] *Austen Chamberlain Diary Letters*, p. 288

[33] Dutton, *Austen Chamberlain*, p. 2

[34] Dutton, *Austen Chamberlain*, p. 154

[35] Charles Petrie, *The Life and Letters of the Right Hon. Sir Austen Chamberlain* (London: Cassell & Company, 1940), Vol. 2, pp. 144; 309; 243; *Chamberlain Papers*, AC5/1/340: Austen to Ida, 6 September 1924

[36] Petrie, *The Life and Letters of Austen Chamberlain*, Vol. 2, pp. 154–5; 246

[37] Dutton, *Austen Chamberlain*, p. 236

[38] *Austen Chamberlain Diary Letters*, p. 326

[39] Dutton, *Austen Chamberlain*, p. 239

[40] Dutton, *Austen Chamberlain*, p. 241

[41] Petrie, *The Life and Letters of Austen Chamberlain*, Vol. 2, p. 261 (n)

[42] Prime Minister Tony Blair, Speech to the US Congress, 17 July 2003, available at http://news.bbc.co.uk/1/hi/uk_politics/3076253.stm

[43] *Austen Chamberlain Diary Letters*, p. 265; Neil Hart, *The Foreign Secretary* (Lavenham: Terence Dalton, 1987), p. 154

[44] Austen Chamberlain, *Down the Years* (London: Cassell & Company, 1935), pp. 43–4

[45] Dutton, *Austen Chamberlain*, pp. 238–9; 241; 243; *Austen Chamberlain Diary Letters*, p. 267

[46] Petrie, *The Life and Letters of Austen Chamberlain*, Vol. 2, p. 261

[47] Dutton, *Austen Chamberlain*, p. 244

48 Petrie, *The Life and Letters of Austen Chamberlain*, Vol. 2, p. 265
49 Petrie, *The Life and Letters of Austen Chamberlain*, Vol. 2, p. 269
50 Dutton, *Austen Chamberlain*, p. 252
51 *Austen Chamberlain Diary Letter*, pp. 267–9
52 *Austen Chamberlain Diary Letters*, p. 268
53 Chamberlain, *Down the Years*, p. 184; Foreign and Commonwealth Office, History Note No. 3, *Locarno 1925: Spirit, suite and treaties* (Revised Edition, August 2000), p. 30
54 *D'Abernon's Diary*, Vol. 3, p. 23
55 *Chamberlain Papers*, AC 5/1/362–3: Austen to Hilda, 16 August 1925
56 Dutton, *Austen Chamberlain*, p. 247
57 *Chamberlain Papers*, AC 5/1/357: Austen to Ida, 27 June 1925
58 *Chamberlain Papers*, AC 5/1/362–3: Austen to Hilda, 16 August 1925
59 *Chamberlain Papers*, AC 5/1/347: Austen to Ida, 1 March 1925
60 *Chamberlain Papers*, AC 5/1/350: Austen to Ida, 19 April 1925
61 *Chamberlain Papers*, AC 5/1/352: Austen to Ida, 3 May 1925
62 *Chamberlain Papers*, AC 5/1/362–3: Austen to Hilda, 16 August 1925; AC 5/1/357: Austen to Ida, 27 June 1925
63 *Chamberlain Papers*, AC 38/1/1: HMG, *Proceedings of the Locarno Conference*, October 1925: Part 1, 'Correspondence leading up to the Conference', No. 35: Mr Austen Chamberlain to Lord D'Abernon (Berlin), 26 September 1925
64 Austen Chamberlain to Lord D'Abernon, 30 September 1925, as published in FCO, *Locarno 1925: Spirit, suite and treaties*, Annex
65 Austen Chamberlain to Sir William Tyrrell, 11 October 1925, as published in FCO, *Locarno 1925: Spirit, suite and treaties*, Annex
66 *Chamberlain Papers*, AC 38/1/1: HMG, *Proceedings of the Locarno Conference*, October 1925: Part 2, 'Proceedings of the Conference', No. 176; No. 187: Mr Austen Chamberlain to Sir W. Tyrrell, 16 Oct 1925 (telegraphic)
67 FCO, *Locarno 1925: Spirit, suite and treaties*, p. 18
68 Chamberlain, *Down the Years*, pp. 174–5
69 *Chamberlain Papers*, AC 38/1/1: HMG, *Proceedings of the Locarno Conference*, October 1925: Part 2, 'Proceedings of the Conference', No. 121: Memorandum of an Interview granted by Mr Austen Chamberlain to British Press Representatives, 9 October 1925
70 Petrie, *The Life and Letters of Austen Chamberlain*, Vol. 2, p. 295
71 Austen Chamberlain to Sir William Tyrrell; Sir William Tyrrell to Austen Chamberlain, 16 October 1925, as published in FCO, *Locarno 1925: Spirit, suite and treaties*, Annex
72 *Chamberlain Papers*, AC 38/1/1: HMG, *Proceedings of the Locarno Conference*, October 1925: Part 1, 'Correspondence leading up to the Conference', No. 4: Memorandum by Mr Austen Chamberlain, Geneva, 11 September 1925, of a Conversation with M. Skrzynski on 9 September
73 Petrie, *The Life and Letters of Austen Chamberlain*, Vol. 2, pp. 238–9
74 Chamberlain, *Down the Years*, pp. 167–8
75 Petrie, *The Life and Letters of Austen Chamberlain*, Vol. 2, p. 290
76 *Austen Chamberlain Diary Letters*, p. 282
77 *Chamberlain Papers*, AC 38/1/1: HMG, *Proceedings of the Locarno Conference*,

October 1925: Part 2, 'Proceedings of the Conference', No. 200: Speech by Austen Chamberlain in the House of Commons, 18 November 1925

78 *Austen Chamberlain Diary Letters*, p. 285

79 Petrie, *The Life and Letters of Austen Chamberlain*, Vol. 2, p. 293

80 Austen Chamberlain to Sir Eric Drummond, 16 October 1925, as published in FCO, History Note No. 3, *Locarno 1925: Spirit, suite and treaties* (Revised Edition, August 2000), Annex

81 Dutton, *Austen Chamberlain*, p. 230

82 FCO, *Locarno 1925: Spirit, suite and treaties*, p. 9

83 *Austen Chamberlain Diary Letters*, p. 293

84 *Austen Chamberlain Diary Letters*, p. 309

85 *Austen Chamberlain Diary Letters*, p. 128

86 Dutton, *Austen Chamberlain*, pp. 277–8

87 *Austen Chamberlain Diary Letters*, p. 313

88 Dutton, *Austen Chamberlain*, p. 281; *Austen Chamberlain Diary Letters*, p. 327

89 Petrie, *The Life and Letters of Austen Chamberlain*, Vol. 2, pp. 373–7

90 Morgan, *Ramsay MacDonald*, p. 119

91 *Austen Chamberlain Diary Letters*, p. 480; Dutton, *Austen Chamberlain*, pp. 304–5

92 Petrie, *The Life and Letters of Austen Chamberlain*, Vol. 2, pp. 391–2

93 *Chamberlain Papers*, AC40/4/14: Austen Chamberlain to E.H. Canning, 17 April 1933

94 *Chamberlain Papers*, AC40/4/1–67

95 *Chamberlain Papers*, AC40/4/7: Anon to Austen Chamberlain, 15 April 1933

96 Dutton, *Austen Chamberlain*, p. 309; *Austen Chamberlain Diary Letters*, p. 482

97 *Chamberlain Papers*, AC40/6/12: Austen Chamberlain to W. Selby, 27 February 1934

98 Dutton, *Austen Chamberlain*, p. 301

99 Dutton, *Austen Chamberlain*, p. 322

100 *Austen Chamberlain Diary Letters*, pp. 14 (fn73); 488

101 Paul Kennedy, 'The Tradition of Appeasement in British Foreign Policy 1865–1939', in *British Journal of International Studies*, Vol. 2 (1976): 195; 205

102 *D'Abernon's Diary*, Vol. 3, p. 175, 10 July 1925

Chapter 7: Bevin and Eden

We are grateful to the Countess of Avon for allowing us access to Anthony Eden's papers in Birmingham University, and for her encouragement and insights into our project.

Alan Bullock's three enormous volumes on Ernest Bevin contain almost everything there is to know about this unlikely but epic Foreign Secretary. But the full drama of Bevin's career would be incomplete without reference to his support for Montgomery's African scheme. We are grateful to Ted Bromund for pointing us towards the work carried out by John Kent in this area and in turn to John Kent's article for steering us towards the relevant files at Kew.

1 Francis Williams, *Ernest Bevin: Portrait of a Great Englishman* (London: Hutchinson, 1952), p. 193

[2] Peter Weiler, *Ernest Bevin* (Manchester University Press, 1993), p. 88; Robert Shepherd, *A Class Divided: Appeasement and the Road to Munich, 1938* (London: Macmillan, 1988), p. 47; Alan Bullock, *The Life and Times of Ernest Bevin* (London: Heinemann, 1960–83) Vol. 1, p. 565

[3] Richard Heller, 'East Fulham Revisited' in *Journal of Contemporary History*, Vol. 6, No. 3 (1971), p. 172

[4] Williams, *Bevin*, p. 192; Bullock, *Bevin*, Vol. 1, p. 567

[5] Shepherd, *A Class Divided*, p. 49

[6] Williams, *Bevin*, p. 193

[7] Bullock, *Bevin*, Vol. 1, pp. 566; 569

[8] Williams, *Bevin*, p. 196

[9] Bullock, *Bevin*, Vol. 1, p. 570

[10] Anthony Eden, Earl of Avon, *Facing the Dictators* (London: Cassell, 1962), p. 548

[11] Eden, *Facing the Dictators*, p. 349

[12] *The Avon Private Papers* (Birmingham University Special Collections), AP 20/6/8

[13] Eden, *Facing the Dictators*, p. 582

[14] John Charmley, *Chamberlain and the Lost Peace* (Basingstoke: Papermac, 1991), p. 49

[15] Robert Rhodes James, *Anthony Eden* (London: Papermac, 1987), p. 193; Eden, *Facing the Dictators*, p. 584

[16] *Avon Papers*, AP 13/1/64F

[17] *Avon Papers*, AP 13/1/64F; D.R. Thorpe, *Eden: The Life and Times of Anthony Eden, first Earl of Avon, 1897–1977* (London: Chatto & Windus, 2003), p. 217; Eden, *Facing the Dictators*, p. 599; Harold Nicolson, *Diaries 1907–1963*, ed. Nigel Nicolson (London: Weidenfeld & Nicolson, 2004), p. 160

[18] Thorpe, *Eden*, p. 19

[19] Thorpe, *Eden*, p. 37

[20] Eden, *Facing the Dictators*, p. 4

[21] Eden, *Facing the Dictators*, p. 4

[22] Bullock, *Bevin*, Vol. 1, pp. 2–16

[23] Weiler, *Bevin*, pp. 27–8; Robert Pearce, 'Ernest Bevin', in *History Review*, 2002

[24] Weiler, *Bevin*, p. 20; Bullock, *Bevin*, Vol. 1, p. 134

[25] Bullock, *Bevin*, Vol. 1, pp. 135–8

[26] Bullock, *Bevin*, Vol. 1, p. 139

[27] Weiler, *Bevin*, p. 96

[28] Bullock, *Bevin*, Vol. 3, p. 106

[29] Bullock, *Bevin*, Vol. 3, pp. 97–8

[30] Weiler, *Bevin*, p. 75

[31] A.R. Peters, *Anthony Eden at the Foreign Office, 1931–1938* (Aldershot: Gower, 1986), p. 22

[32] Peters, *Eden*, p. 57

[33] Thorpe, *Eden*, p. 108

[34] Eden, *Facing the Dictators*, p. 318

[35] Eden, *Facing the Dictators*, p. 220

[36] Thorpe, *Eden*, p. 128

[37] Rhodes James, *Eden*, pp. 135–6

[38] Thorpe, *Eden*, p. 41

[39] Thorpe, *Eden*, pp. 132–3

[40] Eden, *Facing the Dictators*, p. 296

[41] Eden, *Facing the Dictators*, p. 309

[42] Eden, *Facing the Dictators*, p. 366

[43] Peters, *Eden*, p. 195

[44] Weiler, *Bevin*, p. 94

[45] *Avon Papers*, AP 20/5/17

[46] *Avon Papers*, AP 20/5/11 (September 1937)

[47] Eden, *Facing the Dictators*, p. 547

[48] *Avon Papers*, 13/1/58N

[49] *Avon Papers*, AP/20/17/124

[50] Shepherd, *A Class Divided*, p. 1

[51] *Oxford Dictionary of National Biography:* Ernest Bevin

[52] Thorpe, *Eden*, p. 303

[53] Bullock, *Bevin*, Vol. 3, p. 19

[54] Thorpe, *Eden*, p. 303

[55] Thorpe, *Eden*, p. 314

[56] Records of these confidential opinion polls can be found in the US Office of War Information records in the American National Archives at College Park, Maryland – in particular, RG 59: General Records of the Department of State: Office of Public Opinion Studies: 1943–1975, *Special Reports on Public Attitudes Toward Foreign Policy, 1943–65*

[57] Bullock, *Bevin*, Vol. 3, pp. 25; 288

[58] Pearce, 'Ernest Bevin'

[59] Bullock, *Bevin*, Vol. 3, p. 69

[60] Bullock, *Bevin*, Vol. 3, p. 838

[61] Hansard Parliamentary Debates, Fifth Series, Vol. 413, House of Commons, Session 1945–6, 20 August 1945, cc. 312–13

[62] Weiler, Bevin, pp. 145–7

[63] Bullock, *Bevin*, Vol. 3, pp. 82; 97

[64] Duff Cooper, *Diaries: 1915–1951*, ed. John Julius Norwich (London: Phoenix, 2006), pp. 384; 389

[65] Bullock, *Bevin*, Vol. 3, p. 75

[66] *Foreign Office Papers: Soviet Union, 1945–6*, FO 800/501: Top Secret Note of conversation between Bevin and Molotov, 23 September 1945

[67] Bullock, *Bevin*, Vol. 3, p. 121

[68] *Foreign Office Papers: USA, 1945*, FO 800/512: Telegram No. 6444: Halifax to FO, 26 September 1945

[69] Bullock, *Bevin*, Vol. 3, p. 202

[70] Bullock, *Bevin*, Vol. 3, pp. 202–5

[71] *Foreign Office Papers: USA, 1945*, FO 800/512: Ernest Bevin to Sir Stafford Cripps, 20 September 1945

[72] *Foreign Office Papers: USA, 1945*, FO 800/512: Winston Churchill to Ernest Bevin, 13 November 1945

[73] *Foreign Office Papers: USA, 1945*, FO 800/512: Ernest Bevin to Winston Churchill, 17 November 1945

74 Hansard, Fifth Series, Vol. 416, House of Commons, Session 1945–6, 22 November 1945, c. 611

75 Bullock, *Bevin*, Vol. 3, pp. 184; 198

76 Bullock, *Bevin*, Vol. 3, pp. 184–5; 352

77 Bullock, *Bevin*, Vol. 3, p. 198; Hansard, Fifth Series, Vol. 416, House of Commons, Session 1945–6, 22 November 1945, cc. 612–613; 23 November 1945, cc. 784; 785; 786

78 Bullock, *Bevin*, Vol. 3, p. 193

79 Hansard, Fifth Series, Vol. 416, House of Commons, Session 1945–6, 23 November 1945, c. 777

80 Bullock, *Bevin*, Vol. 3, p. 172

81 *Foreign Office Papers: USA, 1945*, FO 800/512: Ernest Bevin to Sir Stafford Cripps, 20 September 1945

82 Bullock, *Bevin*, Vol. 3, p. 178

83 Bullock, *Bevin*, Vol. 3, pp. 179; 181

84 Hansard, Fifth Series, Vol. 426, House of Commons, Session 1945–6, 1 August 1946, cc. 1255; 1253

85 Bullock, *Bevin*, Vol. 3, p. 189

86 Bullock, *Bevin*, Vol. 3, p. 209

87 Bullock, *Bevin*, Vol. 3, p. 211

88 Bullock, *Bevin*, Vol. 3, pp. 220; 311; 282; 495

89 David Reynolds, 'Marshall Plan Commemorative Section: the European Response: Primacy of Politics', in *Foreign Affairs*, May/June 1997

90 Weiler, *Bevin*, p. 160

91 Edward S. Mihalkanin (ed.), *American Statesmen: Secretaries of State from John Jay to Colin Powell* (Westport, CT: Greenwood Press, 2004), p. 93

92 Bevin led the field with 27 per cent support, followed by Eden on 18 and then came Churchill on 13 per cent. See Hadley Cantril and Mildred Strunk, *Public Opinion: 1935–1945* (Princeton University Press, 1951), p. 280

93 Bullock, *Bevin*, Vol. 3, p. 74

94 Bullock, *Bevin*, Vol. 3, p. 88

95 Bullock, *Bevin*, Vol. 3, pp. 340; 353

96 Bullock, *Bevin*, Vol. 3, p. 361

97 Bullock, *Bevin*, Vol. 3, p. 379

98 Bullock, *Bevin*, Vol. 3, p. 402

99 PPS/1: 'Policy with Respect to American Aid to Western Europe', as published in United States Department of State, *Foreign Relations of the United States: The British Commonwealth; Europe*, Vol. 3 (1947), pp. 223–40

100 Bullock, *Bevin*, Vol. 3, pp. 405–6

101 Bullock, *Bevin*, Vol. 3, p. 409

102 Bullock, *Bevin*, Vol. 3, p. 422

103 Duff Cooper, *Diaries*, pp. 442–3

104 Bullock, *Bevin*, Vol. 3, p. 449

105 John Kent, 'Bevin's Imperialism and the Idea of Euro Africa, 1945–49', in Michael Dockrill and John W. Young, *British Foreign Policy: 1945–56* (Basingstoke: Macmillan, 1989), p. 60

106 *Foreign Office Papers: North Atlantic Pact, 1948–50*, FO 800/483: Confidential Note

of meeting between Ernest Bevin and Mr Hamilton Fish Armstrong, 1 June 1948

[107] Kent, 'Bevin's Imperialism', p. 50; Weiler, *Bevin*, p. 176; Bullock, *Bevin*, Vol. 3, p. 488

[108] Bullock, *Bevin*, Vol. 3, p. 659

[109] Kent, 'Bevin's Imperialism', p. 55

[110] Kent, 'Bevin's Imperialism', p. 66

[111] *Foreign Office Papers: Africa, 1946–50*, FO 800/435: f. 10: Montgomery of Alamein to Ernest Bevin, 19 December 1947

[112] *Foreign Office Papers: Africa, 1946–50*, FO 800/435: ff. 11–88: Field Marshal The Viscount Montgomery of Alamein, Chief of the Imperial General Staff, 'Highly Confidential and Top Secret Memorandum, Tour in Africa in Nov/Dec 1947'

[113] *Foreign Office Papers: Africa, 1946–50*, FO 800/435: f. 89: Ernest Bevin to the Prime Minister, 22 December 1947

[114] *Foreign Office Papers: Africa, 1946–50*, FO 800/435: Africa, 1946–50: ff. 97–114: Memorandum by the Secretary of State for the Colonies (undated) ff. 97–114

[115] *Foreign Office Papers: Africa, 1946–50*, FO 800/435: f. 115: Note by F.K. Roberts to Sir O Sargent, Mr Wright, the Egyptian Dept, Mr Hayter, 10 January 1948

[116] *Records of the Cabinet Office:* CAB 129/23: CP (48) 6: Memorandum by the Secretary of State for Foreign Affairs, 'The First Aim of British Foreign Policy', 4 January 1948

[117] *Records of the Cabinet Office:* CAB 128/12: CM (48) 2, 8 January 1948

[118] Bullock, *Bevin*, Vol. 3, pp. 529–30

[119] Bullock, *Bevin*, Vol. 3, p. 610

[120] Hansard, Fifth Series, Vol. 464, House of Commons, Session 1948–9, 12 May 1949, cols 2015–16

[121] Bullock, *Bevin*, Vol. 3, pp. 612; 777; 799

[122] *Cabinet Office Papers:* CAB 129/37: CP(49)208: 18 October 1949: 'European Policy'; Memorandum by the Secretary of State for Foreign Affairs

[123] Bullock, *Bevin*, Vol. 3, pp. 764; 90

[124] Bullock, *Bevin*, Vol. 3, p. 780

[125] Bullock, *Bevin*, Vol. 3, p. 776

[126] Bullock, *Bevin*, Vol. 3, pp. 768; 757

[127] Bullock, *Bevin*, Vol. 3, pp. 883–4

[128] Peter Hennessy, *Having it so Good: Britain in the Fifties* (London: Penguin, 2007), pp. 38–9

[129] *Records of the Cabinet Office: Cabinet Secretary's Notebook: CAB 195/14*, taken from CM 34 (55): Cabinet Meeting held on 4 October 1955 – available at http://www.nationalarchives.gov.uk/releases/2008/may/foreign.htm

[130] Thorpe, *Eden*, p. 367

[131] Thorpe, *Eden*, p. 368

[132] Eden, *Facing the Dictators*, p. 547

[133] Rhodes James, *Eden*, pp. 364–5

[134] Hennessy, *Having it so Good*, pp. 346–8

[135] John Colville, *The Fringes of Power: Downing Street Diaries 1939–1955* (London: Weidenfeld & Nicolson, 2004), p. 700

[136] Colville, *The Fringes of Power*, p. 700

[137] Colville, *The Fringes of Power*, p. 707

[138] Rhodes James, *Eden*, p. 358

[139] We are grateful to Lady de Zulueta for this story.

[140] Eden, *Full Circle* (London: Cassell, 1960), p. 188

[141] Hennessy, *Having it so Good*, p. 308

[142] *Avon Papers*, 20/17/16

[143] Evelyn Shuckburgh, *Descent to Suez: Diaries, 1951–56*, ed. John Charmley (London: Weidenfeld & Nicolson, 1986), p. 15

[144] Colville, *Fringes of Power*, p. 708

[145] Bullock, *Bevin*, Vol. 3, p. 85; Hansard, Fifth Series, Vol. 469, House of Commons, Session 1948–9, 17 November 1949, c. 2233

[146] See Bullock, *Bevin*, Vol. 3, pp. 94–5

[147] As quoted in Bullock, *Bevin*, Vol. 3, p. 88

[148] See Bullock, *Bevin*, Vol. 3, p. 815

[149] As quoted in Bullock, *Bevin*, Vol. 3, p. 99

INDEX

Aberdeen, Catherine, Countess of (*née* Hamilton), 70–2

Aberdeen, George Hamilton Gordon, 4th Earl of, 25–6; dispute with Palmerston, 68, 365; on Battle of the Nations (Leipzig, 1813), 69; background and private tragedies, 70–2, 74, 80; first marriage, 70–2; early political and diplomatic career, 72; travels in Europe, 72–3; first-hand experience of war, 73; death of children, 74, 80; relations and differences with Palmerston, 74–5, 78–9, 90, 93, 100–3, 105–6, 109; remarries (Harriet), 74; on public opinion, 77–8; as Chancellor of Duchy of Lancaster, 78; supports Greek independence, 78; on Palmerston's mercenaries in Spain, 82; Peel appoints Foreign Secretary, 88–9; diplomatic policy, 89–90, 93, 116; hatred of war, 91, 105, 107; brings motion of censure against Palmerston over Don Pacifico, 94; and Peel's death, 97; relations with Peel, 99–100; forms government (1852), 100; attitude to Ottomans, 101, 104–5, 120; letters, 101; and Crimean War, 102–9; Disraeli attacks, 103–4; resigns (1855), 108, 201; death, 109–12; entente with France, 213

Aberdeen, Harriet, Countess of (Aberdeen's second wife), 74, 80

Abyssinia: Mussolini invades and conquers, 284–5, 288–90, 303–4, 306; defeats Italy at Adowa (1896), 303; and Hoare-Laval pact, 305

Acheson, Dean, 340, 342, 362

Adams, John Quincy, 57

Adenauer, Konrad, 354

Adowa, battle of (1896), 189, 303

Afghanistan: British massacred (1841), 86; and Russian threat to India, 167

Africa: British expansion in, 183–4, 187; German ambitions in, 187–8; French expansion in, 188; Italian possessions in, 189, 303; as prospective power bloc with Europe, 332–3, 339; Montgomery reports to Bevin on, 333–5, 369

Agadir crisis (1911), 225–7

Aix-en-Chapelle, Congress of (1818), 40, 43, 48

Albert, Prince Consort: dislikes Palmerston, 76,

97–8; memorandum on Eastern Question, 104; distaste for Ottoman Empire, 120; death, 141–2; optimism, 160

Alexander I, Emperor of Russia, 8, 10, 21, 26–9, 32–3, 36, 38–9, 46, 48–9, 54, 311; death, 61

Alexander II, Emperor of Russia, 108, 141, 153

Alexander of Battenberg, first Prince of Bulgaria, 175, 178

Alexandra, Queen of Edward VII, 113

Alexandria: bombarded by British, 173, 179

Algeciras conference (1906), 217–18

Alsace-Lorraine, 126, 167, 188, 274

American Civil War (1861–6), 111–12

Amery, Leo, 263, 286

Andrassy, Julius, Count, 131, 154

Angell, Norman, 207, 237

Anglo-Russian Treaty (1924), 256

Anglo-Turkish Convention (1878), 171

Annan, Kofi, 367

Anti Jacobin (journal), 4

Antraigues, Count d', 10

Antwerp, 25–6, 30

Aquinas, St Thomas, 367

Arabi, Colonel, 173

Argentina, 55

Argyll House, London, 71

Armenia: Salisbury and, 184–5

Arrow (ship), 110

Ashburton, Alexander Baring, 1st Baron, 89–90

Asquith, Herbert Henry, 1st Earl of Oxford and Asquith: on Boer War, 211; and German naval threat, 223; and outbreak of First World War, 230–1; secrecy before First World War, 234

Atatürk, Kemal, 247n

Atlantic Pact *see* North Atlantic Treaty Organisation

atom bomb, 320

Attlee, Clement (*later* 1st Earl): relations with Bevin, 99, 316; appoints Bevin Foreign Secretary, 313; at Potsdam Conference, 314; on atom bomb, 320; on supporting civil war in Greece, 327; and British economic problems, 343; on Bevin, 360

Austen, Jane: *Sense and Sensibility*, 71

Austria: and Crimean War, 108; and Balkan revolt (1875), 130–1; Balkan claims, 154;